Essentials

of Psychological Ass

Everything you need to know to administer, score, and interpret the major psychological tests.

I'd like to order the following *Essentials of Psychological Assessment*:

- ❏ WAIS®-IV Assessment (w/CD-ROM) / 978-0-471-73846-6 • $46.95
- ❏ WJ III™ Cognitive Abilities Assessment / 978-0-471-34466-7 • $36.95
- ❏ Cross-Battery Assessment, Second Edition
  (w/CD-ROM) / 978-0-471-75771-9 • $46.95
- ❏ Nonverbal Assessment / 978-0-471-38318-5 • $36.95
- ❏ PAI® Assessment / 978-0-471-08463-1 • $36.95
- ❏ CAS Assessment / 978-0-471-29015-5 • $36.95
- ❏ MMPI-2™ Assessment / 978-0-471-34533-6 • $36.95
- ❏ Myers-Briggs Type Indicator® Assessment, Second Edition
  978-0-470-34390-6 • $36.95
- ❏ Rorschach® Assessment / 978-0-471-33146-9 • $36.95
- ❏ Millon™ Inventories Assessment, Third Edition / 978-0-470-16862-2 • $36.95
- ❏ TAT and Other Storytelling Assessments, Second Edition
  978-0-470-28192-5 • $36.95
- ❏ MMPI-A™ Assessment / 978-0-471-39815-8 • $36.95
- ❏ NEPSY®-II Assessment / 978-0-470-43691-2 • $36.95
- ❏ Neuropsychological Assessment, Second Edition / 978-0-470-43747-6 • $36.95
- ❏ WJ III™ Tests of Achievement Assessment / 978-0-471-33059-2 • $36.95
- ❏ Evidence-Based Academic Interventions / 978-0-470-20632-4 • $36.95
- ❏ WRAML2 and TOMAL-2 Assessment / 978-0-470-17911-6 • $36.95
- ❏ WMS®-III Assessment / 978-0-471-38080-1 • $36.95
- ❏ Behavioral Assessment / 978-0-471-35367-6 • $36.95
- Forensic Psychological Assessment, Second Edition / 978-0-470-55168-4 • $36.95
- Bayley Scales of Infant Development II Assessment / 978-0-471-32651-9 • $36.95
- Career Interest Assessment / 978-0-471-35365-2 • $36.95
- WPPSI™-III Assessment / 978-0-471-28895-4 • $36.95
- 5PF® Assessment / 978-0-471-23424-1 • $36.95
- ssessment Report Writing / 978-0-471-39487-7 • $36.95
- anford-Binet Intelligence Scales (SB5) Assessment / 978-0-471-22404-4 • $36.95
- ISC®-IV Assessment, Second Edition (w/CD-ROM)
  3-0-470-18915-3 • $46.95
- BC-II Assessment / 978-0-471-66733-9 • $36.95
- T®-III and KTEA-II Assessment (w/CD-ROM) / 978-0-470-55169-1 • $46.95
- essing Assessment / 978-0-471-71925-0 • $36.95
- ol Neuropsychological Assessment / 978-0-471-78372-5 • $36.95
- itive Assessment with KAIT
- her Kaufman Measures / 978-0-471-38317-8 • $36.95
- sment with Brief Intelligence Tests / 978-0-471-26412-5 • $36.95
- vity Assessment / 978-0-470-13742-0 • $36.95
- ™ Assessment / 978-0-470-28467-4 • $36.95
- ® Assessment (w/CD-ROM) / 978-0-470-22520-2 • $46.95
- ive Function Assessment / 978-0-470-42202-1 • $36.95
- s Behavior Assessments™ / 978-0-470-34633-4 • $36.95
- rament Assessment / 978-0-470-44447-4 • $36.95
- se to Intervention / 978-0-470-56663-3 • $36.95

omplete the order form on the back.
by phone, call toll free **1-877-762-2974**
online: **www.wiley.com/essentials**
by mail: refer to order form on next page

 **WILEY**

Essentials

of **Psychological Assessment** Series

ORDER FORM

Please send this order form with your payment (credit card or check) to:
John Wiley & Sons, Attn: J. Knott, 111 River Street, Hoboken, NJ 07030-5774

QUANTITY	TITLE	ISBN	PRICE
_____	_____	_____	_____
_____	_____	_____	_____
_____	_____	_____	_____
_____	_____	_____	_____
_____	_____	_____	_____

Shipping Charges:	**Surface**	**2-Day**	**1-Day**
First item	$5.00	$10.50	$17.50
Each additional item	$3.00	$3.00	$4.00

For orders greater than 15 items,
please contact Customer Care at 1-877-762-2974.

ORDER AMOUNT _____
SHIPPING CHARGES _____
SALES TAX _____
TOTAL ENCLOSED _____

NAME_____

AFFILIATION_____

ADDRESS_____

CITY/STATE/ZIP _____

TELEPHONE _____

EMAIL_____

❑ Please add me to your e-mailing list

PAYMENT METHOD:

❑ Check/Money Order   ❑ Visa   ❑ Mastercard   ❑ AmEx

Card Number _____ Exp. Date _____

Cardholder Name *(Please print)* _____

Signature _____

*Make checks payable to **John Wiley & Sons**. Credit card orders invalid if not signed.*
All orders subject to credit approval. • Prices subject to change.

To order by phone, call toll free 1-877-762-2974
To order online: www.wiley.com/essentials

WILEY

Essentials of NEPSY®-II Assessment

Essentials of Psychological Assessment Series

Series Editors, Alan S. Kaufman and Nadeen L. Kaufman

Essentials of 16 PF® Assessment
by Heather E.-P. Cattell and James M. Schuerger

Essentials of Assessment Report Writing
by Elizabeth O. Lichtenberger, Nancy Mather, Nadeen L. Kaufman, and Alan S. Kaufman

Essentials of Assessment with Brief Intelligence Tests
by Susan R. Homack and Cecil R. Reynolds

Essentials of Bayley Scales of Infant Development–II Assessment
by Maureen M. Black and Kathleen Matula

Essentials of Behavioral Assessment
by Michael C. Ramsay, Cecil R. Reynolds, and R. W. Kamphaus

Essentials of Career Interest Assessment
by Jeffrey P. Prince and Lisa J. Heiser

Essentials of CAS Assessment
by Jack A. Naglieri

Essentials of Cognitive Assessment with KAIT and Other Kaufman Measures
by Elizabeth O. Lichtenberger, Debra Broadbooks, and Alan S. Kaufman

Essentials of Conners Behavior Assessments™
by Elizabeth P. Sparrow

Essentials of Creativity Assessment
by James C. Kaufman, Jonathan A. Plucker, and John Baer

Essentials of Cross-Battery Assessment, Second Edition
by Dawn P. Flanagan, Samuel O. Ortiz, and Vincent C. Alfonso

Essentials of DAS-II® Assessment
by Ron Dumont, John O. Willis, and Colin D. Elliot

Essentials of Evidence-Based Academic Interventions
by Barbara J. Wendling and Nancy Mather

Essentials of Forensic Psychological Assessment, Second Edition
by Marc J. Ackerman

Essentials of Individual Achievement Assessment
by Douglas K. Smith

Essentials of KABC-II Assessment
by Alan S. Kaufman, Elizabeth O. Lichtenberger, Elaine Fletcher-Janzen, and Nadeen L. Kaufman

Essentials of Millon™ Inventories Assessment, Third Edition
by Stephen Strack

Essentials of MMPI-A™ Assessment
by Robert P. Archer and Radhika Krishnamurthy

Essentials of MMPI-2™ Assessment
by David S. Nichols

Essentials of Myers-Briggs Type Indicator® Assessment, Second Edition

by Naomi Quenk

Essentials of NEPSY®-II Assessment
by Sally L. Kemp and Marit Korkman

Essentials of Neuropsychological Assessment, Second Edition
by Nancy Hebben and William Milberg

Essentials of Nonverbal Assessment
by Steve McCallum, Bruce Bracken, and John Wasserman

Essentials of PAI® Assessment
by Leslie C. Morey

Essentials of Processing Assessment
by Milton J. Dehn

Essentials of Response to Intervention
by Amanda M. VanDerHeyden and Matthew K. Burns

Essentials of Rorschach® Assessment
by Tara Rose, Nancy Kaser-Boyd, and Michael P. Maloney

Essentials of School Neuropsychological Assessment
by Daniel C. Miller

Essentials of Stanford-Binet Intelligence Scales (SB5) Assessment
by Gale H. Roid and R. Andrew Barram

Essentials of TAT and Other Storytelling Assessments, Second Edition
by Hedwig Teglasi

Essentials of Temperament Assessment
by Diana Joyce

Essentials of WAIS®-IV Assessment
by Elizabeth O. Lichtenberger and Alan S. Kaufman

Essentials of WISC-III® and WPPSI-R® Assessment
by Alan S. Kaufman and Elizabeth O. Lichtenberger

Essentials of WISC®-IV Assessment, Second Edition
by Dawn P. Flanagan and Alan S. Kaufman

Essentials of WJ III™ Cognitive Abilities Assessment
by Fredrick A. Schrank, Dawn P. Flanagan, Richard W. Woodcock, and Jennifer T. Mascolo

Essentials of WJ III™ Tests of Achievement Assessment
by Nancy Mather, Barbara J. Wendling, and Richard W. Woodcock

Essentials of WMS®-III Assessment
by Elizabeth O. Lichtenberger, Alan S. Kaufman, and Zona C. Lai

Essentials of WNV™ Assessment
by Kimberly A. Brunnert, Jack A. Naglieri, and Steven T. Hardy-Braz

Essentials of WPPSI™-III Assessment
by Elizabeth O. Lichtenberger and Alan S. Kaufman

Essentials of WRAML2 and TOMAL-2 Assessment
by Wayne Adams and Cecil R. Reynolds

Essentials

of NEPSY®-II Assessment

Sally L. Kemp

Marit Korkman

WILEY

John Wiley & Sons, Inc.

Library of Congress Cataloging-in-Publication Data:
Kemp, Sally L.
  Essentials of NEPSY-II assessment / Sally L. Kemp, Marit Korkman.
    p. ; cm. – (Essentials of psychological assessment series)
  Includes bibliographical references and index.
  ISBN 978-0-470-43691-2 (pbk. : alk. paper); 978-0-470-63461-5(ebk); 978-0-470-63462-2(ebk)
978-0-470-63463-9(ebk)
  1. NEPSY (Neuropsychological test).   2. Neuropsychological tests for children.   3. Brain-damaged children–Psychological testing.   4. Developmentally disabled children–Psychological testing.
5. Developmental disabilities–Diagnosis.   I. Korkman, Marit.   II. Title.   III. Series: Essentials of psychological assessment series.
  [DNLM: 1. Neuropsychological Tests.   2. Child, Preschool.   3. Child.   4. Learning Disorders–diagnosis.   5. Mental Disorders–diagnosis. WS 340 K32e 2010]
  RJ486.6.K462 2010
  618.92'80475–dc22
                                2009050971

Printed in the United States of America

10 9 8 7 6 5 4 3 2 1

This volume is dedicated to all children who struggle with neurological, developmental, and learning disorders, and to the parents and professionals who give them constant support; also to Ursula Kirk, our co-author on NEPSY and NEPSY-II, and to Edith Kaplan, a pioneer in neuropsychology, both of whom passed away in 2009 and whose wisdom will influence neuropsychology for years to come.

Contents

Series Preface

In the *Essentials of Psychological Assessment* series, we have attempted to provide the reader with books that will deliver key practical information in the most efficient and accessible style. The series features instruments in a variety of domains, such as cognition, personality, education, and neuropsychology. For the experienced clinician, books in the series will offer a concise yet thorough way to master utilization of the continuously evolving supply of new and revised instruments, as well as a convenient method for keeping up to date on the tried-and-true measures. The novice will find here a prioritized assembly of all the information and techniques that must be at one's fingertips to begin the complicated process of individual psychological diagnosis.

Wherever feasible, visual shortcuts to highlight key points are utilized alongside systematic, step-by-step guidelines. Chapters are focused and succinct. Topics are targeted for an easy understanding of the essentials of administration, scoring, interpretation, and clinical application. Theory and research are continually woven into the fabric of each book, but always to enhance clinical inference, never to sidetrack or overwhelm. We have long been advocates of "intelligent" testing—the notion that a profile of test scores is meaningless unless it is brought to life by the clinical observations and astute detective work of knowledgeable examiners. Test profiles must be used to make a difference in the child's or adult's life, or why bother to test? We want this series to help our readers become the best intelligent testers they can be.

This volume addresses the administration, scoring, and interpretation of the *NEPSY-II* (Korkman, Kirk, & Kemp, 2007), which is the revision of the *NEPSY, Developmental Neuropsychological Assessment* (Korkman, Kirk, & Kemp, 1998). The book introduces the *NEPSY-II* to individuals who have never used the *NEPSY* and also targets veteran *NEPSY* clinicians who are transitioning to the new instrument. For this reason, the book approaches NEPSY-II at a basic level, walking the reader through the process of preparation, tips on administration, modifications for certain populations, scoring, and providing detailed help in interpretation. Tests newly designed for NEPSY-II are discussed in detail and excerpts from reports, as well as illustrative case reports, are presented to guide clinicians through the scoring and interpretation process. Referral Batteries are new to the NEPSY-II, so this volume has been organized around their use and they are featured in the case reports. The overarching message of the book is that the child's needs are paramount, as decisions for his or her future will be made on the basis of such assessments. This focus can only be achieved by careful preparation for the assessment, and awareness throughout the assessment process of *how* the child performs, as well as of the results of that performance. Sensitive observations of a well-trained clinician grounded in current neuropsychological research will expand the diagnostic power of a neuropsychological assessment immeasurably. Strengths, as well as associated and comorbid disorders, are assessed in order to elucidate a comprehensive picture of the child's functioning. The flexibility of NEPSY-II makes it possible to begin with a Referral Battery that is pertinent to the referral question and to adjust subtest selection based on test findings as the assessment proceeds. In this way, the assessment moves in a focused and parsimonious manner toward a reliable diagnosis that will serve the child well in addressing appropriate interventions impacting his or her future. We believe that this exceptional volume will serve as a guide to elucidate the complexities of the process.

Alan S. Kaufman, Ph.D., and Nadeen L. Kaufman, Ed.D., Series Editors
Yale University School of Medicine

Acknowledgments

The authors would like to thank Alan and Nadeen Kaufman, Series Editors of the *Essentials* books, for conceptualizing the idea and structure of this book. We were honored to have NEPSY included in their series of guides for the administration and interpretation of selected tests. We thank them also for their patience in dealing with all of the time issues that seem to take over our lives these days. Thanks also to Isabel Pratt, our editor at John Wiley & Sons, who bore the brunt of keeping us on track across two continents. Our contact has only been through the magic of e-mail, but her understanding manner comes across even through electronic media. Thanks also to Kara Borbely, our editorial assistant, who worked with us in a kind and patient manner, as she unraveled all of the details of preparing the manuscript. Thanks also go to Kate Lindsay, our production editor. A special note of thanks for Stephen Hooper, PhD, who took time from his already busy schedule to be our external reviewer. He prepared the objective review and analysis of strengths and weaknesses in NEPSY-II to be found in Chapter 5, and for this the authors are most grateful.

Just before work began on this volume, Sally Kemp lost her dear friend and mentor, Ursula Kirk, the second author of NEPSY and NEPSY-II. Her advice was sorely missed by both authors of this book. In addition to her supportive children and grandchildren, above all, however, Dr. Kemp would like to acknowledge and thank her husband, Garry, who has been beyond supportive for so many years of her work in pediatric neuropsychology. He, too, has faced a health crisis in the past few years, but always with inspiring optimism and humor. Thank you also to Dr. Kemp's colleagues Janet Farmer and Steve Kanne at the Thompson Center for Neurodevelopmental Disorders of the University of Missouri, Columbia and to Barbara McEntee, at Tulsa Developmental

Pediatrics and Center for Family Psychology, originally a student, but then a valued friend and colleague, for frequently being a sounding board. Dr. Korkman would like to acknowledge the support and patience of her husband and children, and also that of her research colleagues and team at the university, for tolerating periods when the work on this book was given priority over many other important issues.

One

This book is intended to serve as an in-depth, supplemental handbook to acquaint users with the theoretical basis for the NEPSY II as well as its development (Chapter 1), and to consult on questions concerning NEPSY II administration (Chapter 2), scoring (Chapter 3), and interpretation (Chapter 4). It also presents an objective review and analysis of strengths and weaknesses by an external reviewer, Dr. Stephen Hooper, a respected clinical neuropsychologist and valued colleague (Chapter 5), to whom the authors, Sally Kemp and Marit Korkman are most grateful. Finally, clinical applications of NEPSY-II are presented (Chapter Six) and illustrative case studies complete the discussion (Chapter Seven).

The *NEPSY-II* (Korkman, Kirk, & Kemp, 2007) is the second edition of *NEPSY: A Developmental Neuropsychological Assessment* (Korkman, Kirk, & Kemp, 1998). The original NEPSY comprised 27 subtests designed specifically for children ages 3 to 12. It assessed five domains: Attention/Executive Functions, Language, Sensorimotor, Visuospatial, and Memory and Learning. The NEPSY was based on the clinical methods of Luria and on more recent traditions of child neuropsychology. Rather than dealing with many diverse instruments with different normative populations, the NEPSY was designed to offer the advantage of being able to assess a child across functions and modalities with all subtests standardized on the same population. Therefore, differences in the child's test performance were likely to reflect true discrepancies.

The NEPSY-II has been revised and expanded to be a more sensitive and comprehensive pediatric neuropsychological instrument. Ceiling and floor problems have been addressed, and administration has been simplified. The age range of NEPSY-II has been expanded from 3 to 12 to 3 to 16 years. Most adult neuropsychological assessments begin at age 17, so it is hoped that NEPSY-II will fill a critical gap in pediatric neuropsychological assessment. Further, new tests have been designed specifically for several domains of *NEPSY-II* (Attention/

Executive Functioning, Language, and Visuospatial Processing) and a new domain, Social Perception, has been added to the original five.

The addition of a Social Perception domain to NEPSY-II was the authors' response to recent research showing an apparent increase in the prevalence of autism spectrum disorders. Previously it had been thought that autistic disorder (AD) was found in two to five cases per 10,000 individuals. More recently, prevalence estimates for all autism spectrum disorders (ASD) range from 2 to 6% per 1,000 children (NIMH, 2004b). Recent epidemiological research suggests that prevalence rates for ASD could be as high as 30 to 60 cases per 10,000, possibly due to better screening and to broadening of ASD definitions (Rutter, 2005).

The rationales underlying NEPSY and NEPSY-II will be reviewed subsequently, followed by the history and development of the instruments, as well as the revision goals for NEPSY-II. The changes made between NEPSY and NEPSY-II will be reviewed also.

RATIONALES UNDERLYING NEPSY AND NEPSY-II

Theoretical Foundations

The theory of A. R. Luria has been one of the cornerstones of neuropsychology for more than 45 years (Luria, 1980). The basic concepts in Luria's frame of reference are general principles, most of which apply to both children and adults. Some of them are adopted in NEPSY and NEPSY-II. Working with adults with focal, acute damage, Luria viewed the brain as a "functional mosaic," the parts of which interact in different combinations to subserve cognitive processing (Luria, 1973). He contributed to delineating brain regions that are interactively responsible for specific functions. One area never functions without input from other areas; thus, integration is a key principle of brain function in the Lurian views.

Another level of the principle of integrated neural processes is the functional level. Luria viewed cognitive functions: attention and executive functions, language, sensory perception, motor function, visuospatial abilities, and learning and memory, as complex capacities. They are composed of flexible and interactive subcomponents that are mediated by equally flexible, interactive, neural networks. In other words, multiple brain systems contribute to and mediate complex cognitive functions. Multiple brain regions, for instance, interact to mediate attentional processes (Luria, 1980; see also Barkley, 1996; Mirsky, 1996).

Luria's view of cognitive functions as complex systems based on interrelated neural networks is a general principle applicable to both children and adults. Yet the processes may differ in their composition. For example, in a young child reading involves more deliberate analysis of speech sounds and of the visual signs, more attention, and puts more demands on the not yet very strong working memory, as compared to the overautomatized glancing through a text with immediate sight recognition, of the printed words by an adult reader. Further, the relationship between brain anatomy and function is not clarified in children to the same degree as in adults. Thus, grounds for assuming which parts of the brain may be involved in complex functions are not as firm as they are for adult patients. For one thing, the child's brain is still developing functionally. Further, brain abnormality in a child, whether congenital or acquired, may modify the functional development of different regions.

Lurian theory proposes that impairment in one subcomponent of a function will also affect other complex cognitive functions to which that subcomponent contributes. This is an especially important factor to consider in children, because an early-occurring anomaly or event may well affect the chain of development in a basic subcomponent that occurs subsequent to impairment. (See Rapid Reference 1.1, Summary of Lurian Theory.)

≡ *Rapid Reference 1.1*

Summary of Lurian Theory

A. R. Luria, a Russian psychologist working with adults with focal, acute damage, viewed the brain as a "functional mosaic" (Luria, 1980).

- Luria's concept of interactive brain function
  - Multiple brain functions interact to mediate complex capacities.
  - Complex capacities are composed of flexible interactive subcomponents.
  - Also, the subcomponents are mediated by flexible interactive neural networks.
- Levels of impairment in neurocognitive functioning
  - Impairment in one subcomponent of a function will also affect other complex cognitive functions to which that subcomponent contributes.
  - An early occurring anomaly or event may well affect the chain of development in a basic subcomponent that occurs subsequent to impairment.

In correspondence with the assumption that impairments may have secondary effects, Luria's clinical approach bases its diagnostic principles on identifying the *primary deficit* underlying impaired performance in a complex function (e.g., auditory phonological decoding deficit may underlie a language impairment). The language impairment would be a *secondary deficit* of the auditory decoding impairment. In severe cases this has secondary effects not only on comprehension but also on verbal expression—it is not possible to produce verbalizations without a corresponding verbal comprehension. Luria noted that both impaired performance and qualitative observations are necessary to identify underlying primary deficits (Korkman, Kirk, & Kemp, 1998; Luria, 1980). Therefore, qualitative observations were a part of the structure of NEPSY and, subsequently, became a part of NEPSY-II in the form of scored Behavioral Observations. (See Rapid Reference 1.2, Primary and Secondary Deficits; Behavioral Observations.)

≡ Rapid Reference 1.2

Primary and Secondary Deficits; Behavioral Observations

Primary deficit(s) underlie impaired performance in one functional domain (e.g., auditory decoding deficit). Several different primary deficits can be present in different domains.

Secondary deficits are the effects of the primary deficit(s) on other functions in the same or different domains (e.g., verbal comprehension impairment = secondary deficit due to primary auditory decoding deficit). The deficit may be moderate or severe (e.g., in severe cases a primary deficit in auditory decoding has secondary effects not only on comprehension but also on verbal expression; it is not possible to produce verbalizations without a corresponding verbal comprehension).

Qualitative Behavioral Observations are quantified in NEPSY-II because Luria noted that both impaired performance and qualitative observations are necessary to identify underlying primary deficits (Korkman, Kirk, & Kemp, 1998; Luria, 1980).

Luria formulated a clinical assessment method that permits a comprehensive review and evaluation of disorders of complex functions by assessing subcomponents of these functions with specific tests. Thus, neurocognitive disorders are assessed by administering selective tests that represent the processes relevant for the function that was impaired (Christensen, 1984). In accordance with this approach, NEPSY-II is composed of subtests that assess, as far as possible, the range of basic subcomponents of important complex capacities. Similar to Luria's clinical assessment, NEPSY-II provides great flexibility of assessment. It can be administered as a full NEPSY, a comprehensive, orienting survey of all domains of neuropsychological functioning followed by in-depth assessment in weak areas; or with the General Referral Battery, a briefer version of the full NEPSY-II comprised of the most sensitive subtests. It is also possible to use recommended subtests, Diagnostic Referral Batteries, to focus the assessment on specific referral questions (i.e., poor reading skills). Further, selected subtests can be used individually, if a clinician wishes to supplement other testing.

The NEPSY-II provides information both on basic, fundamental skills required to complete more complex tasks, and on higher-level cognitive processes. Examples of the former are tasks of visual perception or manual motor ability. An example of the latter could be clock reading that puts demands on visuoperceptual and visuospatial skills, and the concept of time. The scores provided in NEPSY-II are also combined with behavioral observations, error analysis, and task analysis. Together these findings provide a basis for evaluating both the nature of a child's disorder by specifying the primary deficit(s) as well as its secondary consequences across other functional domains (Korkman, Kirk, & Kemp, 2007). Such an analysis may suggest the root(s)/primary deficit(s) of the child's problem (often expressed in the referral question), and what other problems might arise in other areas from the presence of the primary deficit(s). These would be secondary deficits.

Neuropsychological Assessment of Children and NEPSY-II

Neuropsychological assessment relies on standardized, objective, reliable measures of diverse aspects of human behavior, allowing for the specification of each individual's profile (Ivnik et al., 2001). Kaplan's "process approach" to assessment taught neuropsychologists to appreciate the value of qualitative observations in understanding *how* an individual arrives at a response (1988). This approach, harking back to Luria, added another layer of clinical information to standardized assessments. Brain behavior relationships in a developing child are both qualitatively and quantitatively different from those of an adult (Baron, 2004, p. 5); therefore, it is essential that the clinician understand child development and the range of normal variation for each age level being assessed. One cannot assess the abnormal accurately until one knows the normal well. Otherwise, appropriate behavior may be misinterpreted as impairment, which may lead to misdiagnoses.

Because neuropsychological assessments are used for placement in special programs, or to formulate treatment/intervention plans, it is essential to understand the whole child, including the context in which the child must operate. The results of an assessment must be tailored to the context in which this information will be used—the child's family, school, and professionals dealing with the child.

Those who see children in clinics may face the challenges presented by children with very diverse conditions. A child may be referred for evaluation due to traumatic brain injury (TBI), closed head injury, a neurological disorder (e.g., epilepsy) or disease (e.g., tuberous sclerosis, cancer), impulse control and behavior problems stemming from attention deficit hyperactivity disorder (ADHD) or autism; psychiatric disorders, such as bipolar disorder and depression, as well as learning disabilities (e.g., dyslexia). It is, therefore, essential that the neuropsychologist be able to weigh the effects of many different factors in assessing a child across a wide spectrum of insults, disorders, and diseases. He or she must have knowledge of and take the following into account: diagnostic clusters of symptoms for certain disorders, age at time of insult or at emergence of the disorder or the disease; location and severity of a lesion, whether or not it is local or diffuse; the role plasticity may play in recovery of function, and the possibility of a condition becoming chronic following an acute insult. Even when children present with signs of brain damage, inferences regarding brain-behavior relationships should be drawn with extreme caution. They should only be made by individuals whose training, expertise, and clinical skills qualify them for such inferences (Hartlage & Long, 1998, p. 5). (See Caution box, following.) Neuropsychological assessment is valuable in assessing the effects of damage on brain function whether the cause is known or not.

CAUTION

Inferences About Brain Pathology

Focal damage is more common in adults, whereas diffuse or multifocal damage is more common in children.

Lateralized or localized damage and neuropsychological findings in children are not usually evident in children with developmental disorders or early neurological insult.

Even with documented lateralized brain damage, the test profiles of children with left damage and with right damage do not differ enough to discriminate these groups.

Inferences concerning underlying brain pathology should be drawn with extreme caution, only by neuropsychologists who are trained in brain-behavior relationships.

Long-term follow-up for children with more severe problems is as essential as the initial evaluation, because cognitive impairment may change with age. For example, a young child with a language disorder may later have less notable language impairment but instead might have a reading disorder. Further, the child should undergo intervention and the clinician needs to follow its effects. For children with acquired damage, following the recovery of function is important in order to identify improved functioning, as well as persistent deficits, and to adapt interventions to changing needs (see also Korkman, Kirk, & Kemp, 1998).

Patterns of deficiencies in children with receptive and/or expressive language disorders and developmental disorders such as autistic spectrum disorders, nonverbal learning disabilities, and Williams syndrome, to name a few, can be detected with neuropsychological assessment. Neuropsychological assessments can, in such cases, assist in the diagnosis.

Subtle deficiencies in children with less severe developmental disorders such as dyslexia, ADHD, or graphomotor problems can be detected as well. It is quite frequent for children with some stated impairment to have problems in other domains as well—problems that are unrelated but coexist; that is, comorbid problems. For example, verbal learning disorders tend to overlap with attention problems, and motor coordination and visuomotor problems (Noterdaeme, Mildenberger, Minow, & Amorosa, 2002; Reinö-Habte Selassie, Jennische, Kyllerman, Viggedal, & Hartelius, 2005; Snowling, Bishop, Stothard, Chipchase, & Kaplan, 2006). Understanding the full spectrum of the child's deficiencies is an important basis for the development of behavioral, educational, and cognitive interventions.

Advanced examiners are able to select NEPSY-II subtests that further clinical utility or that meet clinical or referral needs (Korkman, Kirk, & Kemp, 2008, p. 5). Whatever the clinician's purpose in evaluating a child, the NEPSY-II is designed to be flexible enough to be tailored to specific referral questions. The NEPSY-II contains many traditional neuropsychological tests with appropriate norms for children and adolescents. Also, new tests developed specifically for NEPSY-II are included (e.g., Affect Recognition Theory of Mind, and Memory for Designs). Using the full NEPSY-II provides the additional advantage of conormed subtests, allowing scores to be compared to one another in a test profile.

Examiners who are not trained in neuropsychology can still make extensive use of NEPSY-II by interpreting it at the cognitive processing and more descriptive level. Such assessment is a good basis for developing modifications and interventions for children in the classroom. The test profile gives an idea of the child's relative strengths and weaknesses, in addition to giving information about the child's performance relative to the same-age peers.

Clinicians may use the NEPSY-II to understand children's cognitive processing on both the level of a trained neuropsychologist and on a more descriptive level. In both cases, identifying and explaining the neurocognitive impairments of a child supplies, firm ground for making intervention recommendations to improve functioning in school, home, and social contexts.

Neuropsychological Assessment in Schools

Many school psychologists are obtaining additional training in neuropsychology to improve their neuropsychological assessment skills. The NEPSY-II is designed to aid in assessing school-based problems such as poor academic performance and behavioral control problems. While the use of neuropsychological tests in schools is increasing, it is important that examiners have training in administering and scoring neuropsychological tests and that they restrict their interpretation inferences to a level consistent with their background and training. In cases where the referral question is to determine cognitive consequences of neurological conditions, or to identify signs compatible with brain injury, the examiner should have training and experience in performing such evaluations. Otherwise, he or she should refer the child to a neuropsychologist with the appropriate background.

IDEA Implications for Assessment

The reauthorization of the Individuals with Disabilities Education Act (IDEA) in 2004 produced changes in the criteria used to determine classification of a student with a learning disability. Whether a neuropsychologist in a clinic or private practice is evaluating a child, or a school psychologist with a neuropsychological training is administering the assessment, it is essential that he or she be aware of the new requirements under this law.

The law does not require the use of an ability-achievement discrepancy, and clinicians may consider response to intervention (RTI) when making the determination of a learning disability. A comprehensive assessment is required for all eligibility determinations, but the law allows the clinician to make judgments about the presence or absence of learning problems based on a variety of procedures. Essentially, it is incumbent on the school to demonstrate that scientifically based interventions were provided to the child and that the child did not benefit from these interventions, in order for learning disability classification to be made. This requirement is meant to enable children to receive intervention services sooner, when they are most beneficial, and reduces the number of referrals associated with inadequate instruction. It also may increase the possibility that children will be placed in special education without a formal evaluation. It is strongly recommended that no child be placed in special education at Tier 3 without an evaluation, and it would be preferable for the child to receive an evaluation after Tier 1 at the latest.

The increased emphasis on RTI makes it essential for clinicians to focus the results of their assessment on informing instruction or intervention. It is not sufficient to diagnose a disorder or make a classification. The assessment should provide information relevant to improving services provided to the child. This may be a specific intervention, remediation, or accommodation to provide the best learning environment for the child.

The NEPSY-II is designed to assess cognitive functions not typically covered by general ability or achievement batteries. The NEPSY-II subtests may relate more closely to the source of processing problems manifested in a specific learning or behavior problem than general measures of ability. For instance, poor word reading (decoding) may be a function of impaired phonological processing. This would suggest the child needs intervention related to developing phonological skills; however, if the child has had extensive and appropriate phonological awareness or decoding training and has not improved, the intervention recommendation might suggest that a contextual or whole language approach may be best to improve word reading. (Rapid Reference 1.3 summarizes IDEA and RTI.)

≣ Rapid Reference 1.3

Summary of IDEA and RTI

Reauthorization of the Individuals with Disabilities Education Act in 2004 produced changes in the criteria used to determine classification of a student with a learning disability.

- The law no longer requires the use of an ability-achievement discrepancy.
- A comprehensive assessment is required for all eligibility determinations, but the law allows the clinician to make judgments about the presence or absence of learning problems based on a variety of procedures.
  - Clinicians may consider response to intervention (RTI) in establishing a learning disability.
  - It is incumbent on the school to demonstrate that scientifically based interventions were provided to the child and that the child did not benefit from these interventions, in order for learning disability classification to be made.
    - Meant to enable children to receive intervention services sooner, when they are most beneficial.
    - Reduces the number of referrals associated with inadequate instruction.
    - May increase the possibility that children will be placed in special education without a formal evaluation.

(continued)

(continued)

■ The increased emphasis on RTI makes it essential for clinicians to focus the results of their assessment on informing instruction or intervention.
  ○ It is not sufficient to diagnose a disorder or make a classification.
  ○ The assessment should provide information relevant to improving services provided to the child. This may be a specific intervention, remediation, or accommodation to provide the best learning environment for the child.

NEPSY DEVELOPMENT

Twenty years ago, the scarcity of pediatric neuropsychological instruments led Marit Korkman, a pediatric neuropsychologist from Finland, to develop *NEPS* (Korkman, 1980), a brief assessment designed specifically for children 5.0 to 6.11 years of age. Various aspects of attention, language, sensorimotor functions, visuospatial functions, and memory and learning were each assessed with two to five tasks similar in content to the tasks in Luria's assessment (Christensen, 1975). Although the method proved most useful, the narrow age range was problematic, as was the pass/fail criterion that was built on the medical model (Korkman, 2000).

The NEPS was revised psychometrically by adding more items so that the results could be expressed in graded scores. These were converted to z-scores (mean $= 0 \pm 1$) based on age norms. During this revision new subtests were added, derived from tests that had proven useful in pediatric neuropsychology (e.g., Benton, Hamsher, Varney, & Spreen, 1983; Boehm, 1986; Reitan, 1979; Venger & Holmomskaya, 1978). To complement the test, the shortened versions of the Token Test (De Renzi & Faglioni, 1978), the Motor Free Visual Perception Test (Colarrusso & Hammill, 1972), and the Developmental Test of Visual-Motor Integration (Beery, 1982) were used in their original forms and standardized along with NEPSY. Norms were collected for ages 3.6 to 9.5. The assessment was called *NEPS-U* in Finnish and *NEPSY* in English (Korkman, 1988a, 1988b, 1988c). The Swedish NEPSY for children aged 4.0 to 7.11 was published in 1990 (Korkman, 1990), and the Danish version for the same age range was published in 1993 (Korkman, 1993).

In the spring of 1987, Marit Korkman, Ursula Kirk, and Sally Kemp began to collaborate on the American NEPSY, while keeping in mind international needs. It was planned to incorporate revisions and new subtests based on traditions and views central to contemporary neuropsychological traditions of assessment, as well as to expand the age range to ages 3 to 12. New subtests were designed to serve an extended period of development. The American NEPSY was developed in three phases: Pilot Phase (1987–1989), Tryout Phase (1990–1994), and Standardization and Validation Phase (1994–1996). During the early pilot phase, the original NEPSY subtests were adapted and revised for 3- to 12-year-old children. New items were added, new subtests were developed, and some subtests based on the work of others, such as Fingertip Tapping and Phonemic Fluency (Benton, Hamsher, Varney, & Spreen, 1983; Denckla, 1973), were included. A detailed account of the development of NEPSY is available in the previous volume in this series, *Essentials of NEPSY* (Kemp, Kirk, & Korkman, 2001)

NEPSY, A Developmental Neuropsychological Assessment was published in the United States in January 1998 (Korkman, Kirk, & Kemp). Just prior to its publication, a corresponding version of NEPSY was published in Finland (Korkman, Kirk, & Kemp, 1997). A corresponding version was also published in Sweden (Korkman, Kirk, & Kemp, 2000). After publication of the NEPSY in the United States, its validity was further demonstrated in a number of publications and it has been employed clinically in pediatric neuropsychological assessments in schools, clinics, and hospitals across the United States. (Rapid Reference 1.4 summarizes the history of NEPSY publication).

≋ *Rapid Reference 1.4*

The History of NEPSY

Scandinavia				United States			
Year	Age Range (years)	Country of Publication	Author(s)	Year	Age Range (years)	Phase of Development (U.S.)	Author(s)
1980	5.0–6.11	Finland	Korkman				
1988	3.6–9.5	Finland	Korkman	1987–89	2.0–12.11	Pilot Phase	Korkman, Kirk, and Kemp
1990	4.0–7.11	Sweden	Korkman	1990–94	2.0–12.11	Tryout	Korkman, Kirk, and Kemp
1993	4.0–7.11	Denmark	Korkman	1994–96	3.0–12.11	Standardization	Korkman, Kirk, and Kemp
1997	3.0–12.11	Finland	Korkman, Kirk, and Kemp	1998	3.0–12.11	Publication	Korkman, Kirk, and Kemp
2000	3.0–12.11	Sweden	Korkman, Kirk, and Kemp				

NEPSY-II REVISION: GOALS AND DEVELOPMENT

Revision Goals

In the fall of 2003, the authors began work on the revision of NEPSY in order to incorporate new research in neuropsychology, neuropsychiatry, and education. Client and expert feedback on the NEPSY also needed to be addressed. From author experience and early pilots of revisions and new subtests, four primary revision goals were formulated to:

1. *Improve subtest and domain coverage across the age span.* The first task in order to improve coverage was to review the NEPSY subtests in view of the need to include subtests over a wider age range, from 3 to 16 years. Further, in response to changes and advances in the field demonstrating the importance of executive functioning, new tests were designed to assess executive functioning:

   • Animal Sorting
   • Clocks
   • Inhibition

   The Visuospatial Processing domain had the fewest subtests of any NEPSY domain; therefore, two new subtests were developed to assess mental rotation and visuospatial analysis. Further, a need to include nonmotor, perceptual tests was recognized. Two subtests without motor input were developed that tap spatial location, the ability to deconstruct a picture, and the ability to observe ecological visual details:

   • Geometric Puzzles
   • Picture Puzzles

   The Social Perception domain was created to enhance the assessment of children with autism spectrum disorders or other social perceptual deficits. The domain includes two new subtests measuring:

   • Affect Recognition
   • Theory of Mind

2. *Enhance clinical and diagnostic utility.* In the previous version of the NEPSY, global domain scores often masked subtle deficits. Therefore, the domain scores were dropped from the NEPSY-II in favor of the more clinically sensitive subtest-level scores. On NEPSY-II, the clinician reviews the performance of the child at the level of specific abilities rather than at the global domain level. In this review the clinician may also score the performance for variations in the process of performance. Process scores may, for example, express types of errors.

Other scores, called contrast scores, express a comparison of how the child performs on different conditions or complexity of a task. The child may, for example, find it easier to attend to local visual aspects than to global configurations, or may be able to carry out a simple version of a task but fail to accomplish the task when the instruction is made more complex. The number of behaviors for which base rates in the standardization population are provided has also been increased. These base rates allow the clinician to compare features that may occur as the child performs to average rates of such behaviors in same-age children. Such behaviors may include, for example, out-of-seat behaviors, rate changes, or asking the examiner to repeat the instruction.

Particular attention was paid to the study of how different children with different clinical conditions perform on the tests. To assess the clinical and diagnostic utility of the NEPSY-II, 10 special group studies were conducted during the standardization. The results of these clinical group studies were used as a basis for further modifications of the NEPSY-II. (See Rapid Reference 1.5 for special group samples and instruments used in concurrent validity studies on NEPSY-II.)

3. *Improve psychometric properties.* Scores used to determine eligibility for special programs and for diagnostic purposes should be based on normative data that are both current and representative of the relevant population. The NEPSY-II normative data were collected from 2005 to 2006 and were stratified on key demographic variables according to the October 2003 U.S. Census data (U.S. Bureau of the Census, 2004). However, the Design Fluency, Imitating Hand Positions, List Memory, Manual Motor Sequences, Oromotor Sequences, Repetition of Nonsense Words, and Route Finding subtests were not renormed and were not modified in any way from the 1998 NEPSY. Most of these subtests represent motor skills or other functions that are not sensitive to cultural factors and therefore are not subject to great changes in the population, as will be described in later sections of this chapter.

Increased attention was paid to the floors and ceilings of subtests to ensure adequate coverage across the wide range of abilities in children ages 3 to 16. Subtests were developed for subsets of the age range (e.g., a recognition trial was added to Body Part Naming) and easier and more difficult items were added to many of the subtests. Data collected on children with mild intellectual disability demonstrated improved floors across the subtests. Although ceilings were increased, the focus of the NEPSY-II, as with all neuropsychological assessments, is on identifying impairment in various domains, so the focus on improved floors was critical to the clinical utility of the NEPSY-II. Along with the special group studies described earlier, a number of concurrent studies were conducted to provide evidence of reliability and validity. Retest data are reported for all scaled scores for all ages and by smaller age bands. Evidence of convergent and discriminate validity was provided by correlation studies, with numerous instruments employed in pediatric neuropsychology (see Rapid Reference 1.5).

≡ *Rapid Reference 1.5*

Concurrent Validity Studies for NEPSY-II:

Evidence for the Validity of NEPSY-II Scores in Special Diagnostic Groups

To assess the clinical and diagnostic utility of the NEPSY-II, 10 special group studies were conducted during the standardization. Special group samples included children with the following diagnoses:

- Attention Deficit Hyperactivity Disorder
- Autistic Disorder
- Asperger's Disorder
- Deaf and Hard of Hearing
- Emotionally Disturbed
- Language Disorder
- Mild Intellectual Disability
- Mathematics Disorder
- Reading Disorder
- Traumatic Brain Injury

Instruments Used to Establish Convergent and Discriminate Validity for NEPSY-II

The relationships between the NEPSY-II and the following external measures were examined:

- Pediatric Neuropsychological Instruments: *NEPSY, Developmental Neuropsychological Assessment* (Korkman, Kirk, & Kemp, 1998); *Children's Memory Scale* (CMS; Cohen, 1997); *Delis-Kaplan Executive Function System* (Delis, Kaplan, & Kramer, 2001; D-KEFS)
- General Cognitive Ability: *Wechsler Intelligence Scale for Children—Fourth Edition* ((Weschler, 2003; WISC-IV); *Differential Ability Scales—Second Edition* (DAS-II; Elliot, 2007); *Wechsler Nonverbal Scale of Ability* (Weschler & Naglieri, 2006; WNV)

- Academic Achievement Test: *Wechsler Individual Achievement Test—Second Edition* (Harcourt Assessment, 2005; WIAT-II)
- Basic Concept Test, Receptive & Expressive: *Bracken Basic Concept Scale—Third Edition: Receptive* (BBCS-3R; Bracken, 2006a); *Bracken Basic Concept Scale—Third Edition: Expressive* (BBCS-3E; Bracken, 2006b)
- Behavior Rating Scales: *Devereaux Scales of Mental Disorders* (DSMD; Naglieri, LeBuffe, & Pfeiffer, 1994); *Adaptive Behavior Assessment System—Second Edition* (ABAS-II; Harrison & Oakland, 2003); *Brown Attention-Deficit Disorder Scales for Children and Adolescents* (Brown, 2001); and *Children's Communication Checklist—Second Edition, United States Edition* (Bishop, 2006; CCC-2)

4. ***Enhance usability and ease of administration.*** Flexibility of subtest administration was enhanced by allowing a freer choice of subtests relevant to a specific clinical investigation. The flexible approach to assessment enables the clinicians to reduce testing time by tailoring the assessment to the child's essential problems and the needs at hand.

Instead of fixed rules for subtest selection, referral batteries are proposed in the NEPSY-II that are tailored according to common referral questions. A General Referral Battery is proposed for a situation where the child's problems are not known or fully identified, and to accommodate for the possibility for identification of problems that may be comorbid to a particular referral problem. Eight other Diagnostic Referral Batteries were based on eight of the many special group studies that were undertaken. Clinicians are also free to choose subtests to administer based on clinical, research, or child-specific needs.

Due to the multiple administration order possibilities, most of the NEPSY-II materials are presented in the *Administration Manual* in alphabetical order to make the subtests easier to find. The *Administration Manual* contains only the information required to administer the subtests and score subtest-level data. The normative data are contained in the *Clinical and Interpretive Manual* to allow for a streamlined *Administration Manual* that is not too thick to handle.

NEPSY-II SUBTEST DESCRIPTIONS ORGANIZED BY DOMAIN

Before considering the process of revision and standardization of the NEPSY-II, it will be helpful to the reader to be acquainted with the NEPSY-II subtests (Korkman, Kirk, & Kemp, 2007). Therefore, they are presented here in

Table 1.1 by domain as they appear in the present revised NEPSY-II. For each subtest, the age range and a brief description is given. This review of the NEPSY-II subtests is followed by a detailed account of the development of NEPSY-II and modifications from NEPSY to NEPSY-II.

Table 1.1 NEPSY–II Subtest Description by Domain

Auditory Attention and Executive Functioning

Subtest	Ages	Description
Animal Sorting	7–16	This subtest is designed to assess the ability to formulate basic concepts, to transfer those concepts into action (sort into categories), and to shift from one concept to another. The child sorts pictures into two groups of four cards each using self-initiated criteria.
Auditory Attention and Response Test	5–16 7–16	There are two parts to this subtest: Auditory Attention assesses selective auditory attention and the ability to sustain attention. Response Set assesses complex auditory attention and the ability to inhibit a previously learned stimulus in order to shift to a new set, while still controlling for selective attention to matching stimuli. The child touches a colored circle responding to matching or contrasting stimuli as required.
Clocks	7–16	Planning and organization are assessed, as well as visuoperceptual and visuospatial skills, and the concept of time in relation to analog clocks. The child draws clocks and sets the time, copies clocks, and reads clocks with and without numbers.
Design Fluency	5–12	This timed subtest is designed to assess the child's ability to generate unique designs rapidly by connecting up to five dot patterns in structured and random arrays, using straight lines. Only unique designs are scored.
Inhibition	5–16	The ability to inhibit automatic responses quickly in favor of novel responses is assessed on this subtest, along with the ability to switch between response types. The child looks at a series of black and white shapes or arrows pointing up or down, and names the shape, the direction, or an alternate response depending on the color of the shape or arrow.

Subtest	Ages	Description
Statue	3–6	Assessing motor persistence and inhibition is the aim of this subtest. The child is asked to stand and maintain a body posture with the eyes closed for 75 seconds and inhibit the impulse to talk, move, or open eyes in response to sound distracters.

Language Domain

Subtest	Ages	Description
Body Part Naming and Identification	3–4	This subtest is designed to assess confrontation naming and name recognition, basic components of expressive and expressive language. For Naming items, the child names the parts of the body on a figure of a child or on his or her own body. For identification items, the child points to corresponding parts of the body on a figure as the examiner names them aloud.
Comprehension of Instructions	3–16	This subtest is designed to assess the ability to receive, process, and execute oral instructions of increasing syntactic complexity. For each item, the child points to appropriate stimuli in response to oral instructions.
Oromotor Sequences	3–12	Oromotor programming is assessed on this measure. The child repeats articulatory sequences until the required number of repetitions is reached.
Phonological Processing	3–16	There are two phonological tasks comprising this subtest: Word Segment Recognition requires identification of words from segments. Phonological Segmentation is a test of elision at the level of syllables and phonemes. The child repeats a word and then creates a new word by omitting a syllable or phoneme, or by substituting one phoneme in a word for another.
Repetition of Nonsense Words	5–12	This subtest assesses phonological encoding and decoding. The child repeats nonsense words presented orally by the examiner.
Speeded Naming	3–16	Rapid semantic access to and production of names is assessed. The child rapidly names colors and shapes; colors, shapes, and sizes, or letters and numbers.
Word Generation	3–16	Rapid generation of words in specific semantic and initial letter categories is assessed. The child produces as many oral words as possible in 60 sec.

(continued)

Table 1.1 (continued)

Subtest	Ages	Description
	Memory and Learning Domain	
List Memory, List Memory Delayed	7–12	This subtest is designed to assess verbal learning and memory, rate of learning, and the role of interference in recall for verbal material. List words are read several times, recalling them after each presentation. A delayed memory task follows.
Memory for Designs, MD Delayed	3–16 5–16	MD assesses spatial memory for novel visual memory. A grid of 4–10 designs is shown briefly and removed from view. The child selects the design from a set of cards and places them in the correct location on the grid. A delayed task follows.
Memory for Faces, MF Delayed	5–16	MF is designed to assess encoding of facial features, as well as face discrimination and recognition. The child looks at a photo series of faces and then is shown three photos at a time from which he or she selects a face previously seen. A delayed task assesses long-term memory for faces.
Memory for Names, MN Delayed	5–16	MN is designed to assess the ability to learn the names of children over three trials. The child is shown six or eight cards with line drawings. The cards are then shown again and the child recalls the name for the drawing. A delayed task follows.
Narrative Memory	3–16	This subtest is designed to assess memory for organized verbal material under free recall, cued recall, and recognition conditions. The child listens to a story and then must repeat the story. The child is then asked questions to elicit missing details from his or her recall of the story.
Sentence Repetition	3–6	The ability to repeat sentences of increasing complexity and length is assessed. The child is read a sentence and repeats it verbatim immediately.

Subtest	Ages	Description
Word List Interference	7–16	This subtest is designed to assess verbal working memory, repetition, and word recall after interference. The child hears two series of words and then is asked to repeat each sequence. Then he or she recalls each series in order of presentation.

Sensorimotor Domain

Subtest	Ages	Description
Fingertip Tapping	5–16	This subtest has two parts: Repetitions assesses finger dexterity and motor speed; Sequences assesses rapid motor programming. The child copies a series of rapid finger motions demonstrated by the examiner.
Imitating Hand Positions	3–12	This subtest is designed to assess visual spatial analysis, motor programming, and kinesthetic feedback when imitating static hand positions. The child imitates a series of progressively more complex hand positions.
Manual Motor Sequences	3–12	The ability to imitate a series of rhythmic hand sequences using one or both hands is assessed. The child repeats a required number of series of hand movements demonstrated by the examiner.
Visuomotor Precision	3–12	This timed subtest is designed to assess graphomotor and accuracy. The child uses his or her preferred hand to draw lines inside of tracks ranging from straight to convoluted and wide to narrow.

Social Perception Domain

Subtest	Ages	Description
Affect Recognition	3–16	The subtest is designed to assess the ability to recognize emotional affect from photos of children's faces. One task asks the child whether or not two faces show the same affect. The second task asks the child to select two photos from 3–4 with the same affect. A third task asks the child to select one of four faces that shows the same affect as the photo at the top of the page. Finally, the child is briefly shown a face and then is asked , from memory, to select two photos that depict the same affect as the photo previously seen.

(continued)

Table 1.1 (continued)

Subtest	Ages	Description
Theory of Mind	3–16	This subtest is designed to assess the ability to understand mental functions, as well as the ability to understand that others have their own thoughts/feelings that may be different from one's own. A second part assesses the ability to understand how emotion relates to social context. In the Verbal task, the child is read various scenarios or shown pictures and then is asked questions that require the understanding of another's point of view, as well as figurative language. In the Contextual task, the child is shown a picture depicting a social context and is asked to select a photo from four options that depict the appropriate affect for a child whose face is not visible in the line-drawing picture.

Visuospatial Processing Domain

Subtest	Ages	Description
Arrows	5–16	This subtest is designed to assess the ability to judge line orientation visually. The child looks at an array of arrows arranged around a target and indicates the arrow(s) that points to the center of the target.
Block Construction	3–16	This timed subtest is designed to assess the visuospatial and visuomotor ability to reproduce three-dimensional constructions from models or two-dimensional drawings.
Design Copying	3–16	Motor and visual perceptual skills associated with the ability to copy two-dimensional geometric figures. The child copies figures displayed in the Response Booklet.
Geometric Puzzles	3–16	This subtests aims to assess mental rotation, visuospatial analysis, and attention to detail. The child is shown a grid containing several shapes. For each item, the child matches two shapes outside of the grid to two shapes within the grid.

Subtest	Ages	Description
Picture Puzzles	7–16	Visual discrimination, spatial localization, and visual scanning, are assessed along with the ability to deconstruct a picture into its constituent parts and recognize part–whole relationships. The child is presented a large picture divided by a grid and four smaller pictures taken from sections of the larger picture. The child identifies the location on the grid of the larger picture from which each of the smaller pictures was taken.
Route Finding	5–12	This subtest is designed to assess knowledge of visual spatial relations and directionality, as well as the ability to use this knowledge to transfer a route from a route from a simple schematic map to a more complex one. The child is shown a schematic map with a target house on which he or she can trace the route. Then the child is asked to find that house visually in a larger map with other houses and streets.

NEPSY-II Development

Pilot Phase (2004)

Revision of all 1998 NEPSY Subtests; New Subtests Developed: During the pilot phase, all of the 1998 NEPSY subtests were reviewed, adapted, and revised for children 3 to 12. New items were added, and new subtests were developed for each of the original functional domains. Due to the increasing knowledge and recognition of autism spectrum disorders since the 1998 publication of NEPSY, new subtests (Theory of Mind and Affect Recognition) were designed to address a new Social Perception domain. Other new subtests developed for the pilot phase included the subtests A not B, Body Part Recognition, Face Discrimination, Geometric Puzzles, Inhibition, Memory for Designs, Picture Puzzles, and Word Repetition and Recall.

   Early Piloting of New Subtests Followed by U.S. Pilot Study: An early pilot edition of ten new subtests was administered by the authors to 96 typical children, 24 children diagnosed with Asperger's disorder, and 46 children diagnosed with ADHD. Results of this early piloting were then analyzed and the final pilot version of 13 subtests, including some modified subtests from the

NEPSY, was formulated. It was administered to 109 children across the United States. Children were stratified by age, sex, race/ethnicity, and parent education level. Examiner feedback about subtests and behavioral observations of the test subjects was encouraged in order to assist in further modifications to subtest difficulty, instructions, and materials. Results of the pilot study were reviewed to identify subtests that needed further refinement, and domains that could benefit from the development of new subtests.

Tryout Phase (2005)

Elimination of Some Subtests; Modifications to Address Floor, Ceiling, Stimulus Problems and Difficulty with Administration on Others: Final pilot results, further literature review, and clinical experience with the instruments were integrated. On the basis of these findings, Face Discrimination was eliminated, and other NEPSY subtests and new subtests were modified. Subtests from the original NEPSY (Comprehension of Instructions, Phonological Processing, Speeded Naming, Narrative Memory, Visuomotor Precision) were modified to address ceiling and floor problems. Difficulty with administration on the Auditory Attention and Response Set subtest was addressed by modifying the visual stimulus material so that it requires less manual motor manipulation. Items of rhyming and of reading words that are joined together (the Word Chains subtest) were added as parts of the Phonological Processing subtest. Changes were also made to new subtests from the pilot version, such as Affect Recognition (use of child, rather than adult, faces), Memory for Designs (number and complexity of arrays), and Word Repetition and Recall (modified and renamed Word List Interference). A new subtest, the Animal Sorting subtest, was also developed at this stage for the Attention/Executive domain.

Tryout Phase Data Analysis: Revised, Deleted, Added Subtests; Piloted Subtests from 12-16 years; Full Tryout Version Developed and Administered: The tryout version of NEPSY-II comprised 22 selected subtests and was administered to 205 typical children ages 3 to 12 and to 54 children with clinical diagnoses of ADHD, autistic disorder, or Asperger's disorder. The sample was stratified by age, sex, race/ethnicity, parent education level, and geographical region. Halfway through the tryout phase, data analyses were conducted to evaluate psychometric properties of the subtests and to identify administration and scoring problems. During this review it was decided that the upper age limit for NEPSY-II might be extended from 12 to 16 years. For this reason, a mini-pilot was conducted with 45 adolescents to assess the feasibility of increasing the age range, as well as to test out the new methodology for administering Auditory Attention and Response Set. Because the adolescents' results were positive, the full NEPSY-II tryout version was administered to an additional 51 adolescents, ages 13 to 16. Final revisions were made and testing and scoring procedures were reviewed and modified. Floor and ceiling problems were again addressed by the addition of easier and/or more difficult items. Subtests with poor reliabilities were revised or deleted. The Clocks subtest, based on Edith Kaplan's work (Cohen, Ricci, Kibby, & Edmonds, 2000), was designed for the Attention and Executive Functioning domain and was piloted.

Standardization and Validation Phase (2005–2006)

Final Modifications to Subtests; Age Ranges Determined: Prior to launching the standardization phase of NEPSY-II, final modifications were made to the subtests and age ranges were determined for each subtest. In the Attention and Executive Functioning domain the A Not B subtest was shortened and the Animal Sorting stimuli were modified. The Clocks subtest was finalized with assistance from Edith Kaplan. The Auditory Attention and Response Set subtest was also modified. New items were added to the Comprehension of Instructions subtests in the Language domain and to Arrows and Design Copying in the Visuospatial Processing domain. Recognition of Reversals was added as a subtest. The Rhyming and the Word Chains subtest of the Phonological Processing subtest were dropped, and instead new floor items were added. Fingertip Tapping in the Sensorimotor domain was modified to reduce testing time. Behavioral Observations were added to several subtests.

Some 1998 Subtests Not Expected to Show Flynn Effect Were Not Renormed; Standardization Version Developed and Administered; Concurrent Special Group Validity Studies Undertaken: Due to the length of the standardization battery, subtests that were not modified on the 1998 NEPSY were reviewed closely for psychometric and theoretical issues. The decision was made not to renorm these subtests. These were predominately sensorimotor subtests; therefore normative changes were not expected to show a Flynn effect (a gain in population intelligence test scores over generations; Flynn [1984, 1987]). The normative data for these subtests is based on the 1998 NEPSY sample and is reported with the data collected during the standardization of the NEPSY-II (Korkman, Kirk, & Kemp, 2007).

The standardization version of NEPSY-II contained 29 subtests and 3 delay tasks. It was administered to 1,200 children ages 3 to 16. The normative sample was stratified by age, sex, race/ethnicity, parent education level, and geographical region. The youngest children, ages 3 to 4, took 17 subtests, while ages 5 to 6 took 22 subtests and 2 delayed tasks. Children ages 7 to 12 took 23 subtests and 2 delayed tasks, and the oldest group, ages 13 to 16, took 24 subtests and 3 delayed tasks. An additional 260 children with clinical diagnoses participated, and 1,060 concurrent validity cases were collected.

NEPSY-II *Final Production*

Final Selection of Subtests Based on Standardization and Validity Data; Development of Norm Tables and Manuals: Prior to production, the standardization and validation data were scrutinized and the subtests of the six domains were finalized. Three standardization subtests (A Not B, Recognition of Reversals, and Visual Attention) were dropped due to difficulty with administration or low clinical sensitivity. The norm tables were developed and the two manuals were authored. At this stage, two important developments were undertaken.

New Types of Scores: First, different types of scores were developed in addition to the main scaled scores. The total domain scores were not retained. Instead, more detailed scores were derived from the data to yield a background for clinical interpretation. Process scores were derived to express quantifiable aspects of performance, such as number of errors, performance time, interference effects on memory tasks, and so forth. Norms were also developed for combinations of speed and error scores, or combinations integrating the number of correct responses and the number of errors, when these were not directly dependent on each other.

Some of these process scores are expressed in parametrical standard scores, others as cumulative percentages. Contrast scores were derived to permit a direct, psychometric comparison of scores and subscores. For example, norms are now available that permit an evaluation of whether or not the immediate and delayed memory retrieval scores differ significantly for a child. Further, numerous scores expressing cumulative percentages of different observations, such as rule violations or out of seat behaviors during task performance, were also developed, as was the case also for the NEPSY.

Referral Batteries: The second important step at this stage was the development of recommended selections of subtests—Referral Batteries—based on clinical experience and on the effect sizes seen in the performance of NEPSY-II clinical groups when compared to matched controls. These Referral Batteries permit the examiner to reduce assessment time while still undertaking a sufficiently comprehensive and yet in-depth assessment.

Publication: The final version of NEPSY-II was the result of this comprehensive test development process. It is a comprehensive and reliable instrument that can be used to assess developing cognitive competencies that contribute to children's ability to learn and to perform effectively in and outside of school settings (Korkman, Kirk, & Kemp, 2007, pp. 38–39). In 2007, standardization of the Finnish version of NEPSY-II began, and the final version was published and launched in Helsinki, Finland, in July 2008.

Overview of Modifications From the 1998 NEPSY to NEPSY-II

The process of developing the NEPSY-II led to a number of differences between the NEPSY and the NEPSY-II. To summarize, these differences comprised the following:

- Age range extended upward to age 16 and modifications made to improve the assessment of the upper age range (9 to 16 years), as well as the youngest children (ages 3 to 4).
- New subtests added to enhance assessment within and across domains.
- Changes to subtest content, administration, and scoring procedures.
- Domain scores no longer provided in the NEPSY-II; instead greater attention is paid to qualitative features expressed in the following subtest-level scores:
  - Process scores
  - Contrast scores
  - Additional cumulative percentages and base rates in the standardization population for various Behavioral Observations
  - Proposed subtest selections, Referral Batteries, to facilitate subtest selection and reduce assessment time

(See Rapid Reference 1.6 for a summary of subtests unchanged or modified, and new subtests of NEPSY-II by domain.)

≡ Rapid Reference 1.6

Summary of Subtests Unchanged or Modified and New Subtests of NEPSY-II by Domain

Attention and Executive Functioning:

With increased recognition of the role of executive functions (EF) in learning, it was decided to expand this domain (Klenberg, Korkman, & Lahti-Nuuttila, 2001).

Three subtests were deleted from NEPSY:

Knock & Tap, Tower, and Visual Attention

One subtest unchanged from 1998 NEPSY:

Design Fluency assesses ability to initiate and produce unique designs.

One subtest unchanged from 1998 NEPSY

Statue assesses inhibition of motor response to noise distracters. Age range is now only 3-6 years, because there are more EF subtests for older children.

(continued)

(continued)

One subtest with extensive modifications:

Auditory Attention and Response Set (AA/RS): Administration was simplified so the child listens to a series of words and touches the appropriate circle when he or she hears a target word. Now the child merely touches a colored circle rather than placing a tile in a box. This procedure also makes it easier for the examiner to record the child's response. Scoring changes were made and scoring is no longer weighted; therefore, the influence of motor speed and finger dexterity has been reduced for this measure of attention.

Three new subtests developed; one adapted from an adult measure (Clocks):

- **Animal Sorting** was designed to assess the child's ability to formulate basic concepts, to transfer those concepts into action (i.e., sort pictures into categories), and to shift from one concept to another. The child sorts the cards into two groups of four cards each. (Twelve possible categories) This test was developed specifically for children and the cards designed for the NEPSY-II. No reading is required to complete the task, as it is on some sorting tests.

- **Clocks** includes both drawing and visual items. This subtest is designed to assess planning and organization, visuoperceptual and visuospatial skills, and the understanding of the concept of time in relation to analog clocks. On the drawing items, the child draws the image of an analog clock in the Response Booklet, draws the hands to indicate a specified time dictated by the examiner or from a digital clock displayed in the Response Booklet, or copies a full clock face in the Response Booklet. For visual items the child reads the time on clocks that have hands but either have or do not have numbers. In adults, performance on clock-drawing tasks is frequently impaired in groups with acquired brain injury (see Friedman, et al., 1994). In addition, Cohen, Ricci, Kibby, and Edmonds (2000) found a developmental curve in relation to clock drawing with the ability to draw a clock improving with age. This subtest was modified from the initial drafts of items and administration instructions provided by Edith Kaplan. Scoring criteria were based on her criteria and modified for clarity and ease of use with children.

- **Inhibition** is a timed subtest designed to assess the ability to inhibit automatic responses in favor of novel responses and the ability to switch between response types. It requires the child to look at a series of black and white shapes or arrows and name either the shape, direction, or an alternate response depending on the color of the shape or the direction of the arrow. This subtest is related to the Stroop (1935) procedure in which an overlearned verbal response is inhibited while a conflicting response is given. The Inhibition subtest utilizes the Stroop approach with a nonreading naming task. Naming is assessed first to determine how it might influence the other two conditions: Inhibition and Switching.

Language:

All seven subtests from the 1998 NEPSY were retained.

Two subtests with no changes:

- *Oromotor Sequences* assesses oromotor programming.
- *Repetition of Nonsense Words* assesses oral reproduction of nonsense words (phonological processing).

Three subtests with minimal changes:

- *Comprehension of Instructions* assesses receptive language of increasing complexity; ceiling items added for age range 3–16.
- *Phonological Processing* assesses awareness and analysis of auditory phonological elements of words. Ceiling and floor items added for age range 3–16.
- *Word Generation*—Verbal Fluency from NEPSY—renamed, but otherwise unmodified. Scoring changes.

Other subtests with significant modifications:

- *Body Part Naming and Identification* assesses basic receptive and expressive vocabulary. An identification trial was added to allow for the assessment of receptive as well as expressive vocabulary in young children.
- *Speeded Naming* - Rapid naming assessment. Easier items for 5–6 years (color/shape naming only) added to increase floor. Original item assesses size/color/shape, beginning at 7 years, and more difficult ceiling item requiring naming of letters and numbers alternatively. Age range now 5–16.

Memory and Learning:

Five memory and learning subtests were retained from the 1998 NEPSY.

Three subtests with minor modifications:

- *List Memory* assesses verbal learning, immediate and delayed recall, learning slope and interference from prior/new learning. Responses now recorded verbatim.
- *Memory for Names* assesses name learning and delayed memory for names. Age range now 5–16.
- *Sentence Repetition* assesses ability to recall oral sentences. Now ages 3–6 only.

Two subtests with more extensive changes:

- *Narrative Memory* assesses verbal memory for logical content. Easier and more difficult stories added for extended age range of 5–16. Recognition items added for the first two stories.
- *Memory for Faces* assesses facial recognition, immediate and delayed. Photographs of faces modified to present face only.

(continued)

(*continued*)

Two new measures were developed for NEPSY-II:

- **Memory for Designs** assesses spatial and visual, nonfigurative content memory for novel visual material. A delayed task assesses long-term visual-spatial memory. The child is shown a grid with 4 to 10 designs on a page. The grid is then removed from view, and the child selects the designs from a set of cards and places them on the grid in the same locations as previously shown. The delayed task is administered 15–25 minutes later. It requires the child to select 8 to 10 designs from a set of cards and place the cards on the grid in the same locations as shown during Memory for Designs.

- **Word List Interference** assesses verbal working memory, repetition, and word recall. The child is read two lists of words. He or she repeats each list immediately after it is read and then recalls both lists. In this way, each list serves as an interference task for the other list.

Sensorimotor:

This domain comprised five subtests on the 1998 NEPSY; Four were retained.

Two subtests with no modifications:

- **Imitating Hand Positions** assesses the ability to imitate the examiner's static hand position, using visuospatial analysis, motor programming, and kinesthetic feedback.

- **Manual Motor Sequences** assesses the ability to reproduce rhythmic, sequential movements (manual motor programming).

Two subtests with minor modifications:

- **Fingertip Tapping** assesses fine motor coordination and motor programming of the fingers. Changed from 32 taps and 8 sequences to 20 taps and 5 sequences in line with Denckla's seminal work (Denckla, 1973; 1985).

- **Visuomotor Precision** assesses graphomotor speed and accuracy. Three easier tracks added for younger children. Age range now 3–12.

One subtest dropped due to limited clinical utility in relation to the other subtests:

- Finger Discrimination.

Social Perception Domain

This is a new domain developed for NEPSY-II. It focuses on specific functional areas associated with social perceptual deficits, especially those in autism spectrum disorders (ASD). In addition to Affect Recognition, one of the new tests designed for the Social Perception domain, the Memory for Faces subtest from the Memory and Learning domain, is a relevant test for assessing children with ASD (Dawson, Webb, & McPartland, 2005; Kätsyri, Saalasti, Tiippana, von Wendt, & Sama, 2008.) A poorly developed Theory of Mind is purported to be a core deficit in individuals with ASD (Baron-Cohen, 2001; Baron-Cohen, et al., 1994); therefore, a ToM subtest was developed for NEPSY-II.

Domain comprises two new subtests developed for NEPSY-II:

- ***Affect Recognition*** includes four tasks designed to assess the ability to recognize affect from photographs of children's faces. In the first task, the child simply states whether or not two photographs depict faces with the same affect. In a second task, the child selects two photographs of faces with the same affect from three or four photographs. The third task requires the child to look at a page with five faces and to select one of the four faces that depicts the same affect as a face at the top of the page. Finally, the child is briefly shown a face and, from memory, selects two photographs that depict the same affect as the face previously shown. An Affect Recognition Total scaled score is calculated. Error scores are also provided for each of the emotions displayed in the subtest.

- ***Theory of Mind*** includes Verbal tasks that require knowledge of other individual's perspectives and figurative language. These items assess the ability to understand mental functions, such as belief, intention, deception, emotion, imagination, and pretending, as well as the ability to understand that others have their own thoughts, ideas and feelings that may be different from one's own. In the Contextual task, the child is shown a picture depicting a social situation in which the face of the target individual is not shown. The child is then asked to select that photograph from four options that depict the appropriate affect for the target individual in the picture. The Contextual tasks assess the child's ability to recognize facial affect and to understand how emotion relates to social context, as well as to recognize the appropriate affect given various social cues. It has minimal verbal constraints.

Visuospatial Processing Domain:

Includes four subtests retained from the 1998 NEPSY.

One subtest is unmodified:

- ***Route Finding*** assesses visuospatial relations and directionality and the ability to transfer that understanding from a small schematic map to a complex one.

Three subtests with modifications:

- ***Arrows*** assesses the ability to judge line orientation. Easier and more difficult items have been added for age range of 5–16. Existing items were re-orded. Visual stimulus less cluttered.

- ***Block Construction*** assesses visuospatial constructional ability for 3-dimensional representation. Existing items re-ordered; more difficult items added. Age range now 3–16.

(continued)

(*continued*)
- **Design Copying** assesses visuospatial analysis and visuomotor reproduction of 2-dimensional constructions. There are now diagnostic scores for Motor, Global, and Local Processing separately as well as a Total. There is also, a quick-scoring, Design Copying General score. More difficult items were added for the new age range of 3–16.

Two new subtests:
- **Geometric Puzzles** assesses nonmotor aspects of spatial perception, evaluation of directions, and mental rotation with geometric shapes on a grid.
- **Picture Puzzles** assesses the nonmotor aspects of visual perception from photos of everyday scenes and objects: visual integration, intact local processing, visual scanning, and an understanding of part–whole relationships.

COMPREHENSIVE REFERENCES

The *Clinical and Interpretive Manual of NEPSY-II* (Korkman, Kirk, & Kemp, 2007) and the references for this guide provide comprehensive lists of references for NEPSY-II. The *Manual of NEPSY* (Korkman, Kirk, & Kemp, 1998) and the *Clinical and Interpretive Manual of NEPSY-II* (Korkman, Kirk, & Kemp, 2007) also review studies performed with NEPSY and NEPSY-II, thus far. The *Clinical and Interpretive Manual* further reviews the development of the test and contains descriptions of each subtest, and standardization, reliability, and validity of NEPSY-II. (Rapid Reference 1.7 gives publication information.)

 *Rapid Reference 1.7*

Publication Information

NEPSY Second Edition (NEPSY-II)
Copyright 2007
Harcourt Assessment, Inc.
19500 Bulverde Road
San Antonio, TX 78259 USA
1-800-211-8378
www.Pearson.com
ISBN 0154234354

CONCLUDING REMARKS

In this chapter, we have reviewed the history of the NEPSY and the Revision Goals for NEPSY-II. We have considered the development of NEPSY-II with its improved subtest and domain coverage across an expanded age span, enhanced clinical and diagnostic utility, refined psychometric properties, and increased usability and ease of administration. With this background, in the next chapter, we will discuss the procedures to be followed as the clinician administers the NEPSY-II and observes the manner in which the child approaches the tasks, planning, and strategizing in order to reach problem solution.

🦅 TEST YOURSELF 🦅

Fill in the blanks.

1. **NEPSY-II assesses children in what age range?** _____

2. **Upon what theory is NEPSY based?** _____

3. **The theory upon which the NEPSY is based proposes that impairment in one subcomponent of a function is likely to affect** _____ **to which that subcomponent contributes.**

4. **When many brief instruments are drawn from different sources and their norm groups are different, it is difficult to tell whether differences in performance merely reflect differences in the** _____ .

5. **Because all capacities assessed on NEPSY-II have been normed on the same group,** _____ **trends can be assessed, both within and across a function.**

6. **List the four revision goals for NEPSY-II:**
   (1) _____
   (2) _____
   (3) _____
   (4) _____

7. **Scaled scores on NEPSY-II have a mean of** _____ **and a standard deviation of** _____ .

8. **The new domain on NEPSY-II,** _____ _____ **, addresses concerns about rising frequency of** _____ _____ **disorders.**

9. **Theory of Mind refers to the understanding of** _____ **states and another's** _____ .

Matching:

10. **Match the type of score to the appropriate definition.**

Primary Score _____ (a) assesses more specific abilities and skills or error rates that may not be relevant for all children but provide additional insight into a child's abilities.

Contrast Score _____ (b) combines two measures within the subtest.

Process Score _____ (c) represent the global aspects or key clinical variables of the subtest.

Combined Score _____ (d) compares different aspects of a subtest statistically.

11. _____ _____ allow the clinician to quantify common behaviors seen in clinical groups. Displayed as _____ in the standardization population or as _____ percentages.

12. **List the six domains of NEPSY-II subtests.**

(a) _____

(b) _____

(c) _____

(d) _____

(e) _____

(f) _____

13. **The NEPSY-II is an appropriate instrument for assessing localized brain damage.**

True or False?

14. **Secondary deficits are so named because they are not as important as primary deficits.**

True or False?

15. **The NEPSY-II standardization sample was 1,000 children.**

True or False?

16. **The NEPSY-II standardization sample was stratified by age, sex, race/ ethnicity, parent education level, and geographical region.**

True or False?

17. **The RTI in 2004 produced changes in the criteria used to determine classification of a student with a learning disability.**

True or False?

18. **Animal Sorting is a new Attention/Executive Functioning domain subtest designed to assess the child's ability to formulate basic concepts, to transfer those concepts into action, and to shift from one concept to another.**

True or False?

19. **It is important to report Domain Scores on NEPSY-II.**

    True or False?

20. **Phonological processing is an important subtest to include in the assessment of dyslexia.**

    True or False?

21. **Evidence of convergent and discriminate validity was provided by correlational studies.**

    True or False?

22. **The new Clocks subtest was based on the work of Edith Kaufman.**

    True or False?

Answers:

1. Ages 3 to 16; 2. Lurian; 3. Any function; 4. In norm groups; 5. Developmental; 6. Improve domain coverage across the age span; Enhance clinical and diagnostic utility; Improve psychometric properties; Enhance usability and ease of administration; 7. 10 & 3; 8. Social Perception; autistic spectrum; 9. Mental; perspectives; 10. c, d, a, b; 11. Behavioral Observations, base; cumulative; 12. Attention and Executive Functioning; Language, Memory and Learning, Sensorimotor, Social Perception, Visuospatial Processing; 13. False; 14. False; 15. False; 16. True; 17. False; 18. True; 19. False; 20. True; 21. True; 22. False

Two

HOW TO ADMINISTER NEPSY-II

A standardized test for children provides scores that represent a child's performance compared to other, typically developing children of the same age. In order to obtain results that are comparable to the national norms, the clinician needs to follow the administration and scoring procedures that were used in standardization. On the other hand, an impersonal, robot-like presentation may produce poor results due to distractibility and boredom. The assessment experience must be enjoyable for the child. Both a reasonably individualized, personal manner of administering the test and appropriate testing conditions are essential to good performance.

APPROPRIATE TESTING CONDITIONS

Physical Environment

It is important in any type of assessment that the physical setting is conducive to testing. The room should be quiet, well-ventilated, and well-lit. The temperature should be well-regulated or the child may not be able to concentrate. The testing area should have a table with a smooth surface and of appropriate height for the child to be comfortable. If a low table is not available for testing young children, the clinician may wish to acquire a booster chair to place on a chair of regular height. It is also nice to have a footstool or wooden box available for a child whose feet do not touch the floor. Providing a footrest helps to keep a child from becoming too fidgety because his or her feet are dangling without support. Chairs should be straight-backed, but padded enough to be comfortable throughout the testing session. Arms on the chairs help to contain younger children and provide elbow rests for the clinician. There needs to be ample room for test materials. Some examiners find a clipboard useful, as it facilitates writing responses without exposing the Record Form to the child. For most tests, the clinician should be seated across the table from the child, as this facilitates observation. Watching the child perform the task and recording, not only the formal Behavioral Observations provided on NEPSY-II, but also other observations and impressions, are integral parts of a thorough neuropsychological evaluation. These notations will be invaluable in understanding how the child approaches a specific task. Subsequent to the assessment, such knowledge will aid in the formulation of interventions.

For sensorimotor subtests, the clinician must sit across the table from the child in order to demonstrate the movements and positions and to observe the child from the correct orientation. However, on a few subtests (e.g., Body Part Naming, Arrows) the clinician may be able to administer the subtest more easily if he or she is seated beside or at a right angle to the child. This may facilitate the proper orientation of the materials and observation of the child's response, pointing to the stimuli on the easel. (See Rapid Reference 2.1.)

≣ *Rapid Reference 2.1*
....

Summary of Optimal Physical Environment for Testing

Room: quiet, well-ventilated, and well-lit.; temperature well-regulated to help concentration.

Furniture and Accessories: table with a smooth surface, ample room for materials; appropriate height.

- Use booster chair, if a low table unavailable for testing young children.
- Footstool or wooden box available for child if feet do not touch the floor.
- Comfortable chairs with arms to help to contain younger children; to provide elbow rests for the child and clinician.

Test Materials

Only the test materials being used should be visible on the table during the testing. Other materials may be distracting or cause anxiety for a child who worries about being able to accomplish a task. The clinician may want to place the materials he or she will use on a chair nearby but out of the child's view. The NEPSY-II Stimulus Book easel should be placed so the front cover faces the examiner. The pages of the Stimulus Books are turned toward the child. The child should not be able to see the examiner's side of the easel. The NEPSY-II kit contains all materials needed except the stopwatch, and any extra paper desired for taking notes.

Pencils (red, number two standard) are provided with the kit and need to be well sharpened for the tasks. Extra pencils can be kept available. A clipboard is a useful tool in many subtests as it facilitates observation and recording simultaneously. For young children (ages 3 to 6), use a thick, primary pencil.

Preparation of the Record Form

Prior to testing, mark the start-points for the child's age on the Record Form. Also circle or highlight age-appropriate tests to be administered. The examiner can number the tests in the order she/he wishes to administer them or can prepare a guide sheet with the order, whichever is preferred. The clinician should note whether the child is to take a break or is to perform another subtest between immediate and delayed tasks. Note that if a subtest is to be placed between the immediate and delayed trials of a memory test, it should not be another memory test.

Establishing Rapport

It is important to establish rapport with the child before testing begins. Greet the accompanying adult in a friendly, relaxed manner so the child can be reassured about the way the examiner relates to people. Then greet the child, offering your hand for a handshake. Shaking hands with the child often makes him or her feel that this process is going to be a partnership and that he or she has an important role to play. However, if the child is shy about shaking hands, do not force it. When the child is young, get down on her or his level and chat for a few minutes about some matter to which the child can relate, for example, a toy the child has brought to the testing or an article of clothing. Explain that you will be doing all kinds activities with the child. When an adult refers to the clinician as "doctor," or when the evaluation takes place in a hospital or medical center, the clinician should reassure the child that he or she will not be giving shots or doing anything to hurt the child. Older children need to be reassured that they will not be receiving grades on their performance.

When a young child or a child with a developmental delay has trouble separating from the parent (caregiver), the clinician may wish to invite the parent to walk back to the testing room with the clinician and the child. The clinician should reassure the child that the parent will know exactly where she or he is, and, perhaps, have the parent leave an article (a scarf, a book, etc.) with the child for security. Do not prolong the process. When the mother, father, or both have gone, the examiner may need to play with the child for a while to help him or her feel comfortable before testing is initiated. Occasionally, with a small child or a child with developmental disorders, the parent needs to be present for the testing. When this is the case, talk to the parent prior to the testing about not prompting the child. Most children, however, will perform better if the parent is not present.

Maintaining Rapport

Good rapport is essential to productive assessment. The clinician should introduce the test to the child by talking about the many different activities the child will be doing with the clinician. Explain that each task will be easy at first, and then the items may get harder. The examiner should explain that some tasks are easy and others are hard, but reassure the child that when the items get hard, he or she just needs to do his or her best. This can help reassure the child that he or she is not the only one who finds some items difficult. When items become difficult, the examiner can validate the child's feelings by acknowledging, "Sometimes these get hard," or "That one was tough; let's try a different one." Occasionally, children may need to be reassured by explaining to them that some tasks are really difficult and that they need not know or be able to solve them all, but just try their best.

In general, it is best to praise effort rather than achievement. "You are really working hard!" or "You really kept at that problem until it was solved!" It is fine to use stickers or little treats as reinforcers for small children and for older children with cognitive impairments. These should not be offered as rewards for correct performances but rather for staying on task and working. At best, rewards are offered at the end of the sessions, but may be needed during testing. Older children without developmental delay may find reinforcers "babyish." As subtest materials are being changed for new ones, small talk will help keep the child at ease.

DON'T FORGET

Validate the Child's Feelings

When items get difficult, validate the child's feelings.
- "Sometimes these are hard."
- "That one was tough; let's try a different one."

Praise effort, not achievement.
- "You are really working hard!"
- "You really kept at that problem until it was solved!"

Taking Breaks

A child who becomes fatigued is unproductive and does not perform according to his or her capacity. Watch for signs of fatigue such as squirminess, asking how long it will be, stretching, and so forth. Take a break as soon as possible when any of these signs is observed. It is advisable to have juice and crackers or a similar snack available for the child during the break, but ask permission from the accompanying person to give the child a snack before the assessment begins. Looking out the window with the child for a while may provide a little "mental recess." If necessary, relocate to a playroom or office where some toys are kept or take a short walk with the child. Providing a change of scene and position before returning to work may help.

When the delayed memory section of a subtest is the next one to be administered, the examiner can give the child a break of 15 to 25 minutes or administer another subtest from a different domain until the appropriate time has elapsed before the delayed trial. For example, if Memory for Names has been administered to a young child, the examiner could administer Block Construction or a subtest other than a memory test to fill in the time gap before Delayed Memory for Names is due to be administered. Conversely, breaking for lunch or for the day after an immediate memory subtest has been administered will spoil the delayed trial because the time gap will be too great for the delayed trial to be administered. In such cases only the results of the immediate memory test can be reported.

CAUTION

Do Not Take a Break Between an Immediate and Delayed Memory Test

- Breaking for lunch or for the day after an immediate memory subtest will spoil the delayed trial.
- Time gap will be too great for the delayed trial to be administered.
- Only the results of the immediate memory test can be reported.

To allow for the appropriate delay between memory sections, the examiner can:

- Give the child a break of 15–25 min.
- Administer another subtest from a different domain (not another memory test).

Testing Considerations

It is essential for the assessment to address:

- The referral question
- The needs of the child with respect to particular complaints or problems, and to intervention needs
- Time constraints
- The setting in which the assessment takes place
- The child's age

These questions or circumstances are considered in planning the assessment by selecting the appropriate NEPSY-II subtests or employing a Referral Battery.

Subtest Order

A NEPSY-II normative sample was collected using multiple subtest administration orders. This means that the NEPSY-II subtests are not subject to order effects; they do not have to be administered in the order that they appear in the *Administration Manual*. Subtests can be used individually in any order or the examiner can develop his or her own battery. Because of this flexibility, however, it is essential to plan in advance the order in which the subtests are to be administered. That said, a certain degree of freedom to do online changes in subtest order is advised so as to accommodate for signs of fatigue or frustration that the child may exhibit during the assessment. The subtest order can be varied as the clinician feels is suitable for the child's age, attention, interests, and difficulties. In order to accommodate varying subtest administration orders, subtest administration instructions are presented in alphabetical order in both the Stimulus Books and the *Administration Manual of NEPSY-II*.

CAUTION

Plan Order of Assessment in Advance

- NEPSY-II subtests are not subject to order effects, so do not have to be administered in the order seen in the *Administration Manual*, Record Form, or Stimulus Books.
- Subtests can be used individually in any order or the examiner can develop his or her own battery.

(continued)

(*continued*)
- Select subtests appropriate to the referral question and to the needs and age of the child.
- Plan the order of administration and mark the age-appropriate subtests in the Record Form.
- Can vary order to accommodate for child's difficulties, attention, fatigue, or frustration during assessment.
- To locate easily, subtests are in alphabetical order in Stimulus Books, Record Form, and the *Administration Manual.*

TYPES OF ASSESSMENTS

Full Assessment

Using all of the subtests across six domains, a Full Assessment serves any child encountering problems, either developmental or acquired. In reality, the time and resources for a comprehensive evaluation are not always available. However, a thorough neurodevelopmental evaluation (Full NEPSY-II) is useful in the following conditions:

- The child has been sent for a thorough neuropsychological assessment due to brain damage or dysfunction (e.g., cerebral palsy, epilepsy, hydrocephalus, or brain trauma), or some acute condition affecting the central nervous system (e.g., head injury, cytomegalovirus, herpes infection, or encephalitis) in order to fully establish what consequences these conditions have on the child's brain.
- The child has been exposed to notable neurodevelopmental risk factors (e.g., very low birth weight, birth asphyxia, or alcohol or drug exposure in utero) to establish their consequences.
- The child is being followed over years to facilitate follow-up due to a particularly severe, specific learning disorder or social perception problem.
- The child will receive specific interventions due to some particular impairment such as social perception difficulty or problems with executive functions, to evaluate response to treatment.
- The child undergoes medical treatments that may affect the central nervous system (e.g., chemotherapy, radiation), in order to follow up and establish eventual acquired impairments.

A comprehensive review of neuropsychological functioning will permit an identification of most effects that brain pathology may have on the cognitive capacities of the child. It also facilitates future follow-up by providing the largest possible baseline. Note that all subtests that are appropriate at a certain age level do not necessarily have counterparts at another age level, yet restricting the assessment to those subtests that stay the same may not always capture the aspects of development that are the most age-appropriate. Therefore, a Full Assessment may be the safest solution.

A Full Assessment may be prevented by, for example, motor or cognitive impairments when children with cerebral palsy (CP), intellectual disability, or other conditions are not able to carry out or do not comprehend some tasks. When time constraints or the child's restricted ability to participate prevents a Full Assessment, a General Referral Battery may be administered to establish a baseline.

Abbreviated General and Focused Assessments

General Referral Battery

As noted in Chapter 1, the General Referral Battery (GRB) is a briefer selection of subtests than the full NEPSY-II, but it is still comprehensive and covers most domains of neurocognitive development. It is appropriate when time constraints prevent a Full Assessment, and when a referral question cites multiple problems, because different types of impairment often co-occur in children. It is also appropriate when the referral question is vague. The GRB provides an overview of the child's performance across five of the six functional domains. Selection of subtests for the GRB was determined by psychometric and clinical considerations. It comprises the most sensitive subtests from the special group validity studies. The Social Perception domain is not included routinely in a GRB unless an autism spectrum disorder is suspected. Subtest performance is expressed in scaled scores and percentile ranks.

Diagnostic Referral Batteries

In order to aid in selecting subtests that are tailored to specific referral questions, several recommended batteries have been proposed. Such Diagnostic Referral Batteries are appropriate if a referral question, previous diagnosis, and primary or process score from other testing indicates the possibility of a specific problem, such as a language disorder or attention problem. The NEPSY-II Diagnostic Referral Battery for that disorder should be used when a Full NEPSY-II is not possible and the referral question is fairly specific. These more specific referral batteries are provided in NEPSY-II to guide the clinician in a focused evaluation.

The Diagnostic Referral Batteries include subtests that are critical to a specific diagnosis. They are based on the results of subtests that demonstrated the largest effect sizes for specific validity groups, as well as on findings from the current literature and from clinical experience.

Use of the General Referral Battery and Diagnostic Referral Batteries will be discussed in depth in Chapter 6 in the context of clinical applications of NEPSY-II. Subtests in the GRB and the Diagnostic Referral Batteries are presented there with the special group validity studies from which they were drawn.

A Selective Assessment

Some psychologists use tests other than NEPSY-II for neuropsychological assessments. In such instances, the NEPSY-II may be a complement rather than the main tool of the assessment. Nothing prevents a clinician from selecting particular NEPSY-II subtests as complements to their other habitual tools. The NEPSY-II manuals do not provide guidelines for such use of the test; the appropriateness of the assessment as well as the interpretation will depend entirely on the examiner's knowledge and experience. It is also important to note that an assessment that consists of only a few neuropsychological tests added to a routine test of intelligence should not be called a neuropsychological assessment.

ASSESSING CHILDREN WITH SPECIAL NEEDS

Children With Primary Disabilities

Children who undergo assessments represent children with a wide variety of problems. In some children, primary disabilities in the form of cognitive, sensory, or motor limitations may present specific challenges for the administration of any test. The assessment needs to be adapted to each child's particular needs. First, the administration may need to be individualized while still adhering to the gist of the administration rules. A test is not administered in a standard way if the child does not comprehend or does not hear the instruction, or if motor disabilities prevent the child from carrying them out. Second, the subtest selection may need to accommodate for particular disabilities. The NEPSY-II contains a wide variety of tests and for any child there will be some subtest selection(s) that will suit his or her individual capacity, no matter what the particular disabilities are. Thus, the NEPSY-II can be used to evaluate children with special needs of many kinds.

The NEPSY-II was developed particularly to identify and analyze learning and developmental impairments. Most children who need assessments can take the NEPSY-II subtests as they are presented, but there may be exceptions. Whenever standardized administration is modified, the clinician marks the Record Form as *Modified Administration,* and interprets the results with caution. If major modifications to standardized subtest administration are made, the use of norms may be invalidated. Nonetheless, the clinician can still gain valuable diagnostic information about how the child performed the task.

The discussion that follows concerns evaluating children in special groups, followed by directions for modified administrations of selected subtests for blind and deaf/hard of hearing populations. See Caution box concerning Modifying Standardized Administration. The Referral Batteries and validity studies will be discussed in depth in Chapter 6.

CAUTION

Modifying Standardized Administration

- Mark the Record Form as *Modified Administration.* Note the modifications made.
- Interpret results with caution.
- If major modifications are made to standardized subtest administration, the use of norms may be invalidated. Interpret clinically and discuss, making note that it is a clinical interpretation.
- Do not use such modified subtests to compute the child's personal mean.

Children With Attention Problems

The child brought for evaluation of attention problems should be evaluated in a plain, quiet room with no extraneous stimuli. The assessment is best divided into short testing sessions, if possible. Allow breaks as needed (however, be careful not to break before a delayed memory test has been administered). Provide frequent reminders to wait until the materials have been arranged and/or the directions have been administered before the child can reach for materials. Having the child place his or her hands in the lap, or hands at the edge of the table can help. "Hands back" is a good prompt. Changing position for the testing can be helpful; move to the floor or another table. For children age 5 and up who are impulsive, the "stop and think" prompt may be helpful. Use the child's name, pat the child's hand, or gently alert the child to listen to directions. Stickers or other reinforcers will help younger children to continue working. For adolescents, redirect as needed to maintain rapport and test fluidity. Do note, however, that providing strong support for attention suppresses the child's attention problems so that they may not appear to the extent that is typical for the child in school. Make notes on the Record Form of actions needed to hold the child's attention.

When the referral question is to diagnose or confirm an attention problem or the presence of ADHD, it is recommended that the child should not be evaluated while on medication for the same. When the child receives medication for diagnosed ADHD and the referral question is to determine how the child is functioning with this treatment, NEPSY-II should be administered while the child is on medication. It is essential to work with the child's physician in handling these matters.

Due to the tendency of attention to vary with the child's interest and motivation as well as with the setting, it is advisable to pay particular attention to reports from school and home of the degree and types of attention problems that occur there. Behavioral questionnaires, such as the Brown Attention-Deficit Disorder Scales for Children and Adolescents (Brown, 2001) may be useful for this purpose. (See Rapid Reference 2.2.)

≡ *Rapid Reference 2.2*

Assessing the Child With Attention Problems

- Attention problems may be due to ADHD, Autistic disorder, TBI, depression, and so forth.
- May need multiple short testing sessions.
- May need to be evaluated in a small room with no extraneous stimuli.
- When confirming previous diagnosis of ADHD, evaluate *off medication.*
- If determining how child is functioning with treatment, test on medication.

It is essential to work with the child's physician on medication issues.

Include school and home reports for degree and types of attention problems, adaptive behavior, and ADHD questionnaires.

Children With Autism Spectrum Disorders

Children with autistic spectrum disorders include those with autism or Asperger syndrome. To accommodate a tendency to stereotypic interests and perseverative behavior, it is wise to prepare ahead of time by asking the parent or caregiver on which objects or topics the child is apt to perseverate (e.g., cars, dinosaurs, etc.). The clinician can then remove such toys from the area, can avoid the topic in conversation, and be prepared to redirect the child after a short time if he or she brings it up. If the child is not too perseverative, his or her special object may be used as a reinforcer (e.g., a book about dinosaurs). The clinician should ask about reinforcers that work for the child, as well as anything that is apt to be upsetting to him or her.

It is wise to divide the assessment into a number of 30 to 60 minute sessions, especially if the child is very young or is low-functioning. Many children with autism do not tolerate new situations well. Therefore, it is often best to begin the assessment with an informal play observation for 30 minutes with no formal testing. Thus, the clinician gains valuable information about the child's eye contact, ability to engage, pretend play, language, and so forth, while the child becomes familiar with the setting and the examiner. Children with autism are frequently hypersensitive to certain noises, textures, light, touch, and other stimuli, so try to remove or minimize such distractions. Ascertain from the parents if there is a stimulus (e.g., spinning in a chair) that is soothing to the child. If so, these may be used during breaks. It may be helpful for the child to wear a weighted vest, if he or she has one.

Occasionally, it may be helpful to have a caregiver present during testing; however, instruct the individual not to intervene unless it is requested by the examiner. The clinician needs to be very aware of poor eye contact and should reinforce good eye contact with the prompt the parents use. When the child does not have a prompt, the clinician should prompt, "Look at me" before talking. "Eyes to eyes," gesturing from the child's eyes to yours, can also be used as a prompt. The clinician should use simple, direct language and may need to direct the child to look at each aspect of the materials before a response is given. If language and/ or attention are significantly delayed, the clinician should also review the following instructions for the *Child with Language Disorder* and the *Child with Attention Problems.*

If a cognitive assessment is also to be undertaken as a part of the evaluation of a child on the autistic spectrum, the *Differential Ability Scale—2nd Ed (DAS-II;* Elliot, 2007) is recommended, as it is short and less verbal than some cognitive measures, while still showing good reliability. It also includes a number of manipulatives that capture a child's interest and anchor attention. A nonverbal cognitive measure may be used if language is significantly limited.

≡ *Rapid Reference 2.3*

Assessing Children With Autistic Spectrum Disorders (ASD)

(Includes autism and Asperger's syndrome)

- Prepare ahead of time for stereotypic interests and perseverative behavior and avoid such topics during assessments (e.g., cars, dinosaurs, etc.)
- Ask parent about effective reinforcers and/or "soothers" to use during breaks or to reinforce work (e.g., book about dinosaurs, spinning chair).
- Use simple, direct language—telegraphic speech. Ask parents about prompts used for directing attention and/or eye contact (e.g., "Look at me" or "Stop, look").
- Child may be hypersensitive to sensory input. Remove or minimize distractions and check that the fire alarm will not be tested.
- Child may not tolerate new situations well: 30-to 60-minute sessions for young and low-functioning children. May need a "get acquainted session or an informal play observation initially.
- May be helpful to have a caregiver present during testing; instruct the individual not to intervene unless it is requested by the examiner.
- For cognitive assessment: The Differential Ability Scale—2nd Ed (DAS-II) is recommended: short, less verbal; good reliability; manipulatives to anchor attention. A nonverbal cognitive measure may be used if language is significantly limited.

Children With Emotional Disturbance

This category includes children with a wide variety of problems, from acting out behaviors to internalizing and depressive conditions. It is important to have good background information on a child with emotional disturbance before he or she is evaluated. Interview the teacher as well as the parent(s), so that you are aware of any potential behavioral issues. Children in this category generally should be evaluated in multiple short testing sessions, if possible. The child should also be evaluated in a plain room with no extraneous stimuli. Many of these children will be receiving medication for ADHD, and should be evaluated on the same. However, as noted earlier, because some of these children are subject to ADHD, if the referral question is to diagnose or confirm an attention problem or the presence of ADHD, the child should not be evaluated while on medication for the same.

Children With Language Disorders

Whether a language deficit is developmental or acquired, the clinician should administer language subtests in order to document the deficit. Assessments should be administered in a quiet room. Be sure that the child is looking at you when directions are administered. Use visual cues frequently. The clinician should speak slowly and enunciate words clearly; keep directions as simple and as direct as possible on all subtests. For instance, on Visuomotor Precision, the clinician might abbreviate instructions with telegraphic language: "Draw a line fast" (demonstrating); "No hitting sides" (showing track sides); "No turning paper" (shaking head *no* and demonstrating turning paper); and "Ready, go!" Watch the child closely for signs of confusion, such as asking for repetitions frequently.

If needed, the clinician should use the teaching examples up to three times. Many subtests allow for this repetition; if that is not the case, be sure to note any additional teaching and consider this when interpreting scores. Record verbal responses and utterances heard during testing to analyze for semantic, syntactic, and other language errors later. Children with language impairment can be expected to perform poorly both on language subtests and on verbal memory subtests: such verbal memory deficits are usually secondary to the primary language deficit, rather than being a primary memory deficit. When assessing cognition for children with language disorders, the examiner also needs to include a nonverbal assessment. (See Rapid Reference 2.4.)

≡ Rapid Reference 2.4

Assessing the Child With a Language Disorder

- Whether a language deficit is developmental or acquired, the clinician should administer language subtests in order to document the deficit.

- Administer assessments in a quiet room, speak slowly, enunciate words clearly, and keep directions as simple and as direct as possible. Be sure the child is looking at you: use visual cues.

- Record verbal responses/utterances heard; analyze clinically for semantic, syntactic, and any other errors later.

- The child is apt to perform poorly on verbal memory subtests (e.g., Memory for Names). When assessing cognition include a nonverbal assessment.

Children With Learning Differences in Reading and Children With Learning Differences in Mathematics

These are children who exhibit particular difficulties with the acquisition of reading, spelling, and/or mathematics in spite of normal general cognitive capacity.

Reading Disorder

Ascertain from parents if there is a family history of dyslexia. When administering the NEPSY-II, be aware that language deficits may underlie a reading disorder. These may be subtle, but may affect the child's understanding of directions.

Mathematics Disorder

Mathematics Disorder is another learning difference included in the NEPSY-II special group validity studies. The NEPSY-II can be very helpful in elucidating the primary deficits underlying this complex learning difference. Aside from the obvious visuospatial deficits seen in math disorders, other primary deficits (e.g., attention, executive dysfunction) or comorbid problems (e.g., dysgraphia) may have a negative effect on math performance. Watch for frustration with processing speed across timed subtests. The Referral Battery for Learning Differences—Mathematics is comprised of subtests that aid the clinician in looking at the complexities of this condition. Of course, more achievement-related aspects of mathematics operations should be assessed as well, using academic achievement tests.

Children Who Are Deaf or Hard of Hearing

Children who are deaf or hard of hearing form a heterogeneous population. Further, the validation study group was heterogeneous and small; therefore, only cautious comparison can be made to the average performance of other hearing-impaired children of a specific age and with corresponding characteristics. Given the modifications made during administration for the validity study, only subtests administered to at least ten children are included in the study. The results from the validation study (see Chapter 6) suggest that the NEPSY-II can be modified appropriately for use with children who are deaf or hard of hearing. Nevertheless, the possibility needs to be considered that the child might not have perceived and comprehended the instructions properly. It is also important that appropriate steps be taken to optimize administration.

The clinician should determine before the evaluation which sign system is used by the child: American Sign Language (ASL) or Exact English (EE) or an adapted sign. If certified to do so, and fluent in the appropriate sign language, the clinician may administer NEPSY-II using ASL or EE. Otherwise, a certified interpreter should translate the directions and the child's response. The child needs to be a proficient signer for his or her age in order to have NEPSY-II administered in sign. This is especially true for subtests requiring rapid response in sign, such as Speeded Naming and Word Generation. If the child is proficient in understanding signed directions but cannot sign rapidly, the clinician should not administer the latter two subtests. Also, the examiner needs to be aware of regional colloquialisms in sign or of adapted sign used by the child.

It is best to have an interpreter or teacher who knows the child well interpret for her or him, especially in the case of adapted sign. The clinician may present printed directions if the child reads well. Although a few subtests need modified administration, all except Phonological Processing and Repetition of Nonsense Words can be administered in sign, though as noted before, if the child cannot sign rapidly, Speeded Naming and Word Generation should not be administered. The following subtests need further modification and should be so marked on the Report Form.

- *Statue.* This test can be administered by substituting tactile distracters for auditory ones: blowing on the hand, stroking or touching the arm with a feather, the eraser of a pencil, or a soft fabric (e.g., Kleenex, velvet, velour). Norms can be used as a guideline only for age-appropriate response.
- *Auditory Attention and Response Set.* This test can be administered with significant preparation, not as an auditory attention test, but as a test of response inhibition, of shift of set, and of visual attention to sign. It takes preparation to do this, however, and the clinician will need to videotape the presentation. This modified administration was developed with the help of participants in a 1999 NEPSY training workshop at the North Carolina School for the Deaf, Greensboro, NC.

Practice signing the words printed on the Record Form for the two tasks (Auditory Attention [AA] and Response Set [RS]) at a rate of one per second. Using a digital clock or timer to set your pace will help. Once you feel you are maintaining your pace consistently, videotape the visual equivalent of the audiotape, including directions and a 10-second pause between the end of AA and the directions for RS. However, at the beginning of each section, you need to include the two samples that the examiner usually reads. These can be shown to the child during the teaching phase. Once the videotape is made, you have a permanent tool for modifying this test.

Prior to taping, you need to place the easel with the AA/RS stimulus page just below the video monitor, so that the interpreter on the tape is clearly visible just above it. The child needs to be able to watch the signing and touch the correct color with a minimum of movement of the eyes from the monitor to the stimulus sheet just below it. Practice this with the child, using the samples and the directions in the *NEPSY-II Administration Manual.*

When the child understands the task, administer the test from the videotape. Record responses according to the directions given in the *Administration Manual.* It is best to interpret this subtest clinically, noting patterns of omission, commission, and inhibition errors. Also, on Part B, watch for difficulty with vigilance in responding to *blue,* and difficulty inhibiting the well-learned response to *red* in Part A and shifting set to a *yellow* response on Part B. If you use the typical norms in the *Administration Manual,* do so with great caution. Performance may be compared to mean performance for the sample of hearing impaired children. You may wish to develop your own age norms for children with hearing impairment using this modified administration. (See Rapid Reference 2.5.)

≡ Rapid Reference 2.5

Assessing Children Who Are Deaf or Hard of Hearing

The validation study (see Ch. 6) suggests that the NEPSY-II can be modified appropriately for use with children who are deaf or hard of hearing. It is important that appropriate steps be taken to optimize administration:

- Two subtests require rapid response in sign: If child cannot sign rapidly, do not give Speeded Naming (SN) or Word Generation (WG).
- If certified to do so, and fluent in the appropriate sign language, you can administer NEPSY-II; otherwise use a certified interpreter or the child's deaf education teacher.

The clinician may present printed directions if the child reads well. This is not optimal, however.

All subtests except Phonological Processing and Repetition of Nonsense Words can be administered in sign. Statue and Auditory Attention/Response Set subtests need further modification and should be so marked on the Report Form (Refer to full instructions on pp. 48–50 of this chapter.)

Children With Mild Intellectual Disability (ID)

Mild Intellectual Disability (ID; i.e., mental retardation) refers to subaverage intellectual functioning and concomitant deficits in two or more areas of adaptive skills. When evaluating a child with mild ID, it is important to take into account any special characteristics of an underlying condition (i.e., the talkativeness of a child with William's Syndrome). When assessing a child with intellectual disabilities speak slowly and enunciate clearly as you would for a child with a language disorder. Be aware of motor constraints (e.g., poor motor coordination in children with Down Syndrome may require the use of a primary pencil). Work speed tends to be slow and anxiety results when children with mild ID are rushed. Some children may need frequent breaks. Do not talk down to the child; on the other hand, be aware that behavior may be more typical of a younger child. Praise effort—reinforcers can be helpful in taking a task to completion.

Children With Motor Deficits

Children whose motor deficits are mild, affecting mainly coordination, are usually able to receive the standardized administration. The child with significant spasticity affecting both arms and legs (quadriplegia) obviously cannot complete motor tasks. An additional problem is that these children may be unable to give fluent verbal responses as spasticity may also affect the oral apparatus and the production of speech. Other children can be given the tasks that require only verbal responses. When one side of the body is functional (hemiplegia), assess motor skills on the active side of the body. When only mild motor disability affects one side of the body (hemiparesis), assess both sides of the body as far as is possible in order to demonstrate differences in motor control.

When the child with motor deficits does not finish within the time limits, the clinician may wish to test the limits by recording the child's results when the time runs out and allowing the child to finish the task with the stopwatch continuing to run. When the child finishes, the elapsed time for the full task can be recorded. In this way, the clinician can discuss the child's ability to complete the task, but not quickly. The examiner should provide a primary pencil, if needed. Following are examples of modifications that can be made for children with limited motor control. For all modified tasks, note on the Record Form *Modified Administration* and interpret results taking the modifications in account.

- *Comprehension of Instructions.* A child who can point either with a finger or a pointer should be able to do this task, as long as the easel is placed as close to the child as is needed to facilitate response. The NEPSY-II Stimulus Book is placed flat on the table with the answer sheet shielded with a piece of paper. If the child does not have a pointing response but knows his or her numbers, each shape can be numbered with a small removable adhesive label. The child can then instruct the examiner where to point by number ("2, 4, and then 5"). Because this procedure introduces a second verbal activity that might interfere with the memory traces of the instructions, it may be necessary to repeat the instructions. The modification should be noted on the Record Form and taken into account when scoring and evaluating the results.

- *Block Construction.* The child who can grasp the instruction or demonstration to do so can point to the location in which he or she would like the block placed. The examiner can place the block for the child and receive instructions how to orient it. (See Rapid Reference 2.6.)

≡ *Rapid Reference 2.6*

Assessing the Child Who Has Motor Deficits

- Administer motor subtests to all except the child with quadriplegia; assess children with hemiparesis on both sides to document differences in motor control.
- Provide a primary pencil or a pencil with a gripper.

Modifications may be needed for children with hemiplegia, hemiparesis, or other conditions that limit or preclude the use of one or both hands. (See pp. 51–52)

- For the child with milder motor difficulties, use the standardized administration with modifications. If he or she does not finish within the time limits, do not stop the child; record the time and last item completed. Results can be scored. Allow child to finish to see if child can do the task without time constraints.

The Child Who Is Blind

Blindness will markedly limit the number of NEPSY-II subtests that can be administered. Due to the limited number of subtests that can be employed with this population, children who are blind were not sampled for the validity studies; therefore mean scores are not available for this population. The following NEPSY-II subtests can be used and may provide clinical information to other testing:

- Attention/Executive domain: Statue
- Language domain: Phonological Processing (Phonological Segmentation only), Word Generation, Oromotor Sequences, Body Part Naming, and Repetition of Nonsense Words
- Sensorimotor domain: Fingertip Tapping
- Memory and Learning: List Learning, Narrative Memory (without picture Item 1), and Sentence Repetition

Modifications to administration of specific tests include:

- *Fingertip Tapping.* This subtest can be administered by allowing the child to feel the position of the examiner's hand and a demonstration of the tapping. After the child understands the task, he or she can be assessed according to the regular directions. After completing the tapping part of the subtest, sequencing is demonstrated in the same way, with the child feeling the examiner's hand as the demonstration takes place. Again, when the child understands the task, the clinician can perform regular administration.
- *Body Part Naming.* This test can be administered using a large doll with well-defined features, placing the child's forefinger on the part to be named, the examiner's body, or by touching the corresponding part of the child's body with the eraser end of a pencil. Norms should be interpreted cautiously. The clinician should use the 2 point (doll; examiner's body)/1 point (own body) scoring in the *Administration Manual,* but interpret scores with caution. For the Body Part Identification task, the child can identify the part named by pointing to his or her own body or the doll's body. Score is 1 point for each part correctly identified. (See Rapid Reference 2.7.)

≡ *Rapid Reference 2.7*

Assessing the Child Who Is Blind

Administration of the NEPSY-II for this child is limited to the following subtests, some with modifications:

- Statue, Phonological Processing (Items 23–45 only), Word Generation, Oromotor Sequences, Repetition of Nonsense Words, List Learning, Narrative Memory, Sentence Repetition, Word List Interference
- Body Part Naming, and Fingertip Tapping (See pp. 52–53)

OTHER ADMINISTRATION CONSIDERATIONS

Examiner Practice for Certain Tests

Although this is not true of the majority of the NEPSY-II subtests, certain subtests may be difficult to administer and should be practiced before the first administration. The following subtests need practice before the clinician attempts to administer them: Auditory Attention and Response Set, Inhibition, Memory for Designs, Imitating Hand Positions, and Manual Motor Series. It is recommended that the clinician practice these at least twice with normally developing children and five times with children who have various impairments before administering the test for clinical purposes. See Caution box concerning Subtests Requiring Examiner Practice. Detailed administration directions for each of them can be found in the manual. In particular, the directions designate and show illustrations of specific hands and fingers for the Imitating Hand Positions subtest and the order of movement for Manual Motor Series. If you need time to form the hand positions you may do so on your lap and bring the hand up to the table surface, so the child does not watch you forming the hand position. If needed, for the examiner's benefit, the manual motor movements can also be started in his or her lap and then brought to the table surface when the rhythm is established.

CAUTION

....

Subtests Requiring Examiner Practice

Auditory Attention and Response Set
- Inhibition
- Memory for Designs/MD Delayed
- Imitating Hand Positions

Manual Motor Sequences

Clocks (scoring)

Practice each at least twice with typical children and five times with children who have various impairments before administering the test for clinical purposes. Detailed administration directions for each of them can be found in the Administration Manual and in this chapter of the present volume.

Start and Discontinue Rules

On some of the subtests of NEPSY-II, all items are given to all children. Other subtests have start rules that allow testing time to be shortened for older children, and reverse rules that allow the clinician to go back to earlier items for children unable to succeed at their age level. Most NEPSY-II subtests have Discontinue Rules. Icons are provided on the Record Form to remind the examiner of these points. (See Rapid Reference 2.8.)

≡ Rapid Reference 2.8

Subtest Administration Rules

Start points, reversal rules, discontinue rules, and stop points are discussed and illustrated in the NEPSY-II Administration *Manual*, pp. 21–26.
   Completing the Record Form is discussed and illustrated in the Administration *Manual*, pp. 29–33.
   A summary of each subtest's rules can be found in the Subtest-by-Subtest Rules of Administration section on p. 59.

Recording Responses

There are separate Record Forms for ages 3 to 4 years and 5 to 16 years. Responses are recorded for each test on the appropriate Record Form. Correct responses are printed in violet on the Record Form for ages 3 to 4 and in green on the Record Form for 5 to 16. After the primary subtest scores are computed, they can be plotted on the child's profile, located on the front cover of the Record Form. This is a helpful graph to use when discussing strengths and weaknesses with parents. There are numerous process or contrast scores that provide additional diagnostic information. The examiner is encouraged to use these processes and contrast scores, but they are optional.

Obviously, on all subtests recording of responses is essential, but on a number of subtests, the clinician records information in a way that will allow error analysis later. For example, on Word Generation, the clinician could just tally the number of correct words in each category, because the number of words that the child produces in each category within the time limit is the variable being measured. On the other hand, recording the actual words helps determine if a word is repeated and permits error analysis later. The latter may reveal faulty or particularly efficient strategies or patterns for the child's access to words. Also, on List Learning, when the examiner records the child's words in the order of recall, valuable diagnostic information can be analyzed later. The clinician can see if the child was clustering to aid memory recall. Furthermore, the examiner can also see the type of clustering used, such as semantic (boat, water, fish) or phonemic clustering (window, water, winter). Further, one can see if there is a primacy (most words recalled from the first of the list) or recency effect (most words recalled from the last part of the list).

Behavioral Observations

Recording behavioral observations, both formally (when Behavioral Observations are designated on a subtest) and informally (when the clinician observes interesting aspects of the child's behavior), is necessary for the neuropsychological evaluation. These observations often provide essential diagnostic information about how a child is, or is not, able to perform a function. For many subtests, Behavioral Observations are specified that are specific to the subtest. Some of these are quantifiable and you may compare the scores to base rates in the norm sample (see *NEPSY II Administrative Manual*). After testing is complete, such Behavioral Observations are recorded as present or absent (Y or N) on the inside front cover of the Record Form, while others are totaled. (See Rapid Reference 2.9.)

≡ *Rapid Reference 2.9*

Formal Behavioral Observations That Are Tallied or Recorded

- A list of Behavioral Observations that are tallied or recorded from each domain appears in the *Administration Manual* on p. 34.
- Summarizing scores on the Behavioral Observation page of the Record Form is found on p. 33 in the *Administration Manual*.

Also subtle difficulties may be observed that are not reflected in low scores but rather as unusual effort. There are also general observations that psychologists are accustomed to making during testing sessions. These include, but are not limited to, the following general questions:

- Does the child exhibit signs of anxiety or stress?
- How does the child cope with failure, is he or she easily distressed, or confident, and can the child be easily reassured?
- Is the child able to work attentively or does he or she present signs of poor attention?
- Does fatigue or loss of motivation or attention affect performance?
- Is the child impulsive and/or uncritical with respect to own performance?
- What is the child's general tempo in working?
- Does the child appear to have word-finding problems, attempting to recall words through circumlocutions?

DON'T FORGET

Your Observations are a part of a neuropsychological evaluation.

Watch how the child performs the task and record it. For example:

- How was the task accomplished?
- What strategies were used?
- Did the child verbally mediate the task?
- Record any listed Behavioral Observations for each subtest.
- Record *your own* observations and impressions.

How the child approaches a specific task will aid formulation of intervention.

Timing and Testing the Limits

Many of the NEPSY-II subtests are untimed, but where timing limits are required, this will be noted at the top right of the subtest instructions in the Record Form under *Time Limit (Timing)*. Under the heading *Materials* at the top of each subtest, *stopwatch* will appear if the test is to be timed. The Stimulus Books show a stopwatch icon for the timed subtests. The clinician should record the time rounded to the nearest second. A general timing guideline of a maximum of 10 seconds per item serves to keep the pace from slowing to the point that the child loses interest and to avoid causing a child distress when he or she cannot do an item or is unwilling to perform.

If a child is actively engaged in a task, but it is apparent that he or she will not finish within the time limits, the examiner may wish to test the limits. Record the time when the time limit has expired and the child's response(s) up to that time, but do not stop the child or the stopwatch. Allow the child to complete the task, to a reasonable limit, without saying anything about the time being up. Record the additional elapsed time-to-solution for qualitative analysis later. In this way, the clinician will have the information needed to score the timed subtest, as well as the ability to judge how well the child might have performed without time limits. The latter information can be discussed clinically in the report and may contribute to the interventions recommended.

Prompting, Querying, Self-Corrections, and Item Repetition

As a general rule, prompting ("Keep going," or "Let's give it another try") is permitted on NEPSY-II in order to ensure the child's best performance. The clinician should note the prompt ("Tell me more") with *P*. Some subtests have specific directions for prompting that appear in the manual, Record Form, and Stimulus Books to which the examiner should adhere. Self-corrections are, in general, allowed on NEPSY-II *when they are made before the next item is administered.* The clinician should record *SC* beside the item and write in the correct response. If repetitions are not allowed on a subtest, this will be designated in the manual and Stimulus Books. The clinician should note *R* or *Rep* on the Record Form. On the Phonological Processing, Comprehension of Instructions, and Sentence Repetition subtests, asking for repetition is recorded as a Behavioral Observation to be compared to cumulative percentages for age in the standardization population.

Teaching the Task

The NEPSY-II provides teaching items on many subtests. Directions for these are in both the *Administration Manual* and the Stimulus Books. Unless otherwise specified, the teaching items are presented once, but the child may practice as much as needed to be sure he or she understands the task before the subtest actually begins. If a task actually has to be modified from the standardized directions or format due to the child's disability, the clinician should note the modifications and the reasons for them on the Record Form. The child's performance should be evaluated clinically, and the norms should be used as guidelines and interpreted cautiously.

SUBTEST-BY-SUBTEST RULES OF ADMINISTRATION

The NEPSY-II *Administration Manual* and, when appropriate, the Stimulus Books 1 and 2, provide detailed rules for subtest administration, including Start, Reverse, Discontinue, and Stop rules. This section of the present chapter also provides these crucial elements of administration, including Start, Reverse, Discontinue, and Stop rules, in the same section and in an abbreviated form in a Rapid Reference box for each subtest. In addition, this section presents useful tips for competent administration, and notes key behaviors to observe. Many of the tips are derived from courses and workshops teaching administration of NEPSY-II, and are based on questions that have been raised. Examiners who are new to NEPSY-II may want to spend time studying this advice in depth and using them as a guide to practice. For examiners who have already learned the NEPSY-II, this section can serve as a guide to refresh the memory on important details of subtest administration and to add useful tips. The subtests are presented in alphabetical order in the *Administration Manual* and in this discussion, as the order of administration may be varied. The subtest domain appears in parentheses after the subtest title and the referral batteries, including that specific subtests are indicated by the following abbreviations:

GA = General Administration	R = Learning Differences/Reading	M = Learning Differences/Math
A/C = Attention/ Concentration	B = Behavior Management	L = Language Delays/ Disorders
P/M = Perceptual/Motor Delays/Disorder	SR = School Readiness	S/I = Social/ Interpersonal

If the abbreviation for a referral battery appears in parentheses, the subtest is optional for that battery.

Affect Recognition (Social Perception): Ages 3–16

Referral Batteries: B, S/I (A/C, L, P/M)
This subtest is designed to assess the ability to recognize affect (*happy, sad, neutral, fear, anger, disgust*) from photographs of children's faces in four different tasks (three tasks for ages 3 to 4). (See Rapid Reference 2.10 for Summary of Affect Recognition.)

≡ *Rapid Reference 2.10*

Summary of Affect Recognition Administration Rules
Ages 3–16

Start	Reverse Rule	Discontinue	Stop	Time Limit/Timing
Item 1	Ages 5–16: If 0 on either of first two items, reverse until two consecutive scores of 1, then proceed forward.	After 5 consecutive scores of 0	Ages 3–4, Item 16 Ages 5–6, Item 25	Present each stimulus for 5 seconds

Rules

See Rapid Reference 2.10 for details on Start Point, Reverse Rule, Discontinue, Stop, and Time.

Materials: Stimulus Book 1 is placed flat on the table in front of the child.

Administration: Directions in Stimulus Book 1. The child is to recognize affect (happy, sad, neutral, fear, angry, disgust) from colored photos of children's faces in four different tasks:

- The child states whether or not two photos depict faces with the same affect.
- The child selects two photos with the same affect from three or four photos.
- The child is shown a page with five faces and selects one of the four faces at the bottom of the page that depicts the same affect as the picture at the top of the page.
- The child is briefly shown a face and, from memory, identifies two photos that depict the same affect as the face previously shown.

Recording Behavioral Observations

Each time the child makes a comment about a face, place a tally mark in the *Spontaneous Comments* box on the Record Form.

Tips
- With young children, you may want to demonstrate facial expressions of affect. Say: "See, sometimes I feel like this" (put up a happy face), "sometimes like this" (put up a sad face).
- Items 1–8 show two items (each with two faces) to a Stimulus Book page. Cover the set not being used with a blank piece of paper or card stock. Record spontaneous comments made by the child during this subtest. These are totaled and can be compared to typical children of the child's age. These comments may provide diagnostic information about how the child identifies emotions, and his or her response to specific emotions.

Other Behaviors to Observe
- Impulsivity; not attending to faces before identifying emotions.
- Apparent confusion in identifying *neutral* faces, misinterpreting them as *mad*.
- Mediating each of his or her choices by talking his or her way through the identification of emotions.

Animal Sorting (Attention/Executive Functioning): Ages 7–16

Referral Batteries: B, S/I (A/C, L)

This subtest is designed to assess the executive function of formulating concepts, transferring concepts into action (sorting into categories), and to shift set from one concept to another in sorting cards with animal pictures. (See Rapid Reference 2.11.)

$\equiv$ *Rapid Reference 2.11*

Summary of Animal Sorting Rules Ages: 7–16

Start	Reverse Rule	Discontinue	Stop	Time Limit/ Timing
Ages 3–6, Do not administer Ages 7–16, Teaching Example	None	After 360 seconds of cumulative sorting time, or after all sorts are completed or when the child states that he or she is finished.	None	Allow 360 of cumulative sorting time

Rules

See Rapid Reference 2.11 for details on Start Point, Reverse Rule, Discontinue, Stop, and Time.

> **Materials:** Pack of cards with animal pictures; no Stimulus Book.
>
> **Administration:** Directions in *Administration Manual* (p. 39). The child sorts picture cards as quickly as possible into two groups of four cards each, using self-initiated sorting criteria. There are 12 possible sorts. Animal Sorting does not require the child to respond verbally, nor does he or she need to read.

Recording:

- For each four-card sort completed by the child, record only the three numbers from the backs of the cards in the group that contains the zebra (Card 1). The zebra's number (1) is already on the record form. You do not have to record the other group of four cards. This facilitates recording time.
- After the child's assessment is completed, go back and circle the Y & N for the sort errors and 1 or 0 for a correct or incorrect sort.

Tips

- Determination of a correct four-card sort, novel sort, or repeated sort is based solely on the card numbers recorded, not on anything a child has said.
- Do not start timing until all instructions are read and the Teaching Example is completed. When the last word of the instructions is read, start timing.
- The 360 seconds of sort time reflects only the time the child has the cards in hand and is engaged in sorting activity. Time to record the child's response or to give the child additional instructions should not be included in the 360 seconds of cumulative time. If the child has the cards in hand but does not sort for 2 minutes, discontinue. (See Caution box.)

CAUTION

Determining Cumulative Sorting Time

- To facilitate administration time and accuracy, do not record error types or score until the child's assessment session has been completed.
- If child does not sort the cards exactly into two four-card piles (e.g., sorts three cards in one group and five cards in other group), don't count the sort as a Novel Sort or a Repeated Sort Error.

- If child sorts twice into two unequal piles, stop the watch, remind the child to sort into four-card piles, and re-start stopwatch.
- Do not ask how the child sorted during the administration of the test, as he/she may feel that an explanation must be provided for each sort.
- If you want qualitative information about how the child sorted, place a check mark beside the item. When test is completed, reassemble the item as the child sorted it, and then ask the child how he or she sorted.

Other Behaviors to Observe
- Does the child grasp the concept of the four-card sort easily?
- Does the child sort impulsively without reflection?
- Does the child make many Repeated Sort Errors, suggesting working memory problems or perseverative tendency?
- Does the child make numerous Novel Sort Errors, suggesting problems with concept formation?
- Is the child significantly slow in processing the task, suggesting a problem with fluency?

Arrows (Visuospatial Domain): Ages 5–16

Referral Batteries: (A/C, B, S/I)
This subtest assesses the visual judgment of line and angle orientation. (See Rapid Reference 2.12.)

≡ Rapid Reference 2.12

Summary of Arrows Rules Ages 5–16

Start	Reverse Rule	Discontinue	Stop	Time Limit
Ages 5–6: Teaching Example 1, then Item 1 Ages 9–16: Teaching Example 2, then Item 5	Ages 9–16: If 0 on either item 5 or 6, reverse until two consecutive scores of 1, then proceed forward. If child must reverse, administer Teaching Example 1 before administering Item 4.	After 5 consecutive scores of 0	None	None

Rules

See Rapid Reference 2.12 for details on Start Point, Reverse Rule, Discontinue, Stop, and Time.

Materials: Stimulus Book 1 in flat position.

Administration: Directions in Stimulus Book 1. The child looks at an array of arrows arranged around a target. By judging the line orientation of the arrows in relation to the target, he or she indicates the arrow(s) that will hit the center of the target.

Recording: Circle the child's responses.

Tips

- After the Teaching Example do not let the child trace the arrows path to the target.
- On Items 5–21, if the child chooses only one arrow, prompt for a second arrow if required (and record P).
- Explain that the arrows do not need to be next to each other or in number sequence.

> **CAUTION**
>
> The child is not allowed to trace the arrow's path after the Teaching Example.

Other Behaviors to Observe

- Impulsivity—If impulsive or inattentive, direct the child's attention to each of the arrows before allowing a choice to be made. If the child consistently chooses impulsively, note this on Record Form, interpret results cautiously, and discuss this observation in your report.
- Does child continue to try to trace the path to the house despite reminders?
- Does the child make significantly more errors on one side of space than on the other? Have you noted visual field errors in any other testing?

Auditory Attention and Response Set (Attention/Executive Functioning): Ages 5–16

Referral Batteries: GA, R, M, A/C, B, L, P/M S/I

This assessment has two parts. The AA subtest measures simple, selective auditory attention to rapidly presented auditory stimuli and the ability to sustain attention (vigilance). The second task, RS, assesses both selective attention and inhibition of previously learned responses in order to shift to an alternate response (see Rapid Reference 2.13.)

≡ *Rapid Reference 2.13*

Summary of Auditory Attention and Response Set Rules Ages 5–16

Start	Reverse Rule	Discontinue	Stop	Time Limit/ Timing
Teaching Example for Auditory Attention	None	Do not discontinue.	Ages 5–6: After Auditory Attention	None

Rules

See Rapid Reference 2.13 for details on Start Point, Reverse Rule, Discontinue, Stop, and Time.

Materials: Stimulus Book 1 in flat position in front of the child.

Administration: Follow directions in Stimulus Book 1. The child has a stimulus book before him or her that shows four colored circles (red, blue, yellow, and black). The audio file supplies the auditory stimuli. On the first task (AA) the child listens for the word *Red* among all of the distracter words that he or she hears, and points to the correct circle when *Red* is heard. On the second task, the child must correctly respond to matching (*blue* to *blue*) or contrasting auditory stimuli (*yellow* for *red*/*red* for *yellow*) by pointing to the correct colored circle.

Recording: Follow along in the Record Form as the audio plays. Each time the child touches a colored circle record the corresponding letter for that color in the Response column next to the word being stated.

- R = red   Y = yellow   B = blue   K = black
- W = white if the child purposefully touches the white portion of the page when *white* is stated.
- If the child self-corrects, record both initial response and self-correction on Record Form. Indicate SC beside the self-correction. Apply scoring rules to *Both Responses*.

Recording for Behavioral Observations

- For each instance of inattention or distracted behavior (e.g., looks around the room), place a tally mark in the *Inattentive/Distracted* Off-Task Behavior box on the Record Form.
- Each time the child is out of his or her seat or moves around noticeably in his/her seat during the test items, place a tally mark in the *Out of Seat/Physical Movement in Seat* Off-Task Behavior box on the Record Form.

Tips

- On the Record Form, follow the printed words you hear with your pencil. Watch only the child's hand and record the color (*R, Y, B*) touched in the Response column.
- Practice recording for this test before administering.
- You may present the Teaching Example for each section three times, if necessary.
- The child keeps his or her hands on the edge of the table between items. If child's hands hover over the color circles, gesture for him or her to move hands back to the table's edge. Do not talk because the next word on the tape will not be heard if you do.
- Although the child is told not to try to correct mistakes because of the speed of the tape, spontaneous corrections can be credited, if the correct color is touched <u>before</u> the next item is administered. Record and score both responses. Do not stop the tape.
- Do not allow the child to go back to an item after the next word has been pronounced.

Other Behaviors to Observe

- Salient behaviors (focused attention, excited or frustrated expressions or remarks, oppositional responses) on the two portions of the test. Complex, rapid tasks may be causing similar behavioral responses in the classroom.
- Record boredom, impulsivity, and slips in attention (easier on A.A.).

CAUTION

When Response Set is clearly too difficult, discontinue. You can still score Auditory Attention.

Block Construction (Visuospatial Domain): Ages 3–16

Referral Batteries: Ages 3–6: M, S/I; All ages: P/M, SR

This subtest is a three-dimensional block construction task requiring visuospatial analysis integrated with motor output. (See Rapid Reference 2.14.)

≡ *Rapid Reference 2.14*

Summary of Block Construction Rules Ages 3–16

Start	Reverse Rule	Discontinue	Stop	Time Limit/ Timing
Ages 5–6: Item 6 Ages 7–16: Item 8	If 0 on either of first two items, reverse until two consecutive scores of 1, then proceed forward.	Discontinue after 4 consecutive scores of 0.	None	Items 1–7, Allow 30 sec./per item. Items 8–19, Allow 60 sec./per item. Note: Time bonuses are awarded on Items 11–19.

Rules

See Rapid Reference 2.14 for details on Start Point, Reverse Rule, Discontinue, Stop, and Time.

> **Materials:** Stimulus Book 1 in easel position in front of the child.
> **Administration:** Follow directions in Stimulus Book 1 or on the Record Form. The child uses three-dimensional blocks to reproduce a construction from a three-dimensional block construction or a two-dimensional drawing of a construction.
> **Recording:** Record completion time in seconds for each item. If necessary, you may move your position to verify the correct construction.

Tips

- For error analysis later, you can record imperfect performance by marking *X* on blocks incorrectly positioned, *O* where blocks are omitted, and make a checkmark on each block rotated 45 degrees or more. This is optional qualitative information only.

- Rotations are no longer counted as errors on the more difficult items as they were on NEPSY.

Other Behaviors to Observe
- The child performs well from the three-dimensional model but fails to transition to the two-dimensional stimulus.
- Does the child reflect on the model or stimulus picture before beginning his or her construction?
- Is the child overly precise and obsessive about lining up each block perfectly with the others and perhaps running out of time because he or she keeps adjusting blocks?

Body Part Naming (Language Domain): Ages 3–4

Referral Battery: L (Ages 3–4 only)
This subtest is designed to assess confrontation naming and name recognition of body parts. (See Rapid Reference 2.15.)

≡ *Rapid Reference 2.15*

Summary of Body Part Naming Rules Ages 3–4

Start	Reverse Rule	Discontinue	Stop	Timing
Ages 3–4: Item 1 Ages 5–16: Do not administer	None	BP Naming: Discontinue after 4 consecutive scores of 0, then proceed to BP Identification. BP Identification: Do not discontinue.	None	None

Rules
See Rapid Reference 2.15 for details on Start Point, Reverse Rule, Discontinue, Stop, and Time.

Materials: Stimulus Book 1 in flat position.

Administration: Directions in Stimulus Book 1 and on the Record
Form. For the first task, Body Part Naming, the examiner points to a
body part on the stimulus figure and asks, "What is this called?," or
if the child does not understand, "This is a _____ (pause for response)." If the child is unable to identify the body part on the figure
in the Stimulus Book, the examiner points to the corresponding
body part on the child's body and asks, "What is this called?" For the
second task, Body Part Identification, the examiner, says, "Show me
the (names part)," then asks the child to point to the specified body
part of the figure in the Stimulus Book. The items are on the Record
Form.

Recording: Circle points earned on the Record Form.

Tips
- You may point to the corresponding part of your own body or face if
  it helps the child. Touching the child's body when pointing to it may
  provide tactile feedback and changes the task in comparison with the
  standardization procedure.
- On each Naming item start with the picture, then move to the
  child's body, only if he or she cannot name the body part from the
  picture.
- If the child names a general part rather than a specific part (e.g., head
  instead of nose), query, "What part of the head?" Place a *Q* on the
  Record Form to indicate your query.

Other Behaviors to Observe
- As this subtest is for young children, it is opportune to observe the
  child's articulation. Are there stable misarticulations (e.g., "the" is always /f/) or do sounds that are misarticulated fluctuate?
- Poor eye contact and lack of relatedness?

Clocks (Attention/Executive Domain): Ages 7–16

Referral batteries: A/C, B, P/M, (L)

This subtest assesses the child's understanding of time on an analog clock through
visual items, and planning, organization, and visuospatial skills in regard to drawing clocks. (See Rapid Reference 2.16.)

≡ *Rapid Reference 2.16*

Summary of Clocks Rules Ages 7–16

Start	Reverse Rule	Discontinue	Stop	Time Limit/ Timing
Ages 3–6: Do not administer	None	Do not discontinue.	None	None
Ages 7–16: Item 1 in Response Booklet				

Rules

See Rapid Reference 2.16 for details on Start Point, Reverse Rule, Discontinue, Stop, and Time.

    Materials: Stimulus Book 1: easel position.

    Administration: Follow subtest directions in Stimulus Book 1.

        Items 1–4 in Response Booklet

        Items 5–8 in Stimulus Book 1

        Items 9–10 in Response Booklet

        For each of the drawing items, the child draws the image of a clock and draws the hands where the examiner indicates verbally (e.g., "Now draw the hands at 3 o'clock"). On the digital-to-analog drawing items, the child is shown a picture of a digital clock and is asked to draw the hands on an analog clock so it tells the same time as the digital one. For visual items, the child reads the time on analog clocks with and without numbers.

    Timing: None

    Recording: For *items 1–2* and *9–10*, record the manner in which the child draws the numbers on the clock face. Circle *A* if the child records the anchor numbers first or *S* if the child records the numbers in serial order or reverse serial order. For *items 5–8,* record the child's response verbatim in the space provided on the Record Form.

Tips

- Observation of the child's strategy and careful recording are essential, so it is essential to practice both administering and scoring the test. This will produce good clinical information.

- You may wish to mark your Record Form ahead of time so that you move smoothly between the Response Booklet for Item 4 and the Easel for Items 5–8, then back to the Response Booklet for Items 9–10.
- Provide the child with a sharpened pencil without eraser.

Other Behaviors to Observe
- Is planning apparent or is performance random in arranging numerals on the clock face?
- Are numbers very large or very small, suggesting poor motor control or expansiveness on the former or anxiety/obsessiveness on the latter?
- *After* the child has completed the test you may wish to ask how many minutes the space between numbers represents in order to determine knowledge of time concepts on the analogue clock.

Comprehension of Instructions (Language Domain): Ages 3–16

Referral Batteries: GA, R, M, B, L, SR, S/I
This subtest is designed to assess the ability to perceive, process, and execute verbal instructions of increasing syntactic complexity. (See Rapid Reference 2.17.)

≡ *Rapid Reference 2.17*

Summary of Comprehension of Instructions Rules: Ages 3–16

Start	Reverse Rule	Discontinue	Stop	Time Limit
Age 3–5: Item 1 Age 6–12: Pre-requisite Items for Items 14–33 Ages 13–16: Item 17	6–12: If an incorrect response to either Prerequisite Item is provided, go to Item 1, then proceed forward. 6–16: If a score of zero is obtained on either of the first two items administered, reverse until two consecutive scores of 1 are obtained; then proceed forward.	Discontinue after 7 consecutive scores of 0.	None	None

Rules

See Rapid Reference 2.17 for details on Start Point, Reverse Rule, Discontinue, Stop, and Time.

Materials: Stimulus Book 1 in flat position.

Administration: Follow the subtest directions in Stimulus Book 1 or on the Record Form. For each item, the child points to appropriate stimuli in response to progressively more difficult oral directions, thus demonstrating comprehension of oral instructions (receptive language).

Recording: For all items, reduced versions of the stimuli appear in the Record Form. These are shown from your perspective when sitting directly across from the child. Record the child's responses by numbering, in sequential order, the bunnies or shapes to which he or she points.

For the Prerequisite items, circle *C* if the child points to a correct shape or *I* if the child does not point to the correct shape.

Recording and Scoring During Task Performance

Familiarize yourself thoroughly with the scoring rules that follow.

If an item makes reference to order (e.g., *first, after*), the sequence must be in the correct order.

- If an item makes reference to *a* bunny or *a* shape and the child points to multiple bunnies or multiple shapes that are correct (e.g., *Point to a big bunny,* and the child points to all the big bunnies on the page), the response should be considered correct.
- If an item says specifically, *Point to one bunny*, then the child must point to only one bunny to be correct.
- For any item containing words that indicate direction, these words *make reference to the first shape* in that direction (e.g., *the circle below the white cross* means the circle immediately and directly below the white cross).
- For Items 21 and 29, correct responses may be provided using either a "classroom" row or a traditional row. A response using either the classroom (vertical) row or the traditional (horizontal) row would be considered correct.
  - For Item 21, the *third shape* makes reference to the third shape in the row counting from left to right for a traditional row and counting from the top to the bottom of the page for a "classroom" row. The third shape counting from right to left or bottom to top of the page from the child's perspective would be incorrect.

- For Item 29, the *first row* makes reference to the row at the top of the page from the child's perspective for a traditional row and the row on the left side of the page from the child's perspective for a "classroom" row. The horizontal row at the bottom of the page or the vertical row on the right side of the page would be incorrect responses.
- For Item 27, *diagonal* makes reference to the shape that is at a 45 degree angle from the black and red crosses, which is the red circle and the only correct response. The blue cross is an incorrect response.
- For Item 28, the child must provide three distinct responses. The child cannot receive credit for both *a cross* and *the red cross* by pointing only to the red cross. A response consisting of the black circle, the red cross, and a cross that is not red should be considered correct.

Recording for the Behavioral Observation

Asks for Repetition: Each time the child asks for or otherwise indicates that an item should be repeated, place a tally mark in the *Asks for Repetition* box. Record for both parts of the CI subtest. Do not repeat any items.

Tips

- Although the items should not be repeated, requests for repetition are of interest to see if the child struggles to understand. Tally requests for repetitions in the appropriate box on the bottom of the Record Form page.
- Read directions at a normal rate of speech. Do not stress particular words.
- On the miniatures of the picture stimulus provided on the Record Form, you can number the shapes in the order the child executes the instructions for error analysis later.

Other Behaviors to Observe

- Impulsive responding, which may start before you have completed the instructions.
- Does he or she become more confused as the amount of language increases?
- Does the child appear to have a working memory problem (cannot remember the whole instruction on the longer items)?
- Does the child have more problems on one type of instruction than another (e.g., negation, visual-spatial terms)?

Design Copying (Visuospatial Domain): Ages 3–16

Referral Batteries: GA, M, R, A/C, B, L, P/M, SR, S/I

This subtest is an untimed two-dimensional constructional task that requires the integration of visuoperceptual abilities and motor skills. (See Rapid Reference 2.18.)

≡ Rapid Reference 2.18

Summary of Design Copying Rules Ages 3–16

Start	Reverse Rule	Discontinue	Stop	Time Limit/ Timing
Ages 3–16: Item 1	None	Do not discontinue.	Ages 3–6: Stop after Item 18	None

Rules

See Rapid Reference 2.18 for details on Start Point, Reverse Rule, Discontinue, Stop, and Time.

Materials: Age-appropriate Response Booklet only.

Administration: Directions in the *Administration Manual* (p. 54). The child reproduces paper-and-pencil copies of geometric designs of increasing complexity. No erasures are allowed, nor can the child start over. Neither is the child allowed to turn the paper as he or she draws. The examiner observes the child's planning and execution in order to see if he or she is focused on the task, allows appropriate inspection time before drawing, and employs ordering and sequencing in his or her reproduction. This will enable the examiner to determine if a poor performance and low Motor, Global, and/or Local scores are due to executive dysfunction rather than spatial, detail, or fine motor processing deficits.

Recording: All recording of responses is in the age-appropriate Response Booklet.

Tips

- The first item for 3- to 4-year-olds is imitative. Follow the script for administration.
- Remind the child not to start over with the drawing, and do not allow the child to turn the paper or erase. If the child does turn the page, turn it back and prompt, *remember not to turn the paper.*
- Check that the child has not skipped a page of designs before moving to the next task. Check again before the child leaves.

Other Behaviors to Observe
- Planning and execution are not scored on Design Copying, but your interpretation of the Motor, Global, and Local scaled scores should always take that into consideration. Does poor performance seem to be due to regulatory factors (executive functions) rather than spatial, detail, or fine motor processing deficits?
- Notice whether or not the child approaches the task deliberately, reflecting on the design before he or she begins copying.
- Watch for the ordering and sequencing required to ensure the reproduced design will fit within the space allotted.
- Watch for overflow movements of head and shoulders, around the mouth, or involuntary tongue movements as the child copies.
- Pencil grip is not a Behavioral Observation as it was on NEPSY, but note whether a good tripod grip is present or the child shows an awkward pencil grip that impedes fluid movement.

Design Fluency (Attention/Executive Functioning Domain): Ages 5–12

Referral Batteries: A/C, P/M, S/I (B)
This subtest is designed to assess nonverbal fluency and executive functions through a paper/pencil task generating as many unique designs as possible. (See Rapid Reference 2.19.)

≡ *Rapid Reference 2.19*

Summary of Design Fluency Rules: Ages 5–12

Start	Reverse Rule	Discontinue	Stop	Time Limit/ Timing
Ages 3–4 and 13–26: Do not administer Ages 5–12: Structured Array Teaching Example 1	None	Do not discontinue.	None	Allow 60 seconds for each array.

Rules

See Rapid Reference 2.19 for details on Start Point, Reverse Rule, Discontinue, Stop, and Time.

Materials: Age-appropriate Response Booklet

Administration: Follow subtest directions and general guidelines on pp. 57–58 of the *Administration Manual*. The child is presented a series of structured arrays of five dots. He or she must produce as many unique designs as possible in 60 seconds by joining up two or more dots with straight lines in each array. The child is then presented with a series of random arrays of five dots, and, again, he or she must produce as many unique designs as possible in 60 seconds by joining up two or more dots with straight lines in each array. No erasures are allowed on either series of arrays. Only unique designs count. An organized strategy will enable the child to produce unique designs.

Recording: Child marks all of his or her responses in the Response Booklet.

Tips

- All lines must be straight, or intended by the child to be straight. Two or more dots must be connected. Only unique designs are scored. Prompt child if needed to remember these points.
- The arrows on the Random Array should point toward you and away from the child. This correctly orients the Random Array.
- Use a pencil without an eraser as erasures are not allowed.

Other Behaviors to Observe

- Do poor graphomotor skills appear to affect performance negatively?
- Does the child appear to forget the rules?
- Does the child monitor his or her work to catch errors? Is the child anxious or impulsive?
- Does the child use strategies (e.g., varying designs in a systematic fashion)?
- Does the child draw complex and elaborated figures? This may reduce the number of figures produced.

Fingertip Tapping (Sensorimotor Domain): Ages 5–16

Referral Batteries: B, P/M, S/I

This subtest has two tasks. The first task assesses finger dexterity and fine motor speed, and the second task assesses rapid motor programming. Both finger movement tasks are performed as quickly as possible with preferred and nonpreferred hands. (See Rapid Reference 2.20.)

≡ Rapid Reference 2.20

Summary of Fingertip Tapping Rules: Ages 5–16

Start	Reverse Rule	Discontinue	Stop	Time Limit/ Timing
Ages 3–4: Do not administer	None	Do not discontinue.	None	Items 1–2: Allow 60 sec./item
Ages 5–16: Teaching Example 1, then Item 1				Items 3–4: Allow 90 sec./item

Rules

See Rapid Reference 2.20 for details on Start Point, Reverse Rule, Discontinue, Stop, and Time.

Materials: Age-appropriate Record Form only

Administration: Directions in the *Administration Manual* (pp. 61–62). Correct and incorrect hand/finger positions for Fingertip Tapping appear in Figures 3.6 and 3.7 on p. 61. The examiner demonstrates repetitive finger tapping:

> **The index fingertip is tapped against the pad of the thumb as quickly as possible.**

> After practicing, the child is asked to perform the task as quickly as possible with the dominant hand. The examiner times the child and counts 20 correct Repetitions. The elapsed time for 20 movements is the raw score. The Repetition task is then repeated with the nondominant hand and timed in the same way. Then the examiner demonstrates the motor programming task:

> **The fingers are tapped sequentially against the pad of the thumb (index finger, middle finger, ring finger, then little finger), making a circle with each finger and the thumb.**

After practicing, the child is asked to do Fingertip Tapping Sequences with the dominant hand as quickly as possible. The examiner counts five sequences as he or she is timing. Time for five sequences is the raw score for this task. The child then performs the sequencing task with the nondominant hand. The examiner watches for correct finger position during Repetitions. Errors in position are not counted in the 20 repetitions. Errors in Sequences include incorrect sequences, incorrect finger positions, or movements. The examiner can demonstrate the correct movement but continues to time. No sequence containing an error is counted in the required five sequences.

Recording: Record completion time in seconds for each item on the Record Form.

Recording for Behavioral Observations

- Place a tally mark in the *Rate Change* box on the Record Form each time the child changes rate (variable speed and tempo) during movement sequences.
- Place a checkmark in the appropriate box to note the presence of the following behaviors.
- *Visual Guidance:* The child looks at his or her fingers for the majority of time during an item.
- *Incorrect Position:* The fingers and hand being assessed are positioned incorrectly (e.g., finger overlaps thumb rather than touching tip of it; pincer movement instead of finger and thumb forming an "o" during tapping).
- *Posturing:* The finger or hand not being assessed is extended stiffly at any point during the item.
- *Mirroring:* The finger or hand not being assessed moves involuntarily at any point during an item. The finger movement resembles finger tapping or sequential finger movement.
- *Overflow:* The lips, tongue, jaw, or mouth move involuntarily at any point during an item.

Having the child place his or her nonassessed hand on the table during testing is helpful in order to observe mirroring or posturing.

Tips

- The contralateral hand is resting on the table in plain view, so you can observe associated movements.

- During the Teaching Example for Repetitions, if the child taps with straight fingers, taps with sides of fingers, or does not open the fingers about 2.5 cm (see Figures 3.6 and 3.7 in the *Administration Manual*), stop the child, demonstrate the correct position, saying, "Do it like this," and have the child do it correctly. Repeat the Teaching Example.
- During the Repetition task, if the child taps with straight fingers, taps with sides of fingers, or does not open the fingers about 2.5 cm, it is an error. Stop the child, demonstrate the correct position, saying, "Do it like this," while *continuing to time*.
- During the Teaching Example for Sequential Finger Tapping, be sure the child understands the sequence goes from the index finger to the little finger. Do not allow the child to reverse the sequence from little finger to index finger. Stop the child, have him or her do a sequence correctly, and then repeat the Teaching Example.
- During the Sequences task, if the child reverses the sequence, it is an error. Missequencing (missing a finger or touching the fingers to the thumb out of order) is also an error. Stop the child and demonstrate the correct movement, while saying, "Do it like this," *but continue to time*.
- When you have had to stop the child three times for the same type of error, and he or she slips immediately back into the incorrect finger movement or missequencing, do not stop any more for that error. It is likely that the child is unable to hold the correct finger posture. This is diagnostic in itself. Count any of those same movements as errors and continue to correct any others that may arise. By the time the child has been stopped and corrected three times, the time limit will be nearly up.

Associated movements are discussed in the *Clinical and Interpretive Manual* (p. 167–168). Record these Behavioral Observations on the Record Form. Rate change in motor movements is seen in dyspraxic individuals who have problems with motor programming. Posturing, mirroring, and overflow are often seen in individuals with ADHD, learning disabilities, and other developmental disorders. They are purported to reflect the diffuse, mild, neurological dysfunction these individuals may demonstrate. Associated movements can also coexist with an awkward pencil grip and poor graphomotor skills on the Visuomotor Precision subtest.

Geometric Puzzles (Visuospatial Processing): Ages 3–16

Referral Batteries: GA, M (ages 7–16), A/C, P/M, S/I
This subtest is designed to assess mental rotation, visuospatial analysis, and attention to detail from geometric shapes on a grid. (See Rapid Reference 2.21.)

≡ Rapid Reference 2.21

Summary of Geometric Puzzles Rules: Ages 3–16

Start	Reverse Rule	Discontinue	Stop	Timing
Ages 3–8: Teaching Example 1, then Item 1 Ages 9–16: Teaching Example 2 and 3, then Item 7	Ages 9–16: If 0 or 1 on either item 7 or 8, reverse until two consecutive scores of 2, then proceed forward. Note: If a child must reverse, administer Teaching Example 1 before administering Item 6.	Do not discontinue.	Ages 3–6: Stop after Item 12.	Allow 45 seconds for each item.

Rules

See Rapid Reference 2.21 for details on Start Point, Reverse Rule, Discontinue, Stop, and Time.

Materials: Stimulus Book 1 in flat position.

Administration: Follow the administration directions in Stimulus Book 1. The child is presented with a picture of a large grid containing several geometric shapes. For each item the child matches two shapes outside of the grid to two shapes within the grid.

Recording: Record completion time in seconds for each item. For Items 1–6, reduced versions of the stimuli appear in the Record Form (illustrated from the examiner's perspective when sitting directly across from the child). Circle the shape(s) selected. For Items 7–20, circle the child's responses.

Tips

- To clarify the instruction *turn around* and *flip over* you may use your hand to show a flat, rotating movement of your flat hand (palm down) for turning around; and change position from palm down to palm up for flipping, respectively.
- This subtest is long and all items should be administered. Therefore, sometimes the child may show signs of losing interest. You may have

a short break by closing the stimulus book and chatting with the child for 1–2 minutes. Keep your hand/fingers on the appropriate page in order to find it again when you continue. Say, for example, "Let's breathe some. Most children think these are quite tough but interesting. You need to watch closely. Are you ready to try those that we have left?"

Imitating Hand Positions (Sensorimotor Domain): Ages 3–12

This subtest is designed to assess the ability to imitate static hand/finger positions by using visuospatial analysis, motor programming, and kinesthetic feedback from positions. (See Rapid Reference 2.22.)

≡ Rapid Reference 2.22

Summary of Imitating Hand Positions Rules: Ages 3–12

Start	Reverse Rule	Discontinue	Stop	Timing
Ages 3–4: Item 1, (Dominant Hand) Item 13 (Nondominant) Ages 5–12: Item 3 (DH), Item 15 (NDH) Ages 13–16: Do not administer	For ages 5–12 only: Dominant Hand: If 0 on either Item 3 or 4, go to Item 1 and proceed forward. Nondominant Hand: If 0 on either Items 15 or 16, go to Item 13 and proceed forward.	(DH): 3 consecutive scores of 0 on Items 1–12, then go to NDH. (NDH): 3 consecutive scores of 0 on Items 13–24.	None	20 seconds for each position.

Rules
See Rapid Reference 2.22 for details on Start Point, Reverse Rule, Discontinue, Stop, and Time.

Materials: Age-appropriate Record Form only.

Administration: General Guidelines and Administration in the *Administration Manual* (pp. 65–70). The examiner demonstrates hand and finger positions and the child imitates them. The examiner forms the hand position out of the child's sight, so the child cannot see how to form it. The examiner holds the hand position static as a model for the child for 20 sec./item. The Dominant Hand positions are formed completely first, followed by the Nondominant Hand positions. The examiner uses the hand that corresponds to the child's dominant hand.

Recording: Record completion time in seconds for each item.

Recording for *Behavioral Observations:* Place a checkmark in the appropriate box to note presence of:

> *Mirroring:* The child uses the left hand when the examiner uses the right, or vice versa (echopraxia).
>
> *Other Hand Helps:* The child uses the other hand to help model the position.

Tips

- If the child's dominant hand is right, administer Items 1 to 12 with your right hand; if the child is left-handed, use your left. For the NDH items (13 to 24), use the hand that corresponds to the child's NDH.
- Pictures of the hand positions, including instructions for forming them, are available in the *Administration Manual* on pp.66–70. Practice them before administering the test.
- If you are not very skilled with these items, the hand position is best formed under the table and then brought into view. Do not let the child see you forming the hand position as this changes the task.
- Hold the hand position in full view for the full 20 sec., so the child can analyze it. If the child forms the hand position quickly, you can move on to the next item; if it is incorrect you may wait until the child does not change the position any further. This procedure provides feedback to the child if the child's position is incorrect.
- The last two items are meant to be difficult. If the child is unable to perform them, reassure him or her.
- If you cannot perform the items, you may want to train an assistant or ask a colleague to administer this test.

Other Behaviors to Observe

- Are there significant performance differences in the two hands?
- Does the child form the hand position quickly without checking back to the model?

- Does the child study the model carefully, but form the position inaccurately? If he or she uses the wrong fingers, or reverses the fingers used (index and middle instead of ring and little fingers), there may be a visuospatial deficit. Or is the child very awkward and cannot seem to make the correct fingers move into place, suggesting dyspraxia?
- When a child forms an incorrect hand position, does he or she appear to perceive that the position is wrong? The child may or may not be able to fix it, but indicates that it is incorrect.
- Can the child sequence the fingers into the position fluidly or is motor control poor?

Inhibition (Attention and Executive Functioning): Ages 5–16

Referral Batteries: GA (5–16 only), R, M,A/C, B, L, S/I
This timed subtest is designed to assess the ability to name shapes and arrows, then name them in an inverse fashion, requiring the executive functions of inhibition of automatic responses in favor of novel responses, and the ability to switch between response types. (See Rapid Reference 2.23.)

≡ *Rapid Reference 2.23*

Summary of Inhibition Rules: Ages 5–16

Start	Reverse Rule	Discontinue	Stop	Timing
Ages 3–4: Do not administer Ages 5–16: Teaching Example for Item 1: Naming	None	Do not discontinue.	Ages 5–6: Stop after Inhibition Test Items for Items 1 and 2.	Naming Test Items: Allow 180 seconds. Inhibition and Switching Test Items: Allow 240 seconds.

Rules
See Rapid Reference 2.23 for details on Start Point, Reverse Rule, Discontinue, Stop, and Time.

Materials: Stimulus Book 1 in flat position.

Administration: Follow the Inhibition subtest directions in Stimulus Book 1. For the first condition, Naming, the child looks at a series of black and white shapes (circle and square) or arrows (pointing up and down), and names the shape or direction as quickly as possible. In the second condition, Inhibition, if the child sees a circle he or she says *square* and vice versa. If the child sees an arrow pointing up he or she says *down* and vice versa, again as quickly as possible. The third condition, Switching, requires the child to say a black shape's correct name, but if the shape is white, he or she must say the opposite name as quickly as possible. (e.g., If the child sees a black square, he or she says *square;* then if the child sees a white circle, he or she says *square.*)

Time Limit:
Naming Test Items: Allow 180 sec.
Inhibition and Switching Test Items: Allow 240 sec.

Recording: Record completion time in seconds for the Test Items in each administered condition (i.e., Naming, Inhibition, and Switching).

The correct responses for each set of Teaching Examples and Test Items are listed on the Record Form. Follow along as the child responds.

- Mark a slash through a letter if the child makes an error by providing an incorrect response or skipping a response.
- If the child self-corrects before the next stimulus, write *SC* over the letter.
- If the child does not complete a set of Test Items within the time limit, mark a slash through all stimuli not attempted.

Recording for Behavioral Observations

Place a checkmark in the appropriate box for each item in each condition to indicate whether or not the child pointed to the stimuli as the test was administered.

Tips

Be sure to administer the Teaching Example for each condition.

- If a child commits five or more uncorrected errors on a Teaching Example, do not attempt to administer the subsequent conditions for that item. For instance, the child commits seven errors on the Teaching Example in Naming for Item 1: Shapes; therefore, you would not administer the Naming, Inhibition, or, if age appropriate, the Switching Condition for Shapes. You can proceed to Item 2: Arrows. If the child makes more than five errors on the Teaching Example for Arrows Naming, discontinue the test.

- Place a checkmark in the box (Y or N) for Points to Stimuli for each condition of the test (i.e., Naming, Inhibition, Switching). Tally when scoring.

Other Behaviors to Observe

- Did problems occur in only one condition (i.e., Naming, Inhibition, or Switching) or did they occur across conditions? Was the child able to inhibit response in the Inhibition condition, but not able to inhibit and shift set on the Switching condition?
- Did problems occur in the Naming conditions only? Other naming/ language problems? Compare to Speeded Naming and Memory for Names and language tests.
- Did inattentiveness when directions were read or during the test influence performance?

List Memory (Memory and Learning Domain): Ages 7–12

Referral Battery: A/C

This subtest is designed to assess several aspects of verbal learning and memory. It includes assessment of immediate and delayed recall of a supraspan word list, rate of learning, and the role of interference from prior and new learning. (See Rapid Reference 2.24 for List Memory Rules.)

≡ *Rapid Reference 2.24*

Summary of List Memory Rules: Ages 7–12

Start	Reverse Rule	Discontinue	Stop	Timing
Ages 3–6: Do not administer Ages 7–12: Trial 1	None	Do not discontinue.	None	Present each list at a rate of one word every second.

Rules

See Rapid Reference 2.24 for details on Start Point, Reverse Rule, Discontinue, Stop, and Time.

Materials: None

Administration: Follow the directions for List Memory on pp. 74–75 of the *Administration Manual*. The lists to be read for the memory trials are on the Record Form. The examiner reads the 15-word list aloud, and then the child must recall all of the words he or she can in any order. The list is read and the child recalls it four more times (a total of five Learning Trials with recall after each). The sixth trial is an interference trial of a new list, again with recall after the examiner reads the list. Following the Interference Trial and recall, the child is asked to tell the examiner all of the words that he or she remembers from the *first* learned. Errors are *repetitions* (words repeated in the same recall) and *nonlist words* (not on either list); *wrong-list word* (Interference) is a word that is not from the list the child has been asked to recall, but is a word from the other list.

Recording: For each Trial, record the child's responses verbatim.

Tips
- Read the list over many times to yourself before the test so you will recognize the words easily as you administer the test.
- The child should not see the list, even upside down. Do not emphasize particular words or clusters as you read the words.
- Analyze the child's responses after testing to look for:
  - Semantic clustering: for example, *boat, water, fish*
  - Phonemic clustering: for example, *water, window, winter*
  - A primacy effect (remembering words only from the beginning of the list)
  - A recency effect (remembering words only from the end of the list)
- Numerous Repetitions may suggest perseveration, or a struggle to keep producing words.
- Plan the test session ahead of time so that the Delayed LM may be administered 30 min ± 5 min after the List Memory subtest.
- *Do not read the word list before the child recalls it on the Trial 7 or on the LM Delayed.*

> **C A U T I O N**
>
> The word list is not read before immediate or delayed recall trials.

Other Behaviors to Observe
- Is the child focused on listening to the list as it is being administered?

- Does the child present overt signs of active memorizing, such as silent rehearsal, closing his or her eyes, or putting head down when listening to the words in order to shut out distractions? Or was the child's performance characterized by more automatic production of the words as they come to mind?
- Does the child use clustering techniques as a good memory strategy?
- Does the child seem to try to recall the words in order, though it is not required?

List Memory Delayed (Learning and Memory): Ages 7–12

Referral Battery: A/C
This subtest is designed to assess delayed recall of words. (See Rapid Reference 2.25.)

≡ *Rapid Reference 2.25*

Summary of List Memory Delayed Rules

Start	Reverse Rule	Discontinue	Stop	Timing
Ages 7–12 only: Delayed Recall Trial 1	None	Do not discontinue.	None	None

---

Rules
See Rapid Reference 2.25 for details on Start Point, Reverse Rule, Discontinue, Stop, and Time.

Materials: None
Administration: Administer from the *Administration Manual* and the Record Form. After a 25–35 minute delay, the child is asked to recall the words from List Memory subtest—"the one that started with *Store*." *Do NOT read the Word List* before the child begins the Delayed LM Recall Trial. (See previous Caution box.)
Timing: Administer 25–35 minutes after List Memory. Test is not timed.
Recording: Record the child's responses verbatim.

Tip
- *Do not read the word list before asking the child to recall it.* The Delayed LM is administered as close to 30 min ± 5 min after LM as is possible. Plan this out ahead of time.

Other Behaviors to Observe
- Does the child seem to struggle to recall words? Is performance significantly worse than on Trial 5 (compute LM Delay Effect), suggesting memory decay?
- Does he or she have a strategy for recall?
- Does the child make self-deprecating remarks about his or her memory before attempting to recall the list?
- Does the child perform better than on immediate List Memory, suggesting slow consolidation of the information?

Manual Motor Sequences (Sensorimotor Domain): Ages 3–12

Referral Batteries: R, A/C, P/M, (S/I)
This subtest assesses the ability to imitate a series of rhythmic hand movement sequences (motor programming) using one or both hands (see Rapid Reference 2.26).

≡ *Rapid Reference 2.26*

Summary of Manual Motor Sequences Rules: Ages 3–12

Start	Reverse Rule	Discontinue	Stop	Timing
Ages 3–7: Item 1 Ages 8–12: Item 3 Ages 13–16: Do not administer	Ages 8–12: If a score of 5 is not obtained on Item 3, go to Item 1 and proceed forward.	Discontinue after 4 consecutive scores of 0.	None	Maintain a presentation rhythm slightly faster than one movement every second. Items 9, 11, and 12: First demonstrate one movement every second, then two movements every second.

Rules

See Rapid Reference 2.26 for details on Start Point, Reverse Rule, Discontinue, Stop, and Time.

Materials: None

Administration: Administer from the Record Form and the test directions on pp.78–82 of the *Administration Manual*. Movements are described and illustrated in the *Administration Manual* and on the Record Form. Using the hand directly across the table from the child's dominant hand, the examiner demonstrates each movement sequence three times, keeping a rhythm of slightly faster than one movement every second. The child practices the movement once. Then the child produces five movement sequences and is then stopped. Each sequence is demonstrated by the examiner first, practiced by the child, and then performed.

Recording: Count silently as the child completes each sequence. In the Sequence Number column on the Record Form, circle the sequence number if no error occurs and place an *X* on the sequence number if an error does occur.

If an interruption error occurs, put the *X* on the next number in the sequence. For example, if the child stops after sequence 3 and then restarts, put the *X* on sequence 4.

Recording for Behavioral Observations

Place a tally mark in the *Rate Change* box each time the child demonstrates inconsistencies or changes in rate (variable speed and tempo) during performance of a sequence.

Place a checkmark in the appropriate box to note the presence of the following behaviors.

- *Overflow:* Associated movements of another part of the body (e.g., mouth) in conjunction with the production of movement sequences.
- *Perseveration:* Movements continue for three or more sequences after child is told to stop.
- *Loss of Asymmetrical Movement:* Asymmetrical hand positions become identical (for Items 5, 6, 10, 11, and 12 only), or identical hand movements are performed simultaneously when alternation is required.
- *Body Movement*: Extraneous whole body movements are recruited in conjunction with the production of movement sequences (e.g., rhythmic rocking, rising slowly from seat as hand movements are executed).

- *Forceful Tapping*: The tapping becomes louder during the production of the movement sequences, as the body is recruited into the task.

Tips
- You may demonstrate the rhythm for the child by tapping gently on the table. If the child makes an error in the first or second sequence, demonstrate again and restart the test.
- Count sequences silently or by using your fingers to count the sequences under the table.
- For each item, stop the child after five sequences. If the child attempts to stop before five sequences, encourage him or her to keep going by gesturing or nodding in the same rhythm as the child tapped.
- You need to practice this test sufficiently before you administer it. There are diagrams and written instructions in the *Administration Manual* (pp. 78–82) to help you. You can follow the scheme while demonstrating the sequence. On some diagrams both hands are depicted when only one hand at a time changes position. Circle that hand or cross over the hand that should keep still.
- Train your hand movements before each NEPSY-II evaluation. When you administer the test, perform the sequence two to three times on your lap and then bring it up onto the table in the child's view.
- *Use the hand directly across the table from the child's dominant hand* (i.e., when child is right-handed use your left hand) unless nondominant is indicated in the item instructions. If necessary, point to the hand the child should use. If the child started using the mirror hand, do not stop him or her: You can score the child's performance nevertheless.
- If you cannot perform the items, you may want to train an assistant or ask a colleague to administer this test.

Other Behaviors to Observe
In addition to the Behavioral Observations on the Record Form (Rate Change, etc.), observe and note the following behaviors:

- General rhythm and smoothness of sequences.
- Lack of fluid movement in the hands, jerky movements with hesitations.
- Inattentiveness when the movements are being demonstrated, causing poor performance later.

Memory for Designs (Memory and Learning): Ages 3–16

Referral Batteries: M, P/M, SR, (S/I)
This subtest is designed to assess spatial memory for novel visual material, by placing the correct designs in the correct location on a grid. (See Rapid Reference 2.27.)

≡ *Rapid Reference 2.27*

Summary of Memory for Designs Rules: Ages 3–16

Start	Reverse Rule	Discontinue	Stop	Timing
Ages 3–4: Teaching Example, then Trial 1	None	Do not discontinue.	Ages 3–4: Stop after Trial 4.	Present each trial stimulus for 10 seconds.
Ages 5–6: Teaching Example, then Trial 2			Ages 5–6: Stop after Trial 5.	
Ages 7–16: Teaching Example, then Trial 3				

Rules
See Rapid Reference 2.27 for details on Start Point, Reverse Rule, Discontinue, Stop, and Time.

Materials: Stimulus Book 1 in easel position

Administration: Directions on the Stimulus Book 1 easel for the Teaching Example. Following the Teaching Example, turn to the appropriate Trial for the child's age. The child is shown a picture of a grid with 4–10 designs on a page, which is then removed from view. The child selects the designs from a set of cards and places them in a grid in the same location as was previously seen in Stimulus Book 1.

- Place the memory grid in front of the child between the child and the easel with the word *Examinee* closest to him or her.
- The stimulus plate is exposed for *10 sec.* and then turned to the blank page following the Trial.

- Shuffle the designated cards (e.g., *Cards 1–8 only,* as noted on the Stimulus Book easel and in the Record Form for Trial 2) and *present them in a stack, face up.* Follow the directions for each trial on the easel.
- The maximum number of cards to be used for a correct response is designated (e.g., *4 Designs maximum* on the easel) and in the Record Form for Trial 2.
- When a trial is completed do not allow the child to remove the cards from the grid.
  - First, verify that the correct number *of cards has been* placed in the grid. If more than the designated number of cards has been placed in the grid, this is a Rule Violation.
  - Say "Remember, do not put more than __ cards in the grid," and ask the child to tell you which cards to remove from the grid before you record.

Do not allow the child to remove the cards as the grid or cards may be damaged. Record the c*ards that remain after removing those the child has designated* to be removed.

Recording: Before removing cards, make sure that each card is securely in place, then lift *the edge of the grid closest to you, so you can see* the card identifiers through the holes in the back of the grid. The word *Top* should appear at the top of the grid when lifted correctly. Record the card numbers in the correct location on the Record Form grid, and then remove the cards by pushing your finger through the hole on the back of the grid. (Do not attempt to remove the cards from the front of the grid, as this will damage the cards or the grid.) Place the empty grid in front of the child for the next trial.

If the correct number of cards has been placed, record the card identifiers (numbers) on the Record Form grid just as the child has placed them in the memory grid. If the designated number has been placed, place a checkmark in the box (N) indicating no Rule Violations.

If more than the designated number of cards has been placed, place a checkmark in the box for the presence (Y) of a *Rule Violation,* and use the prompt on the easel to ask the child to designate which cards he or she wants you to remove. After these cards are removed, record the remaining cards.

If fewer than the designated number of cards has been placed, record the card identifiers (numbers) on the Record Form. This is *not a Rule Violation.* Place a checkmark in the box (N) indicating no Rule Violations.

Recording for Content Score:
Circle the numbers of the cards that the child placed in the grid either in the Target column (if it is a correct design) or in the Distracter column (if it is the distracter card—similar, but not correct). If both the Target and the Distracter card are used, circle both. If neither a Target nor a Distracter in a particular row have been placed correctly, neither will be circled and 0 will be scored for that row under Content Score.

Recording for Behavioral Observations:
Place a tally mark in the *yes* (Y) box for each *Rule Violation.*

Tips
- The Record Form shows the number of the correct design in the correct location.
- If more than the designated number of cards is recorded, *this will spoil the Memory for Designs results, which cannot then be used.* Of course, Memory for Designs Delayed cannot be administered under these circumstances.
- If the child places fewer cards than the designated number in the grid, it is not a Rule Violation. Do not remind the child that he or she needs to add more.
- If the child *asks* how many cards he or she needs to place, you may remind him or her.
- If the child asks, the orientation of the cards does not matter when they are placed in the grid.
- If the child has difficulty fitting the cards into the grid, you may assist, but do not assist the child in selecting cards. Do not allow child to use the numbers on the back of the cards to assist in card selection. Plan ahead for the test session so that you can administer the MD Delayed subtest 15 to 25 minutes after the Memory for Designs subtest. If, for some reason, it was not possible to follow through, you can still obtain an immediate MD Content Scaled Score, MD Spatial Scaled Score, and the MD Content vs. Spatial Contrast Scaled Scores.

Other Behaviors to Observe

- Does the child attend closely to directions or is he or she impulsive in reaching for the cards and placing them before the directions are complete?
- If the child has to be reminded to put the designated number of cards in the grid, is he or she more attentive to this number on the next Trial?
- How does the child's ability to remember the design (Content) compare to the child's ability to recall the location (Spatial)? How does this relate to classroom performance?

≣ Rapid Reference 2.28

Summary of Memory for Designs Delayed Rules: Ages 5–16

Start	Reverse Rule	Discontinue	Stop	Timing
Ages 3–4: Do not administer Ages 5–16: Delayed Recall Trial for appropriate age	None	Do not discontinue.	None	Administer 15–25 minutes after Memory for Designs.

Memory for Designs Delayed (Memory and Learning): Ages 3–16

Referral Batteries: M, P/M, (S/I)

This subtest is designed to assess long-term visuospatial and visual detail memory 15–25 minutes after Memory for Designs. (See Rapid Reference 2.28.)

Rules

See Reference 2.28 for details on Start Point, Reverse Rule, Discontinue, Stop, and Time.

Materials: Stimulus Book 1 in easel position.

Administration: Directions on the Stimulus Book 1 easel and in the *Administration Manual* (pp. 89–90) for the MD Delayed Trial. The child selects 8–10 designs from a set of cards and places the cards on a grid in the same location as previously shown in the Memory for Design subtest.

- Place the Memory Grid in front of the child with the word *Examinee* closest to him or her.
- For Ages 5–6, shuffle cards 1–16 and place in a stack *face up* in front of the child. Eight cards max. for Delayed Recall Trial.
- For Ages 7–16, shuffle cards 1–20 and place in a stack *face up* in front of the child. Ten cards max. for Delayed Recall Trial.

Recording:

If the correct number of cards has been placed, record the card identifiers (numbers) on the Record Form grid just as the child has placed them in the memory grid. If the designated number has been placed, place a checkmark in the box (N), indicating no Rule Violations.

If more than the designated number of cards has been placed, place a checkmark in the box for the presence (Y) of a *Rule Violation,* and prompt, "Remember, do not put more than __ cards in the grid." Have the child designate which cards he or she wants you to remove. After these cards are removed, record the remaining cards.

If fewer than the designated number of cards has been placed, record the card identifiers (numbers) on the Record Form. This is *not a Rule Violation.* Place a check mark in the box (N), indicating no Rule Violations.

Recording for Content Score: Circle the numbers of the cards that the child placed in the grid either in the Target column or in the Distracter column. If both the Target and the Distracter card are used, circle both. If neither a Target nor a Distracter in a particular row have been placed correctly, neither will be circled and 0 will be scored for that row under Content Score.

Recording for Spatial Score: The Spatial Score assesses the child's ability to recall the location of a design during the trial. Use the numbers already recorded in the Record Form grid in the cell.

Recording for the Bonus Score: The Bonus Score reflects the child's ability to recall which designs were in which locations for that trial.

Recording for *Behavioral Observations:* For each Rule Violation, place a tally mark in the box.

Tips
- The numbers of the correct cards in the correct location appear on a miniature grid on the Record Form.
- Administer 15–25 min. after MD.
- If the child places more than the designated number of cards in the grid, remind the child not to place more than the designated number (8 or 10) in the grid. Have the child tell you which to remove.

Other Behaviors to Observe
- Is the child confident in his or her ability to remember or does the child state he/she will not be able to remember?
- How does the child's ability to perform on an immediate visuospatial memory task compare to the child's delayed recall ability for visuospatial information? Is memory decay observed or does the child appear

≡ *Rapid Reference 2.29*

Summary of Memory for Faces Rules: Ages 5–16

Start	Reverse Rule	Discontinue	Stop	Time Limit/ Timing
Ages 3–4: Do not administer	None	Do not discontinue.	None	Learning Items: Present each item stimulus for 5 seconds.
Ages 5–16: Learning Items, then Item 1				

to consolidate more information over time? How does this relate to classroom performance?

Memory for Faces (Memory and Learning Domain): Ages 5–16

Referral Batteries: GA (5–16 only) M, B, S/I
Using photographs of children's faces, this subtest assesses encoding of facial features, as well as face discrimination and recognition. (See Rapid Reference 2.29.)

Rules
See Rapid Reference 2.29 for details on Start Point, Reverse Rule, Discontinue, Stop, and Time.

Materials: Stimulus Book 2 in flat position in front of the child

Administration: Administer the subtest from Stimulus Book 2. The child looks at a series of black-and-white photos of children's faces for 5 sec. each and is asked to identify the gender of each. The gender task is not scored, but rather serves the purpose of helping the child attend to the faces. The child is then shown three photographs at a time and is asked to select a face previously seen. There are 16 target faces.

Recording: On the Record Form, circle the child's responses.

Recording for *Behavioral Observations:* Each time the child makes a comment about a face, place a tally mark in the *Spontaneous Comments* box on the Record Form.

Tips

- This is one of the subtests where a delayed task should be administered 15–25 minutes after the immediate recall task. Plan the test session ahead of time to permit this. On the Learning Trials *continue to expose the picture if 5 sec. have not elapsed* when the child identifies the child's gender. If needed, say: "Keep looking."
- Enter the stop time for Memory for Faces on the Record Form
- Check the time you need to begin the Delayed Recall Trial before you begin another test. Choose a test that will fit into the timeframe and allow for transition time from one test to another.

Other Behaviors to Observe

- Discomfort in looking at the faces, or averting his or her eyes after

---

≡ *Rapid Reference 2.30*

Summary of Memory for Faces Delayed Rules: Ages 5–16

Start	Reverse Rule	Discontinue	Stop	Time Limit/Timing
Ages 3–4: Do not administer Ages 5–16: Item 1	None	Do not discontinue.	None	Administer 15–25 minutes after Memory for Faces.

looking at them. Does this correlate with poor or fleeting eye contact with you or others?
- Wanting to move on before the 5 sec. exposure is complete, as opposed to reflecting on them in a focused manner.

Memory for Faces Delayed (Memory and Learning Domain): Ages 5–16

Referral Batteries: GA (5-16 only) M, B, S/I
This subtest is designed to assess long-term memory for faces 15–25 minutes after the Memory for Faces subtest. (See Rapid Reference 2.30.)

Rules
See Rapid Reference 2.30 for details on Start Point, Reverse Rule, Discontinue, Stop, and Time.

Material: Stimulus Book 2 in flat position

Administration: Administer the subtest from Stimulus Book 2; 15–25 min. after Memory for Faces is completed, the child is shown three photos at a time from which he or she selects a face previously seen. There are 16 arrays from which the child must identify a target face.

Recording: On the Record Form, circle the child's responses. Each time the child makes a spontaneous comment about a face, place a tally mark in the Spontaneous Comments box.

Recording for *Behavioral Observations:* Each time the child makes a comment about a face, place a tally mark in the Spontaneous Comments box on the Record Form.

≡ *Rapid Reference 2.31*

. . . .

Summary of Memory for Names Rules: Ages 5-16

Start	Reverse Rule	Discontinue	Stop	Time Limit/ Timing
Ages 3-4: Do not administer	None	Do not discontinue.	Age 5: Do not present cards 7 and 8 during Learning Trials or Trials 1–3	Present each card for 10 seconds.
Ages 5-6: Learning Trial, then Trial 1				

Other Behaviors to Observe
- Discomfort in looking at the faces, or averting his or her eyes after looking at them. Does this correlate with poor or fleeting eye contact with you or others?
- Performing better on Delayed Recall than Immediate Recall, suggesting slowed processing and consolidation.

Memory for Names (Memory and Learning Domain): Ages 5–16

Referral Batteries: R, L
This subtest is designed to assess the ability to learn the names of children over three trials. (See Rapid Reference 2.31.)

Rules
See Rapid Reference 2.31 for details on Start Point, Reverse Rule, Discontinue, Stop, and Time.

Materials: None

Recording: Record the child's responses verbatim for all cards of each trial. Although the presentation order will change for each trial, record the child's response to each card in the space designated for that card.

Administration: Follow the instructions and script in the *Administration Manual,* pp. 93–94. The child is shown six to eight line drawings of children. The examiner says the name of each child on the cards as the card is presented. The child looks at each card and repeats the name. The cards are then shuffled and the child is asked to name each picture one at a time. There are two more trials before which the cards are shuffled, exposed one at time for the child, and named by him or her. Cards 7 and 8 are not used for 5-year-olds.

Tips
- Remove the cards for Sam and Maria before administering the test to a 5-year-old.
- Before you begin the test, order the cards face down out of the child's view, starting with Item 8. Numbers and names are exposed, with Item 1 being on top. Hold the cards in your palm so the pictures are face down and are not exposed as you pull each card sequentially from the top of the deck in your hand.

- Administer the Teaching Presentation with the cards in sequential order. After administration of the Teaching Presentation, shuffle the cards out of the child's view for each learning trial.
- Do not expose the names on the backs of the cards.
- Place the cards face up on top of the pile so that face of the previous card is covered.
- If the child misnames a picture, give the correct name, have the child repeat it, and proceed.
- Note the time the Learning Trials finish on your Record Form, so you can time the Delayed Memory for Faces as close to 30 min. as possible. Select a test to follow MN that will fit into the 30 min. window, including transition time.

≡ Rapid Reference 2.32

Summary of Memory for Names Delayed Rules: Ages 5–16

Start	Reverse Rule	Discontinue	Stop	Time Limit/ Timing
Ages 3–4: Do not administer	None	Do not discontinue.	Age 5: Do not present cards 7 and 8 during Delayed Recall Trial.	Administer 15–25 minutes after Memory for Names.
Ages 5–6: Delayed Recall Trial				

Other Behaviors to Observe

- Does the child recall a correct name but pair it with an incorrect face, suggesting a problem in paired associates learning?
- Does the child perseverate on the same few names and show little learning across Learning Trials?
- If the child does not attend to the name, he or she may fail to encode the information.

**Memory for Names Delayed (Memory and Learning Domain):
Ages 5–16**

Referral Batteries: R, L
This subtest is designed to assess long-term memory for names 25–35 minutes after Memory for Names. (See Rapid Reference 2.32.)

Rules
See Rapid Reference 2.32 for details on Start Point, Reverse Rule, Discontinue, Stop, and Time.

Materials: None

Recording: Record the child's responses verbatim for all cards of each trial.

Administration: Follow the instructions and script in the *Administration Manual,* pp. 95–96. Then, 25–35 minutes after Memory for Names, the cards are shown to the child and he or she names as many as he or she can. Cards 7 and 8 are not shown to 5-year-olds.

Tips
- Plan for MN Delayed trial.
- Do not correct errors.
- Do not allow the child to return to a card once the next card has been presented or to see the names on the backs of the cards.

≡ *Rapid Reference 2.33*

Summary of Narrative Memory Rules: Ages 3–16

Start	Reverse Rule	Discontinue	Stop	Timing
Ages 3–4: Story 1	None	Do not discontinue.	Age 3–4: After Story 1, Recognition Item 13	None
Ages 5–6: Story 2			Age 5–10: After Story 2, Recognition Item 16	
Ages 11–16: Story 3			Age 3–4: After Story 3, Cued Recall Question 17	

Other Behaviors to Observe
- Did the child perform significantly better on the Learning Trials than on the Delay Trial, suggesting memory decay?
- Did the child perform significantly better on Delay than on Learning Trials due to slowed processing and/or delayed consolidation of the information?

Narrative Memory (Language Domain): Ages 3–16

Referral Batteries: GA, L, S/I

This subtest is designed to assess memory for logical verbal material under free recall, cued recall, and recognition conditions. (See Rapid Reference 2.33.)

Rules

See Rapid Reference 2.33 for details on Start Point, Reverse Rule, Discontinue, Stop, and Time.

Materials: Stimulus Book 2 in easel position.

Administration: Follow the administration directions in Stimulus Book 2. Cued Recall and Recognition questions appear in the Record Form. Place Stimulus Book 2 in the easel position in front of the child. Note that there is no visual stimulus for either Story 2 or Story 3. The examiner reads a story to the child, as he or she listens. The child is then asked to repeat the story in the Free Recall condition. For any salient story details that the child did not recall, he or she is asked questions to elicit missing details (Cued Recall). Three- to ten-year-olds also receive a Recognition condition even if they gave the correct responses to the Cued Recall questions. The Recognition questions ask about salient details of the story, giving two possible answers from which the child chooses the correct one (e.g., "Was the boy in the story named Jim or Jeff?").

Recording and Scoring: The Record Form has two recording columns for Narrative Memory.

   In the Free Recall Column, circle 2 if the child recalled the designated story detail in Free Recall.

   In the Cued Recall Column, circle 1 if the child recalled the detail during Cued Recall.

   Circle 0 if the detail is not recalled during Free or Cued Recall.

(Do not award 2 points for Free Recall and then another 1 point for Cued Recall. Maximum score for a detail is 2 points.)

For Recognition, circle the child's response for each item. (The correct response for each item is in color on the Record Form.)

Tips

- If the child has difficulty getting started, provide help by saying, "How did the story start?", or for a young child, "Let's try. The story told about...." For the older child (ages 11–16), ask "How did the passage start?"
- If the child does not respond, say, "Just tell me anything you can remember from the story about the cookies or the dog...." For the older child (ages 11–16), say, "Just tell me anything you can remember from the passage."
- If the child stops before the end of the story, prompt with, "Then what happened?" or "Tell me more," or "What happened next?" For the older child (ages 11–16), say, "Tell me more." Do not prompt more than three times.
- The child's response should have the essential information. It does not have to be verbatim.
- If a detail is provided in Free Recall (FR), do not ask the Cued Recall (CR) questions for those items. If a detail is not provided in Free Recall, ask the Cued Recall Question.
- For children ages 3–10, read each Recognition item in the Record Form to the child, even if correct responses were given to the Cued Recall questions.
- If the child has not yet been questioned on that detail and produces the detail *spontaneously* on Cued Recall (CR), give credit for it in Free Recall.

Other Behaviors to Observe

- The child remembers only the beginning or the end of the story (passage).
- The child remembers the gist of the story but not the details.
- Failing to recall many details in Free Recall, but recalling well with cueing. This suggests an accessing or expressive problem, or a problem with executive functions. The information is there, but the child cannot access it or cannot organize the narration. This may occur developmentally in young children.

≡ *Rapid Reference 2.34*

Summary of Oromotor Sequences Rules: Ages 3–12

Start	Reverse Rule	Discontinue	Stop	Time Limit/ Timing
Ages 3–7: Teaching Example, then Item 1 Ages 8–12: Teaching Example, then Item 4 Ages 13–16: Do not administer	Ages 8–12: If a score of 5 is not obtained on Item 4, go to Item 1 and proceed forward.	Discontinue after 4 consecutive scores of 0.	None	Items 1–8: Present each item at one sequence every second. Items 9–14: Present each item at one sequence every 2 seconds.

• Failing to recall efficiently on either the Free Recall or the Cued Recall trials. This suggests that the child did not encode the information as it was being presented. Attention? Language delay?

Oromotor Sequences (Language Domain): Ages 3–12

Referral Batteries: R, L, P/M
This subtest is designed to assess oromotor programming by repeating articulatory sequences. (See Rapid Reference 2.34.)

Rules
See Rapid Reference 2.34 for details on Start Point, Reverse Rule, Discontinue, Stop, and Time.

Materials: Age-appropriate Record Form only.
Administration: Directions in *Administration Manual*, pp. 99–101. The examiner presents a rhythmic oromotor sequence to the child, who then produces five sequences. The last six of the 14 items are tongue twisters (e.g., *Sue said she should sell shoes*).
Recording:
Count silently or by discreetly counting with your fingers as the child completes each sequence.

Errors:
- Interruptions longer than the time of one sequence. (Encourage the child to complete the five sequences.)
- Omissions, distortions, or substitutions of words.
- Incorrect sequences (changes in word order).

  If no error occurs, in the Sequence Number column on the Record Form, circle the sequence number.

  If an error does occur, place an X on the sequence number.

  If an interruption error occurs, put the X on the next number in the sequence. (For example, if the child stops after sequence 3 and then restarts, put the X on sequence 4.)

Recording for *Behavioral Observations:*
- **Rate Change:** Put a tally mark in the Rate Change box on the Record Form each time the child exhibits inconsistencies or changes in rate (variable speed and tempo) during performance of a sequence.
- **Oromotor Hypotonia:** Weakness or insufficient tone in oromotor musculature. Mild drooling may be evident. Place a checkmark in the appropriate box to indicate presence.
- **Stable Misarticulations:** An error in articulation that is made consistently (e.g., /l/ for /r/). Place a checkmark in the appropriate box to indicate presence.

Tips
- If a child has very poor oromotor control, you need to administer the subtest to document the disability, but reassure the child about how difficult it is and do not rush him or her.
- Keep count of the sequences. With your hand in your lap, you can count them off on your fingers. Practice the oromotor sequences until you feel comfortable with them, before administering the test.

Other Behaviors to Observe
- Oromotor dyspraxia may be evident as poor articulation to the degree that it diminishes the intelligibility of speech or as telegraphic speech in children who have better comprehension.
- No speech impairment, but poor performance on this subtest.

≡ *Rapid Reference 2.35*

Summary of Phonological Processing Rules: Ages 3–16

Start	Reverse Rule	Discontinue	Stop	Time Limit
Ages 3–6: Item 9 Ages 7–8: Item 15 Ages 9–12: Teaching Examples 1 and 2, then Item 23 Ages 13–16: Teaching Examples 3 and 4, then Item 31	Ages 3–6: If a score of 0 is obtained on either Item 9 or 10, go to Item 1 and proceed forward. Ages 7–16: If scores of 0 are obtained on either of the first two items administered, reverse until two consecutive scores of 1 are obtained, then proceed forward.	Discontinue after 6 consecutive scores of 0.	Ages 3–4: Stop after Item 22.	None

Does this relate to classroom performance in reading or language?

Phonological Processing (Language Domain): Ages 3–16

Referral Batteries: R, SR, S/I
This subtest is composed of two phonological processing tasks to assess phonemic awareness. Word Segment Recognition requires identification of word segments. Phonological Segmentation is a test of elision. It assesses phonological processes at the level of word segments (syllables) and of letter sounds (phonemes). (See Rapid Reference 2.35.)

Rules

See Rapid Reference 2.35 for details on Start Point, Reverse Rule, Discontinue, Stop, and Time.

Materials: Stimulus Book 2 in easel position.

Administration: Administration directions in Stimulus Book 2 (in easel position). The young child is asked to blend word segments into common words. The child is first shown three pictures while the examiner names each. Then the examiner presents one of the words in word segments and asks the child to identify the picture with which it goes. Finally, the child is asked to repeat a word and then to create a new word by omitting a syllable or a phoneme, or by substituting one phoneme in a word for another.

Pronounce the words in a conversational tone at a moderate rate while pointing to each of the pictures. Pause. Then say the cue. *Do not repeat* the cue on Word Segment Recognition. You may repeat the auditory stimulus one time on Phonological Segmentation.

Recording:
- For Word Segment Recognition (WSR) and for Phonological Segmentation (PS), circle the response on the Record Form.
- Correct responses for WSR are in color on the Record Form. For PS, correct responses appear in a column titled *Correct Response.*

Recording for *Behavioral Observations:* Each time the child asks for or otherwise indicates the need for a word to be repeated, place a tally mark in the *Asks for Repetition* box on the Record Form.

Tips
- For the presentation of the stimulus words, the sounds are represented by the letter inside slash marks (/*b*/).
- Do not attach a vowel sound to the consonant. It is /*mm*/, not /*muh*/.
- Do not say the name of the letter. The letters in consonant blends are sounded together: /*bl*/, not /*buh*//*luh*/.

Other Behaviors to Observe
- Impulsivity of choice. In Word Segment Recognition, does the child look at all three pictures? Were you able to redirect the child to look at all three pictures?
- Guessing does not necessarily point to attention problems but may indicate real difficulty with the task.

≋ *Rapid Reference 2.36*

Summary of Picture Puzzles Rules: Ages 7–16

Start	Reverse Rule	Discontinue	Stop	Timeing
Ages 3–6: Do not administer	Ages 8–16: If a score of 0 is obtained on either of the first two items administered, reverse until two consecutive scores of 1 are obtained, then proceed forward.	Discontinue after 6 consecutive scores of 0.	None	None
Age 7: Teaching Example, then Item 1				
Ages 8–10: Teaching Example, then Item 5				
Ages 11–16: Teaching Example, then Item 8				

- Does picture reinforcement help on WSR?
- Incorrect sequencing of sounds; confusion in trying to formulate the new sequence.
- Difficulty with working memory on the longer items (31–45) but success prior to that.

Picture Puzzles (Visuospatial Processing): Ages 7–16

Referral Batteries: R, M, (S/I)

This subtest is designed to assess visual discrimination, spatial localization, and visual scanning, as well as the ability to deconstruct complex pictures—photographs of sceneries—into their constituent parts and recognize part–whole relationships. (See Rapid Reference 2.36.)

Rules

See Rapid Reference 2.36 for details on Start Point, Reverse Rule, Discontinue, Stop, and Time.

Material: Stimulus Book 2 in flat position.

Administration: Follow the administration directions in Stimulus Book 2. The child is presented a large photograph divided by a grid with four smaller photos taken from sections of the larger picture placed in the margin. The child identifies the location on the grid of the larger picture from which each of the smaller pictures was taken.

Recording:
- Record completion time in seconds for each item.
- On the Record Form, each item has a grid that represents the item grid in the Stimulus Book. (These are shown from the examiner's perspective when sitting directly across from the child.)
- If the child provides the correct response, circle the response letter (A, B, C, or D) in that cell.
- If a child does not provide a correct response, write the response letter (A, B, C, or D) in the cell chosen by the child.

Tips
- This subtest is long and all items should be administered. Therefore, sometimes the child may present signs of losing interest. You may have a short break by closing the stimulus book and chatting with the child for 1–2 minutes. Keep your hand/fingers on the appropriate page in order to find it again when you continue. Say, for example: "There are quite a few pictures, aren't there? They were taken in many different places. We have a few pictures left. Are you ready to see what scenery comes next?"
- If the child is impulsive, prompt him or her to look at the whole picture and all of the choices before giving a response. Note the prompt.

≡ *Rapid Reference 2.37*

Summary of Repetition of Nonsense Words Rules: Ages 5–12

Start	Reverse Rule	Discontinue	Stop	Timing
Ages 3–6 and 13–16: Do not administer Ages 5–12: Item 1	None	Discontinue after 4 consecutive scores of 0.	None	None

- You may need to remind the child to try to work quickly, if he or she is very slow or dawdling.

Other Behaviors to Observe

- Does the child study the whole picture and the puzzle pieces carefully before making a choice, or is he or she impulsive?
- Were you able to redirect the child to look at all of the pictures? Could the child maintain attention when redirected?
- Does the child use verbal mediation to arrive at a response?
- Does the child seem to attend better to real objects in the pictures than he or she did to the Geometric Puzzles that used abstract shapes?

Repetition of Nonsense Words (Language Domain): Ages 5–12

Referral Battery: L

This subtest is designed to assess phonological encoding and decoding through the repetition of nonsense words. (See Rapid Reference 2.37.)

Rules

See Rapid Reference 2.37 for details on Start Point, Reverse Rule, Discontinue, Stop, and Time.

Materials: Use audio file (CD or tape).

Administration: Follow directions in the *Administration Manual,* p. 104. Check that the test tone has been passed on the audio file and that the sound level on the tape recorder is at an appropriate level. If not, it may startle the child. Nonsense words are played on the audio file and the child repeats each nonsense word after it is presented. Credit only the child's first attempt or spontaneous self-corrections that occur before the next item is presented.

Recording: Record the child's responses verbatim.

Recording for *Behavioral Observations:* Each time a stable misarticulation is heard, make a tally mark in the *Stable Misarticulations* box.

Tips

- If you have administered the Auditory Attention and Response Set Test, the audio file will already be cued.
- You only need to mark incorrect syllables; this will save time. Count unmarked (correct) syllables.

≡ *Rapid Reference 2.38*

Summary of Route Finding Rules: Ages 5–12

Start	Reverse Rule	Discontinue	Stop	Timing
Ages 3–4 and 13–16: Do not administer	None	Discontinue after 5 consecutive scores of 0.	None	None
Ages 5–12: Teaching Example, then Item 1				

- If you need to say something to the child, pause the audio file and restart after you are finished talking.
- Self-corrections are allowed if they are made before the next word is presented.

Other Behaviors to Observe
- Producing the correct syllables in the wrong order (missequencing).
- Stressing the wrong syllable frequently, although this is not an error. Discuss in Test Observations of your report.
- Do results on this subtest compare in level of performance to those on Phonological Processing?

Route Finding (Visuospatial Processing Domain): Ages 5–12

Not a Part of Any Referral Battery
This subtest is designed to assess knowledge of visual-spatial relations and directionality, as well as the ability to use this knowledge to transfer a route from a simple schematic map to a more complex one. (See Rapid Reference 2.38.)

Rules
See Rapid Reference 2.38 for details on Start Point, Reverse Rule, Discontinue, Stop, and Time.

  Material: Stimulus Book 2 is placed flat in front of the child.
  Administration: Follow directions in *Administration Manual,* p. 106. The
    child is shown a simple schematic map with a path to a target house.

With his finger, the child traces the route to the target house on the simple path. Above the simple path is a larger schematic map with more roads and houses. Without tracing with his finger, the child must locate the same target house in the larger map. The schematic maps grow progressively more complex with each item.

Tips
- The child is only allowed to trace with his or her finger on the simple route below the test item, not on the larger map for each item.
- The child is not allowed to turn the stimulus book when attempting to locate the target house.
- You may wish to use a clear, acrylic sheet over the stimulus book pages, because the child will be using his or her finger to trace the simple path. Eventually an uncovered page will become soiled. Also, the spot where the finger has touched the larger map may become marked.

≡ Rapid Reference 2.39

Summary of Sentence Repetition Rules: Ages 3–6

Start	Reverse Rule	Discontinue	Stop	Time Limit
Ages 3–6: Item 1 Ages 7–12: Do not administer	None	Discontinue after 4 consecutive scores of 0.	None	None

- Repeat the teaching if necessary, so the child understands the task before you begin.
- If you have trouble with directionality, you may wish to turn the Record Form upside down so it is in the same orientation with the stimulus book.
- The correct house for each item appears in color on the Record Form.

Other Behaviors to Observe
- Does the child turn his or her head to see the stimulus from another angle?
- Does the child reflect on the task before tracing and making his or her choice, or is the child impulsive?
- Some children with good visual-spatial abilities will not trace the simple route first, but will point directly at the correct target house.

This is permissible. But for the very impulsive child who is incorrect, you should remind the child to trace the simple route before making his or her choice.

Sentence Repetition (Memory and Learning Domain): Ages 3–6

Referral Batteries: (Ages 3–6 only) A/C, B, L, SR
This subtest assesses auditory short-term memory for language with sentences of increasing length and complexity. (See Rapid Reference 2.39.)

Rules
See Rapid Reference 2.39 for details on Start Point, Reverse Rule, Discontinue, Stop, and Time.

Materials: Record Form only.

Administration: Administer according to the directions in the *Administration Manual*, p. 108. The child is read a series of sentences and is asked to recall each sentence immediately after it is presented.

Recording: Draw a line through the omitted word(s) and record any instances in which the child changes or adds a word or changes word order. To assist you, editing symbols are displayed on the Record Form.

Recording for *Behavioral Observations:* Each time the child asks for or otherwise indicates the need for a word to be repeated, place a tally mark in the *Asks for Repetition* box on the Record Form.

≡ *Rapid Reference 2.40*

Summary of Speeded Naming Rules: Ages 3–16

Start	Reverse Rule	Discontinue	Stop	Timing
Ages 3–4: Item 1, Color Naming	None	Do not discontinue.	Ages 3–4: Stop after Item 2.	Allow 300 seconds for each item.
Ages 5–6: Item 3, Color/Shape			Ages 5–6: Stop after Item 4.	
Ages 7–8: Size/Color/Shape				
Ages 9–16 Letter/Number				

Tips
- Present the sentences in normal conversational tone, at a pace comparable to when reading a passage from a book aloud; not too quickly and not too slowly.
- Do not repeat the sentence even when a child asks for a repetition.
- Do not emphasize or stress any particular part of the sentence.
- Reassure the child that the sentences are getting hard when he or she begins to experience failure.

Other Behaviors to Observe
- Does there seem to be a working memory problem? The child's recall may be fine at first, but he or she may make more errors as the sentences become longer and more complex.
- Does the child recall just the first of the sentence (primacy) or just the last part (recency)?

Speeded Naming (Language Domain): Ages 5–16

Referral Batteries: GA, R, M, A/C, B, L, SR, S/I
This subtest is designed to assess rapid semantic access to and production of names of colors, shapes, sizes, letters, or numbers. (See Rapid Reference 2.40.)

Rules
See Rapid Reference 2.40 for details on Start Point, Reverse Rule, Discontinue, Stop, and Time.

Materials: Stimulus Book 2 in flat position. Turn to age-appropriate starting point.

Administration: Follow administration directions in Stimulus Book 2. The child is shown an array of colors, shapes, sizes, letters, and numbers. He or she names them in order as quickly as possible. Some tasks require alternating the names. Stop the child and correct errors as they occur. Have the child repeat the correct response, but leave stopwatch running. Then continue. The errors will be reflected in the time score.

Recording: Record completion time in seconds for each item administered.

The correct responses are printed on the Record Form. Follow along as the child responds. Mark a slash through a word, letter, or number if the child makes an error by providing an incorrect response or skipping a response. If the child *self-corrects before the next stimulus,* write *SC* over the stimulus.

If the child does not complete the item within the 300-second time limit, mark a slash through all unattempted stimuli. Each of these unattempted stimuli is an error.

Correct Responses:

- The correct name for a shape, color, size, letter, or number.
- Although responses for Items 3 and 4 are listed in the Record Form in a specific order (e.g., *Big, Red, Square*), naming in a different or reversed order should not be considered an error (e.g., *Red, Big, Square*), because the name is correct.
- Encourage the use of *big* and *little,* not *large* and *small,* though the latter two are not errors if they occur on the test.
- A *self-corrected error* has occurred when the child provides an incorrect response or skips a shape, color, size, letter, or number, but then corrects the incorrect or skipped response.

Errors:

- Saying an incorrect name for any shape, color, size, letter, or number.
- Skipping a shape, color, size, letter, or number and not self-correcting.

≡ *Rapid Reference 2.41*

Summary of Statue Rules: Ages 3–6

Start	Reverse Rule	Discontinue	Stop	Timing
Ages 3–4 and 7–16: Do not administer Ages 5–6: Introduction to Statue	None	Do not discontinue.	None	75 seconds (**Note:** Execute the distracter tasks at the designated times.) At 10 sec., drop the pencil or pen on the table. At 20 sec., cough once out loud. At 30 sec., knock on the table twice. At 50 sec., say **Ho Hum.** At 75 sec., say **Times Up!**

- Any shape, color, size, letter, or number not attempted by the child due to the time limit should be considered an incorrect response.

Tips

- If the child cannot demonstrate mastery of colors and shapes consistently, do not put him or her under the strain of trying to name them rapidly. If you want a measure of naming, revert to Body Part Naming, though in general it is given only to 3- to 4-year-olds. Interpret with caution.
- During the Teaching, correct the use of *box* for *square,* because this is an error. The use of *large* instead of *big* and *small* instead of *little* is not an error.

Other Behaviors to Observe

- Does the child recruit the whole body into the effort of accessing labels? Does voice volume increase with the effort?
- Is the child very slow, showing a labored performance, or impulsively fast, resulting in errors?
- Anxiety and/or frustration or, alternatively, enjoying the challenge, with time pressure.
- Good naming skills during the Teaching Example, when speed is not required, but poor rapid naming performance.

Statue (Attention/Executive Functions Domain): Ages 3–6

Referral Batteries: *(Ages 3–6 only)* GA, R, M, A/C, B, L, P/M, SR, S/I

This subtest is designed to assess motor persistence and inhibition. (See Rapid Reference 2.41.)

Rules

See Rapid Reference 2.41 for details on Start Point, Reverse Rule, Discontinue, Stop, and Time.

Materials: None

Administration: Follow directions in *Administration Manual*, pp. 112–113. The child stands with feet slightly apart, the left arm at the side and the right arm bent at the elbow so that it is perpendicular to the body. The right hand is in a fist as if holding a flag. The child should place his or her left hand on the table or the back of a chair to aid balance when eyes are closed. (See Figure 3.1 in the manual for a diagram of the position.) The child is asked to maintain this body position with eyes closed during a 75-second period and to inhibit the impulse to respond to sound distracters. (See following.)

Timing: 75 seconds. Execute the distracter tasks at the times indicated on the Record Form.

After the Introduction and directions, begin timing:

- At 10 sec., drop the pencil or pen on the table.
- At 20 sec., cough once out loud.
- At 30 sec., knock on the table twice
- At 50 sec, say **Ho Hum!**
- At 75 sec., say **Times Up!**

Recording: The Record Form breaks the 75 sec. period into fifteen 5-second intervals.

Circle *Y* under the appropriate Errors column for any 5-second interval in which the child moves, opens his or her eyes, or vocalizes.

Circle *N* under the None column for any 5-sec. interval during which no errors occur.

If the child moves, opens his or her eyes, or vocalizes during the subtest, continue timing, but gently and briefly remind the child of the rules, saying "Eyes closed" or "Stay still."

(Involuntary coughing, silent smiling, and small movements of the fingers should not be considered errors.)

Errors:

Movement:

- Dropping the right hand or arm more than 45 degrees
- Turning the head
- Lifting a foot or sliding a foot on the floor

Opening eyes

Vocalizing or laughing

Tips

- Administer the test toward the end of the assessment, so the anxious child has time to feel comfortable with the examiner before closing his or her eyes with a stranger.
- Model the position (see *Administration Manual,* p. 112) for the child, and assist the child into the position, if needed.
- If the child stops trying to complete the task and is unwilling

≡ *Rapid Reference 2.42*

Summary of Theory of Mind Rules: Ages 3–16

Start	Reverse Rule	Discontinue	Stop	Timing
Ages 3–6: Item 1 Ages 7–8: Item 4 Ages 9–16: Item 6	Ages 7–16: If perfect scores are not obtained on both of the first two items administered, reverse until two consecutive perfect scores are obtained, then proceed forward.	**Verbal task:** Discontinue after 4 consecutive scores of 0, then proceed to the Conceptual Task. **Contextual Task:** Do not discontinue.	None	None

to resume the task, note the time and score the remaining 5 sec. intervals as zeroes.

Other Behaviors to Observe

- The child becomes anxious with his or her eyes closed. If the child is upset, discontinue the subtest and note the behavior.
- Other children who have difficulties standing still may keep opening their eyes a bit or moving slightly as if to test the examiner. Such performance may be scored in a standard way, assuming that the score reflects the child's real performance. However, the interpretation of the score should be guarded—did the child's motivation influence the score?
- The child is distracted constantly, and shows poor inhibition, resulting in many errors.
- Does the child sway noticeably when the eyes are closed and he or she ceases to get visual input to judge his or her position in space?

Theory of Mind: Ages 3–16

Referral Batteries: A/C, B, S/I

This subtest is designed to assess the ability to understand figurative language, mental functions, and another's point of view on a Verbal Task. The Contextual

Task uses pictures and a pointing response to assess the ability to relate emotion to social context. (See Rapid Reference 2.42.)

Rules

See Rapid Reference 2.42 for details on Start Point, Reverse Rule, Discontinue, Stop, and Time.

Materials: Stimulus Book 2 in easel position.

Administration: At the age-appropriate Start Point, follow the administration directions in Stimulus Book 2. Through stories, pictures, and questions asked by the examiner, the Verbal task assesses belief, intention, deception, emotion, imagination, pretending, imitation, and the understanding of others' thoughts, ideas, and feelings, as well as comprehension of abstract meanings in figurative language. On the Contextual Task the child is shown pictures depicting children in a social context. For each picture, the child is asked to select one of four photos that depicts the appropriate affect of the target child in the picture.

Tips

- For Verbal Task items with pictures, indicate the picture with your hand, so the child understands that your words pertain to the picture.
- On Item 4 when you use hand/finger gestures to act out the rhyme, you may prompt the child to watch your fingers.
- Take care not to rattle the box containing pencils when placing the

≡ *Rapid Reference 2.43*

**Summary of Visuomotor Precision Rules:
Ages 3–12**

Start	Reverse Rule	Discontinue	Stop	Timing
Ages 3–6: Mouse Track 1	None	Do not discontinue.	None	Mouse Tracks 1–3: Allow 60 seconds for each item.
Ages 5–12: Car				
Ages 13–16: Do not administer				Train, Car, Motorcycle: Allow 180 seconds for each item.

identical boxes on the table for Item 6. Do not allow the child to pick up the boxes.

- Write down the child's words verbatim on Item 9 (Eric pretending to be Daddy). Do not try to score as the child is talking.
- On Items 10 and 14, where there are no pictures for the story, you may prompt the child to listen closely to the story. Record the child's words verbatim and score later. On Item 14, ask both questions, A and B.
- On the Contextual Tasks, do not tell the child if the response is correct or incorrect or provide any feedback on the test items.

Other Behaviors to Observe

- Does the child attend well to your instructions and the test stimuli? Is attention better on the Contextual (pictures) than the Verbal Task or vice versa?
- Does the child provide concrete responses for abstract questions (e.g., "They aren't peas" in response to Item 13 describing the girls as "two peas in a pod")?
- If you prompt the child to use hand gestures on Item 4, does he or she understand that the gestures act out the rhyme?

Visuomotor Precision (Sensorimotor Domain): Ages 3–12

Referral Batteries: M, B, P/M, SR, S/I, (L)

This subtest assesses graphomotor speed and accuracy. (See Rapid Reference 2.43.)

Rules

See Rapid Reference 2.43 for details on Start Point, Reverse Rule, Discontinue, Stop, and Time.

Materials: Age-appropriate Response Book only.

Administration: Use the age-appropriate Response Booklet. Follow the age-appropriate subtest directions and script provided in the *Administration Manual*, pp. 118–119. The preferred hand is used to draw a line inside winding tracks as quickly as possible. Tracks of increasing complexity are executed.

Recording: Record completion time in seconds for each item.

For the Process Score of Pencil Lift, record the number of times the child lifts the pencil from the paper for each item.

Recording for the *Behavioral Observation:* For Pencil Grip, place a checkmark in the appropriate box to characterize the child's pencil grip using the criteria illustrated in Figures 3.14–3.16 in the *Administration Manual.*

Tips
- Use a pencil without an eraser, not a crayon. A primary, thick-barreled pencil is good for younger children.
- Begin timing as soon as the child begins to draw, and stop timing when the child reaches the end of the track or the 60-second time limit

---

⫷ *Rapid Reference 2.44*

Summary of Word Generation Rules: Ages 3–16

Start	Reverse Rule	Discontinue	Stop	Timing
Ages 3-16: Item 1	None	Do not discontinue.	Ages 3-6: Stop after Item 2.	Allow 60 seconds for each item.

---

has been reached. Time discreetly, so you do not convey the idea that time is more important than accuracy. If the child is still working when the time limit is up, say, "Stop."
- If the child turns the Response Booklet while completing the item, turn the Response Booklet back to the original position and say, "Remember, do not turn the paper."

Other Behaviors to Observe
- Does the child begin drawing the line through the track impulsively without attention to accuracy, or is he or she fast, but accurate? Is performance slow, but good graphomotor control is observed, or is performance slow with numerous errors due to poor graphomotor control? Note the style on the Record Form.
- Does the child lift the pencil frequently (mark box) or try to turn the Response Booklet (not allowed) in order to follow the curve of the track?
- Is the child excessively fast as if trying to compensate for poor preci-

sion? Or does the child display anxiety about being fast enough? (Often wants to know if his or her time is "good.")

- Observe associated movements when the child is executing a line within the track. Overflow movements around the mouth or of the tongue may be observed especially.

Word Generation (Language Domain): Ages 3–16

Referral Batteries: A/C, SR, S/I, (B)
This subtest is designed to assess verbal productivity through the ability to generate as many words as possible within specific semantic and phonemic categories. (See Rapid Reference 2.44.)

Rules
See Rapid Reference 2.44 for details on Start Point, Reverse Rule, Discontinue, Stop, and Time.

Materials: None

Administration: Follow subtest directions in the *Administration Manual*, pp. 121–122. The child has 60 seconds to produce as many oral words as possible in each category (Semantic: Animals, Eat/Drink; Initial Letter: *S* & *F*). For each item, begin timing immediately after you say, "Go," and allow 60 seconds to elapse before saying, "Stop."

Recording: Record the child's response verbatim. Record all repetitions and nonsense words.

Repetitions:
- Repetitions of the Teaching Example words for each item should not be considered correct responses. (See list on p. 122 of the *Administration Manual*.)
- The repetition of the same should not be considered a correct response.
- If the child states the same word in two different categories, and it belongs in that category, it is correct in both cases (e.g., *snake* is a correct answer for both Animal and S-words).
- The repetition of a word in the plural form or a different tense should not be considered a correct response for that item (e.g., credit only one correct response for *pie* and *pies* or for *start* and *started*).
- The repetition of a diminutive form of a word already used should not be considered a correct response (e.g., *pig* and *piggy* yields only 1 point; *dog* and *puppy* yields only one point). On the other hand, a

diminutive form on its own is considered correct (e.g., *piggy* given as a single response is correct).

- The repetition of a word using an adjective that does not distinguish it as a different member of the category should not be considered as correct for that item (e.g., credit only one correct response for *bear, furry bear, big bear*). On the other hand, if the adjective is considered as a part of the accepted label for a different member of the category, it should be counted as correct (*Brown Bear, Black Bear, Grizzly Bear* would be three correct labels for animals). A further example: *Brown Bear, furry bear, Grizzly Bear* would be credited as two correct responses, as *furry bear* is not an accepted label for a different member of the category.

Nonsense Words: A nonsense word should not be considered correct.

Noncategory Words: Words generated by the child that are not members of the category are not correct responses.

Proper Nouns: People's names, names of places, and other specific proper names of things should not be considered correct responses for Items 3 and 4. Conversely, if a word has another meaning (e.g., *snickers*) that is not the proper name of a person, place, or thing, the response is correct.

≡ *Rapid Reference 2.45*

Summary of Word List Interference Rules: Ages 7–16

Start	Reverse Rule	Discontinue	Stop	Timing
Ages 3-6: Do not administer Ages 7-16: Teaching Example	None	Discontinue after 3 consecutive Repetition Item scores of 0. Only the Repetition Trial scores are used to determine if the discontinue rule has been met. **Note**: The child must fail both Repetition Trials of an item to receive a Repetition Item score of 0.	None	None

Tips

- Remember that children under 7 do not take the Initial Letter section (Items 3 and 4).
- Do not try to judge correctness as the child is producing words. Record everything for error analysis later.
- Score the test immediately after administering it so that if you did not have time to note all the words completely and clearly, you may remember what word the notations refer to. If it is not possible to score at once, check notations and clarify as needed.
- Begin timing immediately after saying, "Go." Keep timing for the full 60 sec. period.
- If the child stops and does not continue for 15 seconds, prompt with, "Tell me some more," or "What other _____ can you think of?" or, on Phonemic Fluency, "Tell me some more words that begin with _____ ."

Other Behaviors to Observe

- Does the child produce all of his or her responses within the first 20–30 seconds and very little afterwards? Is there a long period of silence and then the child begins producing words in the last 30 seconds, or is there a steady production of the words throughout the 1-minute period?
- Does the child look at objects around the room to cue him or herself for words?
- Does the child's performance on the Phonemic section compare to the level of performance on Phonological Processing or with Repetition of Nonsense Words?

Word List Interference (Memory and Learning): Ages 7–16

Referral Batteries: G, R, M, A/C, L, S/I
This subtest is designed to assess verbal working memory, repetition, and word recall following interference. (See Rapid Reference 2.45.)

Rules
See Rapid Reference 2.45 for details on Start Point, Reverse Rule, Discontinue, Stop, and Time.

Material: None
Administration: Follow the subtest directions on pp. 124-125 of the
Administration Manual. The examiner presents an oral word series, and
the child repeats it. Then a second oral word series is presented and

repeated by the child. Then the child is asked to recall each series in order of presentation. The words presented increase from one to five words over the span of the subtest.

Recording:

For each Repetition Trial, draw a line through any omitted words and record any instances in which the child changes or adds a word or changes the word order. Editing symbols are displayed on the Record Form.

For each Recall Trial, record the child's responses verbatim.

Place a tally mark in the *Asks for Repetition* box on the Record Form each time the child asks for or indicates that a trial should be repeated. Do not repeat any item.

Tips

- Administer the words at the rate of approximately one word/second. Enunciate clearly.
- Administer the Repetition Trial immediately after presentation of each series of words, but do not rush the child. This is not a speed test.
- Administer the two Recall Trials for that item after administering both Repetition Trials.
- *Do not repeat* any Repetition or Recall Trial.
- Mark the errors as noted under *Recording,* but do not attempt to score as you administer the test.

TEST YOURSELF

1. **The subtests that are particularly noted to need extended practice are: (Circle four)**

    (a) Oromotor Sequences

    (b) Inhibition

    (c) Route Finding

    (d) Auditory Attention and Response Set

    (e) Manual Motor Sequences

    (f) Imitating Hand Positions

2. **List three subtests that have delay trials.**

    (a) _____

    (b) _____

    (c) _____

3. If you modify a subtest for a child with special needs, what do you need to note on the Record Form?

_____

4. What is assessed by the three conditions of the Inhibition subtest?

(a) _____

(b) _____

(c) _____

5. A General Referral Battery should be used when

(a) _____

A Specific Referral Battery should be used when

(b) _____

6. Arrows is a subtest measuring _____ .

7. Name the three parts of the Narrative Memory subtest:

(a) _____

(b) _____

(c) _____

8. If you are testing a child to confirm a diagnosis of ADHD, call the parents and ask them to take the child off of meds for the assessment. True or False?

9. The two subtests that measure two-dimensional and three-dimensional constructions are (a) _____ and (b) _____ .

10. A subtest that should not be administered to young children who are very cautious or have PTSD is _____ .

11. Two subtests which assess phonological processing are (a) _____ and (b) _____ .

12. Behavioral Observations that can be compared to base rates are recorded with checkmarks or tally marks to indicate (a) _____ of the occurrences or (b) _____ of the occurrences.

13. A subtest designed to assess motor persistence and inhibition in young children is (a) visuomotor precision or (b) statue.

14. Name two precautions that should be taken when you are going to assess a child with autism.

(a) _____

(b) _____

15. When evaluating a child with hemiparesis, do you assess both hands?

(a) Yes

(b) No

Answers:

1. b, d, e, f; 2. Three from the following: Memory for Faces, Memory for Names, Memory for Designs, and List Learning; 3. Modified Administration; 4. a. Naming Condition: rapid naming speed and accuracy; lexical access to see if naming speed/accuracy will interfere with other two trials. b. Inhibition Condition: inhibition of automatic response in favor of an alternate response. c. Switching Condition: inhibition of response and cognitive flexibility to switch among multiple sets; 5. a. the referral question is vague or multiple problems are suspected. b. referral question points to a specific problem or there is a previous diagnosis; 6. Judgment of line and angle orientation; 7. Free recall, Cued recall; Recognition; 8. False. Ask parents for permission to talk with the child's doctor to ask permission for the child to be off medication for assessment (check amount of time needed) or parents may prefer to call. Work with the child's doctor on this matter; 9. Design Copying, Block Construction; 10. Statue—the child must close his or her eyes and trust a stranger; 11. Phonological Processing, Repetition of Nonsense Words; 12. Presence; number; 13. b. Statue 14. Any two of the following: Find out about stereotypical interests, Find out about sensory issues, Allow time for child to become accustomed to you and the surroundings, Have caregiver available if needed during testing; 15. a

Three

HOW TO SCORE THE NEPSY-II

Scoring an assessment with care is essential. Important decisions about a child's life may be made at least partially on the strength of your scoring. There are many scores on NEPSY-II (see Rapid Reference 3.1). These provide much diagnostic information, but also may increase the possibility of errors in scoring by hand. This chapter will introduce the clinician, step by step, to the process of scoring. You will learn how to compute raw scores, record them, and how to locate the appropriate tables for converting into scaled scores and percentile ranks. You will also learn how to obtain combined and contrast scores for certain subtests. Selected subtests with complex recording and/or scoring will be presented individually. Finally, you will be shown how to record and graph all scores and the use of the Behavioral Observations page.

≡ Rapid Reference 3.1

Types of NEPSY II Scores

Raw Scores The number of correct responses, errors, performance time, or other score that may be directly registered upon completion of a subtest and noted on the record form.

Scaled Scores These scores are obtained by converting raw scores to age-corrected scores expressed in a scale with a mean of 10 and a standard deviation of 3. They represent a child's performance in relation to others of the same age. They can be compared to other normalized scores.

Percentile Ranks

Percentiles are obtained by converting raw scores to age-corrected scores expressed in a percentile scale. They indicate the child's standing relative to same-age peers. A score at the 10th percentile is interpreted as, "the child's score is better than 10% of his or her age group." In NEPSY-II, these scores are usually grouped into ranges of percentiles representing the values <2, 2–5, 6–10, 11–25, 26–50, 51–75, and >75. The expected level for the majority of children at a given age is the 26th–75th percentile range.

Cumulative Percentages (Base Rates)

These scores represent the cumulative percentages of the standardization sample by age or clinical group. They are descriptive base rates and do not represent percentile ranks. A base rate of 10 is interpreted as "10% of the same-age children obtained the same score or lower."

Primary Scores

These scores are the most important age-corrected scaled scores for each subtest. A combined score is a type of primary score.

Combined Scores

Combined Scores are obtained by integrating two different normed scores within a subtest; for example, speed and errors. It does not require age-correction, as the two scaled scores being integrated are already age-corrected. The combined score enables the clinician to see if the subcomponent processes are within normal limits for age (e.g., On Memory for Faces, the score for delayed memory is adjusted for level of performance on immediate memory.

Contrast Scores

These scores are obtained by converting a difference between two subscores to a norm-based value in order to contrast performance on one task with performance on another, or one part of a subtest to another. The combined score represents the child's performance on the designated variable, controlling for performance on the control variable.

Process Scores

Process scores express different aspects of performance; for example, global and local aspects of a Design Copy performance or different emotions recognized on Affect Recognition.

Behavioral Observations

These scored observations are carried out as the child performs tasks and are then tallied or marked for presence or absence. They are expressed in cumulative percentages (base rates) and percents of the standardization population displaying the behavior.

Scoring the NEPSY-II can be very complex but it can also be simplified. For the simplest possible scoring, the Primary Scores may be used to represent results. However, the Primary Scores do not always capture the essential problems of the child. For example, a child may perform a subtest very quickly but make many errors. In such an instance, the two subscores may balance out each other so the Primary Score looks average in spite of the child's problems. Another reason why in-depth scoring may be revealing is when the child has problems with a performance. Then subscores may reveal the nature of the child's problems. Also, comparing scores may demonstrate specific deficits. Yet scoring for types of errors or subtest contrasts is optional.

COMPUTER SCORING

A Scoring Assistant computer scoring program for NEPSY-II is available through the NEPSY-II publisher, Pearson. This software program computes all of the primary, process, combined, and contrast scores and percentiles, and base rates. It then provides a printout of all subtest scores and a plot of scores by domain that can be imported into the Test Results section of your report. This program is appreciated by NEPSY-II examiners because it significantly reduces scoring time. Nonetheless, even if a scoring program is available, it is wise to score NEPSY-II by hand initially, so you are aware how the scores are derived.

PREPARATORY TO SCORING

Immediately following the administration of NEPSY-II and before the child leaves, be sure to take time to look over the Record Form to check that all selected subtests have been administered and all demographic information has been recorded. Give the child a break while you perform this check. In this way, if anything is missing, there may still be time to administer a subtest you meant to give or to obtain missing information before the parent or caregiver and the child depart.

ORDER OF SCORING

All scaled scores are found in Appendix A of the *Clinical and Interpretive Manual,* all combined score tables in Appendix B; Appendix C contains the tables for contrast scores, and Behavioral Observations tables are found in Appendix D. Therefore, many clinicians who are hand scoring prefer to look up all scaled scores and percentiles first and then go back to compute combined and contrast scores. Cumulative percentages and frequency of occurrence in the standardization population for Behavior Observations can be derived last. This method avoids flipping back and forth to different tables in the manual. (See Rapid Reference 3.2.)

≡ Rapid Reference 3.2

Appendices and Order of Hand Scoring

The following scoring tables are found in the following appendices of the *Clinical and Interpretive Manual*:

- Appendix A: Scaled Scores
- Appendix B: Combined Scores
- Appendix C: Contrast Scores
- Appendix D: Behavioral Observations

Hand scoring is easier in the following order:

1) All scaled scores and percentiles across subtests
2) All combined scores across subtests
3) All contrast scores across subtests
4) Behavioral observations cumulative percentage and frequency of occurrence in the standardization population

This method avoids flipping back and forth to different appendices in the manual.

STEP-BY-STEP SCORING

Step 1: Calculating Chronological Age

While this is actually the first step in scoring, it should be accomplished prior to assessment. It is essential that you compute the correct age for the child before assessment, as you will need the child's age for subtest selection, as well as for starting and stopping the subtest at the correct point. Always double-check

CAUTION

Double-Check Birth Date and Age Computation

Example:

	Yr.	Mo.	Day
Date of Testing:	09	10	13
Date of Birth:	95	08	10
	14	02	03

the birth date with the parent or caregiver before testing and check your computation twice. If you have made an error on the age, the scores, not to mention interpretations, will be incorrect. Before you begin to score, check that all items below the start point or basal have been credited and that all parts of a Total Score (i.e., immediate and delayed) have been entered. (See Caution box on the previous page.)

Step 2: Recording Responses

For each subtest, space is provided on the Record Form to record all of the information needed to compute all scores. Be sure to record responses according to the directions in the *NEPSY-II Administration Manual.* The first page of the Record Form provides a place to summarize a child's performance on NEPSY-II. Demographic information is recorded here and primary scaled scores can be plotted to create a visual profile of the child's performance in each of the six domains. The inside front page is for recording raw scores and cumulative percentages for Behavioral Observations. The latter are qualitative observations made during the assessment that can be quantified during scoring and compared to age-level cumulative percentages.

Step 3: Obtain Subtest Scaled Scores and Percentile Ranks

In the *Administration Manual* or in this chapter refer to the scoring section of each subtest for specific instructions on obtaining total raw scores. Refer to the scoring section of each subtest for specific instructions on obtaining total raw scores.

The Record Form also contains schematics to guide you in computing each score. After you have obtained the total raw scores for each subtest, turn to the appropriate table in Appendix A of the *Clinical and Interpretive Manual.* Scaled scores are based on the child's age as calculated on the Record Form. The child's age in years and months determines which page of the table should be used. Each page of Table A.1 provides the scaled scores and percentile ranks for age groups in six-month or one-year intervals. The subtests are listed in the table according to alphabetical order within domain. For each subtest, find the raw score in the column under the subtest name. Then, reading across from this score to the extreme left or right column, find the equivalent scaled score or percentile rank for the subtest. Enter this subtest scaled score in the appropriate box on the subtest Record Form page. Percentile ranks are presented in ranges. See Figure 3.1 for a Record Form example showing the schematic for

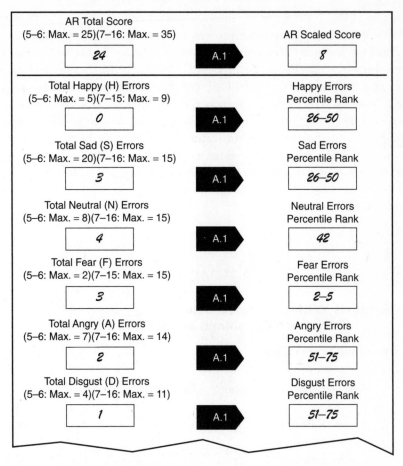

Figure 3.1 A Record Form Sample—Obtaining Affect Recognition Scaled Scores and Percentile Ranks

obtaining Affect Recognition Scaled Scores and Percentile Ranks for a child 12 years, 0 months of age.

Step 4: Obtain Combined and Contrast Scores

For subtests with combined and contrast scaled scores, you first derive the appropriate scaled scores or percentile ranks that are used to calculate that combined or contrast scaled score. These scores are indicated on the Record Form and in the scoring section of the relevant subtests in the *Administration Manual*. A schematic with colored shading (lavender for ages 3–4 and green for ages 5–16) on the Record Form leads you through the process of deriving the combined and contrast scaled scores. The appropriate look-up table in the *Clinical and Interpretive Manual* for each score is indicated by a colored arrow in the schematic on the Record Form, as well. After you derive the normed subtest scores, find the appropriate combined score table in Appendix B or the appropriate contrast score table in Appendix C of the *Clinical and Interpretive Manual*. For each table, find the child's obtained scaled scores for the relevant subtest. Reading across and down from the scores, find the value in the table where the scores meet. This is the combined or contrast scaled score. See Figure 3.2 for an example of deriving the Word Interference Repetition vs. Recall Contrast Scaled Score, where the child obtained a scaled score of 6 on repetition and a scaled score of 4 on recall.

≡ *Rapid Reference 3.3*

Subtests With Combined Scores Only, Contrast Scores Only, Both Combined and Contrast Scores

Combined Scores Only
- Animal Sorting
- The Auditory Attention section of the Auditory Attention/Response Set Subtest
- Speeded Naming
- Visuomotor Precision
- Word Generation

Contrast Scores Only
- Design Copying
- Memory for Designs and Memory for Designs Delayed
- Memory For Faces and Memory for Faces Delayed
- Narrative Memory
- Word Generation

Both Combined and Contrast Scores
- The Response Set section of the Auditory Attention/Response Set subtest
- Fingertip Tapping
- Inhibition

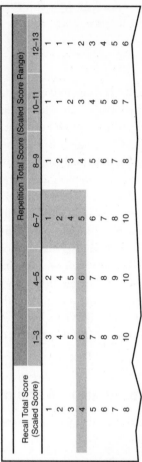

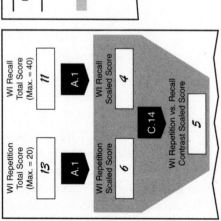

Figure 3.2 A Record Form Sample—Deriving a WI Repetition vs. WI Recall Contrast Score

Some subtests have combined scores only, some have contrast scores only, and some subtests have both combined and contrast scores.

Step 5: Behavioral Observations

Behavioral Observations are scored by tallying Behavioral Observations or checking presence or absence as required. For example, every time the child was inattentive/off-task during the Auditory Attention and Response Set subtest, you recorded a tally mark in the Behavioral Observation Box at the bottom of the page. Those marks are now counted up and the total raw score written in the appropriate bubble on the Behavioral Observation page inside the front cover of the Record Form. After you have recorded totals or presence/absence by checking "yes/no" boxes for all pertinent Behavioral Observations, this qualitative data can be converted to quantitative information by looking up cumulative percentages in Table D.1 or D.4 and the percent in the standardization population in Table D.2 or D.5 in the *NEPSY-II Clinical and Administrative Manual*. An example of a quantified Behavioral Observation would be the frequency with which motor overflow (that is, involuntary movements that accompany, and are similar to, a required motor response) is observed in a child of a particular age. Some motor behaviors are observed more often in younger children than in older children in the normative group, as is indicated in the norms.

TESTS WITH COMPLEX RECORDING AND/OR SCORING

Subtests with Complex Recording and/or Scoring will be addressed individually in this chapter. They include:
- Auditory Attention
- Clocks
- Design Copying
- Inhibition
- Memory for Designs
- Visuomotor Precision

Auditory Attention and Response Set Subtest

The Auditory Attention and Response Set (AA/RS) subtest is made up of two sections, Auditory Attention (AA) and Response Set (RS). Recording and scoring this test may seem complex at first, but with practice, recording and scoring will fall into place. Note that while you record the child's performance you need to keep following the child's performance. This demands divided attention and a certain level of training. Score as outlined in subsequent steps.

Auditory Attention and Response Set Subtest

The Auditory Attention and Response Set (AA/RS) subtest is made up of two sections, Auditory Attention (AA) and Response Set (RS). Recording and scoring this test may seem complex at first, but with practice, recording and scoring will fall into place. Note that while you record the child's performance you need to keep following the child's performance. This demands divided attention and a certain level of training. Score as outlined in subsequent steps.

Step 1: Total Correct Scores and Percentile Ranks

Total Correct Scores are Primary Scores on the AA/RS Tests. In the Auditory Attention (AA) section, look for all of the *R*s that occurred within the two shaded spaces (2 sec.) for each target word *RED*. Circle *1* if you have written *R* next to the target word or the word that follows it in the shaded area. When added, the numbers you have circled will be the AA Total Correct score that you will enter in the appropriate box at the bottom of the AA Record Form page. Use this to find the *AA Total Correct Scaled Score and Percentile Rank* in Table A.1 and enter in the correct box at the bottom of the page.

The RS Total Correct score is derived in the same manner. If the target word is *YELLOW*, to which the child is to respond *Red,* and you have written *R* next to it or next to the word in the space immediately following the target word, circle 1. If the target word is *RED,* and the child correctly points at the yellow circle, a *Y* should be written next to the word *RED* on the Record Form or in the space immediately following. For the word *BLUE*, the child should simply point at the blue circle. If the child responds correctly a *B* should be written beside the target word or in the space immediately following. For any of these correct responses within the 2-second window, the 1 should be circled. When added, the numeral ones that you have circled will be the RS Total Correct raw score that you will enter in the appropriate box and will use to find the *RS Total Correct Scaled Score and Percentile Rank* in Table A.1. Enter these values in the correct box at the bottom of the page on the RS Record Form. Figure 3.3 illustrates recording correct scores.

Step 2: Error Scores

In order to derive the AA and RS error scores, which are Process Scores, one must understand the types of errors and how to record them. This process was discussed in Chapter 2 in the individual subtest instructions for the Auditory Attention and Response Tests, but will be repeated here to give continuity to the scoring process (Figure 3.4 illustrates the recording and scoring of errors on the AA/RS subtest.)

Correct Responses

Auditory Attention				
listen			c	
RED *R*	(1)	o	c	
square			c	
now			c	
yellow			c	i
but			c	
blue			c	i
RED	(1)	o	c	
there *R*			c	

Response Set				
BLUE	(1)		c	
but *B*		o	c	
take			c	
that			c	
RED *Y*	(1)		c	
square		o	c	i
put			c	
YELLOW	(1)		c	
empty *R*			c	i

Figure. 3.3 Scoring and Recording on AA/RS

- **Omission Error:** Circle *o* in the Error column, if the child does not respond at all within the 2-sec. interval.
- **Commission Errors:** Circle *c* in the Error column for any of the following:
  - Any response not within 2 sec. of the target word (shaded area).
  - Incorrect response within the 2 sec. interval. *This is also an Inhibitory Error.*
  - Touching the white page in response to hearing *white*.
  - If child responds correctly two times within the 2 sec. interval, the *second response is a commission error.*
- **Inhibitory Errors:** Circle *i* in Error columns in the following cases:
  - On AA, an Inhibitory Error occurs when any color other than *red* is touched within the 2 sec. interval. *Caution: This is also a Commission Error.*
  - On RS, the child responds to a color word by touching that color within the 2 sec. interval when it is not a correct response. (For example, on RS, the child touches yellow when he or she hears *yellow*, but he or she should inhibit and touch red instead.)
- **Commission Errors (c) in Overlapping Sets:** If the *R* response is outside the shaded area for the second *RED,* or if it is another color within or without the shaded area, a "c" is circled. If it is another color within the shaded area, it is also an Inhibitory Error, so the "i" is also circled.
- **Omission Errors (o) in Overlapping Sets:** If there is no response to the second *RED,* circle "o" to designate an Omission Error. See Caution box concerning recording and scoring errors in overlapping sets on the AA/RS Test.

The Process Scores for AA and RS that are derived from the errors marked on the Record Form include AA Total Commission Errors, AA Total Omission Errors, and AA Total Inhibitory Errors, as well as RS Total Commission Errors, RS Total Omission Errors, and RS Total Inhibitory Errors. Total all of the Commission Errors

Auditory Attention

listen			c	
RED	1	(o)	c	
square			c	
now *R*			(c)	
yellow			c	i
but			c	
blue *B*			(c)	(i)
RED *R*	(1)	o	c	
there			c	

Response Set

BLUE			c	
but	1	(o)	c	
take *B*			(c)	
that			c	
RED *R*			(c)	
square	1	o	c	(i)
put			c	
YELLOW			c	
empty *R*	(1)		c	i

Figure. 3.4 Omission, Commission and Inhibitory Errors on AARS

Omission Error– No correct response within 2-sec. window of target word *Red*.

Two Commission Errors – First *R* response is outside of 2-sec. window and *B* response is to an incorrect color. (Respond only to target word *Red* on Auditory Attention.)

Inhibitory Error – Child did not inhibit response to *Blue*, when should only respond to *Red*.

One Correct Response – Touched red circle within 2-sec. window of target "Red."

Omission Error– No correct response within 2-sec. window of target word *Blue*.

Two Commission Errors – Response to *Blue* outside 2-sec. window and touched red circle when heard "*Red*," but should not have. (In Response Set, touch red circle when you hear *Yellow* and touch yellow when hear *Red*.)

Inhibitory Error – Child did not inhibit touch to the red circle and switch to a yellow response , when heard *Red*.

One Correct Response – Heard *Yellow*, touched red.

CAUTION

Evaluating Overlapping Sets

If two targets have overlapping shaded areas, evaluate from the top of that sequence to score the first response. On Response Set, if the response to the first target word *YELLOW* falls in the shaded space next to the second

(continued)

(*continued*)
target word *RED*, assume that the *R* response you have recorded is the child's response to the first target word *YELLOW* and not to the second, *RED*. Therefore, it is a Commission Error. If you have recorded a *Y* next to the *red* or in the next space by the word *square*, it would be scored as the child's response to the *RED* and would, therefore, receive 1 point.

YELLOW	1		c	
go			c	i
RED *R*	①		ⓒ	
square *Y*			c	i
black			c	
thing			c	i

Commission Errors (c) in Overlapping Sets:

In Auditory Attention, if the first R response is outside the shaded area for the first RED, or if it is another color within or without the shaded area, a "c" is circled. If it is another color within the shaded area, it is also an Inhibitory Error, so the "i" is also circled. The second response to the second RED is also outside the shaded area for the second target word, so it is a commission error, as well.

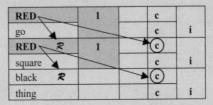

RED	1		c	
go			c	i
RED *R*	1		ⓒ	
square			c	i
black *R*			ⓒ	
thing			c	i

Omission Errors (o) in Overlapping Sets:

In the above Auditory Attention example, if there is no response to the second *RED*, circle "o" to designate an Omission Error. Remember that the *R* beside the second *RED* is the response to the first *Red*.

RED	1		c	
go		o	c	i
RED *R*	1	ⓞ	ⓒ	
square			c	i
black			c	
thing			c	i

(marked "c"), all of the Omission Errors ("o"), and all of the Inhibitory Errors ("i"), and enter the totals for each type of error in the appropriate box on the bottom of the Record Form. The percentile ranks for these raw scores are looked up in Table A.1, and then entered in the appropriate boxes on the bottom of the Record Forms.

Step 3: Combined Scores

The Combined Scores are Primary Scores on the AA/RS Test. The *AA Combined Score* integrates the AA Total Correct Scaled Score and the AA Total Commission Errors Percentile Rank for ages 5–12 (Table B.2) and the AA Total Correct Percentile Rank and the AA Total Commission Errors Percentile Rank for ages 13–16 (Table B.3). *Caution:* These AA Combined Scores are derived in two different ways. For ages 5–12, the AA Total Correct Score is integrated with the Total Commission Errors Percentile Rank. For ages 13–16, the two percentile ranks (Total Correct SS Percentile Rank and Total Commission Errors Percentile Rank) are integrated. See Caution box. The RS Combined Scores are derived in the same way, integrating the RS Total Correct Scaled Score and the RS Total Commission Errors Percentile Rank for ages 7–12 (Table B.4) and the RS Total Correct Percentile Rank and the RS Total Commission Errors Percentile Rank for ages 13–16 (Table B.5). Note that there is pale shading on the Record Form for both AA and RS that guides you in deriving the AA Combined Score and the RS Combined Scores.

Step 4: Contrast Score

The *AA vs. RS Contrast Scaled Score* compares the child's performance on AA (AA Combined Scaled Score) with the child's performance on RS (RS Combined Scaled Score). When you have completed both tests, the AA Combined Score and the RS Combined Score are entered into the appropriate boxes shaded in a pale color at the bottom of the RS Record Form page. Using these scores, the Contrast Score is then looked up in Table C.1 as indicated in white on the colored

---

CAUTION

Deriving AA and RS Combined Scores

AA Combined Scores are derived in two different ways:

- For ages 5–12, the AA Total Correct Score is integrated with the Total Commission Errors Percentile Rank.
- For ages 13–16, the two percentile ranks (Total Correct SS Percentile Rank and Total Commission Errors Percentile Rank) are integrated.

The RS Combined Scores are derived in the same way:

- For ages 7–12, the RS Total Correct Scaled Score and the RS Total Commission Errors Percentile Rank are integrated. (Table B.4)
- For ages 13–16, the RS Total Correct Percentile Rank and the RS Total Commission Errors Percentile Rank are integrated.

arrow that points to the AA vs. RS Contrast Scaled Score box at the bottom of the RS page of the Record Form. The value resulting from this table is entered into the final appropriate box.

This contrast allows one to compare the child's performance on a simple selective auditory attention task (AA) to performance on a complex auditory attention task (RS), during which one must sustain selective attention on one target, while using executive functions to shift set between two other targets.

Step 5: Behavioral Observations

After all quantitative scores have been looked up and recorded, one should tally the frequency of designated AA/RS Behavioral Observations: *Inattentive/Distracted Off-task Behaviors* during AA and during RS separately and *Out of Seat/Physical Movement in Seat Off-Task Behaviors* during AA and during RS separately. Enter each of these totals in the appropriate bubble on the left side of the Record Form at the bottom of each page. These raw score totals are then transferred to the Behavioral Observation summary page on the inside front cover of the Record Form. For ages 5–6, Table D.1 is used to obtain Cumulative Percentages for these raw scores, and for ages 7–16 Table D.4 is used. Enter the Cumulative Percentages in the appropriate rectangular box under Auditory Attention and Response Set. Scoring is complete at this point.

Clocks Subtest

The Clocks (CL) subtest, along with the Design Copying Test that follows it in this chapter, both require clinical judgment in scoring. Therefore, it is important to be familiar with the scoring criteria before you begin administering and scoring these tests.

Step 1: Score the Criteria for Items 1–4 and Items 9–10 and Sum the Item Scores

On pp. 127–133 of Appendix A in the *Administration Manual* are found the Scoring Procedures for the Clock Subtest. The criteria are illustrated with examples of children's performances. Study these carefully and keep them present as you score.

On *Drawing to Command Items 1 and 2,* as well as *Clock Copy Items 9 and 10,* a child's Clock subtest performance is evaluated according to the criteria for:

- Numbers
  - Presence
  - Location
  - Sequence

See the Caution box on the following page: Scoring the Numbers–Sequence Criteria on Clocks.

- Contour
  - Presence
  - Accommodation
  - Closure
  - Symmetry
- Hands
  - Presence
  - Connection
  - Proportion
  - Correct Target
- Center
  - Presence
  - Location

> # CAUTION
>
> ### Scoring the Numbers–Sequence Criteria on Clocks
>
> To score the Numbers-Sequences criteria for items 1–4 and 9–10, the manner in which the child draws the numbers on the clock face *must* be noted during testing.

After these criteria have been evaluated for each of these four items (Items 1–2; 9–10) and scored 0 or 1, add the scores across the row from left to right for each item and place the sum of the scores in the shaded item scoring box on the far right hand side of the page under Item Score.

On the *Digital–Analog* task, Items 3 and 4, the child's performance is only scored for the criteria for:

- Hands
  - Presence
  - Connection
  - Proportion
  - Correct Target
- Center
  - Presence
  - Location

Again, after the items have been carefully evaluated for the aforementioned criteria and scored 0 or 1, add the scores across the appropriate row and place the sum in the shaded box at the end of the row.

Step 2: Score Correct/Incorrect on Items 5–8

On the *Clock Reading without Numbers* and the *Clock Reading with Numbers* tasks (Items 5–8), the child's answer is either correct or incorrect, so the score for each of these items is circled as 1 or 0.

Step 3: Derive the CL Total Score (Raw Score) and CL Scaled Score
Sum the Item Scores in the far right-hand column of the Clocks Record Form, including those in shaded boxes and the Item 5–8 scores of 0 or 1. Place the resulting total in the *CL Total Score* box. The colored arrow shows you that Table A.1 should be used to obtain the *CL Scaled Score*.

Design Copying Subtest

The *Design Copying* (DC) subtest has two scoring methods:
- The *quick scoring method* provides the *DC General* score. This method is a quick and simple way of scoring.
- *DC Process scoring system* provides more diagnostic information as it assesses three skills associated with paper/pencil copying:
  - Motor—the ability to use fine motor control in manipulating a pencil.
  - Global—the ability to reproduce the general gestalt of a design.
  - Local—the ability to reproduce details, shapes, and sizes of a design, as well as the correct relationship between design elements.

DON'T FORGET

Interpretation of Regulatory Factors on DCP

Spatial, detail, or fine motor processing impairments are scored.

Planning and execution are *not* scored, but your interpretation should always take into account whether or not errors are due to

- Regulatory factors (e.g., executive functioning). Executive functions needed for accurate design copying include:
  - Employing ordering and sequencing necessary to see that the design will fit in the allotted space and figure-ground errors are not made.

Be sure that you digest the Scoring Procedures for both types of scoring for the *Design Copying Test* on pp. 135–182 in the *Administration Manual.* Also become familiar with the use of the Scoring Template that came with your NEPSY-II kit. At first, you should score each item in a child's DC subtest while referring to this guide. There you will find General Scoring Considerations as well as descriptions of the criteria and examples for each item. After a good bit of practice, you will internalize the criteria and you will not need to refer to the examples so frequently. However, no matter how experienced you are, if you are in doubt whether a design element meets a criterion, be sure to check Appendix B.

QUICK-SCORING: DESIGN COPY GENERAL (DCG)

If you are using the quick-scoring method, the Scoring Criteria for Design Copying General are found on pp. 159–166 in the *Administration Manual*.

Step 1: Score Each Design 1 or 0
The drawing must meet all of the criteria for an item to receive a score of 1. Circle 1 or 0 in the General column on the left side of the page.

Step 2: Compute DCG Total Score (Raw Score) and DCG Percentile Rank
When you have scored all items, add up the scores for the DCG Total Score (raw score) and enter it in the first box on the left-hand side of the first row of scoring boxes of the DC Record Form. The colored arrow below it directs you to Table A.1 to look up the DCG Percentile Rank, which is entered in the appropriate scoring box to which the arrow points. This is the complete scoring process for DCG.

DESIGN COPYING PROCESS (DCP) SCORING

The Scoring Criteria for the more diagnostic Design Copy Process scoring are found on pp. 167–182. Criteria in this section clearly show which process scores are being addressed. These are denoted as Motor A and B; Global C and D; and Local D and F.

Step 1: Score Motor
Score *Motor A and B* completely, then add those scores and fill in the *DCP Motor Score* (raw score) box that is second from the left in the top row of DC scoring boxes in the Record Form.

Step 2: Score Global
Score *Global C and D* and add the score before filling in the *DCP Global Score* box.

Step 3: Score Local
Score *Local E and F* and add the score before filling in the *DCP Local Score* box.

Step 4: Obtain the DCP Total Score (Raw Score)

Add the *Motor* + *Global* + *Local* raw scores to yield the *DCP Total Score*. Enter this in the far right-hand box on the top row of DC scoring boxes.

Step 5: Derive the DCP Scaled Scores for Motor, Global, and Local

Turn to *Table A.1* as seen on the colored arrow beneath each DCP scoring box. Look up the *DCP Motor Scaled Score (SS)*, the *DCP Global SS*, and the *DCP Local SS*, and enter in the appropriate boxes below the colored arrows.

Step 6: Derive the Contrast Score

You will note that there is a pale colored triangle on the Record Form that encompasses the *DCP Global Scaled Score* and the *DCP Local Scaled Score*, which you have just looked up in Table A.1. Now turn to *Table C.3*, as indicated on the colored arrow in the shaded area. The child's DCP Local Scaled Score is located on the vertical axis and the child's Global Scaled Score range is located on the horizontal axis at the top of Table C.3. Tracing lines across and down, one will

> # CAUTION
>
> ## Deriving the DCP Total Score
>
> If you have scored both ways, be careful not to add the DCG Total Score into the computation for the DCP Total Score. Since one usually uses one scoring method or another, this is not likely to happen, but be aware of the problem if you score both ways for comparison.

find the value of the *DC Global vs. Local Contrast Scaled Score* that will be entered in the appropriate box beneath the C.3 colored arrow. You have now finished scoring the DCP test and are ready to interpret all of the elements of DC individually, as well as the effect of all elements taken together and the contrast between DC Local and Global performance.

Inhibition Subtest

The *Inhibition* (IN) subtest yields many scores that provide a great deal of diagnostic information. However, scoring it looks a bit more intimidating than it actually is. As the Inhibition subtest was administered you recorded the completion time in seconds for Test Item 1 (Shapes) and for Test Item 2 (Arrows) in each condition: Naming, Inhibition, and Switching. You have also checked off whether or not the child pointed to the stimuli as he or she was taking the test. You have also put a slash mark over errors (incorrect response or skipped response on the Record Form). Further, if the child has self-corrected, you have made the notation SC over the response. Therefore, for each of the three conditions, you are actually well-prepared for scoring.

Step 1: Totaling Uncorrected and Self-corrected Errors for Naming, Inhibition, and Switching Conditions

You have already recorded *Completion Time* in the last shaded scoring box in the column for each condition, so that score is done. Further, you have also checked off *Y* or *N* for the *Behavioral Observation—Points to Stimuli* for each condition in Items 1 and Items 2. Now, by moving across the section for each condition row by row, adding the slash marks, you will find the value of *Uncorrected Errors* for each condition for Item 1 and Item 2. Enter this value in the first box in the scoring column for each condition. Then go back and look for all *SC* notations for *Self-corrected Errors,* add them up for each condition, and enter the value in the Self-corrected Errors scoring box for each condition. It is the second scoring box in each column.

Step 2: Computing Total Errors for Shapes and Arrows

Now all of the scoring boxes in each column have been filled, except the third one in each column, which is labeled *Total Errors.* Add together the values in the scoring boxes for *Uncorrected Errors and Self-corrected Errors* for each condition. Enter the value in the appropriate box for each condition in both items. Then add the values in the Total Errors boxes for Item 1 and place this total in the *Item 1: Shapes Total Errors* scoring box beneath the line at the bottom of the left-hand page of the Record Form. Now repeat this step for *Item 2: Arrows Total Errors* and enter the value in the right-hand box below the line at the bottom of the left-hand page of the Record Form.

Step 3: Total Behavioral Observations

Total the *Y* responses for the Naming Condition for Item 1 and for Item 2. Move to the right-hand page of the Inhibition Record Form and under the label *Behavioral Observations,* enter the value in the bubble labeled *INN* (Naming condition) *Points to Stimuli Total.* Now repeat the process for *INI* (Inhibition condition) *Points to Stimuli Total* and *INS* (Switching condition) *Points to Stimuli Total,* and enter the totals.

Step 4: Finding INN, INI, and INS Totals

Next you will find the *INN Total Uncorrected Errors* by adding Uncorrected Errors for Item 1 and Item 2. Enter the resulting total in the Inhibition Naming *INN Total Uncorrected Errors* scoring box, the first box under the Behavioral Observation bubble. Using this same procedure find the Inhibition condition *INI Total Uncorrected Errors* and Inhibition Switching *INS Total Uncorrected Errors* and enter them in the first scoring box in the scoring column for each condition and enter them in the first scoring box in the scoring column for each condition and enter them in the first scoring box in the scoring column for each condition on the right-hand page of the Record Form. Now compute the total of self-corrected errors for each condition by adding together the Self-corrected Error Scores from Item 1 and Item 2. The resulting values will be entered as *INN Total Self-corrected Errors, INI Total Self-corrected Errors,* and *INS Total Self-corrected Errors* in the second scoring box in the first column on the right-hand page of the Record Form. Add the two types of errors for each condition and enter these values as the *INN Total Errors,* the *INI Total Errors,* and the *INS Total Errors.* The fourth scoring box for each condition contains the value computed by adding the Total Completion Time for Item 1 and Item 2 for each condition, resulting in *the INN Total Completion Time,* the *INI Total Completion Time,* and the *INS Total Completion Time.*

Step 5: Tabulating Total Errors for Inhibition Test

Add together the Item 1 Shapes Total Errors and the Item 2 Arrows Total Errors that appear below the line at the bottom of the left-hand page of the Record Form. Enter the resulting raw score in the *IN Total Errors* scoring box at the bottom of the first column on the right-hand page of the Record Form. In *Table A.1,* as indicated by the colored arrow, look up the *IN Total Errors Scaled Score* and enter it in the bottom scoring box in the second column on the right-hand page. This is a Primary Score for the Inhibition Test.

Step 6: Look up Process Scaled Scores and Percentile Ranks

Continuing with *Table A.1,* look up the *scaled scores* or *percentile ranks* as indicated by the colored arrows pointing to the appropriate scoring boxes in the next column. The scores derived will be the Process Score Percentile Ranks for *INN Total Uncorrected Errors, INI Total Uncorrected Errors,* and *INS Total Uncorrected Errors,* as well as for *INN Total Self-corrected Errors, INI Total Self-corrected Errors,* and *INS Total Self-corrected Errors.* These are Process Scores for the Inhibition subtest.

Step 7: Look up Primary Scores for the Inhibition Test

The colored arrows also guide you to look up the *percentile ranks* for the *INN, INI,* and *INS Total Error* scores in *Table A.1,* as well as the *INN, INI,* and *INS Completion Time Scaled Scores.* Both sets of these scores are Primary Scores for the Inhibition subtest. The scoring boxes for these two sets of scores appear in a shaded path that leads to deriving the Combined Scores for the Inhibition Tests.

Step 8: Derive Combined Scores

A different table in Appendix B of the *Clinical and Interpretation Manual* appears on the colored arrow, guiding you to the derivation of each condition's Combined Score. For the *INN Combined Score* you look up the value using the *INN Total*

Errors Percentile Rank and the *INN Total Completion Time Scaled Score* (from Step 7) in *Table B.10*. For the *INI Combined Score* you look up the value using the *INI Total Errors Percentile Rank* and the *INI Total Completion Time Scaled Score* (from Step 7) in *Table B.11*, and for the *INS Combined Score* you look up the value using the *INS Total Errors Percentile Rank* and the *INS Total Completion Time Scaled Score* (from Step 7) in *Table B.11*. The resulting three values are entered in the *INN Combined Scaled Score, INI Combined Scaled Score,* and the *INS Combined Scaled Score* scoring boxes, respectively. The Combined Scores are Primary Scores for the Inhibition Test.

Step 9: Derive Contrast Scores
Dark green arrows and a shaded light green triangular shape encompassing the Combined Scores guide you to the derivation of the Contrast Scores for Inhibition: the *INN vs. INI Contrast Scaled Score* and the *INI vs. INS Contrast Scaled Score*. The value for the first Contrast Score integrating the *INN and INI Combined Scaled Scores* is looked up in *Table C.6* and the value is entered in the top scoring box on the far right side of the Record Form. The value for the second Contrast Score integrating the *INI and INS Combined Scaled Scores* is looked up in *Table C.7* and the value is entered in the bottom scoring box on the far right side of the Record Form.

Using the previously outlined process will make scoring a logical progression and help you accomplish the task fairly quickly. This test is rich in diagnostic information and scoring it by hand for a while will help you understand better how the scores are derived.

MEMORY FOR DESIGNS AND MEMORY FOR DESIGNS DELAYED (MD/MDD) SUBTESTS

The *Memory for Designs (MD)* and *Memory for Designs Delayed (MDD)* subtests assess immediate and delayed spatial memory for novel visual material. Like the Inhibition subtest, accurate recording will simplify the scoring process. There is a miniature grid for each Trial on both MD and MDD. On this you have recorded the numbers of the design cards in the squares where the child placed them during the testing. The numbers you have recorded will be used to derive the Content Score and the Spatial Score.

Memory for Designs

Step 1: Tabulating the MD Content Score
Using the numbers in the grid, circle the numbers the child placed in the grid in the *Target* and *Distracter Columns*. Then score under *Content Score* (Does the child remember the correct designs?) as follows:

- Two points if only the Target card number is circled.
- One point if only the Distracter card number is circled or both the Target card number and the Distracter card number are circled.
- Zero points if neither the Target card number nor the Distracter card number is circled.

Total the numbers circled in the *Content* score column and write the value in the *Content scoring box* for that Trial. Then, proceed to the next Trial grid and compute the Content raw score for that Trial and so on until all Trials attempted are scored.

Step 2: Tabulating the MD Spatial Score

Return to the first Trial the child attempted (not the Teaching Example). Using the numbers recorded and printed in the miniature grid, mark the scores in the *Spatial* score column:

- One point if you have recorded a card number in a cell with a number printed within the cell.
- Zero points if you have not recorded a card number in a cell with a number printed within the cell.

Total the numbers circled in the Spatial Score column and write the value in the *Spatial scoring box* for that Trial. Then proceed to the next Trial grid and compute the Spatial raw score for that Trial and so on until all Trials attempted are scored.

Step 3: Tabulating MD Bonus Score

The next step is to determine if the child has earned *Bonus* points for recalling the correct designs in the correct locations for each. Looking at the miniature grid on the Record Form, score as follows:

- Two points if the card number recorded in the cell matches the printed number in the cell.
- Zero points if the card number recorded in the cell does not match the printed number in the cell.

Total the numbers circled in the Bonus column and write the value in the *Bonus scoring box* for that Trial. Then proceed to the next Trial grid and compute the Bonus raw score for that Trial and so on until all Trials attempted are scored.

Step 4: Totals for Each MD Trial

You now have three raw scores for *Content, Spatial,* and *Bonus* at the bottom of each Trial grid. Total these numbers and write the *Total* in the Total scoring box for each Trial.

Step 5: Tabulate MD Content, MD Spatial, and MD Total Scores

Total all Content Scores for each Trial attempted and record this number in the *MD Content Score* box in the first row of scoring boxes under the colored line on the second page of the Memory for Designs Record Form. *Total all Spatial Scores for each Trial attempted* and record this number in the *MD Spatial Score* box on the first row under the colored line. *Skip the Bonus* score for each trial attempted, but add the *Total* score for each Trial attempted, which will reflect the Bonus points. Place the *MD Total Score* in the third scoring box under the colored line.

Step 6: Look up Primary (MD Scaled Score) and Process Scores (MD Content and MD Spatial Scaled Scores

Using the MD Content Score, the MD Spatial Score, and the MD Total Score, look up in Table A.1, as indicated on the colored arrows under each scoring box, the MD Content Scaled Score, the MD Spatial Scaled Score, and the MD Scaled Score (Total Scaled Score). The MD Scaled Score is the Primary Score for the Memory for Designs subtest, while the MD Content and MD Spatial Scaled Scores are Process Scores.

Step 7: Derive MD Contrast Scaled Scores

The *MD Content vs. Spatial Contrast Scaled Score* is derived next from the *MD Content Scaled Score* and the *MD Spatial Scaled Score,* as indicated by the pale colored shading on the Record Form. The colored arrow pointing to the Contrast scoring box shows that this score will be looked up in *Table C.8.*

Step 8: Total Behavioral Observations

Finally, for the MD *Behavioral Observation* of *Rule Violations,* total the number of *Y (Yes)* boxes in which you have placed a *X* or checkmark during the MD testing.

Memory for Designs Delayed

The scoring for the age-appropriate Delayed Recall Trial is a simplified version of the MD scoring procedure, because there is only one Recall Trial.

Step 1: Compute MDD Content, Spatial, Bonus, and Total Scores

The *MDD Content Score, MDD Spatial Score, Bonus,* and *MDD Total Score* are computed in the same way as on the MD subtest, but there is just one Trial, so these values become the scores. Enter these values in the scoring boxes on the first row under the colored line on the MDD page of the Record Form.

Step 2: Look up MDD Scaled Scores

Using *Table A.1,* as indicated on the colored arrows pointing to the scaled score boxes, look up the *MDD Content Scaled Score,* the *MDD Spatial Scaled Score,* and the

MDD Scaled Score. Write these values in the first, second, and *fourth* scoring boxes of the second row. Now, transfer the *MD Scaled Score* from the MD Record Form page into the third scoring box in the second row of the MDD Record Form page.

Step 3: Look up MDD Content versus MDD Spatial Contrast Score and MD versus MDD Contrast Scores

Two shaded inverted triangles guide you to deriving the *MDD Contrast Scaled Scores*. The inverted triangle on the right encompasses the *MDD Content Scaled Score* and the *MDD Spatial Scaled Score*. The colored arrow indicates that *Table C.9* is to be used to look up the *MDD Content vs. Spatial Contrast Scaled Score*. The resulting value is placed in the scoring box on the left at the bottom of the Record Form. The shaded inverted triangle on the right contains the *MD Scaled Score* and the *MDD Scaled Score*. The colored arrow pointing to the Contrast Score box shows that *Table C.10* is to be used to derive the *MD vs. MDD Contrast Scaled Score*.

Step 4: Total Rule Violations

Finally, the number of Rule Violations for MD and MDD is totaled, yielding the *MD and MDD Rule Violations Total*, which is written in the *Behavioral Observations* bubble, and completes the scoring process.

Visuomotor Precision Subtest

The Visuomotor Precision (VP) subtest, in which the child draws pencil lines through winding tracks as quickly as possible, is scored for both speed and precision, as well as the number of times that the child lifts the pencil while executing the lines.

Step 1: Total Time Raw Scores

Completion Time is recorded for each track when the child completes the task. The Completion Time raw scores for each track are added together to obtain the *Total Time Completion* raw score. This value is entered into the *VP Total Completion Time* box on the Record Form.

Step 2: Score Errors and Pencil Lifts

Errors include:
- **Each segment of the track in which the child's pencil line strays across the outside edge of the track.** There must be white space between the child's line and the outside edge of the track. A good rule of thumb is that if you can place a pencil point between the two lines, the mark is an error. If the child's mark remains outside the outer edge of

the track for more than one segment, each segment counts as an error. You can number consecutively each segment in which an error occurs. In this way the last number recorded in a segment will be the total number of errors for that track. Alternatively, some examiners prefer to mark a line across each segment in which an error occurs, and count them afterwards.

- **Any segments of the track not attempted due to the time limit.**
- **Where the child draws a line that falls outside the edges of the track and then he or she goes back and corrects the error by drawing another line, an error has still occurred.** The line outside of the track should still be used for scoring. Figure 3.5. illustrates errors on Visuomotor Precision.
- **Pencil Lifts are counted for each track.** Every time the child lifts the pencil from the Response Booklet, a pencil lift is recorded on the far right side of the Record Form for Visuomotor Precision. These marks are tallied when the test is over and the resulting number is written in the *VP Pencil Lift Total* box.

Step 3: Compute VP Total Errors
The total number of errors for each track is summed to produce the *VP Total Errors* raw score that is entered in the VP Total Errors box on the Record Form.

Step 4: Derive VP Total Time Scaled Score, VP Total Errors, and VP Pencil Lifts Percentile Ranks.
Using the three raw scores recorded in the first row of boxes, you then look up the *VP Total Completion Time Scaled Score,* the *VP Total Errors Percentile Rank,* and the *VP*

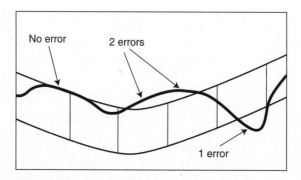

Figure 3.5 Errors on Visuomotor Precision

Pencil Lifts Percentile Rank in Table A.1, as indicated on the colored arrows. These values are entered into the appropriate boxes on the second row of scoring boxes on the VP page of the Record Form.

Step 5: Derive the Combined Score

The shaded inverted triangle that encompasses the VP Total Completion Time Scaled Score and the VP Total Errors Percentile Rank boxes points the path to computing the *VP Combined Scaled Score*. This score integrates the VP Total Completion Time SS and the VP Total Errors Percentile Rank. Use Table B.14 for this score, as indicated in white numbers on the colored arrow pointing to the VP Combined Scaled Score box. The VP Test scoring is now complete and the scores are ready for interpretation.

Step 6: Behavioral Observation

During the testing, you noted in the shaded Behavioral Observations area the *Pencil Grip(s)* used by the child as he or she executed the lines. Check back to the figures in the *Administration Manual* that illustrate various pencil grips (pp. 116–117) to be sure that you have classified the child's grip appropriately. If not, change the mark in the Behavioral Observation area; if so, proceed to the next step. Look up the percent of children of the child's age in the standardization sample using this grip in Table D.2 or D.5. Enter the value in the bubble provided at the bottom of the Behavioral Observations shaded area.

OVERVIEW OF SUBTEST SCORES

The following section presents an overview of the subtest scores to be used as a guide for scoring and demonstrating the NEPSY-II results.

CAUTION

Avoiding Type I Error

It needs to be pointed out that there is a risk of type I errors when multiple scores are presented. This means that the more subtest scores you end up with, the greater is the likelihood that some significant findings—subaverage or significantly different scores—will be obtained by chance. This risk of error is avoided if in the process of interpretation the consistency and meaningfulness of the finding is ascertained, and test findings are validated against reports from the child's daily life.

Affect Recognition (Social Perception): Ages 3–16

Scoring: The correct responses are in color on the Record Form.
Items 1–8 and 13–21
1 point for a correct response.
0 points for an incorrect response or for no response.
Items 9–12 and 22–35
1 point if both responses are correct.
0 points if either response is incorrect or for no response.

Scores:
Primary Scores:
The AR Total Score = The sum of the item scores
(See Table A.1 in the *Clinical and Interpretive Manual* to obtain the AR Scaled Score.)
Process Scores:
Scores are available for each of the six emotions depicted. These are optional scores but may yield diagnostic information. Beneath each incorrect response for Items 9–35 is a letter that corresponds to the emotion expressed by the child for that response (e.g., *H* for Happy). For each of the six emotions, total the number of incorrect responses across all items administered.
(See Table A.1 in the *Clinical and Interpretive Manual* to obtain the Percentile Ranks for Process Scores.)

Behavioral Observations—**Spontaneous Comments made by the child during Affect Recognition: Tally all marks in the Spontaneous Comments Box.**
(See Table D.1 or D.4 in the *Clinical and Interpretative Manual* to obtain the Spontaneous Comments Total Cumulative Percentage.)

Animal Sorting (Attention/Executive Functioning): Ages 7–16

Scoring:
If the card numbers match one of the correct sorts in the *Administration Manual,* p. 40, it is a correct sort.
If the numbers recorded do not match one of the correct sorts, the sort is *always considered a novel sort error.*

If the numbers recorded match the numbers for a previous correct sort, including the Teaching Example, it should always be considered a repeated sort error, even if the child describes a different sorting principle. The child receives:

- 1 point for each correct sort within 360 sec. of cumulative sort time.
- 0 points for each novel or repeated sort or sort without four cards in each group. (See Rapid Reference 3.4 for Correct Animal Sorting Categories.)

Rapid Reference 3.4

Correct Animal Sorting Categories

Animal Sorting Categories

Large/small animal,	Water/no water
Sun/rain,	Fur/no fur—other covering
Facing left/right,	Blue/yellow
Two figures/one figure,	Common pet/uncommon pet
Border/no border,	Stripes/no stripes
Animal moving/still	Tree/no tree

Scores:

Primary Scores:

AS Total Correct Sorts = Total number of correct four-card sorts.

AS Total Errors = Total Novel Sorts + Total Repeated Sorts

AS Combined Scaled Score integrates the AS Total Correct Sorts and the AS Total Errors Percentile Rank.

(See Table A.1 in the *Clinical and Interpretive Manual* to obtain the AS Total Correct Sorts Scaled Score.)

Process Scores:

AS Novel Sort Error—Total the novel errors.

AS Repeated Sort Error—Total the repeated sorts.

(See Table A.1 in the *Clinical and Interpretive Manual* to obtain the AS Novel Sort Errors and AS Repeated Sort Errors Percentile Ranks.)

Arrows (Visuospatial Domain): Ages 5–16

Scoring: The correct response is in color on the Record Form.
Items 1–4
1 point for each correct response.
0 points for an incorrect or no response (Record NR).
Items 5–21
2 points if both responses are correct.
1 point if only one is correct.
0 points if both responses are incorrect or there is no response (Record NR).

Scores:
Primary Score:
The *AW Total Score* = sum of the item scores.
(See Table A.1 in the *Clinical and Interpretive Manual* to obtain the AW Scaled Score.)

Auditory Attention and Response Set (Attention/Executive Function): Ages 5–16

Scoring: (See pp. 136–142 in this chapter for comprehensive scoring.)
Primary Scores:
The AA Total Correct Scaled Scores = The sum of the correct responses provided during AA.
The RS Total Correct Scaled Scores = The sum of the correct responses provided during RS.
The AA Combined Scores integrates the AA Total Correct Scaled Score and the AA Total Commission Errors Percentile Rank for ages 5–12 and the AA Total Correct Percentile Rank and the AA Total Commission Errors Percentile Rank (see Process scores for the latter) for ages 13–16.
The RS Combined Scores integrates the RS Total Correct Scaled Score and the RS Total Commission Errors Percentile Rank for ages 7–12, and the RS Total Correct Percentile Rank and the RS Total Commission Errors Percentile Rank (see Process scores for the latter) for ages 13–16.

Process Scores:

AA Total Commission Errors raw score = The sum of Commission Errors that occurred during AA.

RS Commission Errors raw score = The sum of Commission Errors that occurred during RS.

AA Total Omission Errors raw score = The sum of Omission Errors that occurred during AA.

RS Total Omission Errors raw score = The sum of Omission Errors that occurred during RS.

AA Total Inhibitory Errors raw score = The sum of Inhibitory Errors that occurred during AA.

RS Total Inhibitory Errors raw score = The sum of Inhibitory Errors that occurred during RS.

Contrast Scores:

The AA vs. RS Contrast Scaled Score compares the child's performance on AA with the child's performance on RS.

Behavioral Observations:

For ages 5–6, tally marks are recorded during testing and later totaled separately for:

Inattentive/Distracted Off-task Behaviors during AA.

Out of Seat/Physical Movement in Seat Off-Task Behaviors during AA.

For ages 7–16, tally marks are recorded during testing and later totaled separately for:

Inattentive/Distracted Off-task Behaviors during both AA and RS.

Out of Seat/Physical Movement in Seat Off-Task Behaviors during AA and RS.

Block Construction (Visuospatial Domain): Ages 3–16

Scoring:

Items 1–10

1 point for correct construction completed within time limit.

0 points for incorrect construction within time limit; correct construction over time, or no response.

Items 11–15

2 points for correct construction completed in 1–20 sec.

1 point for correct construction completed within 21–60 sec.

0 points for incorrect construction within time limit; correct construction over time, or no response.

Items 16–19

2 points for correct construction completed in 1–30 sec.

1 point for correct construction completed within 31–60 sec.

0 points for incorrect construction within time limit; correct construction over time, or no response.

Score:

Primary Score:

BC Total Scaled Score = Sum of the item scores. (See Table A.1 in the *Clinical and Interpretive Manual* to obtain the Block Construction Total Scaled Score.)

CAUTION

Rotations Are Not Errors on Block Construction

Rotations are no longer counted as errors on the more difficult items as they were on NEPSY.

Body Part Naming (Language Domain): Ages 3–4

Scoring:

For the Naming items:

The child names the parts of the body on a figure of a child in the Stimulus Book for 2 points.

If the child is unable to name a body part on the picture, he or she can name it on his own body or the examiners body and receive 1 point. No response yields 0 points.

For Identification items:

The child points to the corresponding parts of the body on the figure as the examiner names the body parts aloud. The child receives 1 point for each body part name that he or she is able to recognize.

Scores:

Primary Scores:

BPN Total Score = The sum of the Body Part Naming item scores.

(See Table A.1 in the *Clinica and Interpretive Manual* to obtain the BPN Scaled Score.)

BPI Total Score = The sum of the Body Part Identification item scores.

(See Table A.1 in the *Clinical and Interpretive Manual* to obtain the BPI Scaled Score.)

Contrast Score:

The Body Part Naming vs. Body Part Identification Contrast Scaled Score compares the young child's expressive language at the naming level to receptive language at the identification level. (See Table C.2 in the *Clinical and Interpretive Manual* to obtain the BPN vs. BPI Contrast Scaled Score.)

Clocks (Attention/Executive Domain): Ages 7–16

Scoring: (See pp. 142–144 in this chapter for comprehensive scoring.)

Scores:

Primary Scores:

CL Total Score = The sum of the item scores. (See Table A. 1 in the *Clinical and Interpretive Manual* to obtain the CL Scaled Score.)

> # CAUTION
>
> ## Clocks Scoring Requires Practice
>
> Practice in scoring procedures according to the criteria in Appendix A is essential.

Comprehension of Instructions (Language Domain): Ages 3–16

Scoring:

Items 1–33

1 point for a correct response.

0 for incorrect response or no response.

Scores:

Primary Scores:

CI Total Score = The sum of the item scores.

(See Table A.1 in the *Clinical and Interpretive Manual* to obtain the CI Scaled Score.)

Behavioral Observation:

Total the number of tally marks for *Asks for Repetition* that occurred in the CI subtest.

(See Table D.1 or D.4 in the *Clinical and Interpretive Manual* to obtain the Asks for Repetition Total Cumulative Percentage.)

Design Copying (Visuospatial Domain): Ages 3–16

Scoring: Detailed scoring criteria are discussed on pp. 144–146.
    Design Copying General Scoring:
        1 point if the drawing meets all of the criteria for the item.
        0 points if the drawing does not meet all of the criteria.
    (This is a *quick scoring method* that does not provide the diagnostic information available in the Design Copying Process scoring system following.)
    Design Copying Process Scoring
        Motor:
            Motor A and Motor B
                1 point if the drawing meets all of the criteria for the item.
                0 points if the drawing does not meet all of the criteria.
    Global:
        Global C and Global D
            1 point if the drawing meets all of the criteria for the item.
            0 points if the drawing does not meet all of the criteria.
    Local:
        Local E and Local F
            1 point if the drawing meets all of the criteria for the item.
            0 points if the drawing does not meet all of the criteria.
Scores:
    Primary Scores:
        DCG Total Score = The sum of the Design Copying General item scores.
        (See Table A.1 in the *Clinical and Interpretive Manual* to obtain the DCG Percentile Rank.)
        DCP Total Score = The sum of the points earned for the Motor, Global, and Local criteria on all items administered.
        (See Table A.1 in the *Clinical and Interpretive Manual* to obtain the DCP Scaled Score.)
    Process Scores:
        DCP Motor Score = The sum of the points earned for the Motor A and Motor B criteria on all items administered.

DCP Global Score = The sum of the points earned for the Global C and Global D criteria on all items administered.

DCP Local Score = The sum of the points earned for the Local E and Local F on all items administered.

(See Table A.1 in the *Clinical and Interpretive Manual* to obtain the DCP Motor, DCP Global, and DCP Local Scaled Scores.)

Contrast Scores:

DCP Global vs. DCP Local Contrast Scaled Score compares the child's Global Processing and Local Processing on the Design Copying subtest.

(See Table C.3 in the *Clinical and Interpretive Manual* to obtain the DCP Global vs. DCP Local Scaled Score.)

Design Fluency (Attention/Executive Functioning Domain): Ages 5–12

Scoring:

A design is correct if:

The lines of the design are straight using the 4 mm bar on the Scoring Template included with NEPSY-II.

There are no gaps greater than or equal to 2 mm between a dot and a line drawn for the design.

The design is not a repeat of another design.

(Refer to Appendix B in the *Administration Manual,* Scoring Procedures for the Design Copying subtest, for instructions about measuring line straightness and gaps using the scoring template.)

1 point for each correct design.

0 points for incorrect design.

Scores:

Primary Scores:

DF Total Score = Sum of the correct designs for both the Structured and Random Arrays.

Maximum:

Ages 5–12: 70

(See Table A.1 in the *Clinical and Interpretive Manual* to obtain the DF Scaled Score.)

Process Scores:

DF Structured Array Score = Sum of correct designs on Structured Array.

Maximum:

Ages 5–12: 35

DF Random Array Score = Sum of correct designs on Random Array.

Maximum:

Ages 5–12: 35

(See Table A.2 in the *Clinical and Interpretive Manual* to obtain the DF Structured Array and DF Random Array Cumulative Percentages.)

Fingertip Tapping (Sensorimotor Domain): Ages 5–16

Scoring: For Fingertip Tapping, the completion time for each item is the raw score. Repetition and Sequence errors are not scored, but are reflected in the completion time.

For Items 1–2, if the child is unable to complete 20 repetitions, the completion time for that item is 60 sec.

For Items 3–4, if the child is unable to complete 5 sequences, the completion time for that item is 90 sec.

Scores:

Primary Scores:

FT Dominant Hand (DH) Repetitions Completion Time = Time to complete 20 correct DH repetitions.

FT Nondominant (NDH) Hand Repetitions Completion Time = Time to complete 20 correct NDH repetitions.

FT Dominant Hand Sequences Completion Time = Time to complete 5 correct sequences with the DH.

FT Nondominant Hand Sequences Completion Time = Time to complete 5 correct sequences with the NDH.

(See Table A.1 in the *Clinical and Interpretive Manual* to obtain percentile ranks for aforementioned scores.)

FT Dominant Hand (DH) Combined Scaled Score integrates DH Repetitions Percentile Rank and Dominant Hand Sequences Percentile Rank.

(See Table B.6 in *Clinical and Interpretive Manual* to obtain FT Dominant Hand Combined Scaled Score.)

FT Nondominant Hand (NDH) Combined Scaled Score integrates NDH Repetitions Percentile Rank and Nondominant Hand (NDH) Sequences Percentile Rank.

(See Table B.7 in *Clinical and Interpretive Manual* to obtain FT Nondominant Hand Combined Scaled Score.)

FT Repetitions Combined Scaled Score integrates DH Repetitions Percentile Rank and NDH Repetitions Percentile Rank.

(See Table B.8 in *Clinical and Interpretive Manual* to obtain FT Repetitions Combined Scaled Score.)

FT Sequences Combined Scaled Score integrates DH Sequences Percentile Rank and NDH Sequences Percentile Rank.

(See Table B.9 in *Clinical and Interpretive Manual* to obtain FT Sequences Combined Scaled Score.)

Contrast Scores:

FT Dominant vs. Nondominant Contrast Scaled Scores compares the child's performance on both tasks with the DH to the child's performance on both tasks with the NDH.

(See Table C.4 in the *Clinical and Interpretive Manual* to obtain the FT Dominant vs. Nondominant Contrast Score.)

FT Repetitions vs. Sequential Contrast Scaled Scores contrasts performance with both hands for the Repetitions task with performance with both hands on the Sequences task.

(See Table C.5 in the *Clinical and Interpretive Manual* to obtain the FT Repetitions vs. Sequences Contrast Scaled Score.)

Behavioral Observations:

Rate Change—Total the number of rate changes that occurred during Fingertip Tapping overall.

(See Table D.1 or D.4 in the *Clinical and Interpretive Manual* for Rate Change Cumulative Percentage.)

Visual Guidance, Incorrect Position, Posturing, Mirroring, and Overflow (See Table D.2 or D.5 to obtain the Percent of Standardization Sample that displayed each behavior.)

Geometric Puzzles (Visuospatial Processing): Ages 3–16

Scoring: Correct responses are in color on the Record Form.

Items 1–20:

2 points if two correct responses within the time limit.

1 point if one correct response within the time limit.

0 points if no correct responses within the time limit or no response.

Scores:

Primary Score:

GP Total Score = the sum of the item scores.

Maximum Score:

Ages 3–6: 24

Ages 7–16: 40

(See Table A.1 in the *Clinical and Interpretive Manual* to obtain the GP Percentile Rank [ages 3–6] or the GP Scaled Score [ages 7–16].)

Imitating Hand Positions (Sensorimotor Domain): Ages 3–12

Scoring: A response is considered correct when the imitation is:

Recognizable (miniature illustrations on Record Form)

Involves the correct fingers

Completed within the time limit

All items:

1 point for a correct response.

0 points for an incorrect response or no response.

Scores:

Primary Score:

IH Total Score = Sum of the item scores on Imitating Hand Positions.

Maximum Score:

Ages 3–12: 24

(See Table A.1 in the *Clinical and Interpretive Manual* to obtain the IH Scaled Score.)

Process Scores:

IH Dominant Hand Score = Sum of scores for Items 1–12.

IH Nondominant Hand Score = Sum of scores for Items 13–24.

(See Table A.2 in the *Clinical and Interpretive Manual* to obtain the IH Dominant Hand and the IH Nondominant Hand Cumulative Percentages.)

Behavioral Observations:

For *Mirroring* and *Other Hand Helps*, see Table D.2 or D.5 in the *Clinical and Interpretive Manual* for the Percent of Standardization Sample that displayed the behavior.

Inhibition (Attention and Executive Functioning): Ages 5–16

Scoring: (See pp. 146–149 in this chapter for comprehensive scoring.)
Scores:
Note Abbreviations: INN = Inhibition Naming Trial, INI = Inhibition Inhibition Trial, and INS = Inhibition Switching Trial
Primary Scores:
INN Total Errors = Naming Total Errors for Item 1: Shapes, and for Item 2: Arrows.
INI Total Errors = Inhibition Total Errors for Item 1: Shapes, and for Item 2: Arrows.
INS Total Errors = Switching Total Errors for Item 1: Shapes, and for Item 2: Arrows.
IN Total Errors = INN Total + INI Total + INS Total.
INN Total Completion Time = Sum of INN Completion Time for Item 1: Shapes, and for Item 2: Arrows.
INI Total Completion Time = Sum of INI Completion Time for Item 1: Shapes, and for Item 2: Arrows.
INS Total Completion Time = Sum of INS Completion Time for Item 1: Shapes, and for Item 2: Arrows.
INN Combined Scaled Score integrates the INN Total Errors Percentile Rank and the INN Total.
Completion Time Scaled Score:
INI Combined Scaled Score integrates the INI Total Errors Percentile Rank and the INI Total.
Completion Time Scaled Score:
INS Combined Scaled Score integrates the INS Total Errors Percentile Rank and the INS Total.
Completion Time Scaled Score:
Process Scores:
INN Total Uncorrected Errors = Sum of Inhibition Naming. Total Uncorrected Errors for Item 1: Shapes, and for Item 2: Arrows.
INI Total Uncorrected Errors = Sum of Inhibition Total Uncorrected Errors for Item 1: Shapes, and for Item 2: Arrows.
INS Total Uncorrected Errors = Sum of Inhibition Switching Total Uncorrected Errors for Item 1: Shapes, and for Item 2: Arrows.
INN Total Self-corrected Errors = Sum of Inhibition Naming Total Self-corrected Errors for Item 1: Shapes, and for Item 2: Arrows.

INI Total Self-corrected Errors = Sum of Inhibition Inhibition Total Self-corrected Errors for Item 1: Shapes, and for Item 2: Arrows.

INS Total Self-corrected Errors = Sum of Inhibition Switching Total Self-corrected Errors for Item 1: Shapes, and for Item 2: Arrows.

Contrast Scores:

INN vs. INI Contrast Score compares the child's performance on Naming to the child's performance on Inhibition.

INI vs. INS Contrast Score compares the child's performance on Inhibition to the child's performance on Switching.

Behavioral Observations:

Total the number of Points to Stimuli for each condition (i.e. Naming, Inhibition, and Switching) separately.

List Memory (Memory and Learning Domain): Ages 7–12

Scoring:

1 point for each correct word.

0 points for a repeated word, nonlist word, or a wrong list word. (See the following for operational definitions.)

A *Repetition* has occurred when a word is stated more than once within the same trial (e.g., saying *cat* two times would be one repetition; saying *puppy* three times is two repetitions).

A *Nonlist Word (Novel)* is a word that is not on either the word list or the interference list.

For Trials 1–5, if the child states a word not on the word list, that would be a nonlist word. (In Trials 1–5, if the child states a word that happens to be on the interference list, it would still be considered a nonlist word, because the child has not yet been exposed to the interference list.)

For Trials 6–7, if the child states a word that is not from the word list or the interference list, it is a nonlist word.

A *Wrong-List Word* is a word that is not from the word list that the child is being asked to recall.

For Trial 6 (the Interference Trial), if the child states a word from the word list rather than the interference list, the word is a wrong-list word.

For Trial 7 (Recall after Interference), if a child states a word from the interference list, the word should be considered a wrong list word.

Scores:

Primary Score:

List Memory Total Correct = The sum of words correct for Trials 1–5. This is a raw score used in computing the Learning Effect and LM Interference Cumulative Percentages, as well as LM and LM Delayed Total Correct for the LM Delayed subtest.

Process Scores:

The *LM Repetitions Total* = Sum of repeated words for Trials 1–7. (Do not include repetitions from List Memory Delayed.)

LM Nonlist Words (Novel) Total = Sum of the nonlist words for Trials 1–7. (Do not include nonlist words from List Memory Delayed.)

LM Wrong-List Words (Novel) Total = Sum of the nonlist words for Trials 6–7. (Do not include wrong-list words from List Memory Delayed.)

(See Table A.2 in the *Clinical and Interpretive Manual* to obtain LM Repetitions Total, LM Nonlist Words [Novel] Total, and LM Wrong List Words Total Cumulative Percentages.)

LM Learning Effect = The difference between the total correct words stated during Trial 5 minus the total correct words stated during Trial 1.

LM Interference Effect = The difference between the total correct words stated during Trial 5 minus the total correct words stated during Trial 7.

(See Table D.3 in the *Clinical and Interpretive Manual* to obtain LM Learning Effect and LM Interference Effect Cumulative Percentages.)

List Memory Delayed (Learning and Memory): Ages 7–12

Scoring:

1 point for each correct word.

0 points for a repeated word, nonlist word, or wrong-list word.

(See operational definitions for these errors under List Memory.)

Note: Award 1 point for the word *store,* which is said by the examiner in the administration directions.

Scores:

Primary Scores:

LM and LMD Total Correct = Sum of correct words for Trials 1–5 and the Delayed Recall Trial.

Do not include words from Trial 6 (Interference List) or Trial 7 (Immediate Recall List).

(See Table A.1 in the *Clinical and Interpretive Manual* to obtain the LM and LMD Scaled Score.)

Process Scores:

LM Delay Effect = The difference between the total correct words stated during Trial 5 minus the total correct words stated during the Delayed Recall Trial.

(See Table D.3 in the *Clinical and Interpretive Manual* to obtain the LM Delay Effect Cumulative Percentage.)

Manual Motor Sequences (Sensorimotor Domain): Ages 3–12

Scoring:

Items 1–12:

1 point for each *sequence* correctly completed by the child (maximum of 5 points for each item).

0 points for each sequence not correctly completed by the child or for no response.

Errors include:

An incorrect order of movements.

An interruption longer than the time of one sequence.

Inconsistent pace and slowing of the pace should not be considered errors.

Behavioral Observations:

Tally the number of times that Rate Change occurs during the MM Sequences.

Check presence or absence (Y or N) for the following behaviors:

Overflow: Associated movement of another part of the body (e.g., mouth) in conjunction with the production of movement sequences.

Perseveration: Movements continue for three or more sequences after being told to stop.

Loss of Asymmetrical Movement: Asymmetrical hand positions become identical (for Items 5, 6, 10, 11, and 12 only), or identical hand movements are performed simultaneously when alternation is required.

Body Movement: Extraneous whole-body movements are recruited in conjunction with the production of movement sequences (e.g., rhythmic rocking, rising slowly from seat as hand movements are executed).

Forceful Tapping: The tapping becomes louder during the production of the movement sequences, as the body is recruited into the task.

Scores:

Primary Score:

MM Total Score = Sum of the total correct sequences for all items.

Maximum Score:

Ages 3–12: 60

(See Table A.1 in the *Clinical and Interpretive Manual* to obtain the MM Total Score Percentile Rank.)

Behavioral Observations:

Rate Change: Number of times the Rate Changes during performance of movement sequences.

(See Table D.1 or D.4 in the *Clinical and Interpretive Manual* to obtain the Rate Change Cumulative Percentage.)

(For *Overflow, Perseveration, Loss of Asymmetrical Movements, Body Movement,* and *Forceful Tapping,* see Table D.2 or D.5 in the *Clinical and Interpretive Manual* to obtain the Percent of Standardization Sample that displayed that behavior.)

Memory for Designs (Memory and Learning): Ages 3–16

Scoring: (See pp. 149–152 in this chapter for comprehensive scoring.)

Scores:

Primary Score:

MD Total Score = sum of the total corrects for each trial.

(See Table A.1 in the *Clinical and Interpretive Manual* to obtain the MD Scaled Score.)

Process Scores:

MD Content Score = sum of the content scores for each trials.

MD Spatial Score = sum of the spatial scores for each trial.

(See Table A.1 in the *Clinical and Interpretive Manual* to obtain the MD Content Scaled Score and the MD Spatial Scaled Score.)

Contrast Scores:

MD Content vs. Spatial Contrast Scaled Score compares the child's Content and Spatial Scores on Memory for Designs.

(See Table C.8 in the *Clinical and Interpretive Manual* to obtain the MD Content vs. Spatial Contrast Scaled Score.)

Behavioral Observations:

For ages 3–4, total the number of times that *yes* (Y) has been checked for *Rule Violation*.

(For ages 3–4, see Table D.1 or D.4 in the *Clinical and Interpretive Manual* to obtain the Rule Violation Total Cumulative Percentage.)

Memory for Designs Delayed (Memory and Learning): Ages 3–16

Scoring: (See pp. 151–152 in this chapter for comprehensive scoring of MD and MDD subtests.)

Scores:

Primary Score:

MDD Total Score = sum of the Content, Spatial, and Bonus Scores for the Delayed Recall Trial.

(See Table A.1 in the *Clinical and Interpretive Manual* to obtain the MDD Scaled Score.)

Process Scores:

MDD Content Score = the Content score for the Delayed Recall Trials.

MDD Spatial Score = the Spatial score for the Delayed Recall Trials.

(See Table A.1 in the *Clinical and Interpretive Manual* to obtain the MDD Content Scaled Score and the MDD Spatial Scaled Score.)

Contrast Scores:

MDD Content vs. Spatial Contrast Scaled Score compares the child's Content and Spatial Scores on Memory for Designs Delayed.

(See Table C.9 in the *Clinical and Interpretive Manual* to obtain the MD vs. MDD Contrast Scaled Score.)

MD vs. MDD Contrast Scaled Score compares the child's performance during Memory for Designs with his or her performance on Memory for Designs Delayed.

(See Table C.10 in the *Clinical and Interpretive Manual* to obtain the MD vs. MDD Contrast Scaled Score.)

Behavioral Observations:

Rule Violation (more than designated number of cards placed in grid): Total the number of times that the *Y* has been checked on Memory for Designs and on Memory for Designs Delayed.

Memory for Faces (Memory and Learning Domain): Ages 5–16

Scoring: The correct response for each item is in color on the Record Form.
Items 1–16:
  1 point for a correct response.
  0 points for an incorrect response or no response.

Scores:
Primary Scores:
  MF Total Score = Sum of the item scores for Memory for Faces.
  (See Table A.1 in the *Clinical and Interpretive Manual* to obtain the
  MF Scaled Score.)

Memory for Faces Delayed (Memory and Learning Domain): Ages 5–16

Scores:
Primary Score:
  MFD Total Score = Sum of the item scores for Memory for
  Faces Delayed.
  (See Table A.1 in the *Clinical and Interpretive Manual* to obtain the
  MFD Scaled Score.)
Contrast Score:
  The MF vs. MFD Contrast Scaled Score compares the child's perfor-
  mance during Memory for Faces to his or her performance during
  MF Delayed.
  (See Table C.11 in the *Clinical and Interpretive Manual* to obtain the
  MF vs. MFD Contrast Scaled Score.)

Behavioral Observations: Tally the marks for Spontaneous Comments.

Memory for Names (Memory and Learning Domain): Ages 5–16

Scoring: A correct response:
  The child says the name in the exact form it was presented.
  A diminutive form of a name (e.g., *Sammy* for *Sam*) is used.
  Stable misarticulations (e.g., *Tham* for *Sam*)
  1 point for a correct response.
  0 points for an incorrect response or no response.
  For each trial, sum the scores to obtain the trial total.

Scores:

Primary Score:

MN Total Score = sum of the trial totals for Memory for Names.
(See Table A.1 in the *Clinical and Interpretive Manual* to obtain the MN Scaled Score.)

Memory for Names Delayed (Memory and Learning Domain): Ages 5–16

Scoring:

1 point for a correct response.

0 points for an incorrect response or no response.

Sum the scores to obtain the trial total.

Scores:

Primary Score:

MND Total Score = Sum of the trial totals for the Delayed Recall Trial.
(See Table A.1 in the *Clinical and Interpretive Manual* to obtain the MND Scaled Score.)
MN and MND Total Score = Sum of the MN Total Score and the MND Total Score.
(See Table A.1 in the *Clinical and Interpretive Manual* to obtain the MN and MND Scaled Score.)

Memory for Names Delayed (Memory and Learning Domain): Ages 5–16

Scoring:

1 point for a correct response.

0 points for an incorrect response or no response.

Sum the scores to obtain the trial total.

Scores:

Primary Score:

MND Total Score = Sum of the trial totals for the Delayed Recall Trial.
(See Table A.1 in the *Clinical and Interpretive Manual* to obtain the MND Scaled Score.)

MN and MND Total Score = Sum of the MN Total Score and the MND Total Score.

(See Table A.1 in the *Clinical and Interpretive Manual* to obtain the MN and MND Scaled Score.)

Narrative Memory (Memory Domain): Ages 3–16

Scoring
Free and Cued Recall

2 points if the detail is recalled during Free Recall.

1 point if the detail is recalled during Cued Recall.

0 points if the detail is recalled during Free Recall and Cued Recall.

Do not award 2 points for Free Recall and then another 1 point for Cued Recall. The maximum score for a detail is 2 points.

Free Recall

1 point for each detail recalled during Free Recall.

0 points for each detail not recalled during Free Recall.

Recognition

The correct response for each item is in color on the Record Form.

1 point for a correct response.

0 points for an incorrect response or no response.

Scores:
Primary Scores

NM Free and Cued Recall Total Score is the sum of the points earned on Free and Cued Recall for the story administered.

(See Table A.1 in the *Clinical and Interpretive Manual* to obtain the NM Free Cued Recall Scaled Score.)

Process Scores

NM Free Recall Total Score is the number of details recalled during Free Recall.

(See Table A.1 in the *Clinical and Interpretive Manual* to obtain the NM Free Recall Total Score.)

NM Recognition Total Score is the sum of the Recognition item scores for the story administered.

(See Table A.1 in the *Clinical and Interpretive Manual* to obtain the NM Recognition Percentile Rank.)

Contrast Score

NM Free and Cued Recall vs. Recognition Scaled Score compares the child's performance on the Free and Cued Recall to the child's performance on Recognition.

(See Table C.12 in the *Clinical and Interpretive Manual* to obtain the NM Free and Cued Recall vs. Recognition Scaled Score.)

Oromotor Sequences (Language Domain): Ages 3–12

Scoring:
Items 1–14:

1 point for each sequence correctly completed by the child (maximum of 5 points for each item).

0 points for each sequence not correctly completed by the child or for no response.

Behavioral Observations:
Tally the marks for Rate Change. Note also the general pace and rhythm of the child's production.

Total the checkmarks for Oromotor Hypotonia.

Total the checkmarks for Stable Misarticulations.

Scores:
Primary Score:

OS Total Score = Sum of the total correct sequences for all items.

(See Table A.1 in the *Clinical and Interpretive Manual* to obtain the OS Percentile Rank.)

Behavioral Observations:
Rate Change = Total Rate Changes that occurred during OS.

(See Table D.1 or D.4 in the *Clinical and Interpretive Manual* to obtain the Rate Change Cumulative Percentage.)

(For Oromotor Hypotonia and Stable Misarticulations, see Table D.2 or D.5 in the *Clinical and Interpretive Manual* to obtain the Percent of the Standardization Sample that displayed that behavior.)

Phonological Processing (Language Domain): Ages 3–16

Scoring:
Items 1–45

1 point for a correct response.

0 points for an incorrect response.

Scores:

Primary Score:

The *PH Total Score* is the sum of the item scores.

(See Table A.1 in the *Clinical and Interpretive Manual* to obtain the PH Scaled Score.)

Behavioral Observations: Total the tally marks in the Asks for Repetition box.

(See Table D.1 or D.4 in the *Clinical and Interpretive Manual* to obtain the Asks for Repetition Total Cumulative Percentage.)

Picture Puzzles (Visuospatial Processing): Ages 7–16

Scoring: An item is correct if the child provides four correct responses within the time limit.

Items 1–20:

1 point if four correct responses are given within time limit.

0 points if four correct responses are not given within the time limit or for no response.

Scores:

Primary Score:

The *PP Total Score* is the sum of the item scores.

(See Table A.1 in the *Clinical and Interpretive Manual* to obtain the PP Scaled Score.)

Repetition of Nonsense Words (Language Domain): Ages 5–12

Scoring: The number of syllables for each item is provided on the Record Form. Each syllable is scored independently.

A response is considered correct:

If the syllable is pronounced correctly—even if the wrong syllable is stressed in repeating the nonsense word or if a stable misarticulation is present.

A response is incorrect:

If distortions (other than a stable misarticulation) and omissions of syllables are present.

Items 1–13:

1 point for each correct syllable.

0 points for an incorrect syllable or for no response.

The item score is the sum of correct syllables for the item.

Score:

Primary Score:

RN Total Score = The sum of the item scores.

(See Table A.1 in the *Clinical and Interpretive Manual* to obtain the RN Scaled Score.)

Behavioral Observation:

Stable Misarticulations Total—total the tally marks in the Stable Misarticulation Box.

(See Table D.2 or D.5 in the *Clinical and Interpretive Manual* to obtain the Percent of the Standardization Sample.)

Route Finding (Visuospatial Processing Domain): Ages 5–12

Scoring: The correct responses are in color on the Record Form.

Items 1–10:

1 point for a correct response.

0 points for an incorrect response or for no response.

Score:

Primary Score:

The *RF Total Score* is the sum of the item scores.

(See Table A.1 in the *Clinical and Interpretive Manual* to obtain the RF Percentile Score.)

Sentence Repetition (Memory and Learning Domain): Ages 3–6

Scoring: The correct responses are in color on the Record Form.

Items 1–10:

1 point for a correct response.

0 points for an incorrect response or for no response.

Score:

Primary Score:

The *RF Total Score* is the sum of the item scores.

(See Table A.1 in the *Clinical and Interpretive Manual* to obtain the RF Percentile Score.)

Speeded Naming (Language Domain): Ages 5–16

Scoring:

1 point for a correct response or a self-corrected response.

0 points for an incorrect response or a response that has not been attempted.

Correct responses:

The correct name for a shape, color, size, letter, or number.

Although responses for Items 3 and 4 are listed in the Record Form in a specific order (e.g., *Big Red Square),* naming in a different or reversed order should not be considered an error (e.g., *Red Big Square),* because the name is correct.

Encourage the use of *big* and *little,* not *large* and *small,* though the latter two are not errors if they occur on the test.

A *self-corrected error* has occurred when the child provides an incorrect response or skips a shape, color, size, letter, or number but then corrects the incorrect or skipped response.

Errors:

Saying an incorrect name for any shape, color, size, letter, or number.

Skipping a shape, color, size, letter, or number and not self-correcting.

Any shape, color, size, letter, or number not attempted by the child due to the time limit should be considered an incorrect response.

Score:

Primary Scores:

SN Total Completion Time = the sum of completion times for all items administered.

(See Table A.1 in the *Clinical and Interpretive Manual* to obtain the SN Total Completion Time.)

SN Total Correct = the sum of all correct responses and all self-corrected responses for all items administered.

(See Table A.1 in the *Clinical and Interpretive Manual* to obtain the SN Total Completion Time.)

SN Combined Scaled Score integrates the SN Total Completion Time Scaled Score and the SN Total Correct Percentile Rank.

(See Table B.13 in the *Clinical and Interpretive Manual* to obtain the SN Combined Scaled Score.)

Process Score:

SN Total Self-corrected Errors = The sum of the self-corrected errors for all items administered.

(See Table A.1 in the *Clinical and Interpretive Manual* to obtain the SN Total Self-corrected Errors Percentile Rank.)

Statue (Attention/Executive Functions Domain): Ages 3–6

Scoring:

Errors: Body movements, eye-openings, and vocalizations. Only one error of each type can be counted within one 5-sec. interval. (e.g., Moving the body twice in one 5-sec. interval would be one Body Movement Error; opening eyes three times in a 5-sec. interval would be one Eye-Opening Error.)

2 points for no errors during a 5-sec. interval.

1 point for one error during a 5-sec. interval.

0 points for two or more errors during a 5-sec. interval.

Scores:

Primary Scores:

Statue Total Score = Sum of the scores for each 5-sec. interval.

(See Table A.1 in the *Clinical and Interpretive Manual* to obtain the Statue Scaled Score.)

Process Scores:

ST Body Movement Total = Sum of body movements errors during Statue.

ST Eye-Opening Total = Sum of eye-opening errors during Statue.

ST Vocalizations Total = Sum of vocalization errors during Statue.

(See Table A.1 in the *Clinical and Interpretive Manual* to obtain the ST Body Movement Total, ST Eye-Opening Total, and ST Vocalization Total Percentile Ranks.)

Theory of Mind: Ages 3–16

Scoring: For Items 1–15, use the criteria included with each item in the Stimulus Book to score the item. *Note:* For Items 1–5, use the criteria included with each item in the Stimulus Book to obtain the item score. For Items 16–21, the correct response for each item is in color on the Record Form.

1 point for a correct response.

0 points for incorrect or no response.

Scores:

Primary Scores:

TM Total Score = Sum of the item scores.

(See Table A.1 in the *Clinical and Interpretive Manual* to obtain the TM Scaled Score [ages 3–6] or TM Percentile Rank [ages 7–16].)

Process Scores:

TM Verbal Score = Sum of the scores for Items 1–15.

(See Table A.1 in the *Clinical and Interpretive Manual* to obtain the TM Verbal Percentile Rank.)

Visuomotor Precision (Sensorimotor Domain): Ages 3–12

Scoring: (See pp. 152–154 in this chapter for comprehensive scoring.)

Scores:

Primary Scores:

VP Total Completion Time = Sum of completion times for all items administered.

(See Table A.1 in the *Clinical and Interpretive Manual* to obtain the VP Total Completion Time Scaled core.)

VP Total Errors = Sum of all errors for all items administered.

(See Table A.1 in the *Clinical and Interpretive Manual* to obtain the VP Total Errors Percentile Rank.)

The *VP Combined Scaled Score* integrates the VP Total Completion Time Scaled Score and the VP Total Errors Percentile Rank.

(See Table B.14 in the *Clinical and Interpretive Manual* to obtain the VP Combined Scaled Score.)

Process Scores:

The *VP Pencil Lift Total* is the sum of pencil lifts for all items administered.

(See Table A.1 in the *Clinical and Interpretive Manual* to obtain the VP Pencil Lift Total Percentile Rank.)

Behavioral Observation:

(For *VP Pencil Grip*, see Table D.2 or D.5 in the *Clinical and Interpretive Manual* to obtain the Percent of the Standardization Sample that displayed that grip.)

Word Generation (Language Domain): Ages 3–16

Scoring:

Repetitions:

Repetitions of the Teaching Example words for each item should not be considered correct responses. (See list on p. 122 of the *Administration Manual* and further correct Scoring and Response examples on p. 123.)

The repetition of the same word in a category should not be considered a correct response (e.g., if *bird* is said twice in Item 1, only 1 point is awarded).

If the child states the same word in two different categories, and it belongs in that category, it is correct in both cases (e.g., *snake* is a correct answer for both Item 1 and Item 3).

The repetition of a word in the plural form or a different tense should not be considered a correct response for that item (e.g., credit only 1 point for *pie* and *pies* or for *start and started*).

The repetition of a diminutive form of a word already used should not be considered a correct response (e.g., *pig* and *piggy, dog* and *puppy*). On the other hand, a diminutive form on its own is considered correct (e.g., *piggy* given as a single response is correct).

The repetition of a word using an adjective that does not distinguish it as a different member of the category should not be considered as correct for that item (e.g., credit only 1 point for *bear, furry bear, big bear*). On the other hand, if the adjective is considered as a part of the accepted label for a different member of the category, it should be counted as correct (*Brown Bear, Black Bear, Grizzly Bear* would be three correct labels for animals, receiving 3 points total). A further example: *Brown Bear, furry bear, Grizzly Bear* would receive 2 points total, as *furry bear* is not an accepted label for a different member of the category.

Nonsense Words: A nonsense word should not be considered correct, but verify with a dictionary.

Noncategory Words: Words generated by the child that are not members of the category are not correct responses.

Proper Nouns: People's names, names of places, and other specific proper names of things should not be considered correct responses for Items 3 and 4. Conversely, if a word has another meaning (e.g., *snickers*) that is not the proper name of a person, place, or thing, the response is correct.

Scores:

Primary Scores:

WG Semantic Total Score = The sum of the correct responses for Items 1 and 2.

WG Initial Letter Total Score = The sum of the correct responses for Items 3 and 4.

(See Table A.1 in the *Clinical and Interpretive Manual* to obtain the WG Semantic and WG Initial Letter Scaled Scores.)

Contrast Scores:

WG Semantic vs. Initial Letter Contrast Scaled Score compares the child's performance on Semantic items to the child's performance on Initial Letter Items.

(See Table C.13 in the Clinical and Interpretive Manual to obtain the WG Semantic vs. Initial Letter Contrast Score.)

Word List Interference (Memory and Learning): Ages 7–16

Scoring:

Repetition Items:

2 points if the child repeats all words for both Repetition Trials in the correct order.

1 point if the child repeats all words for one Repetition Trial in the correct order.

0 points if the child does not repeat all words for both Repetition Trials in the correct order or for no response.

Recall Trials:

2 points if the child recalls all words for both Recall Trials in the correct order.

1 point if the child recalls all words for one Recall Trial but not in the correct order.

0 points if the child does not repeat all words for the Recall Trial or for no response.

Scores:

Primary Scores:

WI Repetition Total Score = The sum of the Repetition Item scores.

WI Recall Total Score = The sum of the Recall Trial scores.

(See Table A.1 in the *Clinical and Interpretive Manual* to obtain the WI
Repetition and the WI Recall Scaled Scores.)

Contrast Scores:

The *WI Repetition vs. Recall Contrast Scaled Score* compares the
child's performance on Repetition to the child's performance on
Recall.

(See Table C.14 in the *Clinical and Interpretive Manual* to obtain the
WI Repetition vs. Recall Contrast Scaled Score.)

Behavioral Observation:

Total the number of *Asks for Repetition(s)* that occurred during the
Word List Interference subtest.

(See Table D.1 or D.4 in the *Clinical and Interpretive Manual* to obtain the Asks for Repetition Total Cumulative Percentage.)

SUMMARIZING NEPSY-II SCORES

The NEPSY-II Score Summary by Domain is found on the front page of the Record
Form. Not all of the scores from each test are summarized here, but the Primary
Scaled Scores, including some Combined Scores, are graphed and also some Process Scores. Simply transfer the designated scores from the appropriate scoring
box to the summary sheet. This will allow you to compare key results with and
across domains.

The NEPSY-II Behavioral Observations Summary is found on the inside front page
of the Record Form. Simply transfer the Behavioral Observation raw score to
the bubble beside the appropriate subtest area under the correct domain. Then
transfer the Cumulative Percentage or the Percent of Standardization Sample as
they appeared when you scored the Record Form to the scoring box beside the
bubble. In some cases, you enter *Y* or *N* for presence or absence of a Behavioral
Observation.

These summaries provide a way to "eyeball" the data and for parents to see
how a child performs compared to the typical child of his or her age. They can be
a very helpful adjunct to the clinician's report.

Finally, it is important to remember that it is not necessary to calculate and
consider all process, combined and contrast scores for the subtests that have
been administered. These may be regarded as optional, supplemental scores.
However, they provide qualitative data that make the picture of the child's abilities and stumbling points much richer and may provide a fuller understanding of
the child's situation.

CONCLUDING REMARKS

Scoring is somewhat of a mechanical process, but it is essential to the validity of the clinician's interpretation of the child's performance that it be handled professionally and with precision. The process of interpretation begins, of course, with administration, as one observes the child's performance and begins to form hypotheses concerning the presenting problem(s). Interpretation continues as the clinician scores and formulates further hypotheses and/or verifies previous hypotheses or rejects them. The scores come alive through this process. In the next chapter, interpretation of a child's scores will be presented, along with how one identifies diagnostic clusters and verifies results. These are crucial steps in any assessment process and can have an enormous impact on the ultimate outcome for the child being assessed.

🖎 TEST YOURSELF 🖎

1. **The subtests that are more difficult to score than most are (check all that apply):**
   (a) _____ Memory for Names.
   (b) _____ Inhibition
   (c) _____ Phonological Processing.
   (d) _____ Design Copying.
   (e) _____ Auditory Attention and Response Set (AARS).
   (f) _____ Arrows.
   (g) _____ Speeded Naming.
   (h) _____ Clocks

FILL IN THE BLANKS AND TRUE/FALSE

2. **A Commission Error on AARS can also be an inhibitory error**
   (a) true_____   (b) false_____

3. **The Design Copy Process Scoring Total Score comprises three scores: DCP Motor Score that reflects fine motor control in copying designs; DCP Score that reflects_____; and the DCP Score that reflects_____ .**

4. **A pencil mark went outside the track in VMP and came back into the track in the next segment. It would count as _____ errors.**

5. The _____ confidence interval is recommended when one is computing statistical differences.

6. A performance >75% of the standardization sample would be described as being _____ according to the **NEPSY-II Manual.**

7. A cumulative percentage of 10 would be interpreted as "the child's score is better than 10% of his or her age group."

    (a) true _____   (b) false_____.

MATCHING

8.	_____ **A scaled score of 4**	a.	most important age-corrected scaled scores for each subtest
9.	_____ **A base rate of 4**	b.	Above Expected Level
10.	_____ **A scaled score of 14**	c.	express different aspects of performance
11.	_____ **Primary score**	d.	Below Expected Level
12.	_____ **Type I error**	e.	more than the designated number of cards placed in the grid
13.	_____ **MD Rule violation**	f.	At Expected Level
14.	_____ **Process scores**	g.	avoid by validating scores with evidence from child's daily life
15.	_____ **26–75%**	h.	"4% of the same-age children obtained the same score or lower."

Answers:

1. b, d, e, g, h; 2. true; 3. (*Answers can be in any order*) Global—reflects accuracy in reproducing configuration of design; Local—reflects accuracy in reproducing the design details; 4. 2; 5. .95; 6. above expected level; 7. False. This would be the interpretation of a score at the 10th percentile rank; 8. d; 9. h; 10. b; 11. a; 12. g; 13. e; 14. c; 15. f

Four

HOW TO INTERPRET THE NEPSY-II

This chapter presents a systematic method of interpreting NEPSY-II. After the discussion of some background concepts, the three goals of interpretation and their implementation will be discussed in depth. Interdomain and Intradomain differences at the subtest level, as well as the meaning of such differences, will be discussed, and interpreting various scores and quantifying Behavioral Observations as a means of teasing apart a problem will be presented. Finally, the chapter will discuss the integration of results and patterns of findings that Bernstein and Waber (1990) have termed "diagnostic behavioral clusters."

GOALS OF INTERPRETATION AND IMPLEMENTATION OF GOALS

The First Goal: Consider and Describe Strengths and Weaknesses

The first straightforward goal of NEPSY-II interpretation is to consider the child's neurocognitive development comprehensively. Implementing this goal involves not only looking at the child's performances in terms of psychometric test scores, but interpreting the data in terms of the child's strengths and weaknesses as well as needs.

Interpretation at this level accomplishes the first goal of considering the child's neurocognitive development comprehensively. The clinician develops a comprehensive overview of the child's neurocognitive development through the NEPSY-II test profile and assesses the child's strengths and weaknesses. This level of interpretation may be an end in itself or the first step in the next level of interpretation. A psychologist without special training in neuropsychology may feel comfortable in drawing these kinds of conclusions. The purpose of any evaluation in the final analysis is to provide a basis for rehabilitation and/or intervention plans. The results at this level of interpretation are interpreted for "behavior-behavior relationships" (Taylor & Fletcher, 1990). For example, the clinician might discuss a child's reading disability in terms of his poor performance on the Phonological Processing subtest in comparison to other children his age. Interpretation at this level is carried out in three steps: (1) describing the child's performance in comparison to the normally developing child of his or her age, (2) looking at the child's performance in terms of his or her own functioning, and (3) relating these results to observed areas of difficulty in learning or in everyday life. This last part of the interpretation is the ultimate goal of all neuropsychological assessments.

How the Child Functions in Comparison to the Typical Child of His or Her Age in the NEPSY-II Standardization Population

First, examine psychometrically the profile of primary, process, and contrast scores, percentile ranks, and cumulative percentages derived from the assessment, comparing the child's performance to the NEPSY-II subtest mean of 10 ± 3. The subtest mean on NEPSY-II reflects the performance of the typical child on any of the NEPSY-II subtests. Comparison is also made to the descriptive classification levels for scaled scores and percentile ranks. (See Rapid Reference 4.1 for descriptive classification of scores.)

≡ Rapid Reference 4.1

Qualtitative Descriptions of Scaled Scores and Percentile Ranks

Scaled Score	Percentile Rank	Classification
13–19	>75	Above Expected Level
8–12	26–75	At Expected Level
6–7	11–25	Borderline
4–5	3–10	Below Expected Level
1–3	≤2	Well Below Expected Level

Some qualitative Behavioral Observations are quantified on NEPSY-II so that the percentage of children in the standardization sample who displayed this behavior can be used as a reference point for interpreting a child's performance. Cumulative percentages (base rates for age) and the percent of the Standardization Sample Displaying a Specific Behavior may also be used. These are found in Appendix D of the *Clinical and Interpretive Manual of NEPSY-II*. (See Rapid Reference 4.2.)

≡ Rapid Reference 4.2

Appendix D

Behavioral Observations Are Quantified on NEPSY-II

- Cumulative percentages (base rates for age) or the percent of the Standardization Sample displaying a specific behavior are found in Appendix D of the *Clinical and Interpretive Manual.*
- These may be used as a reference point for interpreting a child's performance.

How the Child Performs in Terms of His or Her Own Functioning on NEPSY-II

The second step is to describe the child's relative strengths and weaknesses in terms of his or her own functioning on NEPSY-II. The clinician will focus on how the child's performance on a particular task was deviant from the child's performance on other subtests within and across domains. The clinician describes the strongest subtest results, the weakest, and those that fell in between. As there are many possible scores, there is a need to be critical in order to avoid Type 1 errors, which is to see weaknesses when there actually are none. Psychological assessments are influenced by many situational factors—for example, the child may lose interest or be momentarily thinking of something external to the task. The likelihood of some sporadic poor test findings is greater the more subtest scores we end up with. Therefore, when describing the test profile, strengths or weaknesses that appear in a consistent fashion over several scores or observations are the ones of interest, not single findings that appear to be isolated or sporadic.

CAUTION

A weakness in a single score that is not validated by other findings may be a sporadic finding or an artifact of testing.

Relate the Child's Performance to Observed Areas of Difficulty in School and in Everyday Life

Finally, the third step in interpretation at the descriptive level is to relate the child's performance not only to that of age peers, and to his or her own pattern of strengths and weaknesses, but also to observed areas of difficulty in school and in everyday life. An example of behavior-to-behavior relationships (Taylor & Fletcher, 1990) in interpretation is seen here:

EXAMPLE (*One segment of a full report, not meant to imply conclusions were based on one subtest*): Ricky, age 7, displayed a significantly poor performance (PP scaled score 5) on the Phonological Processing subtest in relation to the NEPSY-II subtest mean (10 ± 3) for a child of 7 years. This result suggested a deficit in the phonological awareness that has been shown in numerous studies across the years to underlie efficient reading decoding and spelling (Betourne & Friel-Patti, 2003; Bishop & Snowling, 2004; Bradley, 1989; Fraser & Conti-Ramsden, 2008. Ricky also displayed a relative weakness in phonological awareness in terms of his own average performance on NEPSY-II subtests overall (Personal mean = 11 ± 3), suggesting that this is an area that is apt to cause him significant difficulty in school and everyday life in relation to his other abilities. These results relate to background history collected from Ricky's teachers and family. His parents have noted, and Ricky's teachers have reported, marked struggles in reading decoding and spelling since reading instruction began last year. In particular, he has struggled with phonics. Family history revealed that a paternal uncle was diagnosed as dyslexic in childhood, although he had overcome his reading problems by middle school. This background information lent support to the finding of a deficit in phonological awareness, one of the core symptoms in dyslexia. (Rapid Reference 4.3 provides guidelines for describing strengths and weaknesses.)

⟰ Rapid Reference 4.3

Interpreting by Describing Strengths and Weaknesses

1. Describe child's strengths and weaknesses compared to development of typical child of his or her age in standardization population (scaled score mean = 10 ± 3).
   - Remember strengths are as important as weaknesses.
2. Describe child's relative strengths and weaknesses compared to his or her own functioning (personal subtest mean across/within domains).
   - Remember the diagnostic essence of NEPSY-II is at the subtest level.
3. Relate child's NEPSY-II results to behavioral observations and to developmental, medical, family, educational, and emotional history.
   - Use behavior-to-behavior relationships (e.g., relate child's poor Phonological Processing results to his or her weak reading decoding skills).

The Second Goal: Specify and Analyze the Child's Impairments

The second goal of interpretation is to identify impairments, and wherever possible, to analyze the child's impairments (Korkman, Kirk, & Kemp, 2007). The first step at this level aims to discover *what* function is specifically impaired, while the second step addresses the question of *why* a particular activity is so difficult for the child (Korkman, 1999). A third step in the clinical interpretation may answer the question, *which* disorder might be present, based on a recognition of diagnostic behavioral cluster composed of the observed primary and secondary impairments. A diagnostic behavioral cluster is not always present, however. The clinician should then analyze the specific impairments instead. The clinical level of the interpretation process involves three separate steps, described as follows:

Identify Specific Impairments

To do so, the clinician must delineate some aspect of performance derived at the descriptive level on which the child tends to exhibit specific problems in a fairly consistent fashion. Such impairments need to meet certain criteria, that is, they are demonstrated:

(a) When specific subtests in one domain are impaired both in relation to the age norm and in relation to the child's results in other domains.

EXAMPLE: Specific impairments of this type are language impairments, attention problems, social perceptual differences, sensorimotor problems, or visuospatial impairments. These disorders, which may affect subtests in one domain differentially, will often show effects on the subtests of other domains (e.g., a language impairment affecting verbal memory performance).

(b) When two or more subtest scaled scores, percentile ranks, or Behavioral Observations within a domain or across domains indicate that a certain aspect of performance is impaired either in relation to the age norm or in relation to the child's own mean.

EXAMPLE: An example of consistent findings across domains is when a child has weak scores on the Inhibition subtest and on the Response Set task of the AARS subtest in the Attention/Executive Function domain, and also performs poorly on the List Learning subtest in the Memory and Learning Domain due to a flat learning curve. Together, these findings suggest executive dysfunction related to planning, programming, and monitoring performance.

Another example might be dysnomic or semantic problems evident on the Speeded Naming and Comprehension of Instructions subtests in the Language Domain, but also the Memory for Names and Narrative Memory subtests in the Memory and Learning domain, all of which suggests a language problem with associated verbal memory deficits and deficits of name learning or retrieval.

Finally, a third example would be motor coordination problems that may affect not only sensorimotor tasks, such as Fingertip Tapping and Visuomotor Precision, but also the Design Copying subtest in the Visuospatial domain, despite good visuospatial skills on Geometric Puzzles, which has no motor component.

This step in interpretation differs from the more straightforward behavioral interpretation of findings at the descriptive level. Interpretation at this level is richer if the clinician has current knowledge of patterns to look for based on familiarity with the pediatric neuropsychological research. Identifying specific impairments is not exactly the same thing as defining strengths and weaknesses behaviorally. The problem may be more subtle or complex than describing a behavior in relation to the norm. It often takes place through error analysis. The more neuropsychological training and expertise a clinician has, the more skillful he or she is in inferring the role of deficits. (See Rapid Reference 4.4.)

≡ Rapid Reference 4.4

Interpretation at the Clinical Level

The three steps of the interpretation process at this level are:

1. To identify specific impairments.
2. To analyze specific impairments.
   - Analyze separately, as far as possible, the subcomponents known to be a part of that function.
   - Specify and discuss what part of the process is deficient.
   - Specify and discuss primary and secondary deficits.
3. Identify diagnostic behavioral clusters that characterize particular diagnostic groups.
   - Look for a diagnostic behavioral cluster to describe a disorder.
   - Just because a cluster of symptoms is present does not necessarily mean a disorder is present.
   - Interpret by anatomic axes only with neuropsychological training.
   - Do not propose focal brain lesions or dysfunction and assume such only if there are clear neuroimaging data to suggest this.

Analyze Impairments by Specifying Primary and Secondary Deficits, Whenever Possible

The impairments the clinician identifies should be further analyzed to determine why the function was impaired.

(a) *Analyze separately, as far as is possible, all subcomponents that are known to be a part of the function in question.* In the Lurian tradition, specific NEPSY-II subtests represent subcomponents of complex processes. For instance, the NEPSY-II subtests Phonological Processing and Comprehension of Instructions address receptive language deficits. Studies have shown that receptive language deficits include errors when discriminating among phonemes, morphemes, and other speech sounds, particularly when a task is complex or involves high memory load (Bishop & McArthur, 2005; Burlingame, Sussman, Gillam, & Hay, 2005; Coady, Kluender, & Evans, 2005). Expressive language deficits are apparent, for example, as restricted expressions in narration and impaired word finding (American Psychiatric Association, 2000; Klee, Stokes, Wong, Fletcher, & Gavin, 2004). The NEPSY-II subtests that address such problems include holding a verbal sequence in memory long enough to process its content (Sentence Repetition subtest); attaching verbal labels to things and concepts, and retrieving them smoothly (Speeded Naming, Inhibition Naming, Memory for Names); as well as organizing articulatory sequences (Oromotor Sequences) and the details of a narration (Narrative Memory) (American Psychiatric Association, 2000). In a similar way, the clinician can analyze subcomponents used in the organization of other complex tasks: visuomotor performance, reading, solving arithmetical problems, and so forth (Korkman, Kirk, & Kemp, 1998, 2007).

(b) *Specify what particular part of the process is deficient and whether the deficit contributing to the dysfunction is primary or is secondary to another deficit.* The Lurian view, upon which NEPSY was originally based, and upon which, along with other theoretical substrates, NEPSY-II rests as well, suggests that cognitive capacities are functional systems composed of basic and complex interactive subcomponents (Christensen, 1984; Luria, 1973, 1980). Therefore, a primary deficit in one functional system could affect performance in other functional systems, causing secondary deficits. For example, on the NEPSY-II List Learning subtest, the child may be unable to learn a long list of isolated words, due not to a language disorder, but to executive dysfunction. The child cannot organize and monitor the mental list as he or she hears the words repeated. On the other hand, verbal working memory deficits (phonological and functional working memory) may be a clinical marker for language disorders and may be related to morphological and lexical language deficits (Montgomery, 2003). On the NEPSY-II Narrative Memory subtest, for example, children with language difficulties may have problems telling a story after hearing it, not because of a memory problem *per se,* but because of a language disorder. In this case, the verbal memory problem is secondary to the child's language disorder. Each subcomponent performs its role in the chain of subprocesses. When one of them is deficient, the whole functional system may be disturbed. On the other hand, a disorder such as dyslexia may have more than one underlying deficit.

Kaplan's (1988) view, that a process approach to assessment can provide information about a child's problem that cannot be obtained from an analysis of primary scores alone, also underlies NEPSY-II. Therefore, where Primary Total Scores are provided, NEPSY-II often provides Process Scores, as well, so that different aspects of a global score can be considered separately (e.g., speed and accuracy) in order to facilitate identifying and interpreting primary and secondary deficits. For instance, the clinician can break down the Speeded Naming Combined Scaled Score that integrates time to completion on the test overall with overall accuracy by inspecting the Total Completion Time and the Total Correct. In this way, the clinician can consider whether a naming deficit is evident, or whether the child is slow in accessing words, or both. A naming deficit might be further confirmed by a weak performance on the Memory for Names performance and/ or on the Inhibition Naming condition of the Inhibition subtest. A more generalized processing speed problem, on the other hand, might be supported through inspection of Visuomotor Precision Total Completion Time and other timed tests that were administered, for instance, from the WISC-III or the DAS-II.

After Administering the Appropriate Subtests, the Clinician Should Analyze the Findings by Determining the Deficient Subcomponent That Appears to Cause the Overt Dysfunction

Because all human performance is more or less complex, most test results will depend on many capacities. For example, on the NEPSY-II Arrows subtest in the Visuospatial domain, the child must judge the orientation of lines and angles by pointing to the two arrows that will hit the target on each item. The child needs not only to perceive and judge the direction and orientation of the arrows correctly, but also to attend to the lengthy task and to look actively at each of the eight arrows before responding. Sometimes a poor performance on the Arrows subtest is the result, not of poor visuospatial perception, but of poor visual attention or executive dysfunction. The former problems would be characterized by the child's inability to focus attention on the task or to sustain attention across the task. The latter could lead to responding impulsively, because the child could not inhibit the impulse to point to the first two arrows seen. In this case, the primary deficit would be visual inattention or a more pervasive dysexecutive function if many executive functions were affected. A secondary effect would be weak ability to perform on visual tasks requiring focused attention. Underlying primary deficits may have to be inferred in this way, by using error analysis and looking at the pattern of findings.

Specifying primary deficits in children is complicated by the high degree of comorbidity of deficits (e.g., Watemberg, Wasserberg, Zuk, & Lerman-Sagie, 2007; Willcutt, Pennington, Olson, & DeFries, 2007). When a child suffers from several co-occurring deficits, such as an attention disorder and a language disorder, both of which can affect many types of performance, it can be difficult to specify primary and secondary weaknesses. Inattention affects language processing, but poor language processing can contribute to inattention. In these cases, it may be sufficient to provide a comprehensive description of the child's neurocognitive status. The clinician may not always be able to specify primary and secondary deficits. In such instances, one may have to describe the total test profile and identify specific impairments, but not perform an in-depth analysis of the disorders.

Identify Diagnostic Behavioral Clusters That Characterize Particular Diagnostic Groups

Bernstein and Waber (1990) discuss the need to locate "diagnostic behavioral clusters." This term refers to the process of recognizing specific patterns that usually characterize different diagnostic groups, such as children with ADHD, dyslexia, autistic spectrum disorders, Fetal Alcohol Syndrome, Asperger's Syndrome, William's Syndrome, and so forth. Such disorders may be of neurological, genetic, or unknown etiology. The identification process is based primarily on clinical expertise and knowledge of the literature, and, secondarily, on the pattern of the child's specific psychometric scores.

The fact that a child shows a pattern of scores similar to that seen in a disorder does not necessarily mean the child has the disorder. Unless the child's functioning is consistent with the disorder and the medical, genetic, and environmental factors that are consistent with the disorder are present, the disorder should not be identified. For instance, a girl might have a visuospatial deficit and a math learning disability, but be very sociable, maintain good eye contact, and be expressive during the evaluation. Her history reveals that she has many friends and participates successfully in several group activities. In this case, identifying Nonverbal Learning Disability would be inappropriate, because there is no evidence of social perceptual difficulties.

Sometimes, however, the parent may not report a family history of the disorder because he or she has forgotten about it, is embarrassed, or did not make the connection between the child's problem and the presence of a similar problem in a member of the extended family. These are the kind of cases in which the importance of the diagnostic interview, the depth of the clinician's knowledge of the literature, and the level of clinical insight can prove most valuable.

EXAMPLE: Suppose that Sonia has been referred for an evaluation of a reading problem. Achievement testing shows particular difficulty with reading decoding and spelling. There is no record of any familial dyslexia or reading problem on the history form. You notice, however, that there are many misspellings on the history form that was filled out by Sonia's mother, who has a college degree. In your diagnostic interview you ask if there was anyone in the family who had a reading difficulty, and the response is negative. But when you ask if anyone had or has trouble pronouncing new words, you learn that the family playfully teases Sonia's maternal aunt for that. When you ask if anyone has trouble finding words when he or she is talking (word-finding problems, dysphasia), you discover that Sonia, her mother, her maternal aunt, and her maternal grandfather all have this problem. You then ask if anyone has had difficulty learning a foreign language, and even though Sonia's mother has not been able to express this on the history form, she now tells you that she had a great deal of difficulty getting her college degree because she had trouble passing French. She also reports that Sonia's older sister, who is a very good student, is really struggling with French, too, because she cannot seem to master the pronunciation or spelling. Finally, when you ask if anyone has dropped out of school early, Sonia's mother reveals that her own father left school after ninth grade because he "just couldn't keep up." A little more gentle discussion reveals that, despite the fact that he runs a successful retail business, he has marked difficulty reading and spelling. He keeps it very secret, and his wife does all of the ordering and bookkeeping for him. Through a skillful clinical interview, you have established a family history of dyslexia.

Being able to recognize diagnostic behavioral clusters rests on the clinician's ability to gain as much training and expertise in clinical neuropsychological practice as possible, and it is one of the reasons why clinicians must stay current with the literature. As the clinician performs his or her evaluation, he or she needs to know the direction to follow to confirm the hypotheses. For instance, if the clinician suspects dyslexia, as in Sonia's case, he or she needs the background knowledge to look for primary deficits in phonological processing deficits and naming.

When Sonia was evaluated subsequently, the clinician found performance *Well Below Expected Level* on the Phonological Processing and Repetition of Nonsense Words subtests, establishing a primary deficit in phonological analysis. Speeded Naming performance was *Below Expected Level.* The Total Completion Time Scaled Score revealed *Borderline* speed of access as well as accuracy in naming that was *Well Below Expected Level*. Performance on Memory for Names and Memory for Names Delayed Scaled Score was *Below Expected Level,* as well. The latter included both individual scaled scores for immediate and delayed learning. Therefore, a primary naming deficit was identified that was associated with a secondary deficit in learning and retaining people's names, which might have social implications. Difficulty with access to semantics seen on Speeded Naming was confirmed when Sonia, despite performance showing receptive language *At Expected Level* on the Comprehension of Instructions subtest, had problems on the Free Recall Trial of the Narrative Memory subtest, reflecting an NM Free Recall Scaled Score that was *Below Expected Level*. When the Cued Recall Trial was administered, however, Sonia was able to access story details well, which caused the NM Free and Cued Recall Scaled Score to be *At Expected Level*. Sonia had encoded the language in the story, but could not access it. The questions provided cues for accessing the details that were in her memory and she just needed a cue to the story details.

Sonia's difficulties with speed of processing on Speeded Naming appeared to be more generalized than just accessing language. On Visuomotor Precision, Sonia's Total Completion Time SS was *Below Expected Level,* although accuracy for graphomotor control on the VP Total Errors Percentile Rank was *At Expected Level*. Graphomotor control did not appear to be a problem on Design Copying either, because the DC General Percentile Rank was *Above Expected Level* on an untimed test. Further, on the Inhibition subtest, Sonia showed weak performance on the IN Naming condition, further supporting the finding of a naming problem, but she also demonstrated difficulty in speed of processing on the INN, INI, and INS Completion Time Scaled Scores. The latter confirmed the more generalized slow processing speed, rather than just slow performance on naming tasks. Therefore, there appeared to be a primary deficit in processing speed, which was also apparent on Sonia's WISC-III results, such as Coding, with a secondary deficit in speed of lexical access, which was further complicated by her primary naming deficit. Performance in all other domains was compatible with that of the general population and in terms of Sonia's own performance within or across domains.

Academic achievement testing revealed reading decoding and spelling discrepancies with predicted achievement based on Sonia's ability level, though reading comprehension was average and within the range of Sonia's ability as measured by the WISC-III. Familial history of dyslexia was present, and Sonia was reported to have marked struggles in mastering phonics and learning to read. She often experienced word-finding problems, and this difficulty was observed informally during her evaluation in her frequent use of "thing" when she could not access

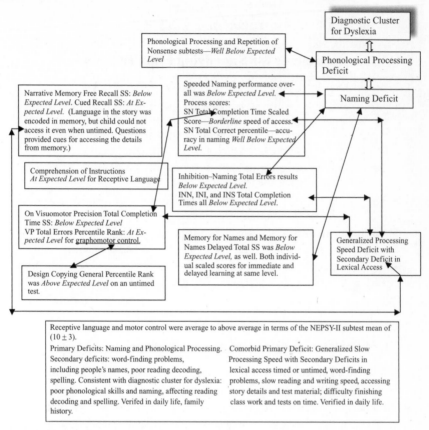

Figure 4.1 Integrating Results from Subtests Reflecting a Diagnostic Behavioral Cluster

a word. The diagnostic behavioral cluster for dyslexia was present. (Figure 4.1 illustrates the integration of results from subtests reflecting a diagnostic behavioral cluster.)

If a diagnostic behavioral cluster is not present, the clinician should identify and analyze primary and secondary deficits. If this is not possible, the clinician should identify neurocognitive strengths and weaknesses. The clinician should not attempt the diagnosis of disorders for which he or she has no neuropsychological training or background. Rapid Reference 4.5 summarizes guidelines for specifying impairments. The last step in Sonia's evaluation would be to verify the results by integrating all available information about the child.

Rapid Reference 4.5

Guidelines for Specifying Impairments

- Specific impairments may be demonstrated when:
  - (a) Two or more subtest scaled scores (SS) or Behavioral Observations within or across a domain indicate that a certain aspect of performance is impaired either in relation to the age norm or in relation to the child's own mean.
  - (b) This finding corresponds to or explains the child's problems in daily life or is confirmed by the child's history.
- The neuropsychological and ecological significance of the findings is as important as the statistical significance.
- The problem may be more subtle or complex than describing a behavior in relation to the norm (e.g., often takes place through error analysis).
- Current knowledge of pediatric neuropsychological research facilitates analyzing impairments for diagnostic clusters (patterns).

The Third Goal: Integrate and Implement Findings

The third goal of interpretation is to integrate results with all developmental, neurobiological, medical, educational, and environmental information about the child in order to formulate recommendations. This, as well as both of the first two levels, leads to a final step to make meaningful recommendations and formulate treatment plans, materials, and assessments for response to intervention (RTI).

This step is intimately connected to all diagnostic conclusions. After integrating the results of the evaluation with all other developmental, neurobiological, medical, educational, and environmental information about the child, the clinician analyzes presenting problems and the child's situation in detail with an eye to providing recommendations for compensatory methods, remediation techniques, and/or treatment options. The entire assessment is geared toward providing help and advice to those involved in the interventions with, and education of, the child. The following is an example of recommendations drawn up following Sonia's evaluation.

EXAMPLE: Following Sonia's evaluation, the clinician might recommend that she work with a reading specialist, if possible, on a multisensory, phonological approach to decoding. At the very least, Sonia's teacher should use individualized Orton Gillingham methods with her in the classroom while monitoring her progress. The clinician recommended that Sonia's weekly spelling list be modified to 10 rather than 20 words. Further, she suggested that Sonia have a multiple choice spelling test with no dictation sentences, because children with dyslexia have marked difficulty spelling in context. A further recommendation was made that Sonia have drill and practice with the Dolch Sight Words in order to give her a ready sight vocabulary for reading. Her teachers would be asked not to require Sonia to read aloud in front of classmates. Software programs were recommended for help with reading decoding and spelling both at school and at home. Another recommendation was that spelling in context not be penalized when Sonia was required to write a story or essay. It was recommended that Sonia and the teacher draw up a list of five words that Sonia needed to use often in her writing and misspelled frequently. These would be the only words circled for correction. When Sonia had begun to spell one of the words correctly on a regular basis, another frequently misspelled common word would be added to the list. The list would be circulated to all of her teachers, so that she could use the same system, no matter what the subject. Mother and Father were shown several multisensory methods to consider, which Sonia could use for studying spelling.

Word-processing instruction was recommended immediately, so that Sonia could learn to use the computer for any written expression. The software program "Inspiration" was recommended to help Sonia organize her thoughts in writing.

Because Sonia's school started foreign language study in the third grade, the clinician further recommended that this be delayed for Sonia until her reading was fluent, unless she was able to be in an immersion program. If she wanted to study a foreign language, Spanish was recommended because of its simple phonetic structure. Latin was recommended as an excellent alternative, because it helps to build word analysis and vocabulary skills in English due to the great number of Latin roots, prefixes, and suffixes in English.

Finally, it was recommended that Talking Books be ordered through the Library of Congress for Sonia. In this way she could "read" books that other children were reading but that she could not yet handle. She could read the book along with the CD, however. This was also recommended for her social studies and science books, as these texts are particularly difficult content reading. Parents were informed that recorded textbooks can be obtained through Recording for the Blind and Dyslexic, and the clinician made sure that both parents and teachers had the appropriate Web site to order the service. Because Sonia was comfortable reading to her mother, she was to read for 10 minutes each night with her. Her parents were asked to read to her nightly from a book of her choice. Sonia loved ballet, so it was recommended that Sonia's mother consult the children's librarian at the public library about simple books that Sonia could read on that topic. Sonia's parents were given a bibliography of books that would help them understand dyslexia and another list of books that they could read to Sonia to help her learn about famous people who had overcome dyslexia. (See Rapid Reference 4.6 for guidelines to specifying primary and secondary deficits and diagnostic clusters.)

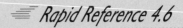

Rapid Reference 4.6

Guidelines to Specifying Primary and Secondary Deficits and Diagnostic Clusters

1. Analyze separately, if possible, all subcomponents that are known to be a part of the function in question.
   - Specific NEPSY-II subtests represent subcomponents of complex processes (e.g., Speeded Naming and Inhibition-Naming assess the ability to attach labels to things and concepts and the speed of access to retrieve them smoothly).
2. Specify what particular part of the process is deficient and whether the deficit contributing to the dysfunction is primary or is secondary to another deficit.
   - A primary deficit in one functional system can affect performance in other functional systems, causing secondary deficits (e.g., primary deficit: language disorder; secondary deficit: poor verbal memory).
   - Each subcomponent has a role in the chain of subprocesses. If one is deficient, the whole functional system may be disturbed. Some disorders (e.g., dyslexia) may have more than one underlying deficit.
   - Look within and across subtests to identify and interpret primary and secondary deficits.
     - Process Scores separate subcomponents (e.g., speed of access and accuracy in naming).
     - Look across subtests (e.g., Speeded Naming, Inhibition Naming, Memory for Names).
       For example: Primary generalized processing speed deficit (e.g., Speeded Naming, Visuomotor Precision, IN-Naming (timed subtest). Secondary deficits: slow reading and graphomotor speed, inability to finish tests.

- Specifying primary deficits in children is complicated by high comorbidity of deficits:
  - The clinician may not always be able to specify primary and secondary deficits. He or she may have to describe the total test profile and identify specific impairments.
3. Identify diagnostic behavioral clusters (patterns) that characterize particular diagnostic groups.
   - Identification process based primarily on clinical expertise, knowledge of literature, and, secondarily, on the pattern of the child's specific psychometric scores.
   - Child's functioning must be consistent with disorder, and the medical, genetic, and environmental factors are present (e.g., poor Phonological Processing results, but no reading problems).
   - Be thorough in reviewing records and history with parents/caregiver.

LOCALIZING BRAIN DYSFUNCTION IS NOT A GOAL FOR INTERPRETATION

Traditionally, one aim of neuropsychological assessment was to localize brain damage or dysfunction by specifying which part of the brain, judging from neuropsychological evidence, seemed to be dysfunctional. With the advent of neuroimaging techniques, this aim is no longer essential in clinical neuropsychology. Furthermore, certain aspects of interpreting neuropsychological performance in children make it a particularly hazardous endeavor in comparison to the possibilities of relating neuropsychological impairment to brain damage in the adult population.

CAUTION

Cautions Against Localizing Brain Functions in Children

With neuroimaging techniques, localization is no longer essential in clinical neuropsychology. Interpreting neuropsychological performance in children is a hazardous endeavor in comparison to relating neuropsychological impairment to brain damage in the adult population for several reasons:

(*continued*)

(continued)
Widespread and diffusely distributed neural networks:

- Children may have more widespread and diffusely distributed networks of neural processes that underlie cognitive functions than adults have. There is also a high degree of neural redundancy in childhood.

- During development, neural substrates are organized and crystallized, increasing efficiency, but decreasing redundancy and plasticity, as neural circuits become committed to specific functions.

Functional organization of the young brain may be modified:

- Evidence from children with lateralized brain damage shows that the ongoing functional organization of the brain may be modified following early brain damage; therefore, in the young child functional organization may not be predictable.

Genetic etiology and diffuse brain dysfunction:

- Children tend to have diffuse or multifocal brain dysfunction (Korkman, Kirk, & Kemp, 2007). In the adult, because development is complete, a lesion in one area will usually cause predictable, circumscribed deficits.

- Because children are still developing, a deficit in one area may cause subtle, diffuse dysfunction in multiple areas due to subsequent development affected by the original lesion.

Pediatric Neuropsychologists May Interpret by Neuroanatomic Axes

In spite of the fallacies involved in attempting to localize brain dysfunction in a child, pediatric neuropsychologists may nevertheless interpret results by implicitly—not explicitly—thinking in terms of the functional organization of the brain, by reference to the three primary neuroanatomic axes of the brain: left/right hemisphere; anterior/posterior; and cortical/subcortical. They reference these three axes without assuming that there is any focal brain lesion or focal dysfunction (Bernstein & Waber, 1990). That is, it is common to think of neuropsychological processes in terms of frontal lobe functions, posterior brain processes, and left and right hemisphere functions, without presupposing any direct relationship between test findings and underlying brain dysfunction. In these cases, the neuropsychologist's training and knowledge of current research form an integral part of the interpretation. This type of interpretation is not a necessary step in applying the NEPSY-II and should be undertaken only by those with specialized training in pediatric neuropsychology. These important neuropsychological concepts having been noted, we will proceed to the key process of interpreting the results of a pediatric assessment. (See Rapid Reference 4.7.)

≡ *Rapid Reference 4.7*

Pediatric Neuropsychologists May Interpret by Neuroanatomic Axes

Pediatric neuropsychologists may interpret results by implicitly—not explicitly—referencing the functional organization of the brain through three primary neuroanatomic axes of the brain:

- Left/right hemisphere
- Anterior/posterior
- Cortical/subcortical

No assumption of focal brain lesion or focal dysfunction, nor a direct relationship between test findings and underlying brain dysfunction/ neuropsychological processes expressed in terms of:

- Frontal lobe functions
- Posterior brain processes
- Left and/or right hemisphere functions

The neuropsychologist's training and knowledge of current research form an integral part of the interpretation.

- This type of interpretation not a necessary step in applying the NEPSY-II.
- Undertaken only by those with specialized training in pediatric neuropsychology.

STEP-BY-STEP INTERPRETATION OF NEPSY-II PERFORMANCE

During the scoring procedures addressed in Chapter 3, the clinician recorded all available scores on the Record Form. In this section the interpretation of the actual test scores will be presented. First, the clinical meaning of the different types of scores will be clarified. Thereafter, how to decide which results are psychometrically significant is explained. Finally, interpretation at the clinical level is clarified.

The first step in interpretation focuses on psychometric scores and describes strengths and weaknesses as based on psychometric discrepancies. However, the clinician should remember from the previous discussion in this chapter that this is just one level in the interpretative process. After psychometric discrepancies have been considered and strengths and weaknesses defined, the subsequent steps of identifying and analyzing primary and secondary deficits, identifying diagnostic behavioral clusters, and interpreting the findings still lie ahead. Therefore, even in the process of entering the scores, and during test administration, the clinician should keep in mind any preliminary hypotheses he or she may have derived from the review of the records, diagnostic interview with the parents and the child, and the results of the assessment itself. The clinician should continue to formulate and refine hypotheses when working with the psychometric test results. The scores and their interpretations can be seen as two levels of interpretation: the surface layer and the deeper, diagnostic level.

Step 1: Enter Psychometric Test Data on the NEPSY-II Data Worksheet

In the Appendix of this volume, there is a NEPSY-II Data Worksheet that will help you organize a child's test results to facilitate interpretation. For all subtests administered, transfer all scaled scores for Primary, Combined and Contrast Scores, their percentile ranks, and the cumulative percentages (base rates) or percent in the standardization sample for Process Scores and Behavioral Observations. As you perform these steps, consider any hypotheses concerning deficits that may have been formulated during testing. The NEPSY-II Data Worksheet can be reproduced for your future use. (See Rapid Reference 4.8.)

≡ Rapid Reference 4.8

NEPSY Data Worksheet in Appendix A

The Appendix of this volume contains the NEPSY Data Worksheet (reproducible), which will help you:

- Organize and integrate the child's test results.
- Identify the primary and secondary deficits.
- Make decisions on significant deficits in functioning.
- With interpretation and formulation of recommendations.

Alternatively, the Scoring Assistant computer program may be used to obtain a record with the scores. When you enter the raw scores and the child's age, the computer scoring program prints out all scores, percentiles, descriptors, and so forth.

Step 2: Inspection of the Scores on NEPSY-II Preparatory to Interpretation

Three types of scores in NEPSY-II can be expressed as standard scores: subtest-level Scaled Scores, Combined Scaled Scores, and Contrast Scaled Scores. Interpretation of these scores varies. Further, as was already evident from the previous chapter, results may also be expressed in percentile ranges and base rates.

Standard Scaled Scores

The standard scaled scores represent a child's performance relative to his or her same-age peers. Generally, the NEPSY-II subtest scaled scores can also be compared to other types of normalized scores (See Rapid Reference 4.9 for a summary of the relationship between scaled scores, standard deviations from the mean, and percentile rank equivalents.) The NEPSY-II subtests have a scaled score mean of 10 ± 3. One standard deviation below the mean corresponds to the extreme 15% of the general population, and can be considered just outside normal variation (Kaufman & Lictenberger, 1999). Therefore, test results at or below a standard scaled score of 7 should be used as a marker of low performance. When comparing scores to other scores it is important to note, further, that a statistically significant discrepancy between two values may occur too frequently in normally developing children to be considered abnormal. Inspect all scaled scores in relation to the mean of 10 ± 3 on the NEPSY-II Data Worksheet and the percentile rank for each scaled score, followed by the descriptive classification. (Refer to Rapid Reference 4.1 on p. 186 of this chapter for qualitative descriptions of scaled scores and percentile ranks.)

EXAMPLE: Jeannie showed a scaled score of 5 on the Arrows subtest, which assesses judgment of line orientation. Given the subtest mean of 10, Jeannie's score was $-1\frac{2}{3}$ standard deviations from the mean, comparable to the 5th percentile. Therefore, in terms of the typical child of Jeannie's age, her performance would suggest a significant deficit in judgment of line orientation.

≡ Rapid Reference 4.9

Relation of Scaled Scores to Standard Deviations From the Mean and Percentile Rank Equivalents

	Scaled Score	Number of Standard Deviations from the Mean	Percentile Rank Equivalent
	1	−3	0.1
	2	−2⅔	0.4
	3	−2⅓	1
	4	−2	2
	5	−1⅔	5
	6	−1⅓	9
	7	−1	16
	8	−2/3	25
	9	−1/3	37
Average Range	10	0(Mean)	50
	11	+1/3	63
	12	+2/3	75
	13	+1	84
	14	+1⅓	91
	15	+1⅔	95
	16	+2	98
	17	+2⅓	99
	18	+2⅔	99.6
	19	+3	99.9

Combined Scores

The Combined Scores integrate two normed scores (e.g., one scaled score and one percentile or two percentiles) obtained during one subtest. The Combined Score functions as a composite total score for two measures within a subtest. A conversion table places the two scores on roughly the same metric or differentially weights errors versus time based on the construct being measured. This allows the clinician to determine if the subcomponent processes are within normal limits for the child's age.

EXAMPLE: On the Inhibition Trial of the Inhibition subtest, Dan might be *Above Expected Level* on the INI Total Completion Time (SS: 15) but *Well Below Expected Level* for accuracy (INI Total Error Percentile Rank: 5th percentile). The INI Combined Scaled Score would be 7 (11th to 25th percentile) in the *Borderline* range. While the combined total may be in the borderline range, inspection of the separate subcomponent scores allows the clinician to understand *how* Dan achieved that score. The clinician might interpret these results in Dan's report in the following way: "Dan's completion time on the Inhibition Trial of the Inhibition subtest (INI) was Above Expected Level for age, but accuracy was poor (Well Below Expected Level), better than only 3 to 10% of children of his age. Essentially, his performance was fast and inaccurate. It appears to be very difficult for Dan to inhibit response when he must complete a task quickly. He can either be slow and possibly inhibit response more efficiently, or sacrifice accuracy and finish the task quickly. Under time pressure in the classroom, Dan is more apt to do the latter."

The scaled score derived for the combined score does not require age correction, as the variables used to derive the new total are already age-corrected. It is interpreted in the same manner as a single scaled score, but the subcomponent scores should always be taken into account and discussed.

Contrast Scaled Scores

These scores are derived by a new method that describes differences in scores and yields normative data on one measure while controlling for the ability of the child on a control variable. The resulting score represents the child's ability on the designated variable, adjusted for the child's ability on the control measure. These scores are consistent with the process approach (Kaplan, 1988) in clinical neuropsychological assessment. Such scores provide a way to compare and interpret two parts of a measure (e.g., Word Generation Semantic Scaled Score vs. Word Generation Initial Letter Scaled Score) or to contrast two related measures (e.g., Memory for Faces vs. Memory for Faces Delayed) in order to help the clinician identify the deficit contributing to poor performance more precisely. It is important to inspect these scores well before proceeding with further analysis so that you understand the full range of the child's functioning on that particular subtest.

EXAMPLE: On Memory for Faces, Leia achieved an immediate memory performance *At Expected Level* (SS: 10) with a Memory for Faces Delayed scaled score of

6 (*Borderline*). This would yield an MF vs. MFD Contrast Scaled Score of 5 (*Below Expected Level*). The MF vs. MFD Contrast score might be interpreted thus: "Leia's immediate recall of faces was *At Expected Level,* but her delayed recall of faces was only *Borderline.*" Therefore, the MF vs. MFD Contrast Scaled Score reveals a performance *Below Expected Level* when compared to children of a similar initial encoding ability (*At Expected Level*). In other words, most children who perform in the average range on the immediate Memory for Faces test would recall nearly the same or the same number of faces 15–25 minutes later on the Memory for Faces Delayed test. Given the fact that Leia appeared to be attending to the faces when the test was administered, her results suggest that she is not consolidating the facial information in long-term memory; she is processing slowly and/or she is subject to memory decay.

It is important to note that the Contrast Scaled Score expresses differences irrespective of level. The contrast scaled score is interpreted in the same manner across all age and ability levels. The child who shows delayed memory recall right at the NEPSY-II subtest mean of 10 in relation to immediate encoding ability right at the mean of 10, will, therefore, show an MF vs. MFD Contrast Scaled Score of 10. However, a child who scores *Above Expected Level* at an SS of 16 on Memory for Faces and performance on Memory for Faces Delayed *At Expected Level* (SS: 9) would still show an MF vs. MFD Contrast Scaled Score of 4 *(Below Expected Level).* This is because the average level of the child's delayed memory recall at the 37th percentile (SS: 9) is significantly below expected level for children who show very high levels of immediate encoding ability (SS: 16) at the 98th percentile. If the child shows excellent immediate encoding of faces (SS: 16) with excellent delayed memory recall at an SS of 14, the MF vs. MFD Contrast Scaled Score would be *At Expected Level* (SS: 10). The reason for this is that the delayed memory performance is what one would expect from a child with excellent immediate encoding of faces.

Conversely, occasionally one sees a child who shows a poorer score on immediate recall of faces than on the delayed trial of Memory for Faces. So, if a child showed an SS of 5 (*Below Expected Level*) on Memory for Faces, with a marked improvement to *Expected Level* (SS: 10) on Delayed Memory for Faces, the MF vs. MFD Contrast Scaled Score would be 14 (*Above Expected Level*). In this case, the interpretation might be that Joanie showed immediate encoding of faces *Below Expected Level* for age, but, interestingly, 20 minutes later her performance was *At Expected Level,* suggesting that it is taking a prolonged period of time for Joanie to consolidate the facial information. Joanie's delayed recall of faces is *Above Expected Level* when compared to that of other children with her initial encoding skills. The long delay in her ability to consolidate facial features may well be contributing to social difficulties. (See Rapid Reference 4.10 for summary of interpretation of Combined and Contrast Scores.)

≡ Rapid Reference 4.10

Interpreting Combined and Contrast Scores

Combined Scores

- Integrate two normed scores (e.g., one scaled score and one percentile or two percentiles) from one subtest.
- Function as a composite total score for two measures within a subtest.
- Conversion table places the two scores on roughly the same metric or differentially weights errors vs. time based on the construct being measured.
- Allow the clinician to determine if the subcomponent processes are within normal limits for the child's age.
- Separate subcomponent scores allow understanding of how a combined score was obtained.
- Subcomponent scores should always be taken into account and discussed.

Contrast Scaled Scores

- Describe differences in scores; yields normative data on one measure while controlling for the ability of the child on a control variable.
- Resulting score represents the child's ability on the designated variable, adjusted for the child's ability on control measure.
- Way to compare and interpret two parts of a measure (e.g., Word Generation Semantic SS vs. Word Generation Initial Letter SS) or to contrast two related measures (e.g., Memory for Faces vs. MF Delayed).
- Help identify the deficit contributing to poor performance more precisely.
- A Contrast Scaled Score expresses differences irrespective of level and is interpreted in the same manner across all age levels and ability levels.

Percentile Ranks

Some of the subtests on NEPSY-II do not have scaled scores. Because the distributions are skewed, they cannot support a scaled score. The skills assessed in these subtests tend to develop early in normally developing children, so most children in the standardization group were able to achieve "high" total scores. One way to compare the performance of the child with an impairment to that of the normally developing children in the standardization sample is to use smoothed percentile ranks and percentile rank ranges.

The percentile ranks indicate the percentage of children in the normative sample who scored at or below a given raw score. The percentile rank is an indication of a child's standing relative to other children of the same age. Midpoint percentiles are interpreted in the same way as percentiles derived for scaled scores. Percentile ranks typically range from 1–99 with 50 as the mean and the median. Children with a percentile rank of 15 perform as high as or higher than 15% of children the same age (or perform the same or lower than 85% of other children the same age). Since we are recommending a stringent percentile rank of 10 to indicate a significant deficit, the clinician needs to look for scores at this level when defining weaknesses. (See Rapid Reference 4.11.)

≡ Rapid Reference 4.11

Is a Significant Difference Different Enough?

A statistically significant discrepancy in two values may occur too frequently in normally developing children to be considered abnormal.

- The extreme 15% of the general population, or one standard deviation from the mean (e.g., for the NEPSY-II mean of 10 + 3, a scaled score of 7) can be considered outside normal variation (Kaufman & Lictenberger, 1999).
- Use 10% or lower (scaled score of 6) as a stringent marker of low frequency for a statistically significant difference.
- A frequency of 25% means that one-quarter of the children that age exhibited the behavior, so it would not be a significant-enough difference to be outside the range of normal variation.

EXAMPLE: On NEPSY-II, the percentile ranks are presented in ranges. The 26th to 75th percentile represents the expected level at which the majority of children in each age group of the standardization population performed. One might, therefore, interpret a percentile rank as, "Tony's performance on Theory of Mind at the 26th to 50th percentile placed him *At Expected Level* in understanding another's perspective, figurative language, and other components of this core deficit of Autistic Disorder. His performance suggests a level better than or equal to 26–50 out of 100 children his age on Theory of Mind tasks." Since the average percentile range on NEPSY-II is 26th to 75th percentile, Toby's performance falls within that range, suggesting that he is not displaying this core symptom of autism. This does not rule out autism entirely, however, as 30% of children with autism do not show a deficit on the Theory of Mind subtest. Other subtests, particularly Affect

Recognition and Memory for Faces, need to be taken into account, as well as other measures and autism spectrum symptom checklists.

Cumulative Percentages (Base Rates)

Cumulative percentages (base rates) of the standardization sample by age or clinical group are also presented as scores on NEPSY-II. These scores are descriptive base rates and do not represent percentile rank scores. The interpretation of the two scores is slightly different. A score at the 10th percentile is interpreted as, "The child's score is better than or equal to 10 children of his or her same-age peers." A base rate of 10% is interpreted as, "Ten percent of the children in the same age group obtained the same score or a lower score."

Base rates are usually considered in terms of rareness of the finding rather than how the person's performance compares to a normalized distribution, that is, distance from average performance on the task.

EXAMPLE: Interpretation of Cumulative Percentages on List Memory process scores might be, "Shandra, at 8 years of age, learned 3 words on Trial 1 of the List Learning Test, but after five learning trials, Shandra recalled only 7 of the 15 words on the list. This level of learning across repeated trials showed a cumulative percentage of 39 for children in the same age group. This result suggests that 39% of children in the same age group score at the same level or below it. After the Interference Trial was administered, Shandra was asked to recall as many of the Trial 5 words as she could. At that point, she was only able to recall 3 of the 7 words on Trial 6 she had learned on Trial 5. The cumulative percentage for the Interference Effect was 98, suggesting that 98% of children of Shandra's age scored at the same level or lower than Shandra did. This result suggests that most children of 8, therefore, are likely subject to interference on such a task. New, similar information is apt to reduce recall of previously learned material. Fifteen to twenty-five minutes later, when Shandra was asked to recall the 7 words she had learned by Trial 5, she was able to recall 6 of them. She had continued to learn and consolidate her learning over time. This result yields a Delay Effect Cumulative Percentage of 88, suggesting that 88% of children in the same group score at or below this level. Therefore, over time, Shandra learned well."

Behavioral Observations

Many observations should be recorded during the administration of NEPSY-II. Some of these are the very important qualitative observations of the child's performance that are informally recorded. Others are a part of the formal structure of the NEPSY-II and the presence or absence of them is checked off or they are tallied to be summed later. Scores for Behavioral Observations are cumulative percentages or percents of the standardization samples displaying the behavior. These Behavioral Observation scores are found in Appendix D of *The Clinical and Interpretive Manual.* (See Rapid Reference 4.12 for summary of the percentile ranks, cumulative percentages, and behavioral observations.)

EXAMPLE: Jeff, age 7.11, displayed average cumulative percentages for the Behavioral Observation *Asks for Repetition* on several subtests, but his cumulative percentage for Rule Violations on Memory for Designs and Memory for Designs Delayed was only 3 to 10%. Thus, when Jeff was instructed that subtest stimuli could not be repeated, his cumulative percentage score for the Behavioral Observation, *Asks for Repetition,* was 26 to 75% on three subtests—Comprehension of Instructions, Phonological Processing, and Word List Interference—which was *At Expected Level* for inhibiting himself from asking for repetition when it was not allowed. However, when Jeff was told to remember a simple rule for reproducing the design grid on Memory for Designs and Memory for Designs Delayed, he made two rule violations, yielding a cumulative percentage for his performance of 3 to 10%. This result suggests that 3 to 10% of Jeff's same-age peers performed at the same level or lower, a result *Below Expected Level for Age.* Jeff appears to have more difficulty than most children his age in carrying out rule-bound behavior in hands-on visuospatial memory tasks.

≡ *Rapid Reference 4.12*

Smoothed Percentiles and Cumulative Percentages— How and Why

A. Problems in standardizing a neurospsychological instrument are:

- Typically developing children acquire many basic skills at an early age, which tends to cause skewed distributions in corresponding tests.

- Some children have impairments in these skills and neuropsychological assessment needs to identify the impairments.

- Assessing these children requires that their performance is compared to that of typically developing children; therefore, normed tests are necessary.

B. For some subtests, total raw scores are converted to percentile ranks, not scaled scores.

- Smoothed percentile ranks are derived by inspecting progression of scores within and across ages and eliminating minor sampling irregularities by smoothing.

- Percentile ranges, not exact percentile values, are chosen because identification of a specific percentile value could be misleading when there is not a normal distribution.

C. Behavioral Observations are presented as cumulative percentages, representing the pure base rates of occurrence in the standardization sample.

Step 3: Moving From Psychometric Examination of Score Differences to Descriptive Interpretation of Performance

By this point the clinician will have chosen the type of comparisons he or she wants to make, or the clinician may have computed all possible differences to note any interesting discrepancies. Also, the clinician will have recorded all scores, significant discrepancies, and performance levels on the NEPSY Data Sheet (Appendix A). It is likely, therefore, that he or she will have discarded some hypotheses, and the results are beginning to converge on specific areas of concern.

Variability in the child's performance is important for understanding neurocognitive strengths and weaknesses for that child. Psychometrics merely supply the observations from which the final steps of interpretation start. Considering strengths through which the child can feel success and that may be avenues for remediation or rehabilitation is just as important as identifying weaknesses. In a psychological assessment, differences between scores or between the scores and the normative data are judged through psychometric analysis. There are several ways to make psychometric comparisons on NEPSY-II. These will help elucidate the child's strengths and weaknesses and ultimately lead to the identification and interpretation of primary and secondary deficits. (Comparisons are outlined in Rapid Reference 4.13.)

≡ Rapid Reference 4.13

Ways to Make Comparisons

Psychometrics will help elucidate the child's strengths and weaknesses for descriptive interpretation and will ultimately pinpoint primary and secondary deficits. Comparisons can be made:

- **In relation to typically developing agemates:** Comparisons can be made between a child's subtest scaled score and the NEPSY-II mean across domains (10 + 3) or the child's personal mean across domains to the NEPSY-II test mean.

- **Within subject**: Compare child's specific subtest performance to the child's personal mean across domains.

- **Within a test**: Comparisons made within a test using Combined and Contrast Scaled Scores.

It is important to note that the diagnostic thrust of the NEPSY-II is at the subtest level; therefore comparisons between domain means are not encouraged as deficits can be masked in that way. However:

(continued)

(continued)

- A child's subtest score from a particular domain compared to the child's own domain mean may be useful, if at least three subtests have been administered in that domain (e.g., Bridget's poor score on Phonological Processing in relation to her average Language domain mean. See the second example in Step 4 of Interpretation.

There are numerous scores to be compared and it is not necessary to study all possible differences in detail. A general review of the test profile will help to decide which contrast scores and which subscores to analyze in greater detail. Areas that are generally well performed by the children and are not problems in daily life may well be looked at through the Primary Scores. These areas are nevertheless important to report as strengths on which to build the child's self-esteem and to give the parents a positive view of the child's capacities. These areas may also serve as points of comparison for the more poorly achieved performances. Primary scores that show poorer performance and that correspond to difficulties in daily life need to be analyzed. The clinician will record all these scores and related significant discrepancies on the NEPSY Data Sheet (Appendix A). In this process hypothesis testing continues, some hypotheses will be discarded, and the results will begin to converge on specific areas of concern.

Step 4: Inspect NEPSY Data Worksheet for Interpretation at the Clinical Levels

The process of interpretation really began as the assessment was taking place, and the clinician was testing hypotheses. The clinician may have begun the testing with a General Assessment Battery if the referral question was vague or a more specific Referral Battery for a narrower referral question. In many cases this approach will be sufficient, but in others it will become apparent that the child's difficulty is more complex than first suspected from the referral. This is where a good background in neuropsychology is extremely advantageous. As results accumulated during the testing session, the clinician may have noted indications of a problem and carried out additional tests to elucidate the problem. Further subtests may have been administered within one or more domains or across domains to look for suspected diagnostic behavioral clusters. In a few cases, the clinician may have proceeded with a Full NEPSY-II Assessment to test further hypotheses that evolved during the evaluation process.

Identifying Strengths and Weaknesses

At this point, you have interpreted NEPSY-II starting from the descriptive level to look at neurocognitive development comprehensively. You will now move on to interpret at a clinical level, identifying deficits, analyzing their contribution to dysfunction as primary or secondary, and locating diagnostic behavioral clusters, which may point to a specific disorder.

Look at the NEPSY Data Worksheet (Appendix) that you filled in earlier to locate strengths and weaknesses for your comprehensive overview of neurocognitive development in relation to typical children. It is important to discuss individual strengths reflected in the child's subtest performance, but also to highlight the child's relative strengths in terms of his or her ability. For this comparison, you have computed the child's subtest mean:

EXAMPLE (*A segment of a report only*): "In relation to her average performance across domains for all NEPSY-II subtests administered, Maria displayed a relative strength in visuomotor integration. This can be observed in her very good performance in paper/pencil copying of geometric figures on the Design Copying subtest and her fast and accurate performance on Visuomotor Precision where she had to draw pencil lines through winding tracks while staying within their borders."

If a child's personal mean is low, there may still be areas in which he or she can feel success in terms of his or her own functioning. It is just as important to identify strengths as it is to identify weaknesses (Korkman, Kirk, & Kemp, 1998). A child's learning might well be directed through the strong area or areas, while remediation is addressed in weak areas. An obvious example is that in which seven-year-old Maria meets the *DSM-IV-TR* criteria for a Receptive and Expressive Language Disorder (Developmental Language Disorder), but has well-developed visual perceptual and visuomotor skills. Pictures, charts, models, and manipulatives, as well as copying or tracing diagrams, can be used to teach her.

An area of strength can also provide an extracurricular area of success. For instance, in the present example, Maria may enjoy and be successful with crafts, art projects, model-building, or constructional activities. Developing a successful hobby will help Maria's self-esteem so that she can better face the daily challenge of coping with weak language skills. Speech and language therapy, by contrast, will focus on strengthening receptive and expressive language skills.

After strengths are interpreted, significant weaknesses should be considered next. Again, for interpretation at the descriptive level, you compare performance to the NEPSY-II subtest mean to see how a particular child's neurocognitive development compares to that of the normally developing child, as represented by the NEPSY-II standardization sample. Do the weaknesses all fall in one domain?

Are they evident across domains? You should also compute relative weaknesses in terms of the child's own ability as you did for the strengths. Obviously, it is helpful to know which weaknesses are apt to affect the child's learning. Remediation or rehabilitation should focus the most on these areas. The child's strengths may provide compensatory means for circumventing a problem. A child might have a specific deficit within one domain or a pattern of deficits across domains.

EXAMPLE: The child's significant strengths and weaknesses are identified in relation to the standardization population (using the NEPSY-II scaled score mean of 10 ± 3), and to the child's own functioning (personal subtest mean) in a particular domain. Suppose that Bridget, aged 7, was referred for an evaluation due to reading difficulties. On the NEPSY-II, she achieved a scaled score of 4 on the Phonological Processing subtest. The clinician interpreted this score in terms of the general population of Bridget's age as *Below Expected Level* with a percentile rank of 3 to 10% when compared to NEPSY-II scaled score mean of 10 ± 3. Bridget's score met the stringent tenth percentile level for a reliable weakness in terms of typical children of her age. The clinician also wanted to determine if this was a relative weakness for Bridget in terms of her Language domain performance overall. The clinician averaged the scaled scores of the Language domain subtests that he had administered (Speeded Naming Combined: 8; Comprehension of Instructions: 11; Word Generation-Semantic: 12; Word Generation Initial Letter: 8; Phonological Processing: 4). He determined that her language subtest mean was 8.6, or 9.0 rounded up, which is average, or *Within Expected Level,* according to NEPSY-II classification. The clinician then compared Bridget's Phonological Processing scaled score of 4 to her own Language domain subtest mean 9.0 and found a difference of 5, which is −1 2/3 SD from Bridget's mean of 9.0. According to Table 6.1 (p. 134) in the *Clinical and Interpretative Manual,* a standard deviation at this level would have a percentile rank equivalent of 5, which would indicate a relative weakness in phonological skills for Bridget in relation to her own language functioning. Furthermore, her phonological processing skills were a significant weakness in terms of the standardization population for her age (NEPSY-II scaled score mean = 10 ± 3).

A possible interpretative report is written as the following (*only a segment of a report*): "Bridget displayed understanding of linguistically complex oral instructions *At Expected Level* for age in her performance on the Comprehension or Instructions Subtest (63rd percentile). Therefore, receptive language skills for Bridget were at a level better than 63 out of 100 children of eight years. On the WISC-III, her expressive vocabulary performance was in the high average range (Vocabulary, 13), and verbal abstract reasoning was average (Similarities, 11). Bridget does not appear, therefore, to be subject to a generalized language disorder that often underlies a reading disability."

Bridget's Speeded Naming Combined Score was on the lower border of *Expected Level* for age, however. Inspection of the two scores integrated into the SN Combined Score revealed an SN Time Completion Scaled Score of 10, *At Expected Level* for age (26–75% of the standardization sample), but an SN Total Correct Percentile Rank at the 6th to 10th percentile (*Below Expected Level* for age). Bridget's results revealed average speed of access but a weakness in naming ability, contributing to her dyslexia and causing the word-finding problems reported by parents and her teacher. Her weakness in the basic expressive language ability of naming was also seen in her Memory for Names performance, which was *Below Expected Level*. Therefore, despite her well-developed receptive language skills and her average to high average verbal abstract reasoning skills and expressive vocabulary, Bridget does appear to have a specific dysnomia (naming deficit) sometimes found in children with dyslexia.

Bridget's phonological processing skills are not only significantly poor in terms of the general population of Bridget's age, as represented by the NEPSY-II standardization sample, but they also appeared as a relative weakness in terms of Bridget's language performance on the NEPSY-II Language domain. Phonological processing is the ability to conceptualize speech-sound patterns and to manipulate those patterns. It is the underlying process in reading decoding and spelling. Bridget displayed a significant deficit in this area (5th percentile). It would appear that Bridget's deficits in phonological processing and naming are related to her marked difficulty in reading decoding and spelling.

Academic achievement testing revealed that performance on the Basic Reading subtest (decoding) was in the low average range (Standard Score, 80; mean = 100 ± 15), Spelling was borderline (75), but results on the Reading Comprehension subtest were in the average range (99). The latter result suggests that Bridget is "finessing" the meaning from passages, even though she cannot decode all the words. This profile is typical of dyslexics with good reasoning ability. Bridget's WISC-III Full Scale IQ was 106 (66th percentile), and there was no significant discrepancy between the Verbal and Performance Scales. Therefore, Bridget's FSIQ should be a reliable indicator of the level of her cognitive functioning overall. Both reading decoding and spelling skills showed a significant discrepancy with Bridget's ability level. Therefore, Bridget's test results provided evidence of a Reading Disorder and Disorder of Written Language (spelling), and she should be referred for learning disability intervention. To address her weakness in phonological processing, intensive work in multisensory phonological analysis of words is recommended, along with training to automatize access to high frequency words and irregular spellings.

Specifying Primary and Secondary Deficits

As noted earlier in this chapter, interpretation involves specifying and analyzing primary and secondary deficits, locating diagnostic behavioral clusters (patterns of symptoms that cluster together and point to a specific disorder), and discussing all of the above in the context of all the factors impacting the child. You have inspected and interpreted the NEPSY-II data for differences, strengths, and weaknesses in relation to the normally developing child in the first step of interpretation at the descriptive level. As you carried out this first step you identified areas of weakness, which you will now analyze more actively.

Poor performance in one area or across domains may suggest deficits converging on a particular function. By studying the deficits observed through the test results and in your observations of the child's performance during testing, you should analyze which deficits appear to be at the root of a dysfunction (primary deficit) and which deficits appear to be the result of the primary deficit adversely affecting another function (secondary deficit). Figure 4.1 demonstrates an example of a diagnostic cluster.

Using the preceding case of Bridget, let us see how the next step in interpretation at the clinical level should proceed.

EXAMPLE (*A segment of a report only; not meant to encompass all possible findings or conclusions*): "Bridget displayed the diagnostic behavioral cluster associated with dyslexia, including a primary deficit in phonological processing, which underlies the secondary deficit in mastering phonics, and marked difficulty in spelling and in decoding words. Her reading comprehension was significantly better than reading decoding skills or spelling, which often occurs in dyslexics who have good verbal reasoning ability. She had difficulty spelling in context, a particular problem for dyslexics. Furthermore, Bridget displayed another deficit known to be comorbid with dyslexia, naming ability that was *Below Expected Level* for age. Her primary deficit in naming (dysnomia) contributed to two secondary deficits, her word-finding problems reported by parents and teachers, as well as observed during the evaluation, and her poor performance in learning and recalling names of people. The latter was seen in her Memory for Names performance, which was *Below Expected Level.* As is true of some dyslexics, Bridget did not appear to have any language deficits other than naming. Her receptive language understanding was good on NEPSY-II, and expressive vocabulary was within normal limits on the WISC-III. Finally, dyslexia is a highly heritable disorder, and family history showed evidence that there is a familial reading disorder in the paternal great-grandfather and the paternal uncle. Therefore, Bridget's primary and secondary deficits, as well as comorbid deficits, comprise a diagnostic behavioral cluster consistent with dyslexia."

Recommendations for this report should include learning disability assistance, as well as intensive work in multisensory phonological analysis of words to address her phonological processing deficit, along with training to automatize access to high-frequency words and irregular spellings due to her poor performance in lexical access. (Recommendations would actually be enumerated at length—see Chapter 7.)

The case of Sonia earlier in this chapter also illustrates how primary deficits may be identified. In Sonia's case it was found that primary problems both of phonological analysis and of naming underlie her reading problems.

Diagnostic behavioral clusters refer to patterns of symptoms that cluster together and point to a specific disorder. Findings that help to identify diagnostic clusters frequently cut across domain boundaries much more comprehensively than in Bridget's case. Subtests that are not in the target domain of interest for the referral question may lend a great deal of clinical information to the diagnostic picture for the clinician who is very observant and is well-versed in the research literature. Furthermore, the clinician's own neuropsychological background can be key to the diagnosis. The behavioral clusters may suggest medical diagnoses or syndromes in which specific cognitive and behavioral features are typical. These may include, for example, disorders within the autism spectrum or attention deficit hyperactivity disorder. Needless to say such diagnoses are identified in collaboration with pediatric or neuropediatric expertise, often in the context of a neuropediatric team. However, it may be in the context of the neuropsychological assessment that the diagnostically defining features are identified.

EXAMPLE: Five-year-old Bill came for assessment due to what was thought to be a severe reaction to the birth of a younger brother one-and-a-half years earlier. Bill had started to stammer; later he became restless, his speech deteriorated, and he refused to obey or even react to verbal commands. An assessment revealed complete inability to comprehend the NEPSY-II instructions or carry out any purely verbal task whatsoever. In contrast, his nonverbal capacities—visuospatial and visuomotor—were generally average, provided that he understood the instruction. *He was good at picking up nonverbal cues and reacted adequately to them, which gave the impression that he understood verbally.* A discussion with the neuropediatrician and the neuropediatric team resulted in an EEG recording. As this daytime recording was inconclusive, a nightly video telemetry recording during sleep was taken. This recording demonstrated no epileptic seizures but epileptiform activity during slow-wave sleep. This finding confirmed a suspicion of acquired aphasia typical of the Landau-Kleffner syndrome (epilepsy, acquired aphasia, and continuous spike-wave discharges during sleep) (Kleffner & Landau, 2009).

Step 5: Integrate and Verify NEPSY-II Interpretation With Other Assessment Results and Developmental, Neurobiological, Medical, Educational, and Environmental Information

Throughout the process of scoring, analyzing, and interpreting results, the clinician should hold the referral concerns in mind. Having carefully selected an appropriate Referral Battery, the clinican should ask him or herself questions concerning possible causes of the problem by comparing NEPSY-II scores, Behavioral Observations, additional testing, achievement, and comprehensive information available about the child and his family. Verification is not just a matter of verifying patterns within the assessment, but it is also an external process of comparing one's conclusions on impairments and diagnostic clusters with data from history, the child's problems in everyday life, reports from school, and literature concerning such impairments.

In some cases, it may be useful to refer to subtest intercorrelations to see what components may be included in the performance of different subtests (see shared abilities, following). Note, however, that these may be different in the normally developing children of the standardization sample than in children with developmental or acquired disorders. If the clinician returns to the referral question and presenting symptoms periodically as he or she undertakes the interpretative process, the clinician can be assured that concerns will be appropriately addressed in the final report.

Internal and External Verification of NEPSY-II Results

The process of verification that follows is dependent not only on inspecting results of other subtests within a domain for similar deficits, but also on reviewing performance *on subtests across domains that share abilities with the subtest being verified*. In this way, it is possible to review performances across domains and subtests, including Primary Scaled Scores, Combined Scaled Scores, Process Percentile Ranks, and Behavioral Observation cumulative percentages (base rates), or percent of the standardization samples displaying the behavior. This will help the clinician trace a diagnostic thread and corroborate the results seen on the test he or she is interpreting.

EXAMPLE: Suppose the clinician observed a lack of response inhibition on the Inhibition subtest in 11-year-old Peter's performance on a Full NEPSY-II evaluation. Before interpreting it as a deficit, he or she would want to look at other measures where this component might have adversely affected performance.

In the Attention/Executive domain the clinician needs to look at scaled scores for commission errors, which represent impulsivity or a lack of response inhibition, on AA and RS to see if they occurred at a significant level.

He or she would want to know if a lack of response inhibition was present on the simple, on the complex, or on both tasks of these subtests. He or she could then compare the patterns on AA and RS to those on the different conditions of the Inhibition subtest. The Behavioral Observations for Off-Task Behavior on those two subtests might also reveal impulsive, off-task behavior. Furthermore, the clinician would want to inspect the notes he or she made during administration of other subtests to see if Peter worked impulsively on them. He or she might also find that Peter displayed impulsive responding on Design Fluency, perhaps more so on the Random Array than on the Structured Array, which structures response. Statue is another subtest of inhibition of motor response that can provide information about inhibition in young children.

After reviewing other subtests within the same domain, the clinician will want to review similar results on other subtests that also require response inhibition. In the Language domain, both Comprehension of Instructions and Phonological Processing can elicit impulsivity. Peter may have demonstrated this by not waiting for the whole oral instruction or the whole phonological pattern before he began to respond. This fact would be present in the clinician's notes.

In the Sensorimotor domain, the clinician may have noted impulsive responding on Imitating Hand Positions and Manual Motor Sequences. Peter's SS for Time may be *Above Expected Level*, despite the fact that he made many errors. (Accuracy was *Below Expected Level*.) This suggests that he was impulsive and sacrificed accuracy for speed. Similarly, on DC in the Visuospatial domain, Peter may have executed his designs impulsively. The clinician's observational notes may reveal that he responded impulsively on Arrows, not looking at all eight arrows before making his choices. On Route Finding, the clinician may also have found impulsive responding.

In the Memory and Learning domain, Peter may have just glanced at the photos of children, so the clinician had to remind him to look for the full 5 seconds. If Sentence Repetition was administered, it may have revealed a significant level on the Behavioral Observation for Off-Task Behavior. Finally, Peter's QOs for List Learning may show that he was not able to inhibit Novel Intrusions or Interference Intrusions on List Learning.

Thus, by looking within the same domain and across domains to establish a deficit pattern, the clinician can verify his interpretation of NEPSY results. Poor performance on one subtest in the absence of corroborating evidence is not sufficient to identify a dysfunction or disability (Korkman, Kirk, & Kemp, 1998). Significant findings for verification of interpretation would include:

- Performance level *Below* or *Well Below Expected Level.*
- Subtest results with scaled scores of less than 7.
- If a result is *Borderline,* it needs to show a significant discrepancy with other performances within or across domains.

When two or more significant findings, such as the following, point to the same deficit, then the working hypothesis can be accepted and the interpretation internally verified.

- Two subtest performances
- A subtest performance and a qualitative observation
- A subtest performance and supplemental score

However, if the assessment has been very complete and many test scores have been derived, there is a need for even stronger corroborative evidence. Interpretations must also:

- Be logical and consistent with the research investigating mechanisms of a disorder.
- Have ecological validity that is related to actual events occurring in the child's life.

This means, for example, that findings that seem to indicate some primary deficit that is contrary to accumulated research evidence and current theory need to be very critically examined and not readily accepted as explanations.

EXAMPLE (*A segment of a report only; not meant to encompass all possible findings or conclusions*): Nine-year-old Johnny came for an assessment due to reading disorder. His test profile revealed several scaled scores below 7 and percentile ranks *Below Expected Level.* Findings were, among others, impairments in Phonological Processing, Comprehension of Instructions, Memory for Faces, and Memory for Designs. In spite of the consistent findings of problems with memorizing visual material, the conclusion would not be drawn that the primary deficit was one of visual memory. This is because, at least so far, such an explanation has not been presented by theory formation or research evidence. The findings of poor visual memory may be signs of a comorbid problem or a more generalized learning difference. Regarding the ecological validity, findings need to make sense and correspond to observations and visual memory problems reported at home or in school. The examiner would certainly need to consider the possibility that external factors, momentary lapses of attention, or similar could have influenced performance in the test session.

The clinician would want to find external verification of primary visual memory problems in the literature on reading disorders, in other assessments, and in parental and school concerns about visual memory problems contributing to the child's reading disorder before one could consider the possibility of a primary deficit in visual memory. On the other hand, verifying these concerns with parents and school might reveal problems with attention not reported previously, and the clinician could then discuss with parents the need to assess further for ADHD as a possible co-morbid problem.

Finally, it is essential to remember that typical children frequently show performance discrepancies or even below average performance on assessments for which they compensate well in everyday activities. It is the child who displays a deficit and is also struggling at school or home who needs intervention. (Korkman, Kirk, & Kemp, 2007, p. 133)

Integration of NEPSY Interpretation

The final step before arriving at a diagnosis is to integrate NEPSY-II results with all other information available about the child in order to corroborate the findings with and verify your interpretation of them. Integrating the NEPSY-II results in this way helps you to understand the impact of the primary and secondary deficits on the child's life, and to formulate an effective intervention and/or a treatment plan. This step allows you to obtain as complete a picture of the child's functioning as is possible, including not only the strengths and weaknesses of his or her neuropsychological profile, but also the particular demands in the child's environment. (Korkman, Kirk, & Kemp, 1998, p. 147; Rourke, Fisk, & Strang, 1986).

The clinician will then be ready to formulate interventions for the child based on testing and on the realities of his or her life. The final and decisive test of the assessment and interpretation of results is to design and implement an intervention program and evaluate its efficacy. Many examples of interventions based on test results have been presented thus far; for example, those of Sonia. Additionally, in Chapter 7, illustrative case histories with interventions will be presented.

The NEPSY-II approach, with its specifications of underlying primary deficits, lends itself particularly well to planning interventions, an important part of Luria's approach. However, with 29 subtests in the NEPSY-II , the scope of this book must, by necessity, be restricted to assessment. Advice for intervention will, therefore, be left in the hands of the future. (See Rapid Reference 4.14 for a final summary of the verification process.)

≡ *Rapid Reference 4.14*

Final Summary of the Verification Process

A. The process of verification is dependent on inspecting results of other subtests within a domain for similar deficits, and reviewing performance on subtests across domains that share the same abilities.

- Review all Primary and Process scores computed, and Behavioral Observation cumulative percentages (base rates) or percent of the standardization samples displaying the behavior.
- Trace a diagnostic thread and corroborate the results seen on the test.

B. Poor performance on one subtest in the absence of corroborating evidence is not sufficient to identify a dysfunction or disability. Significant findings for internal verification of interpretation would include:

- Performance level Below or Well Below Expected Level.
- Subtest results with scaled scores of less than 7.
- A significant discrepancy with other performances within or across domains, if a result is Borderline. When two or more significant findings point to same deficit, the working hypothesis can be accepted and the interpretation internally verified through: two subtest performances, a subtest performance, and a qualitative observation-as-subtest performance and supplemental score.

If the assessment has been very complete and many test scores have been derived, there is a need for even stronger corroborative evidence in order to avoid Type I error (a high degree of false positives).

C. After internal verification, the interpretation must still be externally verified with logical and consistent findings in terms of:

- The referral question.
- Other assessment results.
- Developmental, medical, and environmental (school/home) history.
- Ecological validity related to actual events occurring in the child's life.
- Current research in the field related to mechanisms of a disorder.

It is your responsibility as a neuropsychologist to keep abreast of the research in order to be capable of discussing pertinent details of research, resources, and treatment with the child's parents.

In the next chapter, Dr. Stephen Hooper, Ph.D, external reviewer of NEPSY-II for this volume, presents a detailed, objective critique of the instrument. Specific strengths and weaknesses are highlighted for: Test Development, Standardization, Psychometric Properties (i.e., Reliability, Validity), Test Administration and Scoring, and Interpretation.

 TEST YOURSELF

1. **Strengths and weaknesses on NEPSY-II should be interpreted for "behavior-behavior relationships."**
   True or False?

2. **A weakness that appears in a single score is always a valid result.**
   True or False?

3. **The ultimate goal of a NEPSY-II assessment is to assess performance.**
   True or False?

4. **To look at a child's neurocognitive development, the clinician would use the NEPSY-II subtest mean.**
   True or False?

5. **It is recommended that the clinician analyze the subcomponents contributing to a function.**
   True or False?

6. **A good clinician can always specify primary and secondary deficits.**
   True or False?

7. **Being current with the research helps clinicians to be aware of comorbid deficits.**
   True or False?

8. **Phonological awareness studies show that it underlies efficient reading decoding and spelling.**
   True or False?

9. **One of NEPSY-II's most important purposes is to pinpoint focal brain dysfunction very precisely.**
   True or False?

10. **Identifying specific impairments is more subtle than defining strengths and weaknesses behaviorally.**
    True or False?

11. **The NEPSY-II includes quantified _____ that are compared to base rates in the standardization sample.**

12. **List the three goals of interpretation.**

(a) _____

(b) _____

(c) _____

13. **List three aspects of neuropsychological development in children that makes brain localizing hazardous.**

(a) _____

(b) _____

(c) _____

14. **Specific impairments can be interpreted when a minimum of _____ findings are present on NEPSY-II.**

15. **A _____ score integrates two normed scores.**

(Each letter can be used only once for matching.)

16. _____ **Diagnostic behavioral cluster**   (a) multifocal and diffuse

17. _____ **is consistent with Kaplan's**   (b) points to a disorder
    process approach

18. _____ **An individual with this**   (c) a contrast score
    training can interpret using
    neuroanatomic axes without   (d) results at 12th percentile
    implication of focal dysfunction
    or damage.   (e) neuropsychological

19. _____ **Damage or dysfunction**
    in children is usually _____.

20. _____ **Outside normal variation**
ranks.

Answers:

1. True; 2. False; 3. False; 4. True; 5. True; 6. False; 7. True; 8. True; 9. False; 10. True; 11. Behavioral Observations; 12. Describe strengths and weaknesses; Specify and analyze the child's impairments; Integrate and implement findings; 13. Widespread and diffusely distributed neural networks; Functional organization of the young brain may be modified; Genetic etiology and diffuse brain dysfunction; 14. 2; 15. combined; 16. b; 17. c; 18. e; 19. a; 20. D

Five

STRENGTHS AND WEAKNESSES OF NEPSY-II

Stephen R. Hooper

INTRODUCTION

Test development is an incredibly arduous process that requires significant fore-sight and planning, attention to detail, and ultimately, the recognition that there will be strengths and weaknesses regardless of the Herculean effort to produce a quality measurement tool. The NEPSY-II (Korkman, Kirk, & Kemp, 2007) is no different. Although the authors and test developers had the experiences and lessons learned from the original NEPSY (Korkman, Kirk, & Kemp, 1998) upon which to base many of their insights, thoughts, and decisions, the process of modification requires an equal amount of foresight, planning, and attention to detail as new test construction. As such, the NEPSY, and its current version the NEPSY-II, maintain the distinction of being the first well-normed and standard-ized neuropsychological batteries for children and adolescents. This distinction is significant given the need for such a tool in the field of child neuropsychology, but such tests should receive detailed critique with respect to their ultimate utility in both clinical and research endeavors, and with respect to its appropriate applica-tion in the larger evaluation process.

Although it is recognized that specific strengths and weaknesses of a measure will surface once users have had sufficient time to use the tool, this chapter provides an initial detailed examination of the specific strengths and weaknesses that are present in the NEPSY-II as it moves into its real-time phase. Specific strengths and weak-nesses are highlighted for: Test Development, Standardization, Psychometric Prop-erties (i.e., Reliability, Validity), Test Administration and Scoring, and Interpretation.

TEST DEVELOPMENT

For this revision, the test developers took into account several key pieces of information: evidence-based findings in the field of child neuropsychology, child development, and related neuroscience fields; customer feedback; author experiences with the NEPSY; and pilot data in the early phases of revision. In addition, there were four specific goals for the NEPSY-II: (1) to improve domain coverage across a wider age range; (2) to improve clinical and diagnostic utility; (3) to improve psychometric properties; and (4) to improve its ease of administration and, ultimately, its usability. The developers have addressed each of these issues in the *Clinical and Interpretive Manual* and, in general, have been successful in addressing each of these goals. Additionally, the developers are commended for engaging in an iterative process of subtest inclusion and elimination via pilot and tryout phases prior to their national standardization. It was during the tryout phase that the extension of the NEPSY-II into the adolescent years was examined, with the data suggesting additional subtest modifications (e.g., lowering test floors and raising ceilings), although only 45 adolescents were included in the tryout phase. They also followed test construction guidelines espoused by the *Standards for Educational and Psychological Testing* (American Educational Research Association, American Psychological Association, & National Council on Measurement in Education, 1999). (See Rapid Reference 5.1 on the following page.)

Similar to its predecessor, the NEPSY-II continues to be based on the theoretical foundation of Luria (1966), wherein designated brain functions correspond with selected assessment tasks. While other concepts from Lurian Theory, such as functional systems and zones of proximal development, are not clear with respect to their integration into the NEPSY-II, the domains provided are clearly multidimensional and representative of the broad range of neurocognitive functions espoused by most neuropsychological models. Consistent with the NEPSY, the NEPSY-II includes the domains of Attention and Executive Functioning, Language, Memory and Learning, Sensorimotor, and Visuospatial Processing. The NEPSY-II also includes the new domain of Social Perception. Although the manual mentions a range of neuropsychological studies documenting the inclusion of selected dimensions within each domain, there is not a clear model underlying any of the domains that may have strengthened its theoretical underpinnings. Also, it is important to note that the neuropsychological domains are not empirically derived, or even statistically independent. Although this is clearly noted in the manual and, indeed, noted that the intent was not to create empirically derived domains, the user is left to determine how specific subtests relate within and across domains—and, importantly, how these relationships may change over the age range proposed by the NEPSY-II. Based on available research on the NEPSY, including information provided in the original NEPSY Manual, the NEPSY-II does not provide individual domain

≡ *Rapid Reference 5.1*

Strengths and Weaknesses of NEPSY-II Test Development

Strengths	Weaknesses
Theoretically driven domains of function.	Domains are not empirically derived or necessarily independent.
Each domain is multidimensional in its conceptualization.	
No domain scores derived.	Although theoretically derived, the use of specific models of each domain may have contributed to a different battery of task.
New subtests included based on clinical sensitivity and utility, including new tasks measuring social cognition, executive functions, and visual-spatial abilities.	
Developed for use with neurodevelopmental and neurological disorders.	Little available data on preschool tasks.
Expanded age range of 3 through 16 years.	
Proposes eight different referral batteries to facilitate subtest selection, which replaces standard administration order.	
Pilot and tryout phases prior to national standardization.	
Followed APA guidelines for test construction.	

or composite scores. Although a variety of different types of scores can be generated from the NEPSY-II, the use of subtests to guide interpretation of results is emphasized.

Further, the NEPSY-II not only modified and expanded subtests within the domains to be more representative of different dimensions of a neurocognitive domain, they extended the number of domains to include subtests measuring social cognition (i.e., Affect Recognition, Theory of Mind). This latter addition is innovative with respect to its inclusion in such assessment batteries, will assess an important brain function to a certain degree, be applicable to certain clinical groups (e.g., Autism Spectrum Disorders), and provide an additional avenue for assessment from the neuroscience literature that has not been routinely available to most clinicians. The addition of new subtests reflecting various aspects of executive functioning (e.g., Animal Sorting, Clocks, Inhibition); language (e.g., Word Generation); memory (e.g., Memory for Designs); and visual-spatial abilities (e.g., Geometric Puzzles, Picture Puzzles) also is noteworthy in the NEPSY-II. The extension of tasks into the middle adolescent years (i.e., up to age 16.9 years) required the addition of new items to a number of subtests (e.g., Arrows, Design Copying), but clearly will serve its users well with respect to having options for neuropsychological testing in this developmental period.

Similar to its early development, as well as the NEPSY, the NEPSY-II utilized available data to showcase its utility with both neurological and neurodevelopmental disorders. The utility with neurological disorders continues the long-standing standard use of such tests and procedures with frank neurological conditions, but the inclusion of neurodevelopmental disorders—conditions that presume neurological involvement—clearly expand the overall application of this test to a wide variety of potential clients. To facilitate this process, the manual proposes eight different referral batteries from which to facilitate subtest selection, and they designed the standardization in such a fashion as to reinforce this process; thus, replacing the need for a standard administration order.

Finally, the NEPSY and the NEPSY-II represent significant efforts to extend neuropsychological testing into the preschool years. Quite frankly, outside of selected intellectual batteries and single test approaches, there are few batteries that have attempted to provide neuropsychological measurement for such a young population. This should facilitate increased precision with respect to description of neurocognitive functions for a wide variety of children with both neurological and neurodevelopmental disorders and, subsequently, prescription of specific treatment strategies and interventions. It is important to note, however, that few empirical data were provided with respect to the utility of the preschool battery for the NEPSY—either from the publisher or from independent investigators—and the same seems to be true with respect to the release of the NEPSY-II. The field will need to determine the ultimate clinical utility of the preschool version of this test.

STANDARDIZATION

With few exceptions, the standardization of the NEPSY-II was well conceived and nicely executed. The normative sample was extracted from the most recently available census data, with excellent concurrence with the available census

≡ Rapid Reference 5.2

Strengths and Weaknesses of NEPSY-II Standardization

Strengths	Weaknesses
Normative sample extracted from most recent census data; has excellent match with 2003 census figures, particularly for minority representation and parent education.	Several subtests are not renormed and continue to employ 1998 norms (e.g., Design Fluency, Imitative Hand Positions, Route Finding).
Stratified by age, race, parent education, and geographic region; sample evenly divided between gender.	The use of 50 children per age band is relatively weak, especially for preschool years.
Procedures for quality assurance of examiners in standardization administration.	Little empirical data provided for use of six-month intervals in the age-splitting of the normative data—was this in line with the empirical data showing developmental changes?
Examined flexibility systematically via four different administration orders.	
Inclusion of Contrast Scores that are based on the normative data and not regression or simple discrepancy methods.	

figures. The normative sample was well-matched on race, parent education, and geographic region of the country, with the minority representation being particularly noteworthy across nearly all of the stratification cells. The NEPSY-II also was stratified by chronological age and evenly divided by gender. (See Rapid Reference 5.2.)

The NEPSY-II was standardized on 1,200 children across the ages of 3 through 16 years. Of the 29 possible subtests included in the standardization, 17 were administered to children ages 3 to 4 years; children 5 to 6 years of age were administered 22 subtests and 2 delay tasks; children ages 6 to 12 years were given 23 subtests and 2 delay tasks; and the adolescent children, ages 13 to 16 years, received 24 subtests and 3 delay tasks. Final adjustments to the final composition of subtests were made following the standardization process (e.g., deletion of several subtests due to low clinical sensitivity and/or administration challenges), and scoring nuances were determined. Of note with respect to the scoring nuances, the NEPSY-II provides new scores for selected subtests, Contrast Scores, which are a quantification of the difference between one measure and a comparison measure. In addition to being new to the NEPSY-II when compared to the 1998 NEPSY, the development of these scores utilized a normed contrast/comparison variable wherein normative data on the specific variable are produced by controlling for the ability of the children on the control variable. As such, this score does not assume equal base rates across different ages and ability levels, and the variances can be different across the range of the control variable.

One modification asserted for the NEPSY-II was to provide increased flexibility in the order of subtest administration. Although this was present in the 1998 version of the NEPSY, it was not clear how different orders of subtest administration would affect scores in a larger test profile. For the NEPSY-II, the test developers examined the flexibility systematically via four different administration orders during the standardization process. By not showing any order effects, they were successful in being able to document that the subtests in the NEPSY-II could be administered in a variety of orders without affecting results. This should facilitate subtest administration, particularly in difficult-to-test samples of children (e.g., child psychiatric disorders, ADHD-Hyperactive Type), and this benefit will extend into both the clinical and research realms. While it is recognized that all possible test orders could not be assessed given the possible number of permutations and combinations, this is one of the first times that a test developer has examined the evidence for order effects to such an extent, and it was critical to the NEPSY-II given the expressed option of a flexible subtest administration order.

Throughout the standardization process, the developers of the NEPSY-II made significant efforts in addressing the quality of the data being obtained. Specifically, they ensured that the examiners had testing experience with children, with the majority of the examiners having professional credentials to conduct psychological testing. Examiners were then trained using a videotape of NEPSY-II administration and scoring procedures, and needed to pass a quiz with 90% accuracy on these procedures. Ongoing follow-up also was provided via monthly Internet meetings. Prior to engaging in the standardization phase, examiners were required to provide a practice case, with direct feedback being provided by the test publisher within 48 hours of submission. Once standardization testing ensued, cases were reviewed within 72 hours of receipt in the event of errors in administration and/or scoring, and a periodic newsletter was provided to all examiners indicating where commonly occurring errors appeared on the protocols. Once data were obtained, information was double-entered into the database, and all data were checked routinely for ranges, extreme values, and derivation of the starting and stopping points, scores were determined using empirically-based findings.

Despite the aforementioned strengths, the NEPSY-II does have several potential weaknesses. As can be seen in Rapid Reference 5.2, as a strategy to facilitate obtaining the normative data from the lengthy standardization battery, a number of subtests were not included. These subtests were not included in an effort to shorten the time required for a child to complete the standardization battery, but also because the development team determined that tasks required no modifications and likely would show little change in normative values. Consequently, these subtests (i.e., Design Fluency, Oromotor Sequences, Repetition of Nonsense Words, Manual Motor Sequences, Route Finding, Imitative Hand Positions) were not included in the standardization version and retained the normative scores from the 1998 version of the NEPSY. Despite these efforts, there are no data provided, in either the pilot or tryout phases of the NEPSY-II, to suggest that the 1998 version of these tasks is equivalent to the 2007 version. This creates a potential problem with interpretation and, in many respects, hinders one of the major benefits of a battery of tasks (i.e., all tasks normed on the sample population). If these versions are not equivalent in their normative data, then unknown error variance will be created when these subtests are compared to the newly normed subtests in a profile of scores. How this may affect interpretation is not known.

Second, the use of 50 children per age band is relatively weak, especially for the preschool years where there is significantly more potential error variance in test data given the relatively lower reliability of test scores in a younger population. Further, the test developers provide little empirical data to support the use of six-month intervals in their age-splitting of the normative data. It is unclear if this was in line with their empirical data showing developmental changes on tasks over time.

PSYCHOMETRIC PROPERTIES

Reliability

The area of reliability is critical in test construction; not only does it determine the test's capabilities of replicating results, but it also sets the upper limit on validity (Bracken, 1992). A summary of the strengths and weaknesses for the reliability of the NEPSY-II is presented in Rapid Reference 5.3 on the following page.

≡ *Rapid Reference 5.3*

Strengths and Weaknesses of NEPSY-II Reliability

Strengths	Weaknesses
Most subtests were adequate to high for internal consistency estimates.	Lowest reliability coefficients were achieved on Response Set Total Correct, Inhibition Total Errors, Memory for Designs Spatial, Total Score, and Delay Total.
Good inter-rater reliability for Clocks, Design Copying, Memory for Names, Theory of Mind, Word Generation, Visual Memory Delayed, and Visual Motor Precision, ranging from .93 to .99.	
	Practice effects most noted on Memory for Designs, Memory for Faces, and Inhibition.
Test-retest reliability across seven age groups revealed little change in scores, with test intervals ranging from 12 to 51 days ($M = 21$ days).	Less focus on improved ceilings, which may place a limit on interpreting neurocognitive strengths; at present, from ages 3 to 5.9, there are 0–5 subtests; from ages 6.0 to 9.9 there are 3–8 subtests; and from 10.0 to 16.9 there are 11–17 subtests.
Focused on improving the test floors, with nearly all subtests across age bands having at least a 2 standard deviation limit; more tasks at the 3.0 to 4.5 ages (5–13) do not reach this criterion, while 0–1 from ages 9.0 to 16.9.	
Standard error of measure ranged from .85 to 2.18 across subtests and ages.	
Reliability of subtests was relatively stable for both typical and impaired samples.	

For the NEPSY-II primary and process scaled scores, most subtests have adequate to high internal consistency estimates, and the standard error of measure for all of the subtests ranged from 0.85 to 2.18 across all of the age ranges. Temporal stability of the NEPSY-II subtests across seven age groups (i.e., ages 3 to 4, 5 to 6, 7 to 8, 8 to 9, 9 to 10, 11 to 12, 13 to 16), revealed little change in scores over an average of a three-week period (range 12 to 51 days), suggesting that there was little practice effect across a relatively short time frame. This is critical in a test where alternative form reliability is not available, and provides an evidence-based foundation to use many of the subtests in various types of intervention studies. The largest score differences were noted on the Memory for Designs, Memory for Faces, and Inhibition subtests. In general, the highest reliability coefficients were achieved for the subtests: Comprehension of Instructions, Design Copying, Fingertip Tapping, Imitating Hand Positions, List Memory, Memory for Names, Phonological Processing, Picture Puzzles, and Sentence Repetition. The lowest reliability coefficients were noted for the subtest variables: Response Set Total Correct, Inhibition Total Errors, Memory for Designs Spatial and Total Scores, and Memory for Designs Delayed Total Score. Given the potential application of the NEPSY-II, it also is important to note that the reliability of the subtests was relatively stable for both typical and impaired samples.

The NEPSY-II also examined inter-rater agreement across all cases ascertained for standardization and clinical validity studies by employing two independent scores. For the more objective types of subtests (e.g., Comprehension of Instructions), rates were quite high, ranging from .98 to .99. This also speaks to the integrity of the data included in the standardization phase. Scoring for several of the subtests require clinical judgment (e.g., Clocks, Design Copying) or implementation of specific scoring rules (e.g., Memory for Names, Word Generation), thus necessitating the generation of inter-rater reliability estimates. For these subtests, the inter-rater agreement ranged from .93 (Word Generation) to .99 (Memory for Names, Theory of Mind). These findings suggest that these specific subtests will require more scoring attention from trainers and administrators of the NEPSY-II, but that a high degree of scoring reliability can be achieved on these subtests.

Finally, although not directly related to reliability, the issue of tests' floors and ceilings can have a direct effect on reliability by potentially restricting the range of scores available. For the NEPSY-II, the test developers focused significant resources on this issue, with targeted resources being devoted to improving the test floors. This is absolutely critical for a test that is designed to uncover neurocognitive weaknesses across different presenting problems and disorders. In this regard, nearly all of the NEPSY-II subtests across the age bands have at least a two standard deviation limit. There is a difference across the age range, however, with all or nearly all of the subtests having at least this floor from ages 9.0 to 16.9, but 5 to 13 of these subtests not reaching this floor for ages 5 to 13 years. In general, the number of subtests having at least a two standard deviation floor increases with age. Conversely, the test developers were not as focused on having at least a two standard deviation ceiling on the subtests. Although this is consistent with the notion of assessment via the NEPSY-II, this is unfortunate, as it may place a limit on determining the presence of neurocognitive strengths; consequently, the concept of utilizing neurocognitive strengths to facilitate intervention may be limited. This notion is apparent in the NEPSY-II normative data, as from ages 3.0 to 5.9 few subtests meet this criterion (0 to 5 subtests); from ages 6.0 to 9.9 only 3 to 8 subtests meet this criterion, and from ages 10.0 to 16.9 only 11 to 17 subtests meet this criterion.

Validity

As noted in the test manual, "contemporary definitions of validity describe lines of evidence of validity as opposed to different types of validity" (p. 79). Evidence lines for validity may be the most important aspect of a test such as the NEPSY-II, where interpretation issues are critical to the ultimate clinical utility of the test (American Educational Research Association et al., 1999). According to the *Standards for Educational and Psychological Testing* (1999), key lines of validity include content, construct, and criterion-related. Strengths and weaknesses of the NEPSY-II for these lines of validity are presented in Rapid Reference 5.4.

Content validity (i.e., do the subtests adequately sample the targeted constructs of interest?) for the NEPSY-II had the benefit of the 1998 NEPSY upon which to

⟰ *Rapid Reference 5.4*

Strengths and Weaknesses of NEPSY-II Validity

Strengths	Weaknesses
Content, concurrent, and construct validity issues all adequately addressed.	Although the NEPSY-II is driven by a subtest model, users are still left with the issue of how tests are clustered, especially at different developmental epochs.
Subtests have strong theoretical (Lurian) and evidence-based foundations.	
Subtest intercorrelations fit a multitrait-multimethod model.	No subtest specificity estimates were provided to reinforce interpretation strength of the NEPSY-II.
	No relationships with adaptive behavior as measured by the ABAS-II.

Strengths	Weaknesses
Correlations with intellectual batteries (WISC-IV, DAS) and other task cognitive batteries (NEPSY) are moderate to strong.	Research criteria not employed for many of the special group studies, leaving them too heterogeneous and likely not generalizable to the larger contemporary research corpus.
Correlations with achievement batteries (e.g., WIAT-II) are moderate to strong.	
Correlations with specific neurocognitive batteries (e.g., DKEFS, CMS, BBCS) are moderate to strong.	The special groups were not compared to show differential profiles.
Correlations with Devereux Scales of Mental Disorder show specific relationships with Autism (Comprehension of Instructions) and Conduct Disorder (Affect Recognition).	
Correlations with ADHD Scale show relationships between Inhibition Subtest and Focus Cluster.	
Employed 10 special group studies (e.g., ADHD, RD, MD, TBI, ASD, etc.).	

base its modifications. The 1998 NEPSY was based on Lurian neuropsychological theory, but capitalized on recent advances in the field of child neuropsychology. For the NEPSY-II, this theoretical foundation remained, but the research that utilized the 1998 version of the NEPSY was reviewed as to its relevance for test revision and specific modifications. The pilot and tryout phases of test development further facilitated the examination of specific items within subtests, as well as the subtests proper, with a particular focus on content gaps, and following the standardization phase additional analysis was conducted to determine the adequacy of content at the specific item level, content biases, and associated psychometric properties. This process also extended into examination of the child's responses such that traditional and atypical responses were considered with respect to whether the item or subtest was capturing the intended information. Taken together, these procedures produced a battery of tasks that adequately sample the targeted constructs of interest.

Construct validity pertains to the internal structure of a test, particularly with respect to the interrelationship of subtests or components. This is important, given the theoretical neurocognitive domains espoused by the NEPSY-II, as it will drive how the components of the test are viewed for interpretation. The NEPSY-II provides an interesting challenge for construct validity in that while there appears to be an overarching set of neuropsychological domains (e.g., Language, Visuospatial Processing, Social Perception), the test is not designed to provide scores for these domains. As such, and in accordance with the guidance in the *Clinical and Interpretive Manual*, the administration and interpretation of the NEPSY-II should be guided by the subtests. The 1998 version of the NEPSY did not present any factor analysis data, but two subsequent reports did address this issue via exploratory (Stinnett, Oehler-Stinnett, Fuqua, & Palmer, 2002) and confirmatory factor analytic methods (Mosconi, Nelson, & Hooper, 2008). Consistent with this philosophy, the NEPSY-II continues to focus on the subtests and their interrelationships. For the NEPSY-II, the test developers hypothesized that there would be a subtest intercorrelation pattern wherein the subtests within a domain would correlate more highly than subtests across domains. This multitrait-multimethod model for construct validity was supported in both the normative and clinical samples, with the correlations within many of the domains being higher in the clinical samples. Of note, subtests within the Language domain produced the highest intercorrelations, and many of these subtests also were more highly correlated with verbally based subtests in the other neurocognitive domains. The test developers use this pattern of correlations as support for the structure of the NEPSY-II.

Although the NEPSY-II is driven by a subtest model, with the authors and test developers arguing that this is the best approach for interpreting the data, users are still left to wonder about how these subtests cluster within and across domains, and across developmental epochs. As noted earlier, there were at least two efforts to examine the factor structure of the 1998 version of the NEPSY (Mosconi et al., 2008; Stinnett et al., 2002), with mixed support being provided. Stinnett and colleagues (2002) conducted an exploratory principle axis factor analysis using the correlation matrix for the 5- to 12-year-old children from the standardization sample ($n = 800$) and found that it yielded a 1-factor solution—a language/comprehension factor—and accounted for only 24.9% of the variance. Results also indicated that numerous subtests cross-loaded on multiple factors in two-, three-, and four-factor solutions, and that the same 11–12 subtests loaded on the first factor for each of these models. These findings suggested that the NEPSY five-domain model was not supported, but Stinnett and colleagues (2002) suggested that confirmatory factor analysis would provide more convincing support of the test's structural validity.

In that regard, Mosconi and colleagues (2008), using the standardization sample from the 1998 version of the NEPSY, conducted a confirmatory factor analysis for ages 5 though 12, as well as for the younger (5 to 8 years, $n = 400$) and older (9 to 12 years, $n = 400$) age bands. This latter question was important in the exploration of possible differences in test structure at different developmental epochs. Using four standard fit indices, results indicated that a five-factor model was less than adequate for the entire sample, and produced negative error variance for the younger and older age groups, making any solutions for the two subgroups statistically inadmissible. A four-factor model without the Executive Function/Attention Domain subtests produced satisfactory fit statistics for the entire sample and the younger group, but did not fit the data as well for the older group. In contrast to Stinnett and colleagues' (2002) findings, a one-factor model did not fit well for the full sample. These results indicated that the structure of the 1998 NEPSY was not invariant across development, with the four-factor model best fitting the data for the younger age group and for the entire school-age sample.

It is unfortunate that these additional analyses were not explored, or at least presented in the *NEPSY-II Clinical and Interpretive Manual*, as this structure would support data reduction strategies for research and would provide some sense of linkage to the theoretical model that underlies the NEPSY-II. In support of the test developers' contentions, however, it is likely that different factor structures would be present across different clinical groups, much as is seen in the pattern of intercorrelations of subtests between clinical samples and the normative sample; this question will require ongoing examination.

Finally, with respect to construct validity, there are no data provided with respect to subtest specificity estimates. Subtest specificity estimates provide an index for what proportion of a subtest's variance is reliable and unique to the subtest. For any assessment tool where subtest interpretation is possible, subtests with low specificity (i.e., $< .25$, and greater than the proportion of error variance; McGrew & Murphy, 1995) should not be interpreted as measuring a specific function. Given the strong emphasis on utilization and interpretation of the NEPSY-II at the subtest level, it would seem that empirical data would have been provided with respect to the strength of specific subtests and its assessment of unique variance, and the specificity estimates would have been examined across each age block encompassed by the NEPSY-II. This would have facilitated interpretation and utilization of the subtests in the way they were intended, but with empirical evidence as to their ability to measure a specific function.

Criterion-related validity was determined primarily by using concurrent validity studies (i.e., the relationship of the NEPSY-II with other tests measuring similar constructs). The NEPSY-II was concurrently administered with a wide range of measures, including intellectual batteries (e.g., Wechsler Intelligence Scale for Children—Fourth Edition; WISC-IV); achievement batteries (e.g., Wechsler Individual Achievement Test—Second Edition; WIAT-II); specific neuropsychological measures (e.g., Delis-Kaplan Executive Function System; DKEFS); behavior (e.g., Devereux Scales of Mental Disorders); and adaptive behaviors (e.g., Adaptive Behavior Assessment System-II). The concurrent administration of the NEPSY-II and other tasks included a sufficient number of participants to gain relatively stable validity coefficient.

As can be seen in Rapid Reference 5.4, the NEPSY-II correlated in a moderate to strong fashion with the intellectual and achievement batteries—the latter being particularly important with respect to its importance for use with children being referred for a variety of learning problems. When specific neurocognitive batteries were examined, the NEPSY-II subtests that were most similar to the items being tapped by the battery generally aligned in a moderate to strong manner.

For example, the NEPSY-II Memory and Learning subtests correlated most highly with selected subtests from the Children's Memory Scale; NEPSY-II Attention and Executive Function subtests correlated most highly with selected subtests from the DKEFS; and NEPSY-II Language subtests correlated most highly with the Bracken Basic Concept Scale—Third Edition Receptive and Expressive scales. The NEPSY-II subtests did not correlate with the Children's Communication Checklist. Given the potential usage of the NEPSY-II for children with emotional/behavioral disturbance and intellectual disabilities, correlations with several behavioral measures (e.g., Devereux Scales of Mental Disorders, Brown Attention-Deficit Disorders Scale, Adaptive Behavior Assessment System-II) also were examined. For the Devereux, the NEPSY-II subtests of Comprehension of Instructions and Affect Recognition showed moderate negative correlations with Autism and Conduct Disorder, respectively. The NEPSY-II Affect Recognition also correlated with the Devereux Externalizing Composite score. For the Brown Attention-Deficit Scale, the Focus Cluster moderately and negatively correlated with the NEPSY-II Inhibition-Switching Combined scaled score, reflecting declining inhibitory control with increasing ADHD symptoms. None of the NEPSY-II subtests correlated significantly with the Adaptive Behavior Assessment System, perhaps an indication of its lack of association to ecological, day-to-day behaviors. These findings support a convergent validity line of evidence for the NEPSY-II; however, it is important to note that these patterns of correlation may change depending on the age of the child, the presenting clinical condition, and the method of assessment (e.g., parent rater, clinician ratings, etc.), and this will require additional examination as the NEPSY-II begins to be employed in a variety of clinical settings.

The special group studies conducted with the NEPSY-II are noteworthy in that the test developers employed 10 different clinical conditions (i.e., Reading Disability, Math Disability, Traumatic Brain Injury, Autism Spectrum Disorder, Attention-Deficit Hyperactivity Disorder, Language Disorders, Intellectual Disability, Asperger's Disorder, Hearing Impairment, Emotional Disturbance). Comparison groups were derived from the normative sample and matched on chronological age, gender, race, and parent education levels. These studies have promised to determine the differential sensitivity of the NEPSY-II to the neuropsychological profiles that can be manifested by specific disorders.

Findings from these special group studies generally support the clinical utility of the NEPSY-II in the assessment of children referred for different conditions and disorders. More specifically, the special groups typically differed from the typical groups on variables where they would be expected to deviate, as well as in a wide range of other variables. For example, the special group study using children with ADHD showed significant differences on NEPSY-II subtests assessing attention and executive functions, verbal memory, and sensorimotor abilities. Similarly, children with language disorders showed significant differences on NEPSY-II subtests measuring language-related functions, and children with intellectual disabilities and autism spectrum disorders performed more poorly than the typical group on nearly all of the NEPSY-II subtests. The separate examination of the newly added Theory of Mind Subtest for the Autism Spectrum Disorders versus Controls and for the Asperger's Disorder versus Controls also provided support for the use of this subtest with these types of clinical referrals.

While the test developers should be commended on the inclusion of the various clinical disorders and conditions, and the findings generally support the separation of these groups from the typical group, there are several concerns with respect to these clinical studies that require mention. First, many of the studies employed small sample sizes, with group sizes ranging from 10 (Traumatic Brain Injury) to 55 (ADHD). Second, although inclusion and exclusion criteria for participation in these studies are provided in Appendix F of the

Clinical and Interpretive Manual, it does not appear that strict research criteria were employed for many of the special group studies, such as use of state Department of Education criteria and use of the Diagnostic and Statistical Manual-IV-TR (American Psychiatric Association, 2000) without acknowledgement of any reliability checks. This type of ascertainment can contribute to the potential for significant heterogeneity in the samples, and is magnified by the small sample size. Third, the comorbidity apparent in many of these clinical samples is not mentioned or examined in the data presentations, thus leading to additional variables that could contribute to group differences. Finally, it is unclear why the different clinical groups were not compared in some fashion. While the differences from typical performance are important to document, this clinical differentiation, if present, might have provided more useful information with respect to its clinical utility and uncovering neuropsychological profiles for specific clinical populations.

ADMINISTRATION AND SCORING

For the NEPSY-II, there is a separate *Administration Manual* that provides detailed, manualized procedures for administration and scoring of each subtest. The domain, description, materials, starting points, discontinue rule, timing, recording, general guidelines, and specific administration and scoring details are provided for each subtest. These details are particularly important for several subtests, such as Clocks, Design Copying, Visuomotor Precision, and Word Generation, where increased attention to detail in administration and scoring is required. In fact, the *Administration Manual* provides specific appendices for scoring procedures for the Clocks Subtest (Appendix A) and Design Copying Subtest (Appendix B), for which inter-rater reliability probably should be obtained for any new examiner. Additional positive administration features and potential improvements over the 1998 NEPSY include: (a) the alphabetical arrangement of the subtests, which should facilitate administration efficiency; (b) the inclusion of eight different assessment batteries suggested by the referral question, which should assist new examiners in their use of the NEPSY-II; and (c) an increased age range for the NEPSY-II, which extends its clinical use into the adolescent years. As such, the manual is clear and user friendly, and should assist in learning the procedures in a standardized fashion for both clinical and research settings.

The materials provided in the NEPSY-II kit are easy to use, colorful, and attractive, and appear to be relatively durable. Separate test forms are provided for the preschool battery (ages 3 to 4) and the school-age battery (ages 5 to 18). The

NEPSY-II test forms are clear, providing additional guidance to the examiner without the need for referring to the manual and include key information such as materials needed, starting and stopping points, time limits, and specific administration rules (e.g., reversal rules). Space is provided on the cover sheet for profile presentations of the subtests by domain so that normative findings can be viewed immediately, and on the second page for the specific behavioral observations. Other specific scores (e.g., Contrast scores) are provided space associated with their specific subtest.

The innovative addition of teaching items for selected subtests, and the modifications to the Auditory Attention and Response Set Subtest also are noteworthy in that they should improve the chances of obtaining a reliable administration on these tasks. With respect to the Auditory Attention and Response Set Subtest, the administration "gymnastics" that were needed to administer this subtest were significant and likely contributed, in part, to its low correlation to other subtests in the 1998 version of the NEPSY. For the NEPSY-II, specific changes included: (a) when each of the components of this task are administered (i.e., ages 5 to 6 years are no longer given the Response Set component); (b) the method of response has been changed from selecting colored foam squares to a simple pointing response to a stimulus book within 2 seconds of the target word presentation; (c) elimination of partial credit for a slower response. These changes purportedly have minimized the effects of motor speed and finger dexterity in this attention task.

Scoring procedures for the NEPSY-II subtests are clearly presented in the *Administration Manual*. While most of these can be calculated by hand, the efficiency of their use likely will increase with use of the NEPSY-II computer scoring program. To obtain the various scores on the NEPSY-II, however, the *Clinical and Interpretive Manual* also will be needed as this is where the normative tables are located. If the computer scoring program is utilized, it will be important for the examiner to consult the *Clinical and Interpretive Manual* to determine how to use these scores, especially when employing the various contrast scores and behavioral observations that are calculated. The deletion of the NEPSY domain scores should facilitate the scoring process, but it will require additional knowledge with respect to how various subtests interrelate for a selected clinical population of interest. Perhaps the only concern at this time for the administration and scoring of the NEPSY-II will be to determine the clinical utility of the various combined scores and contrast scores, as limited evidence was provided for their use. See Rapid Reference 5.5 on the following page for a summary of strengths and weaknesses of administration and scoring of the NEPSY-II.

≋ *Rapid Reference 5.5*

Strengths and Weaknesses of NEPSY-II Administration and Scoring

Strengths	Weaknesses
Detailed *Administration Manual* is clear and user friendly.	Limited evidence provided for combined scores, and they may require additional validity, especially from developmental perspective.
Subtests are arranged in alphabetical order and should facilitate ease of administration.	
Reduced administrative "gymnastics" of Auditory Attention Response Set Subtests.	
Test forms are clearly marked with age-specific starting and stopping points to reduce frustration and testing time.	
Eight different assessment batteries suggested by referral question.	
Teaching items are present for selected subtests.	
Provides for a wide range of scores: primary, process, contrast, and behavioral observations; combined scores and contrast scores are new.	
Contrast scores based on methods that take into account a child's functioning on a control variable.	
Behavioral observations probably represent some of the best data for clinical behaviors; unheralded advance that addresses base rates for certain functions (e.g., mirroring).	
Deletion of domain scores consistent with psychometric properties.	

INTERPRETATION

Just like other neuropsychological assessment approaches, the interpretation of the NEPSY-II requires a certain amount of examiner knowledge with respect to brain functioning and, at a minimum, a knowledge base in the underlying neurocognitive functions of selected conditions. So, while this battery is available to all psychological examiners, and its administration relatively straightforward, its interpretation does require additional knowledge that will facilitate its use and, ultimately, its clinical utility across settings and patient populations. This will be especially pertinent to the nonneuropsychologist.

The NEPSY-II, like the 1998 version, provides a selection of tasks that have empirical or theoretical linkages to various clinical problems. This linkage is critical for identification of underlying neurocognitive contributors to specific problems not only from a diagnostic perspective, but from an intervention perspective as well. The interpretation is facilitated by a good normative base, a variety of scores—including base rates for a number of pathognomonic signs, and a nice array of subtests that will provide data relevant to level of function, pattern of function, pathognomonic signs and, to some extent, left-right differences. This latter level of inference, left-right differences, probably represents a weakness in the overall battery, as subtests providing these types of information are limited and likely better obtained by complementary measures.

The *Clinical and Interpretive Manual* also provides a wide range of specific hypotheses by neuropsychological domain, specific steps for moving through the interpretive process—including a verification step (i.e., a problem or impairment is present when there are similar findings on two or more primary subtest scores), and detailed suggestions for secondary factors that could influence a performance. These sections are noteworthy, even for the trained neuropsychologist, but especially for the examiner new to neuropsychological testing.

Specific strengths and weaknesses for the interpretation of the NEPSY-II are listed in Rapid Reference 5.6.

≡ *Rapid Reference 5.6*

Strengths and Weaknesses of NEPSY-II Interpretation

Strengths	Weaknesses
Facilitates selection of tasks that have empirical or theoretical linkages to referral concerns.	Depends on knowledge base of examiner to select tasks, so test continues to require a high degree of neuropsychological sophistication—especially from the nonneuropsychologist.
Provides steps for interpretation, including a verification step.	

(continued)

(continued)

Strengths	Weaknesses
Provides a variety of scores, including base rates.	Lateralizing signs may be difficult to extract and may require additional measures.
Provides rich hypotheses by domain.	
Each section has purpose, subtest use, and primary and secondary factors influencing performances.	
Provides level, pattern, pathognomonic signs, and some left-right differences.	

OVERVIEW OF STRENGTHS AND WEAKNESSES

The NEPSY-II is the second iteration of the American version of the NEPSY. The 1998 version of the NEPSY likely represented one of the first well-normed, well-standardized neuropsychological batteries that was available to child neuropsychologists and other child practitioners, and its revision continues in the same tradition. This revision was able to capitalize on the available information from the 1998 NEPSY, and provide a nicely packaged update to both clinicians and researchers alike. From an initial review of the strengths and weaknesses apparent in the NEPSY-II, suffice it to say that the test authors and test developers have done an exceptional job in producing a quality tool.

The NEPSY-II maintains a wealth of strengths that have been described in this chapter but, like most assessment tools, also presents some weaknesses of which users should be aware. Specific weaknesses include the limited availability of data on the preschool tasks and their application; the use of 1998 normative data for certain subtests; the relatively low ceilings on many of the subtests, particularly as children get older; the heterogeneity of their clinical groups and the likely presence of comorbid conditions; the lack of subtest specificity estimates, especially given the subtest approach espoused; and the relative lack of coverage to examine left-right differences in the sensorimotor domain, which will be critical for determining the presence of lateralizing signs. While none of these specific weaknesses or the few others that were mentioned in this chapter are significant enough to offset the wide array of strengths of this assessment tool, recognizing these limitations should facilitate intelligent use of this NEPSY-II in both clinical and research settings.

Of importance here is that the NEPSY-II manuals certainly provide the information from which to evaluate the NEPSY-II. So, as in all tests, there are relative strengths and weaknesses, but this test can be evaluated from data presented in the manual, and additional evaluative aspects of this test will appear with its usage over the next decade. Of course, while this initial review is positive, it remains for the field to determine its ultimate use and utility across different venues.

🐾 TEST YOURSELF 🐾

Fill in the blanks.

1. Chapter 5 highlights strengths and weakness for: Test Development, Standardization, _____ _____ , Test Administration and Scoring, and _____ .

2. Name four specific goals for the Revision of NEPSY when developing NEPSY-II:

   (a) _____

   (b) _____

   (c) _____

   (d) _____

3. The NEPSY-II developers are commended for engaging in an iterative process of subtest inclusion and elimination via _____ and _____ phases prior to their national standardization.

4. A strength for NEPSY-II Test Development, according to Hooper, was the following of construction test guidelines espoused by the

   _____ .

5. Name three weaknesses of NEPSY-II Reliability:

   (a) _____

   (b) _____

   (c) _____

6. Name three strengths of NEPSY-II Reliability:

   (a) _____

   (b) _____

   (c) _____

7. Strengths and weaknesses of NEPSY-II Standardization, according to Hooper, show that the normative sample is an excellent match with 2003 census figures in the United States, particularly for _____ representation and _____ parent education.

8. The standardization sample for NEPSY-II was stratified by age, race, parent education, and _____ _____, with a sample evenly divided between _____.

9. The summary of Strengths and Weaknesses of NEPSY-II Validity shows that the following types of validity were adequately addressed: (a) _____, (b) _____, (c) _____.

10. On NEPSY-II, the development of Contrast scores utilized a normed contrast/comparison variable wherein normative data on the specific variable are produced by controlling for the ability of the children on the _____ variable. As such, this score does not assume equal _____ _____ across different ages and ability levels, and the _____ can be different across the range of the control variable.

11. The ability to infer left-right differences probably represents a strength in the full battery.

    True or False?

12. Of 29 possible subtests in the standardization, 17 were administered at ages 3–4.

    True or False?

13. The *NEPSY-II Clinical and Interpretation Manual* provides steps for interpretation, including a verification step.

    True or False?

14. Correlations with specific neurocognitive batteries (e.g., DKEFS, CMS, BBCS) are weak to moderate.

    True or False?

15. No subtest specificity estimates were provided to reinforce interpretation strength of the NEPSY-II.

    True or False?

16. Correlations with Devereux Scales of Mental Disorder show specific relationships with Autism (Comprehension of Instructions) and Conduct Disorder (Affect Recognition).

    True or False?

17. Hooper sees a strength in the fact that no domain scores are derived for NEPSY-II.

    True or False?

18. Several subtests are not renormed and continue to employ 1998 norms.

    True or False?

19. Subtests are arranged in order of administration in the *Administration Manual*.

    True or False?

20. **The use of 50 children for each six-month age band between 3.0–4.11 (making 100 children for age 3 and 100 for age 4) is a relative weakness, especially for preschool years, according to Hooper.**

True or False?

Answers:

1. Psychometric Properties, Interpretation; 2. (a) to improve domain coverage across a wider age range; (b) improve clinical and diagnostic utility; (c) to improve psychometric properties; and (d) to improve its ease of administration and, ultimately, its usability; 3. pilot, tryout; 4. *Standards for Educational and Psychological Testing* or APA guidelines; 5. and 6. See Rapid Reference 5.3; 7. minority, education; 8. geographic region, gender; 9. content, concurrent, and construct validity; 10. control; base rates, variances; 11. False; 12. True; 13. True; 14. False; 15. False; 16. True; 17. True; 18. True; 19. False; 20. True

Six

CLINICAL APPLICATIONS OF THE NEPSY-II

APPLICATIONS OF NEPSY-II DERIVED FROM STUDIES OF DISORDERS

Children with virtually all types of developmental problems may be assessed with NEPSY-II. Because the brain organizes all behavior, an evaluation that assesses the various brain processes underlying complex behavior is, in principle, applicable to all situations where disordered development is of concern. The problem often lies in time constraints: how can the clinician, with a restricted amount of time, direct his or her efforts in the most efficient way and choose among the wide variety of NEPSY-II subtests as well as other instruments? How can he or she understand and organize the various results? The best way to answer these questions is for the clinician to review the types of findings he or she may expect in various disorders as well as research findings that may provide explanations and theories concerning the disorders. Along with a thorough grounding in child neuropsychology, one must gain experience in assessment and how it is used diagnostically. Experience naturally comes with assessing children with many types of disorders. However, one should also build on the experience of others and the findings in current research.

This chapter focuses first on the use of the NEPSY-II Referral Batteries as a guide for subtest selection and parsimonious assessment when constraints preclude a full NEPSY-II assessment. In addition to the subtests of the General Referral Battery, the subtests for the specific Diagnostic Referral Batteries will be presented as pertinent cases are discussed later in the chapter. These Referral Batteries serve to guide the clinician to subtests that address hypotheses relevant to the referral question.

After the general discussion of the Referral Batteries, the discourse turns to the clinical applications of the NEPSY-II (Korkman, Kirk, & Kemp, 2007) in various developmental and acquired disorders. The focus is on test results that are characteristic of different diagnostic groups and that may clarify the nature and underlying mechanisms of various disorders. The review also serves as a guide to help clinicians recognize patterns of results (diagnostic behavioral clusters) that are characteristic of different types of disorders. The review does not encompass all possible disorders, but considers some syndromes that are representative of types of disorders, both developmental and acquired, in which the NEPSY-II has been shown to provide helpful diagnostic information. Obviously, however, no two children with a disorder will produce identical results on an assessment.

What follows is a discussion of performance for groups of children with particular disorders. The discussion of each group is organized in the same manner. First a brief survey of research findings for the special group is presented as background, followed by the results of the NEPSY-II validity studies in relation to that group. The diagnostic cluster for the group resulting from the validity study is then presented with primary and secondary deficits, as well as co-occurring deficits. From the validity studies, as well as from findings in current research, the Referral Batteries have been formulated; therefore, the specific Diagnostic Referral Battery for the validity group will be presented last with all subtests and test ages. This discussion can serve as a guide for selecting the appropriate Referral Battery.

It should also be noted that many of the clinical groups in the validity studies are small and the data here are, therefore, to be considered as suggestions. Most often the results are, however, concordant with other research findings. The flexibility of the NEPSY-II is apparent in the fact that the clinician is also free to select any combination of subtests appropriate for a specific evaluation and the child's age range. Further, the clinician may also decide to employ selected NEPSY-II subtests to supplement his or her standard psychological or psychoeducational tools. Under these circumstances, training in neuropsychology will allow the clinician to select subtests that he or she believes will be sensitive to determining the underlying neurocognitive impairments associated with the child's presenting condition. Therefore, a fixed battery or flexible approach can be employed with NEPSY-II.

THE NEPSY-II REFERRAL BATTERIES

To assist examiners in selecting subtests that tap the relevant aspects of performance, Referral Batteries have been developed for the NEPSY-II. The nine Referral Batteries are designed to provide both a general overview across domains with the General Referral Battery (GRB) that is briefer than a full NEPSY-II or a focused assessment with one of the eight, specific Diagnostic Referral Batteries meant to address common referral questions (e.g. ADHD, Mathematics Disorder, and so forth). The Referral Batteries facilitate subtest selection and guide examiners to obtain a competent assessment.

Applying the Referral Batteries also directs the examiners to gain thorough knowledge and experience of useful tests. It is important to remember, however, that Referral Batteries are guidelines only and should not replace clinical experience and judgment. (See Caution box.)

CAUTION

Referral Batteries Are Guidelines

The batteries are designed as guidelines. They should not replace clinical experience and judgment.

The General Referral Battery

The General Referral Battery (GRB) is recommended when the exact nature of the child's problems is not expressed in the referral question, or to identify comorbid problems. Ideally, a full NEPSY-II is the most helpful approach in looking at primary and secondary deficits. Unfortunately, however, time or other constraints do not always allow for such a comprehensive evaluation. This is where the GRB can be particularly helpful, because this battery is composed of the most sensitive tests within each domain. The GRB is essentially a shortened form of the full NEPSY-II assessment and consists of subtests from all domains except the Social Perception domain. The General Referral Battery can be applied to most clinical conditions and can be expanded with additional subtests to cover deficits specific to the clinical condition or referral. There are seven subtests in the GRB for children 3-4 years old. For children 5-6, there are 10 subtests, and for children 7-12 there is a slightly different selection of 10 subtests. The GRB for children 13-16 years of age includes nine subtests. (See Rapid Reference 6.1 on the following page for subtests included in the GRB for two specific age ranges: 3-4 years and 5-16 years.)

The case of Julianne D. in the next chapter, Illustrative Case Reports (pp. 340) is an example of a situation in which the clinician chose to employ the GRB because she knew that the subtest selection would be sensitive to revealing deficits when the referral was vague and time was of the essence. Additional subtests can always be added to the GRB as diagnostic questions arise during the evaluation, more support is needed to verify a diagnosis, or after the initial scanning of domains has been completed, and it is clear that, ultimately, a full NEPSY-II will be needed. However, whenever a clinician is selecting subtests for an evaluation, whether they are a part of a Referral Battery or not, care must be taken that they are age appropriate. (See Caution box on the following page.)

≡ *Rapid Reference 6.1*

The General Referral Battery and GRB Subtests in Two Age Ranges

The General Referral Battery is comprised of the most sensitive subtests from five functional domains; the Social Perception domain can be added, if needed. The GRB is recommended when the exact nature of the child's problems is not expressed in the referral question, or to identify comorbid problems.

Ages 3-4	Ages 5-16
Comprehension of Instructions	Auditory Attention and Response Set
Design Copying	Comprehension of Instructions
Geometric Puzzles	Design Copying
Narrative Memory	Geometric Puzzles
Speeded Naming	Inhibition
Statue	Memory of Faces/MF Delayed
Visuomotor Precision	Narrative Memory
	Speeded Naming
	Statue (Ages 5-6)
	Visuomotor Precision (Ages 5-12)
	Word List Interference

CAUTION

NEPSY II Subtests Differ for Age Ranges

The clinician may select any combination of subtests appropriate for a specific evaluation, but care needs to be taken in selecting subtests appropriate to the age range, particularly in preschool and adolescent children.

Diagnostic Referral Batteries

By the time a child is referred for a neuropsychological evaluation, a more re-fined referral question is often available. Addressing referral questions with preselected, circumscribed, but thorough, focused assessments is a new feature of NEPSY-II that grew out of the extensive empirical data available from the validity testing undertaken during the development of NEPSY-II. There are eight Diagnostic Referral Batteries (DRB) for common referral questions that are designed to help the clinician select useful subtests to address the presenting problem. Some subtests will appear in one DRB but not in others. Subtests for the Referral Batteries have been selected according to the largest effect sizes for differences between the particular validity group and typical controls, as well as their identification with particular diagnostic clusters in the current literature. For instance, problems with phonological processing are closely identified with learning differences in reading, but not with learning differences in math. Therefore, the Phonological Processing subtest appears in the DRB for reading, but not in the DRB for math. Ability to handle visuospatial concepts is especially important to math learning, but not so key in reading; therefore, these tasks appear in the DRB for math, but not in the reading battery. Other subtests may be in only one or two of the batteries. For example, the Affect Recognition and Theory of Mind subtests are not included in many of the DRBs because difficulty recognizing facial emotion and/or another's perspective is identified with few of the other validity groups, but is key to the DRB for Social-Interpersonal problems, especially autism spectrum disorders (ASD). However, if a child with a reading difference, for example, is also having social difficulties, behavior problems, or an autism spectrum disorder is suspected, then Affect Recognition and/or Theory of Mind should be administered. As with the GRB, additional subtests can be added to a Diagnostic Referral Battery when appropriate to address specific questions.

For your convenience when testing, in the *Administration Manual* (p. 11) is a list of the subtests in the GRB and on page 12 is found a chart of the subtests by age for each Diagnostic Referral Battery (DRB) of NEPSY-II. When scoring, you can consult the DRB chart in the *Clinical and Interpretive Manual* (p. 24) with a more comprehensive discussion of Referral Batteries on pp. 13-18 of that manual. The eight Diagnostic Referral Batteries appear in Rapid Reference 6.2. The individual subtests in each Diagnostic Referral Battery will appear later in this chapter with the pertinent validity study from which the subtests were selected (pp. 258 to 327 in this chapter).

EXAMPLE: The use of a Diagnostic Referral Battery plus selected subtests is illustrated by the following case.

The clinician is preparing to evaluate 7-year-old Grant, who was referred by the classroom teacher. The teacher's monitoring record revealed weak word attack skills, spelling difficulties, and significant handwriting problems. From the teacher's referral, the comprehensive history form endorsed by the parents, as

≡ *Rapid Reference 6.2*

The Diagnostic Referral Batteries

Eight Diagnostic Referral Batteries to address a specific presenting problem. Subtests selected according to

- The largest effect sizes in scores with significant differences between clinical group and matched controls in the validity studies.
- Clinical experience and Identification in the current literature with particular diagnostic clusters.
- Some subtests will appear in one referral battery but not in others.
- The eight specific referral batteries are:
  1 Learning Differences—Reading
  2 Learning Differences—Mathematics
  3 Attention/Concentration
  4 Behavior Management
  5 Language Delays/Disorders
  6 Perceptual-Motor Delays/Disorders
  7 Social Perception
  8 School Readiness

well as parent/child interviews, the clinician formulates diagnostic hypotheses of dyslexia and dysgraphia. The parent interview reveals that the child's father is dyslexic, and Grant's profile suggests the same.

In order to test the hypothesis of dyslexia, the clinician chooses to use the NEPSY-II Referral Battery for Learning Differences—Reading. Results of this focused assessment revealed deficits on the Phonological Processing and Speeded Naming subtests, as well as a poor performance on the Memory for Names (immediate and delayed), and Design Copying subtests. These results suggest the presence of the diagnostic behavioral cluster of phonological and naming deficits associated with dyslexia, whereas performance on attention subtests was generally average. The phonological deficits in dyslexia affect both decoding (word attack) and encoding (spelling).

Further, Grant's difficulty with paper/pencil copying suggested a visuomotor deficit underlying his handwriting problems, especially because the diagnostic Motor Score for Design Copying was significantly weak. In order to lend support to the diagnosis of dyslexia and dysgraphia, the clinician added two subtests to the referral battery: Repetition of Nonsense Words to assess phonological processing further, and Visuomotor Precision to assess the ability to manipulate a pencil quickly and accurately. The weak results yielded by these two subtests explained the classroom results of the teacher's monitoring record and verified the diagnoses.

With this type of targeted Diagnostic Referral Battery, the examiner can feel confident that he or she is addressing the child's specific problems and that it will be possible to use the data to formulate helpful interventions and modifications for the child. In order to select appropriate additional subtests across domains and to interpret results on any type of NEPSY-II assessment, however, it is imperative for the clinician to stay current with pediatric neuropsychological research.

Selecting the appropriate Referral Battery for the referral question will focus the assessment and help the clinician address the problem in a parsimonious but thorough manner. In the spirit of the flexible approach to neuropsychological

---

☰ *Rapid Reference 6.3*

Components Recommended for Inclusion in an Assessment

- **History of child** from parent that includes detailed information about the child but also any neurological, developmental, psychological, or medical problems in the immediate and extended family.
- **General adaptive behavior scales** endorsed by parents and teachers
- **Checklists pertinent to the referral question** (e.g., ADHD, autism, etc.).
- **Comprehensive cognitive assessment** should be administered.
- **Comprehensive achievement tests**, including language/reading/ spelling areas. In the interest of time or presence of other constraints, a school assessment of cognition and achievement may be used to supplement neuropsychological assessment.
- **Observational notes** should be kept throughout the assessment.

Additional age-appropriate NEPSY-II subtests or other measures can be added, if areas of concern arise as testing proceeds.

- All measures should be reviewed for patterns of deficits that corroborate or disconfirm the NEPSY-II hypotheses.
- All educational, medical, developmental, and psychoemotional factors should be used to verify the NEPSY-II results and diagnostic cluster.

assessment, however, other subtests can be added to the battery if the clinician feels that an area needs further probing.

Other Measures to be Included in an Assessment

The NEPSY-II was constructed to yield information concerning the child's neurocognitive test profile and to analyze problems. It is not primarily intended to give a diagnosis that may be expressed in a diagnostic category or code, although it may provide information that is helpful in making specific diagnoses. Other assessments are also used for that purpose. Thus, a diagnosis that refers to the child's intellectual ability will require assessments with a test of intelligence. For diagnoses that refer to behavioral features, such as attention disorder or conduct disorder, questionnaires for evaluating these features are useful. Diagnoses that refer to learning disorder or motor disability will necessitate evaluation of academic or motor performance, respectively. Frequently, assessments will include all of these other measures in order to provide a complete diagnostic picture of the child. (See Rapid Reference 6.3 on the previous page for a summary of other measures for inclusion in an assessment.)

DEVELOPMENTAL DISORDERS AND NEPSY-II

Application of the NEPSY-II in Diagnosing a Learning Difference

Specific learning disabilities (e.g., reading, mathematics), in which a child exhibits a significant discrepancy between intellectual functioning and academic achievement, represent a relatively high incidence (2–10%; American Psychiatric Association, 2000) of disorders in child development. When NEPSY-II is used to diagnose a learning disability, it should be combined with a cognitive assessment, achievement testing, and, of course, information from the comprehensive history (developmental, medical, educational, family, etc.), as well as additional summaries of functioning gathered from the child's teachers, records of any previous assessments, and copies of standardized testing. The following is a discussion of findings on NEPSY-II associated with reading and mathematics disorders in the validity studies. NEPSY-II can also address the diagnosis of other learning disabilities. In addressing the diagnosis of any learning difference, however, it is important to keep current with the research literature, so that diagnostic behavioral clusters and diagnostic factors will be recognized. (See Rapid Reference 6.4 for the location of criteria for NEPSY-II validity group membership.)

≡ Rapid Reference 6.4

Locating Criteria for NEPSY-II Validity Groups

Appendix F of the NEPSY-II *Clinical and Interpretive Manual* contains full inclusion and exclusion criteria for all validity groups.

Reading Disorder

Background

Developmental reading disability (dyslexia) affects a significant proportion of otherwise normal children. Dyslexia has been defined as a specific learning disability that affects accurate/fluent word recognition, spelling, and decoding. It is neurological in origin and unexpected in relation to intellectual functioning and school instruction (International Dyslexia Association, 2008; Lyon, S. E. Shaywitz, & B. A. Shaywitz, 2003). Dyslexia exists on a continuum of severity from the lowest readers to those with milder cases (Olson, 2006). A core deficit in dyslexia is in the operation of a decoding process that performs grapheme to phoneme conversions at a sublexical level, known as phonological assembly (Lundberg & Hoien, 2001). Byrne, Fielding-Barnsley, and Ashley (2000) found that for children who participated in a highly structured preschool training program for phoneme awareness, the best preschool predictor of their later reading development was the number of training sessions needed for them to reach a criterion level for phoneme awareness. Olson (2006) argued that direct genetic influences on slow learning rates for phoneme awareness and grapheme/phoneme correspondences may be an important causal influence on dyslexia (see also Snowling & Hayiou-Thomas, 2006). Olson and Wise (2006) found that computer programs focused on phoneme awareness and phonological decoding substantially improved those skills.

Stanovich (2000) maintains that both phonological and orthographic factors must be taken into account in looking at the performance of good readers. He states that good readers read *graphemes,* rather than *letters,* because skilled readers "chunk" orthographic units. While reading unfamiliar or infrequent words is grounded in strong phonemic awareness, skilled readers also learn to read frequent, common words instantly (in less than one-third of a second); therefore, "sight word reading" is involved in skilled reading. Reading words becomes automatic (a) if a word is read using mediation (decoding) over and over (an average of 14 times), and (b) if they are practiced repeatedly as frequent, common words are. This skill may partly be related to the capacity for word retrieval.

Rapid naming has shown a highly correlated relationship with reading accuracy and fluency consistently from the time of Denckla and Rudel's seminal work in developing the Rapid Automatized Naming (RAN) tasks. The RAN also discriminates between dyslexic and nondyslexic reading groups. (Denckla & Rudel, 1976). The component processes of RAN that are responsible for its relationship with reading ability remain underspecified, however (Jones, Branigan, & Kelly, 2009). Jones and colleagues designed a study of dyslexic and nondyslexic adult groups that experimentally manipulated RAN formats to elucidate how different components of RAN differentially influence dyslexic and nondyslexic performance. The dyslexic group showed a pervasive deficit in rapid access of individually presented items. Additionally, they showed a significant impairment when multiple items were presented, whereas nondyslexic readers showed marginal facilitation for this format. Semrud-Clikeman and colleagues found that children with reading disabilities were slower on letter- and number-naming tasks and made more errors on all tasks than normal controls or children with ADHD and no reading problems. There was an age effect for the RAN tasks (rapidly naming colors, letters, numbers, and objects) and on the RAS tasks, (alternating letters/numbers and letters/numbers/colors). Younger children with reading disabilities showed poorer performance on all tasks, while the older children with reading disabilities showed poorer performance only on the letter- and number-naming tasks (Semrud-Clikeman, Griffin, & Hynd, 2000). Young children assessed on RAN tasks at the beginning and end of kindergarten and the beginning and end of Grade 1 showed highly stable pause time that developed significantly from the beginning of kindergarten to the end of Grade 1. It was highly correlated with both reading accuracy and reading fluency. Articulation time was less stable, did not develop, and was only weakly correlated with reading measures (Georgiou, Parrila, & Kirby, 2006). Rapid naming, along with phonological processing, appears to be a core deficit in dyslexia.

Weakness in organization, using codes (verbal or mathematical), memory, sequencing, time concepts, directionality, and multitasking often make home life, social life, and school life frustrating for children with dyslexia (Mortimore, 2003; S. E. Shaywitz & B. A. Shaywitz, 2003). Daily routines that are automatic to individuals without learning disabilities often demand closer attention, inordinate amounts of time, and intense energy for people with learning disabilities (Mortimore, 2003).

Regarding the etiology of reading disorder, some early postmortem studies demonstrated neuronal anomalies that indicated disordered migration of neurons to their final destination in the cortex (abnormally placed neurons and disorganized cortical layering) in the left hemispheres of dyslexics (Galaburda & Eidelberg, 1982; Galaburda & Kemper, 1979; Galaburda, Sherman, Rosen,

Aboitiz, & Geschwind, 1985). Modern "functional" imaging methods examine task-related changes in cerebral activation as indices of regional cortical engagement. Simos and colleagues (2000) employed magnetoencephalography (MEG), also known as magnetic source imaging (MSI), to look at the pattern of spatiotemporal brain activation in dyslexia. The MSI reflects where activity occurs in the brain. Pronounced differences in spatiotemporal activation profiles between dyslexic and age-matched nondyslexic children were evident on a case-by-case basis. The most dramatic differences (left posterior superior temporal and inferior parietal cortex) support the view that developmental dyslexia is linked to a functional deficit in the brain mechanism that supports phonological analysis of print and an aberrant pattern of functional connectivity between brain areas normally involved in reading, namely ventral visual association cortex and temporoparietal areas in the left hemisphere.

Heritability estimates for dyslexia assessed through a composite-reading measure in a large sample of twins demonstrated that greater than 50% of the group deficit is attributable to genetic influences (Raskind, Hsu, Berninger, Thomson, & Wijsman, 2000). More recently, Fletcher (2009) noted that dyslexia has a heritable component that accounts for 50 to 80% of the variance in reading outcomes. Analysis of the cognitive components of reading (phonological decoding, orthographic representation/coding, and phoneme awareness) also revealed similar results (Raskind, Hsu, Berninger, Thomson, & Wijsman, 2000).

Meng and colleagues (2005) identified markers in a noncoding region of the DCDC2 gene that were significantly associated with dyslexia in a twin and sibling sample. They demonstrated that "knocking out" the DCDC2 gene in mice resulted in grossly abnormal neuronal migration during brain development. This same gene was also associated with dyslexia (specifically severe spelling disability) in a German sample (Schumacher et al., 2006). Studies in the United Kingdom by Cope and colleagues (2005) and more recently by Paracchini, Scerri, and Monaco (2006) have focused their attention on the nearby KIAA0319 gene that also has shown significant association with dyslexia. They have observed a similar disruption of neuronal migration when they interfered with the expression of the KIAA0319 gene in rats. Olson (2006) maintained that while there are promising developments in research on how the DCDC2 and KIAA0319 genes may influence brain development and dyslexia, there most certainly are other genes yet to be discovered, particularly for less severe cases of dyslexia.

Grigorenko and Naples (2007) report that currently there are nine regions of the genome and six candidate genes are under active investigation. Thus far, it would appear that there are no dyslexia-specific genes, but rather a number of genes that reflect multiple small effects (Pennington et al., 2009).

Comorbidity is relatively common in reading disorder, particularly in the form of reading disorder and ADHD combined. Willcutt and colleagues (2003) have shown that there is a significant (about 30%) shared genetic etiology between dyslexia and the attention deficit component of ADHD, but not with the hyperactivity component. Pennington (2006) also found that ADHD often co-occurs with reading disability.

To conclude, impaired phonological processing and rapid naming (lexical access) stand out as the most characteristic primary disorders of reading disorder, whereas the jury still seems to be out concerning the impact of visual processing problems. A genetic background is frequent, as are comorbid problems, particularly ADHD. Given the relatively pervasive problems outlined for children with dyslexia, it is essential that an early diagnosis be made and intervention, preferably one-on-one or in a small group, be undertaken.

Validity Study Results—Reading Disorder

A sample of 36 children diagnosed with reading disabilities (RD), according to the State Department of Education or Special Education criteria for the child's home state or by a qualified mental health professional, was assessed with the NEPSY-II. Children with neurological and/or psychiatric diseases or disorders were excluded from the study. Additionally, they had normal or corrected vision and no hearing deficits. The IQ was greater than 85. Full inclusion and exclusion criteria for all validity groups is found in Appendix F of the NEPSY-II *Clinical and Interpretive Manual.* (See Rapid Reference 6.4: Locating Criteria for NEPSY-II Validity Groups.) The performance of children with RD on the NEPSY-II was compared to the performance of a matched control sample that was derived from the normative group and matched on age, sex, race/ethnicity, and parent education level (Korkman et al., 2007).

Children with reading disabilities exhibited significantly poorer performance ($p < .01$) on all subtests in the Language domain. The *Phonological Processing* (pH) and *Speeded Naming* (SN) subtests assessing consistent deficits in dyslexia were most sensitive to impairments in children with reading disabilities, with large effect sizes observed in these subtests (pH effect size: .94; SN Total Completion Time and SN Combined Scaled Score effect sizes: 1.10 for both). Large effect sizes are those ranging from .80 to 1.0 or greater. A moderate effect size of .66 (range .50–.79) was seen for the *Comprehension of Instruction* performance in the clinical group for reading. On a language subtest unchanged from the 1998 NEPSY (except for a name change), the RD group demonstrated significant differences with matched control performance on the *Word Generation* (previously Verbal Fluency) Semantic Score ($p < .03$) assessing rapid verbal production of words in categories. In the Attention and Executive Functioning domain, performance was significantly different from matched controls on *Clocks* ($p < .03$) and on the *Naming* Total Completion Time Scaled Score of the *Inhibition subtest* ($p < .01$). Performance on both subtests showed moderate effect sizes (.51 and .55, respectively). In the Visuospatial domain, *Picture Puzzle* performance was lower ($p < .03$) in the clinical reading group than in matched controls with a moderate effect size (.52). On a visuospatial processing subtest unchanged from the 1998 NEPSY, *Route Finding*, the sample of children with RD showed a significantly lower performance ($p < .02$) than matched controls on this task, designed to assess visuospatial concepts of orientation and directionality. In the Memory and Learning domain performance one of the subtests unchanged from the 1998 NEPSY, *Memory for Names*, showed a significant difference ($p < .0001$) when compared to matched controls. This was an assessment of learning and recall of the names of children; again showing that naming deficits are fairly generalized in children with reading disorders. On another subtest unchanged from the 1998 NEPSY, differences were seen in the Sensorimotor domain on *Oromotor Sequences* ($p < .001$), designed to assess oromotor coordination and programming for producing articulatory sequences, and *Manual Motor Sequences* ($p < .02$) that assess motor programming in reproducing rhythmic motor sequences (Korkman, Kirk, & Kemp, 1998). Lowest scores across all subtests were seen on *Speeded Naming*. A scaled score lower than 7 was obtained on *Phonological Processing*. These findings support the differential validity and sensitivity of the NEPSY-II to deficits in cognitive functioning exhibited by children diagnosed with Reading Disorder.

The NEPSY-II Reading Disorder Diagnostic Cluster

The results from NEPSY-II performance suggest that children with reading disorders show the following.
- Primary deficits in:
  - Phonological processing, showing high effect size.
  - Rapid naming, both for time and accuracy, showing high effect sizes.
  - More basic language, with moderate effects, as seen in comprehension of oral instructions, and the production of words in categories. This means that in some children a more pervasive language impairment may underlie the reading disorder.
- Secondary deficits in:
  - Reading and spelling acquisition.
  - Learning and studying through reading.

- Naming on tasks assessing factors other than naming alone, such as naming on the Inhibition subtest and immediate and delayed recall of children's names on a memory task.
- Reading time on a clock task that is mediated with name learning; learning verbal labels of directions and left-right may also be secondary to naming problems.
- Comorbid deficits often occur in:
  - Executive dysfunction in planning and strategizing.
  - Visuospatial analysis and processing with moderate effects for visual discrimination, spatial localization, and visual scanning, as well as part-to-whole relationships, and inability to judge orientation and directionality.
  - Motor programming for sequential oromotor and manual motor movements. (See Rapid Reference 6.5 for a summary of NEPSY-II reading disorder diagnostic cluster.)

≡ Rapid Reference 6.5

NEPSY-II Diagnostic Cluster for Reading Disorder

The results from NEPSY-II performance suggest that children with reading disorders show the following.

Primary deficits:

- High effects in
  - Phonological processing
  - Rapid naming, both for time and accuracy

Moderate effects in:

- Basic language; In some children, a more pervasive language impairment may underlie the reading disorder.
  - Comprehension of oral instructions
  - Production of words in categories

Secondary deficits in:

- Reading and spelling acquisition
  - Learning and studying through reading
  - Naming on tasks assessing factors other than naming alone (e.g., immediate and delayed recall of children's names on a memory task)

(continued)

(continued)

- Reading time on a clock task, mediated with name learning (learning verbal labels of directions and left-right may also be secondary to naming problems)

Comorbid deficits often occur:

- High effects in
  - Executive dysfunction in planning, strategizing
  - Visuospatial analysis and processing
- Moderate effects in
  - Visual discrimination, spatial localization, and visual scanning, as well as part-to-whole relationships
  - Inability to judge orientation and directionality
  - Motor programming for sequential oromotor and manual motor movements

Because the performance of children with RD may vary, all of these factors are not present in every child who has a reading disability or dyslexia. Consistent findings have been seen in the primary deficit of phonological processing and naming speed and accuracy, however. As a part of the assessment, it is important to have parents complete a history that includes not only detailed information about the child but also about reading and spelling problems in the immediate and extended family. Parents and teachers should also complete general adaptive behavior scales, as well as a checklist pertinent to ADHD, in order to help rule out this possibly comorbid condition. Further, the clinician should administer a comprehensive cognitive assessment, and comprehensive achievement tests, including language/reading/spelling areas. If there are any areas of concern as testing proceeds, additional NEPSY-II subtests or other measures can be added. Observational notes will, of course, be kept throughout the assessment. All measures can then be reviewed for patterns of deficits that corroborate or disconfirm the NEPSY-II hypotheses. See Rapid Reference 6.6 on the following page for other measures for inclusion in a NEPSY-II assessment. All educational, medical, developmental, and psychoemotional factors should be used to verify the NEPSY-II results and diagnostic cluster. Together these measures should yield enough information to confirm or discard the diagnosis of RD reliably, according to the DSM-IV-TR criteria.

Rapid Reference 6.6

Components Recommended for Inclusion in an Assessment

- Parents should complete a history that includes detailed information about the child but also any neurological, developmental, psychological, or medical problems in the immediate and extended family.
- Parents and teachers should also complete general adaptive behavior scales, and checklists pertinent to the referral question (e.g., ADHD, autism, etc.).
- A comprehensive cognitive assessment should be administered.
- Comprehensive achievement tests should be administered, including language/reading/spelling areas. In the interest of time or presence of other constraints, a school assessment of cognition and achievement may be used to supplement neuropsychological assessment.
- Observational notes should be kept throughout the assessment.
- If areas of concern arise as testing proceeds, additional age-appropriate NEPSY-II subtests or other measures can be added.
- All measures should be reviewed for patterns of deficits that corroborate or disconfirm the NEPSY-II hypotheses.
- All educational, medical, developmental, and psychoemotional factors should be used to verify the NEPSY-II results and diagnostic cluster.

Referral Battery for Learning Differences—Reading Disorder

(Note subtest age range. Subtests in parentheses are optional.)

Age	Subtest	Designed to Assess
	Attention/Executive Functioning Domain	
Ages 3–6	Statue	Inhibition of motor response to interfering noise
Ages 5–16	Auditory Attention and Response Set	Selective auditory attention and vigilance (AA)
Ages 5–16	Inhibition	Shift and maintenance of new auditory set; inhibition
		Shift and maintenance of new visual set; inhibition

(continued)

(*continued*)

Age	Subtest	Designed to Assess
Language Domain		
Ages 3–16	Comprehension of Instructions	Receiving, processing, and executing oral instructions
Ages 3–16	Phonological Processing	Phonological processing at the level of word segments (syllables) and letter sounds (phonemes)
Ages 3–16	Speeded Naming	Rapid semantic access and production of names
Memory and Learning Domain		
Ages 5–16	Memory for Names and MN Delayed	Name learning, immediate and delayed recall
Ages 7–16	Word List Interference	Verbal working memory; repetition and recall after interference
Sensorimotor Domain		
Ages 3–12	Manual Motor Sequences	Imitation of rhythmic manual movement sequences (programming)
Social Perception (no subtests recommended, unless added for social concerns)		
Visuospatial Processing		
Ages 3–16	Design Copying	Motor and visuoperceptual skills in copying 2-D designs
Ages 7–16	Picture Puzzles	Visual discrimination, spatial localization, visual scanning, and the ability to deconstruct a picture into constituent parts and recognize part-whole relationships

Mathematics Disorder

Background

Mathematics Disorder (MD), or dyscalculia, has been defined as a specific learning disability that affects one's ability to do mathematics. It is based on atypical brain organization and is unexpected in relation to intellectual functioning and school instruction (Geary, 2000; Geary & Hoard, 2001). Between 5 and 8% of school-age children have some form of memory or cognitive deficit that interferes with their ability to learn concepts or procedures in one or more mathematical domains (Geary, 2003). As with other forms of learning disabilities, twin and familial studies, although preliminary, suggest both genetic and environmental contributions to mathematics disorders (Light & DeFries, 1995; Shalev et al., 2001). For instance, Shalev and colleagues studied familial patterns of MD in number and arithmetic. They found that parents and siblings of children with MD are 10 times more likely to be diagnosed with MD than are members of the general population.

The many factors contributing to mathematical thinking and operations make it difficult to identify clearly the diagnostic cluster that defines a learning disability in mathematics. Ginsburg (1997) emphasizes that researchers should consider such factors as the adequacy of classroom instruction, the availability in children of informal knowledge, the role of motivation, the effects of specific interventions, the role and operation of different cognitive processes in constructing mathematical understanding, children's difficulties across different areas of mathematics, and the development of children's thinking throughout the school years. Geary and colleagues note that the goal of defining the cognitive pattern of math learning differences is further complicated by the task of distinguishing poor achievement due to inadequate instruction from poor achievement due to an actual cognitive disability (Geary, Brown, & Samaranayake, 1991).

Cutoff scores are frequently used to determine which participants have math learning differences. Some researchers apply more restrictive cutoffs than others (e.g., performance below the 10th versus below the 35th percentile). Different cutoffs may lead to groups of children that differ in their profile of math and related skills, including reading, visuospatial, and working memory skills. In a recent study (Murphy, Mazzocco, Hanich, & Early, 2007), it was found that despite some similarities, qualitative group differences were observed in the profiles of math-related skills across groups. These results highlight differences in student characteristics based on the definition of learning disability in mathematics and illustrate the value of examining skill areas associated with math performance in addition to math performance itself.

> # DON'T FORGET
>
> Examine skill areas associated with math performance in addition to math operations.

The visuospatial system appears to be involved in representing and manipulating mathematical information that is cast in a spatial form, as in a mental number line (Zorzi, Priftis, & Umiltá, 2002). An MD would be manifest as a deficit in conceptual or procedural competencies that define the mathematical domain, and these, in theory, would be due to underlying deficits in the central executive or in the information representation or manipulation (i.e., working memory) systems of the language or visuospatial domains. Thus, deficits underlying MD appear to cut across several domains.

Investigating core information processing deficits in developmental dyscalculia and low numeracy, Iuculano and colleagues found that *low numeracy was related not to a poor grasp of exact numerosities, but to a poor understanding of symbolic numerals* (Iuculano, Tang, Hall, & Butterworth, 2008). Numerous children with MD have difficulties retrieving basic arithmetic facts from long-term memory, and these difficulties often persist despite intensive instruction on basic facts (e.g., Howell, Sidorenko, & Jurica, 1987). A retrieval deficit resistant to instructional intervention might be a useful diagnostic indicator of arithmetical forms of MD (Geary, 2000).

Ostad (2000) also notes that disruptions in the ability to retrieve basic facts from long-term memory might be considered an essential feature of arithmetical forms of MD. When children with MD retrieve arithmetic facts from long-term memory, they commit many more errors than do their typically achieving peers, and they show error and reaction time patterns that often differ from the patterns found with younger, typically achieving children (Geary, 1993; Geary, Hamson, & Hoard, 2000). Geary (2000) demonstrated that children with MD and children with RD committed more retrieval errors than did their typically achieving peers, even after controlling for IQ. Hanich, Jordan, Kaplan, and Dick (2001) found a similar pattern.

Mathematics disabilities often coexist with language, spatial, attentional, and psychomotor disabilities (McCarthy & Warrington, 1990). Many children with MD have comorbid disorders, including reading disabilities (RD) and attention deficit hyperactivity disorder (ADHD; Gross-Tsur, Manor, & Shalev, 1996). Mazzocco and Myers (2003) found that reading-related skills were correlated with math achievement, as were select visual spatial skills. Reading disability was relatively more frequent in a group of children with math disabilities persisting for more than one grade level than in the remaining groups (25% versus 7%) who displayed transient math problems, poor achievement, or an IQ–achievement discrepancy. There was minimal overlap between groups who met either a "poor achievement" criterion or an "IQ-achievement discrepancy," and the latter was far less stable a measure over time than the former.

As a group, children with MD/RD or only MD commit more counting errors and use developmentally immature procedures (e.g., "counting all" rather than "counting on" from the largest number; that is, in adding 3 + 8, one would start with the higher number and count the next 3 digits: 9, 10, 11) more frequently and for more years than do their peers. The differences are especially pronounced for children with MD/RD, as children with MD only appear to develop typical levels of procedural competency more quickly than do children with MD/RD (Geary, Hamson, et al., 2000; Jordan & Montani, 1997).

Factors related to poorer mathematics outcomes include lower birth weight and gestational age (GA), neonatal complications, and possible abnormalities in brain structure (Taylor, Espy, & Anderson, 2009). Children with very low birth weight (< 1500 g) or very preterm birth (< 32 weeks GA) have more mathematics disabilities or deficiencies and higher rates of mathematics learning disabilities than normal birth weight term-born children (> 2500 g and > 36 weeks GA). Mathematics disabilities are found even in children without global disorders in cognition or neurosensory status and when IQ is controlled. They are associated with other learning problems and weaknesses in perceptual motor abilities and executive function.

Children with chromosomal disorders may show a pattern of learning differences, including math deficits. Mazzocco (2001) found that young girls with Turner syndrome or fragile X syndrome were significantly more likely to reveal specific math difficulties relative to their control group. A larger effect size was demonstrated by the group with Turner syndrome. By contrast, young children with Neurofibromatosis, Type 1, had a heterogeneous profile not suggestive of specific MD.

To conclude, math disorders have been studied particularly on the level of the arithmetical operations and concepts involved. Underlying deficits, such as spatial concepts, working memory, and executive functions, have been implicated in MD and appear to cut across several domains.

Mathematics Disorder NEPSY-II Validity Study

A sample of 20 children diagnosed with mathematics disabilities (MD), according to the State Department of Education or Special Education criteria for the child's home state, or by a qualified mental health professional, was assessed in the NEPSY-II validity study. To be included in the study, these children were required to be free of other psychiatric or neurological disorders, to have normal or corrected vision, normal hearing, and to have an IQ greater than 85. The performance of the children with MD disabilities on the NEPSY-II was compared to a matched control sample that was derived from the normative group and matched on age, sex, race, ethnicity, and parent education (Korkman et al., 2007).

The clinical sample of children with mathematics disabilities (MD) exhibited significantly poorer performance than matched controls on the subtests of the Attention and Executive Functioning (A/E), and on Memory and Learning domain subtests, as well as on subtests in the Visuospatial Processing domain. Subtest performance of the MD sample on the Language, Sensorimotor, and Social Perception domains was similar to that of the matched controls.

In the A/E domain, high effect sizes were seen on the scores of the *Response Set* (RS Total Correct SS effect size: .86; RS Combined SS effect size: .99), a measure of complex auditory attention, inhibition, and cognitive flexibility. A large effect size was also seen on the group comparison of Auditory Attention vs. Response Set Contrast (.94), revealing that the MD sample's performance on *Response Set*, controlling for simple selective auditory attention on *Auditory Attention* required to perform the task, was markedly poorer than expected given AA performance. The children with math disabilities were also impaired when compared to matched controls on the *Inhibition* subtest of the A/E domain, with high effect sizes. On the IN Inhibition Total Combined score comparison the effect size was greater than 1.0 (1.14). The score in question reflects errors integrated with completion time. Further, on the IN Naming vs. Inhibition Contrast SS, the group difference yielded an effect size of 1.12. The latter suggests that given the MD sample's ability to name shapes and directions, which showed no significant difference with matched controls, performance on the inhibition condition of the *Inhibition* subtest was particularly poor. In other words, inhibition of response rather than naming was a significant problem for children with MD. A high effect size (.99) was also seen for the MD sample on the IN Total Errors, an indication of errors on the *Inhibition* subtest as a whole across all three conditions. Executive dysfunction appears to make a significant contribution to poor performance in mathematics.

In the Memory and Learning domain, *Memory for Designs* and *Memory for Designs Delayed (MDD)* performance of children with MD was lower than that of the control group, yielding effect sizes in excess of 1.0 on the Memory for Design Content scores, both immediate and delayed (effect sizes: 1.05 and 1.04, respectively). Group differences also appeared on the Memory for Designs Spatial Score that showed a high effect size (.96) for immediate recall of location, as did the MDD Spatial Score (effect size: 88). Thus, while children with math disabilities had problems with both immediate and delayed spatial recall for location of the designs in a grid, they showed more deficits in recalling the designs themselves in both immediate and delayed conditions. Consistent with the mentioned differences, the Memory for Designs Total Score (effect size: 1.18), and its delayed counterpart (effect size: 1.27) differed between the groups.

While children with MD displayed no significant difference with matched controls on a measure of immediate recall of faces ($p < .28$), they showed a significant difference ($p < .02$) with high effect size on the Memory for Faces Delayed subtest (effect size: 88), because, given their performance on immediate recall, they would have been expected to perform better than they did on the delayed task. These children also displayed a significant difference ($p < .04$) with moderate effect size (.71) in performance on the *Word Interference* subtest WI Recall Total Score despite the fact that there was no difference ($p < 1.00$) in their performance when compared to matched controls on the WI Repetition subtest. Thus, children with MD were able to repeat the word series as well as matched controls, but they could not recall them after interference at the same level as the typical children. Again, executive dysfunction appeared to be a confounding factor. Consistent with these results, children with math disabilities showed a significant difference compared to the control group ($p < .05$), with a moderate effect size (.77) in their performance on the WI Repetition vs. WI Recall Contrast SS.

In the Visuospatial Processing domain, the MD sample showed significantly poorer performance ($p < .01$) with effect sizes equal to or greater than 1.0 for performance on *Geometric Puzzles* (effect size: 1.23) and *Picture Puzzles* (effect size: 1.00) when compared to matched controls. These results are of particular interest since both are nonmotor tasks, reflecting pure visuospatial deficits. There was also a significant difference ($p < .03$) in performance between the sample of children with MD and matched controls on the Block Construction Total Score with a high effect size (.88).

The lowest scores across all subtests were obtained on the Memory for Designs subtest. Scaled scores lower than a 7 were also obtained on the Clocks and Picture Puzzles subtests, both tests of visuospatial processing. However, Clock subtest performance for the MD sample was not significantly lower ($p < .09$) than that of matched controls. The findings support the differential validity and sensitivity of the NEPSY-II to deficits in cognitive functioning exhibited by children with Mathematics Disorder.

The NEPSY-II Learning Difference—Mathematics Diagnostic Cluster

The results from NEPSY-II performance suggest that children with learning differences in mathematics show impairment in several areas.

- Primary deficits in:
  - Executive dysfunction as seen in the Attention and Executive Functioning domain subtests, including complex auditory attention, inhibition (time and errors, due to inhibition and switching errors, not naming), and cognitive flexibility.
  - Visuospatial processing seen in deficits reproducing a 3-D block construction from a model or 2-D picture; on a nonmotor geometric puzzle task, assessing visuospatial analysis, mental rotation, and attention to detail; on a nonmotor Picture Puzzle subtest assessing

visual discrimination, spatial localization, visual scanning, and part-to-whole relationships.

- Secondary deficits caused by the above primary deficits in:
  - Visual design and spatial memory, both immediate and delayed.
  - Delayed facial memory.
  - The ability to reproduce a 3-D design from a model or 2-D picture.
  - Recall of word series due to inability to inhibit interfering words. This weakness may be secondary to the more general inhibition problem (executive dysfunction). (See Rapid Reference 6.7 for the NEPSY-II diagnostic cluster for Mathematics Disorder.)

≡ Rapid Reference 6.7

NEPSY-II Diagnostic Cluster for Mathematics Disorder

Language, social perception, and sensorimotor areas were similar to those of typical children of the same age, but children with learning differences in mathematics show impairment in several areas on NEPSY-II.

Primary deficits:

- High effects seen in
  - Executive dysfunction as seen in the Attention and Executive Functioning domain subtests, including complex auditory attention, inhibition (time and errors, due to inhibition and switching errors, not naming), and cognitive flexibility.
  - Visuospatial processing seen in deficits on a nonmotor Geometric Puzzle task, assessing visuospatial analysis, mental rotation, and attention to detail; on a nonmotor Picture Puzzle subtest assessing visual discrimination, spatial localization, visual scanning, and part-to-whole relationships.

Secondary deficits caused by the aforementioned primary deficits were seen in

- Visual design and spatial memory, both immediate and delayed.
- Delayed facial memory, possibly due to executive dysfunction in inhibiting interfering stimuli.
- The ability to reproduce a 3-D design from a model or 2-D picture.
- Recall of word series due to inability to inhibit interfering words. This weakness may be secondary to the more general inhibition problem.

Typically, children with math problems do not seem to differ from controls with respect to Language, Sensorimotor, and Social Perception. The subtests unchanged from the 1998 NEPSY are not available for this specific group as there was no math validity group on the original NEPSY.

For the MD sample in particular, it is important to rule out ADHD, due to the executive dysfunction seen in the group profile. As a part of the assessment for MD, it is very important to have parents complete a history that includes not only detailed information about the child but also about visuospatial and math problems in the immediate and extended family. Parents and teachers should also complete general adaptive behavior scales, as well as a checklist pertinent to ADHD in order to help rule out this possibly comorbid condition. If the latter is positive, further assessment for ADHD should be considered. Further, the clinician should administer a comprehensive cognitive assessment, and comprehensive achievement tests, including all mathematics operations and mathematics reasoning areas.

If there are any areas of concern as testing proceeds, additional NEPSY-II subtests or other measures can be added. Observational notes will of course be kept throughout the assessment. All measures can then be reviewed for patterns of deficits that corroborate or disconfirm the NEPSY-II hypotheses. All educational, medical, developmental, and psychoemotional factors should be used to verify the NEPSY-II results and diagnostic cluster. Together these measures should yield enough information to confirm or discard the diagnosis of MD reliably, according to the *DSM-IV-TR* criteria. Because the performance of children with MD may vary, all of these factors may not be present in every child who has a learning difference in math. Most children with math problems, however, will likely have either primary deficits of executive dysfunction or of visuospatial processing, or of both.

Referral Battery for Learning Differences—Mathematics

(Note subtest age range. Subtests in parentheses are optional.)

Age	Subtest	Designed to Assess
	Attention/Executive Functioning Domain	
Ages 3–6	Statue	Inhibition of motor response to interfering noise
Ages 5–16	Auditory Attention and Response Set	Selective auditory attention and vigilance (AA)
		Shift and maintenance of new auditory set; inhibition

(*continued*)

(*continued*)

Age	Subtest	Designed to Assess
Ages 5–16	Inhibition	Shift and maintenance of new visual set; inhibition

Language Domain

Age	Subtest	Designed to Assess
Ages 3–16	Comprehension of Instructions	Receiving, processing, and executing oral instructions
Ages 3–16	Speeded Naming	Rapid semantic access and production of names

Memory and Learning Domain

Age	Subtest	Designed to Assess
Ages 3–16	Memory for Designs and MD Delayed	Spatial memory for novel visual designs; immediate and long-term visuospatial memory
Ages 5–16	Memory for Faces and MF Delayed	Encoding of facial features, as face discrimination and recognition; immediate and long-term memory for faces
Ages 7–16	Word List Interference	Verbal working memory; repetition and recall after interference

Sensorimotor Domain

Age	Subtest	Designed to Assess
Ages 3–12	Visuomotor Precision	Graphomotor speed and accuracy

Social Perception (no subtests recommended, unless added for social concerns)

Visuospatial Processing

Age	Subtest	Designed to Assess
Ages 3–6	Block Construction	Visuospatial and visuomotor ability to reproduce 3-D constructions from models or 2-D drawings
Ages 3–16	Design Copying	Motor and visuoperceptual skills in copying 2-D designs
Ages 3–16	Geometric Puzzles	Visuospatial analysis, mental rotation, and attention to detail; nonmotor
Ages 7–16	Picture Puzzles	Visual discrimination, spatial localization, visual scanning, and the ability to deconstruct a picture into constituent parts and recognize part-whole relationships

APPLICATION OF THE NEPSY-II IN DIAGNOSING ADHD

Background

Attention deficit hyperactivity disorder (ADHD) is a relatively common disorder of development that is found in 3 to 7% of children younger than 18 years old, with 70% of these children continuing symptoms into adulthood (*DSM-IV-TR*, 2001). Research on gender differences demonstrated that ADHD has been reported for 4% of girls and 8% of boys in preschool (Gadow, Sprafkin, & Nolan, 2001), and for 2 to 4% of girls and 6 to 9% of boys in middle childhood. Psychiatric disorders commonly associated with ADHD include oppositional defiant disorder (the most common comorbidity), found in 54 to 67% of clinic-referred ADHD children (Angold, Costello, Erkanli, & Worthman, 1999); conduct disorder, found in 20 to 50% of ADHD children and 44 to 50% of ADHD adolescents (Barkley 1998; Lahey, McBurnett, & Loeber, 2000; Lahey et al., 2000.); anxiety, found in 10 to 40% of clinic-referred ADHD children (Biederman, Newcom, & Sprich, 1991; Tannock, 2000); and depression, found in 26% of ADHD individuals (Biederman, Faraone, & Keenan, 1992). Children with ADHD can have marked difficulty staying focused on a task, cannot sit still, act without thinking, and rarely finish anything (National Institute of Mental Health [NIMH], 2004a). These children are also at risk for comorbid learning disabilities and language disorders. As noted earlier, Willcutt and colleagues (2003) have shown that there is a significant (about 30%) shared genetic etiology between dyslexia and the attention deficit component of ADHD, but not with the hyperactivity component. The manifestation of symptoms and comorbid problems vary by subtype of ADHD. The *DSM-IV-TR* (American Psychiatric Association, 2000) recognizes three subtypes of ADHD: Predominately Inattentive Type, Hyperactive/Impulsive Type, and Combined Type. Early diagnosis and treatment is essential.

An essential feature of ADHD is a problem with executive functions. These have been defined as neurocognitive processes that are involved in maintaining an appropriate problem-solving set to obtain a later goal (Willcutt, Doyle, Nigg, Faraone, & Pennington, 2005). A 2005 meta-analysis (Willcutt et al., 2005) of 83 studies that administered EF measures to groups with ADHD ($N = 3,734$) and without ADHD ($N = 2,969$) found significant impairment of ADHD individuals on all EF tasks. The strongest and most consistent effects were obtained on measures of response inhibition, also evident as continuous performance task (CPT) commission errors, vigilance omission errors, verbal working memory, spatial working memory, and planning. Deficits in working memory (WM) are prominent. Martinussen, Hayden, Hogg-Johnson, and

Tannock (2005) in a meta-analysis of 46 studies of WM, indicated that ADHD children showed deficits in both verbal and spatial WM relative to normal controls, but spatial storage WM was more problematical with greater effect sizes than those for verbal storage. These findings are consistent with Barkley's (1997) model of executive function and ADHD in which the primary deficit is response inhibition, and the secondary deficits are poor working memory, inadequate internalizing of speech, an inability to separate affect from content in order to arouse attention and motivation, and an inability to reconstitute information. Poor motor performance can be a comorbid disorder in ADHD, but it can also be adversely affected by poor executive control, according to Barkley (2006).

Language deficits in ADHD include delayed onset of language (up to 35% of ADHD children), speech impairments (10 to 54% of ADHD children), excessive conversational speech, poor organization and inefficient expression of ideas in conversation (i.e., pragmatic deficits), as well as delayed internalization of speech (Barkley 2004). Pennington (2006) found that ADHD often coexists with reading disability. Although ADHD children do not differ from normal children in their capacity to understand emotional expressions of other children, ADHD children with ODD/CD are more likely to interpret ambiguous emotional expressions as anger and to respond with anger (Casey, 1996).

Although limited, research on ADHD and processing speed indicates that ADHD children show slower and more variable responses on processing speed tasks. For example, Willcutt, Pennington, Olson, and DeFries (2007) found that relative to healthy controls, ADHD children showed significantly slower responses on Stroop Word, Stroop Color, Stroop Color-Word, Symbol Search, and an overall factor score representing composite performance on all processing speed tasks. Problems with visuospatial tasks in ADHD appear to be due more to inattention and executive dysfunction, rather than visuospatial deficits per se. These difficulties include slow responses on a visuospatial orienting task (Wood, Maruff, Levy, Farrow, & Hay, 1999), errors due to premature responding on a visual search task (Mason, Humphreys, & Kent, 2003), "looking away" on a continuous performance task involving nonpredictable stimuli (Borger & van der Meere, 2000), and a failure to adjust to feedback on a test of vigilance (Swaab-Barneveld et al., 2000). A meta-analysis of 14 studies of covert visuospatial attention by Huang-Pollock and Nigg (2003) revealed inconsistent or no evidence of visuospatial deficits. Sensorimotor deficits in ADHD include deficits in fine motor coordination, muscle tone and balance (arm, leg balance), foot/leg coordination (walk backward and skip), hand/arm coordination (writing and drawing), and complex coordinated sequences of motor movements, among other neurological "soft sign" deficits (Barkley, Fischer, Edelbrock, & Smallish, 1990; Hern & Hynd, 1992; Iwanaga, Ozawa, Kawasaki, & Tsuchida, 2006).

To conclude, ADHD is related to executive dysfunction, particularly response inhibition but also poor selective attention, for vigilance may be a factor. Impaired attention and executive functions may cause various secondary problems on, for example, working memory or visuospatial tasks. They may be comorbid with verbal learning problems, sensorimotor deficits, and behavioral problems.

NEPSY-II Validity Study for ADHD

A sample of 55 children (mean age 9.9 ± 1.8) who met the *DSM-IV-TR* criteria for ADHD, Combined Type, and were free of other psychiatric or neurological diagnoses, had normal or corrected vision, normal hearing, and IQs greater than 85, were evaluated with NEPSY-II. The performance of the clinical ADHD, Combined Type group on the NEPSY-II was compared to that of matched controls from the NEPSY-II standardization sample. They were matched for age, sex, ethnicity, and parent education level.

In the Attention/Executive Functioning domain, the performance of the children with ADHD differed significantly ($p < .01$ to $p < .05$) from that of the nonclinical controls on over 80% of the scores for the *Auditory Attention and Response Set, Clocks,* and *Inhibition* subtests with small to moderate effect sizes (.42–.73). The largest effect sizes were seen on Response Set Total Correct Scaled Score (.73), Response Set Combined Scaled Score, integrating RS Total Correct and RS Commission Errors Percentile Rank (.70), and the IN-Inhibition condition (INI) Total Completion Time Scaled Score (.64). These measures are related to vigilance and failure to inhibit automatic responses. In the A/EF domain, only Animal Sorting did not reach significance. Evidently, the children with ADHD were able to formulate concepts on Animal Sorting and transfer them into action (sort) in a manner similar to matched controls.

Discrepancies were also seen in the Language domain on NEPSY-II on *Phonological Processing* ($p < .03$), but with a small effect size of .44 and on the *Speeded Naming* ($p < .01$) subtest with moderate effect sizes of .52 on SN Total Completion Time and .62 on the SN Combined Score that integrates completion time and accuracy. The Phonological Processing subtest requires close attention to auditory stimuli that is likely problematical for some children with ADHD, Combined Type. The Speeded Naming results also highlight the role of attention underlying a variety of language tasks (e.g., rapidly and accurately naming common shapes, colors, and sizes), but may speak further to slowed processing speed in this clinical group.

In the Sensorimotor domain, performance on the *Visuomotor Precision* Total Completion Time Scaled Score ($p < .03$) but with a small effect size (.49) was lower among the ADHD group than among the matched controls. Again, speed of processing may be the issue in the group differences. In the Memory and Learning domain, the ADHD group demonstrated poorer performance on *Memory for Faces* Total Score ($p < .04$) with a small effect size (.44). The *Narrative Memory* subtest also showed significant differences with matched controls on NM Free Recall ($p < .02$), NM Free and Cued Recall ($p < .05$), *Word List Interference* (WI) Recall ($p < .01$), and WI Repetition vs. Recall Contrast SS ($p < .01$), but effect sizes were small for all (.41, .35, .45, and .41, respectively). These results are reflections of the problems seen in working memory in ADHD, but they may also reflect auditory inattention if the child was not focused on the oral story as it was being administered.

Affect Recognition results from the Social Perception domain were lower ($p < .04$) in the clinical ADHD group than in matched controls, but the effect size was small (.37). This result may reflect visual inattention to the facial emotions portrayed. Visuospatial Processing domain subtests were generally performed at a level consistent with matched controls, with the exception of *Arrows* ($p < .02$) and *Geometric Puzzles* ($p < .03$), both with a small effect size of .46. Both of these subtests require attention to detail.

The lowest scores across all subtests were obtained on *Auditory Attention and Response Set*, assessments of auditory attention and executive function, requiring the child to inhibit a well-learned routine, and shift set to an alternate stimulus.

Subtests unchanged from the 1998 NEPSY that demonstrated significant differences include *Repetition of Nonsense Words* ($p < .001$), a test of phonological processing that requires close attention to auditory stimuli; *Word Generation* (Verbal Fluency) ($p < .01$), a test of rapid production of words in categories; *Oromotor Sequences* ($p < .001$), a test of oromotor programming for reproducing articulatory sequences; *Manual Motor Sequences*, another test of motor programming for hand movement sequences ($p < .001$); and *Imitating Hand Positions* ($p < .001$), an integrative subtest requiring visuospatial analysis, motor programming to move the fingers into the modeled position, and kinesthetic feedback from the position. Two memory tests also showed significant differences with matched controls: *Sentence Repetition* ($p < .04$), a test of repetition and immediate recall of sentences, and *List Learning* ($p < .001$), in which the child learns a long list over trials and then recalls the words after interference with immediate memory and later, long-term memory (Korkman et al., 1998).

The NEPSY-II ADHD Diagnostic Cluster

Thus, the results from NEPSY-II suggest that children with ADHD, Combined Type show impairment in many areas, especially those outlined in the following.

- Primary deficits in:
  - Executive functions for:
    - Planning, strategizing, and monitoring.
    - Adopting, maintaining, and switching set.
    - Inhibition of automatic responses.
  - Selective attention, particularly auditory attention and attention to detail.
- Secondary deficits in:
  - Verbal repetition and recall, as well as verbal working memory.
  - Rapid naming for time and accuracy and affect recognition, possibly as secondary effects of inattention and slowed processing.
  - The behavioral level (conduct, depression).
- Comorbid deficits in:
  - Verbal learning, possibly secondary to executive dysfunction.
  - Sensorimotor programming.

(See Rapid Reference 6.8)

Because the performance of children with ADHD may vary, all of these factors may not be present in every child who has ADHD. Caution: ADHD, and particularly the hyperactivity component, are not always captured by psychological tests in the controlled assessment setting. Therefore, as a part of the assessment, it is very important to have parents and teachers complete adaptive behavior scales pertinent to ADHD and to administer a computerized continuous performance measure. (See Caution box.)

CAUTION

Capturing ADHD Symptoms in an Assessment

In addition to NEPSY-II, it important to obtain at least one adaptive behavior scale pertinent to ADHD, filled out by each parent and the child's teachers and to administer a computerized continuous performance test.

≡ *Rapid Reference 6.8*

The NEPSY-II Diagnostic Cluster for Attention Deficit Hyperactivity Disorder (ADHD)

Children with ADHD, Combined Type, show impairment in many areas on NEPSY-II.

Primary deficits:

- Executive functions for
  - Planning, strategizing, and monitoring.
  - Adopting, maintaining, and switching set.
  - Inhibition of automatic responses.
- Selective attention, particularly auditory attention and attention to detail.

Secondary deficits:

- Verbal repetition and recall, as well as verbal working memory.
- Rapid naming for time and accuracy and affect recognition, possibly as secondary effects of inattention and slowed processing.
- (Not assessed on NEPSY-II, but watch for secondary effects at the behavioral level, conduct, depression, etc.)

Comorbid deficits:

- Verbal learning, possibly secondary to inattention to stimuli and the lack of inhibition of interfering stimuli.
  - Sensorimotor programming.

Further, in order to get a broad picture of functioning in children with ADHD, the clinician should also administer a cognitive assessment, and achievement tests. These can be reviewed for patterns of deficits that corroborate or disconfirm NEPSY-II hypotheses. In other assessments, the clinician should look for evidence of auditory short-term memory deficits, dysgraphia, working memory problems, inattention, impulsivity, and distractibility, as well as executive dysfunction. Observational notes, results of a classroom observation (if possible), and the comprehensive history covering all educational, medical, developmental, and psychoemotional factors should be combined with the NEPSY-II results. Together these measures should yield enough information to confirm or discard the diagnosis of ADHD reliably, according to the *DSM-IV-TR* criteria.

Referral Battery for ADHD

(Note subtest age range. Subtests in parentheses are optional.)

Age	Subtest	Designed to Assess
Attention/Executive Functioning Domain		
Ages 3–6	Statue	Inhibition of motor response to interfering noise
Ages 5–12	Design Fluency	Planning, strategizing, monitoring for rapid problem solution
Ages 5–16	Auditory Attention and Response Set	Selective auditory attention and vigilance (AA)
		Shift and maintenance of new auditory set; inhibition
Ages 5–16	Inhibition	Shift and maintenance of new visual set; inhibition
Ages 7–16	Clocks	Planning and organization; visuospatial skills; concept of time
(Ages 7–16)	(Animal Sorting)	Concept formation; ability to transfer concepts to action; shift
Language Domain		
Ages 3–16	Speeded Naming	Rapid semantic access and production of names
Ages 3–16	Word Generation	Verbal productivity; generation of words in categories
Memory and Learning Domain		
Ages 3–6	Sentence Repetition	Repetition and immediate recall of sentences
Ages 7–12	List Memory/LM Delay	Verbal learning, immediate/delayed recall; learning curve; interference from prior and new learning
Ages 7–16	Word List Interference	Verbal working memory; repetition and recall after interference
Sensorimotor Domain		
Ages 3–12	Manual Motor Sequences	Imitation of rhythmic manual movement sequences (programming)

(continued)

(*continued*)

Age	Subtest	Designed to Assess
(Ages 3–12)	(Imitating Hand Positions)	Imitation of static hand/finger position using visual spatial analysis, motor programming, and kinesthetic feedback
Social Perception (if social concerns)		
Ages 3–16	Theory of Mind	Ability to understand mental functions and another's point of view
		Ability to relate emotions to social context
(Ages 3–16)	(Affect Recognition)	Ability to recognize emotional affect
Visuospatial Processing		
Ages 3–16	Geometric Puzzles	Mental rotation, visuospatial analysis, and attention to detail
Ages 3–16	Design Copying	Motor and visuoperceptual skills in copying 2-D designs
(Ages 5–16)	(Arrows)	Ability to judge line orientation

APPLICATION OF THE NEPSY-II IN CHILDREN WITH EMOTIONAL DISTURBANCE

Background

Many terms are used to describe emotional, behavioral, or mental disorders. In 1994 when Public Law 94-142 was passed to provide special education services for this group in public schools, the term Serious Emotional Disturbance (SED) was used. The characteristics for this category were defined as:

[A] condition exhibiting one or more of the following characteristics over a long period of time and to a marked degree, which adversely affects educational performance:

An inability to learn which cannot be explained by intellectual, sensory, or health factors.

An inability to build or maintain satisfactory interpersonal relationships with peers and teachers.

Inappropriate types of behavior or feelings under normal circumstances.

A general pervasive mood of unhappiness or depression.

A tendency to develop physical symptoms or fears associated with personal or school problems.

In the 1997 recertification of the law, the federal definition included children who were diagnosed as schizophrenic, but excluded socially maladjusted children "unless it is determined that they are seriously emotionally disturbed." Although autism was formerly included under the SED designation, in 1981 it was transferred to the category of "other health impaired" (Zabel, 1988).

Currently, under the Individuals with Disabilities Education Act (2004), students with such disorders are still categorized as having a Serious Emotional Disturbance with the same characteristics listed. As defined by the 2004 bill, however, serious emotional disturbance includes schizophrenia but does not apply to children who are socially maladjusted, unless it is determined that they have a serious emotional disturbance. [See Code of Federal Regulation, Title 34, Section 300.7(c)(4)(ii).]

In a study of 1,285 students, the IDEA criteria, as defined in the state of Texas, was applied by Narrow and colleagues (1998) to identify emotionally disturbed children. Nearly 12% of children qualified for a diagnosis of emotional disturbance. The diagnoses included demonstrated the variety of diagnoses included under this IDEA category: anxiety, mood, substance abuse, disruptive behavior, and psychotic and other disorders. In the 2000–2001 school year, 473,663 children and youth with an emotional disturbance were provided special education and related services in the public schools (U.S. Department of Education, 2001).

The causes of emotional disturbance have not been adequately determined. Although various factors such as heredity, brain disorder, diet, stress, and family functioning have been suggested as possible causes, research has not shown any of these factors to be the direct cause of behavior problems. Some of the characteristics and behaviors seen in children who have emotional disturbances include:

- Hyperactivity (short attention span, impulsiveness)
- Aggression/self-injurious behavior (acting out, fighting)
- Withdrawal (failure to initiate interaction with others; retreat from exchanges of social interaction, excessive fear or anxiety)
- Immaturity (inappropriate crying, temper tantrums, poor coping skills)
- Learning difficulties (academically performing below grade level)

Children with the most serious emotional disturbances may exhibit distorted thinking, excessive anxiety, bizarre motor acts, and abnormal mood swings and are sometimes identified as children who have a severe psychosis or schizophrenia.

Many children who do not have emotional disturbances may display some of these same behaviors at various times during their development. However, when children have serious emotional disturbances, these behaviors continue over long periods of time. Their behavior thus signals that they are not coping with their environment or peers (NICHY, 2001).

Wagner and Davis (2006) describe five principles they identified from the literature on exemplary practices to help students with emotional disturbances (ED) have positive secondary school experiences and successful trajectories into early adulthood:

- Relationships
- Rigor
- Relevance
- Attention to the whole child
- Involving students and families in goal-driven transition planning.

The authors evaluated implementation of these practices for middle and secondary school students with ED by using data from a nationally representative longitudinal study of students receiving special education services. The results suggest that exposure to best practices has improved since the 1980s and is similar to that for students with other disabilities, but significant opportunity for improvement remains.

Benner, Nelson, Allor, Moody, and Tai (2008) investigated the mediating role of academic processing speed (i.e., academic fluency in completing school work quickly and accurately). The neuropsychological concept of processing speed may underlie the same on the relationship between (a) the externalizing behavior and academic skills of K–12 students with ED, and (b) language skills and academic skills of students with ED. Results indicate that academic processing speed mediated the influence of both language skills and externalizing behavior on academic skills of this population.

Milsom and Glanville (2009) found students with emotional disturbance or learning disabilities to be at risk for academic difficulties and school dropout. Using data from the National Longitudinal Transition Study-2 database, the relationships between social skills and grades were examined for these students. Results revealed significant direct and indirect effects of social skills on grades.

In a meta-analysis, Reddy and colleagues (Reddy, Newman, DeThomas, & Chun, 2008) evaluated the effectiveness of school-based prevention and intervention programs for children and adolescents at risk for and with emotional disturbance. Twenty-nine published outcome studies from December 1988 to March 2006, including 1,405 children and adolescents, were reviewed. Each investigation was coded on several variables describing the child, parent, and teacher samples, as well as reported outcome results. The overall mean weighted effect size was large (1.00 at post-test and 1.35 at follow-up). Mean weighted effect sizes were a moderate 0.42 for between-subjects design studies, a high 0.87 for within-subjects design studies, and a very high 1.87 for single-subject design studies. Prevention programs yielded a moderate mean weighted effect size of 0.54, but intervention programs produced a strong mean weighted effect size of 1.35. Therefore, it would appear from this meta-analysis that the best outcomes for children with emotional disturbance are apt to be through well-designed intervention programs.

In conclusion, children with very varying conditions and behavioral patterns related to emotional and social adjustment are included in the educational category of emotionally disturbed children. Consistently, few studies have been undertaken on such heterogeneous groups. Various primary or secondary neurocognitive problems may be expected to occur in these children.

Validity Study for IDEA Category of Emotional Disturbance

The sample collected with the NEPSY-II is meant to demonstrate the wide variety of abilities seen in children classified as emotionally disturbed (Korkman et al., 2007). Caution: It is essential to remember that this Referral Battery is not meant to delineate a pattern for a single diagnostic cluster, but rather cuts across diagnostic categories as does the class composition in the IDEA category, Emotional Disturbance. (See Caution box.)

CAUTION

Referral Battery for Emotional Disturbance Not Meant to Delineate a Single Diagnostic Cluster

This diagnostic cluster cuts across diagnostic categories as does the class composition in the IDEA category of Emotional Disturbance.

A sample of 30 children categorized as emotionally disturbed, as defined by the child's school district, was assessed with the NEPSY-II. A control group matched for age, sex, race/ethnicity, and parent education level was derived from the NEPSY-II normative sample. Each child was required to have normal vision and hearing, and an IQ greater than 80. Diagnosis was not restricted, and children could be taking medications related to their emotional disturbance. While the majority of children did not carry a formal *DSM-IV-TR* diagnosis, five (17%) were diagnosed with conduct disorders, twelve (40%) were diagnosed with mood or anxiety disorders, and two (7%) were diagnosed with ADHD. The variety of diagnoses demonstrates the variability of children classified as emotionally disturbed (Korkman et al., 2007).

Reflecting the heterogeneity of the sample, impairments were seen in nearly every domain of the NEPSY-II assessment. In the A/E domain, lower scores ($p < .01$) were seen on the executive function subtests *Animal Sorting* (AS), *Response Set* (RS), *Clocks* (CL), and *Inhibition* (IN). Large effect sizes were seen on the AS Combined Score difference (.85), integrating types of errors and correct responses in formulating concepts and shifting set, and on the IN-Switching Total Completion Time Score difference (1.12), assessing the ability to inhibit an automatic response and switch to an alternate response quickly. Moderate effect sizes were seen when the clinical group's performance was compared to matched controls on AS Total Correct Sorts (.74) and Response Set Combined Score (.65), integrating correct responses and commission errors, and on the RS Total Correct score (.63). Executive functions and rapid concept formation appear to be problematical for the ED students.

In the Language domain, the sample with ED achieved lower scores ($p < .01$) than did matched controls on *Comprehension of Instructions* (CI) and *Speeded Naming* (SN) subtests, although performance was similar to that of matched controls on *Phonological Processing*. Large effect sizes were seen in comparing performance of the clinical and control groups on the CI Total Score (.99) and on SN Total Completion Time (1.05), with a moderate effect size on SN Combined Score (.77), a score that integrates both time and accuracy. Rapid and accurate lexical access, language understanding, and ability to carry out oral instructions were all of concern in the ED sample. Slowed processing, inattention, and oppositional behaviors, as well as language difficulties, may all have been instrumental in the Language domain subtest results of this special group because, interestingly, they showed no verbal memory problems on the Memory and Learning domain subtests.

Usually, individuals with language deficits also show verbal memory deficits. The one significantly lower performance ($p < .01$) on the Memory and Learning Domain subtests was in the *Memory for Faces Delayed* performance. Facial recognition was similar to matched controls on immediate recall, but apparently, memory decay set in, or attention on task motivation faded, and negatively impacted long-term facial memory. On Affect Recognition in the Social Perception Domain, performance of the children with ED was similar to matched controls.

The *Visuomotor Precision* Combined SS from the Sensorimotor domain was significantly lower ($p < .01$) with a large effect size (.84) for the ED sample when compared to matched controls. This score integrates the speed and accuracy of graphomotor performance that would adversely affect written output in the classroom. On the *Fingertip Tapping* subtest, both FT Dominant Hand Combined (repetitions and sequences) and the FT Sequences Combined (both hands) were significantly lower ($p < .04$) than matched controls, but effect size (.55) was moderate for both. These results do indicate, however, that the ED sample seems to have difficulty with motor programming bilaterally and may not be well lateralized for manual coordination and programming.

When compared to matched controls, ED performance on subtests of the Visuospatial domain revealed significant ($p < .01$) problems in several different areas with large effect sizes: judgment of line orientation assessed by the *Arrows* subtest (Total Score effect size: 80), and visual perceptual and visuomotor skills associated with the ability to copy 2-D geometric figures as assessed by the *Design Copying* (DC) Process Total Score (effect size: 85) and the DCP Motor Score (effect size: 90). Moderate effect sizes were seen for DCP Local Score (.74) and for DCP Global (.59). The *Block Construction* Total Score was also lower ($p < .04$) for the ED sample than for matched controls, but effect size was moderate (.55). This clinical population appears to have significant visuospatial processing problems in judging line orientation and in perceiving global (outer configuration) and local (details) stimuli along with significant visuomotor copying deficits.

Children referred to the ED classroom show numerous deficits across domains, raising the question of whether or not some of these young people may be individuals who have had significant learning deficits since they were young children and may have ended up in ED classrooms due to acting out as a result of frustration. It is particularly concerning that they show language deficits. Rapid and accurate lexical access, language understanding, and ability to carry out oral instructions were all of concern in the ED sample. On the other hand, this group did not show verbal memory deficits as would be usual for children with language deficits. Therefore, slowed processing, inattention, and oppositional behaviors, as well as language difficulties, may all have been instrumental in the Language domain subtest results of this special group. Effects of depression and mood disorders may have impacted results, rather than the other way around. Executive dysfunction was also pervasive, including concept formation and cognitive flexibility. Further, the children in the ED group showed visuospatial and visuomotor deficits that may impact math achievement and underlie dysgraphia. Clearly, this population presents a complex picture.

Referral Battery for Behavior Management

(Note subtest age range. Subtests in parentheses are optional.)

Age	Subtest	Designed to Assess
Attention/Executive Functioning Domain		
Ages 3–6	Statue	Inhibition of motor response to interfering noise
(Ages 5–12)	(Design Fluency)	Planning, strategizing, monitoring for rapid problem solution
Ages 5–16	Auditory Attention and Response Set	Selective auditory attention and vigilance (AA)
		Shift and maintenance of new auditory set; inhibition
Ages 5–16	Inhibition	Shift and maintenance of new visual set; inhibition
Ages 7–16	Clocks	Planning and organization; visuospatial skills; concept of time
Ages 7–16	Animal Sorting	Concept formation; ability to transfer concepts to action; shift
Language Domain		
Ages 3–16	Comprehension of Instructions	Receiving, processing, and executing oral instructions
Ages 3–16	Speeded Naming	Rapid semantic access and production of names
(Ages 3–16)	(Word Generation)	Verbal productivity; generation of words in categories
Memory and Learning Domain		
Ages 3–6	Sentence Repetition	Repetition and immediate recall of sentences
Ages 5–16	Memory for Faces and MF Delayed	Encoding of facial features, as face discrimination and recognition
		Immediate and long-term memory for faces

Age	Subtest	Designed to Assess
Sensorimotor Domain		
Ages 3–12	Visuomotor Precision	Graphomotor speed and accuracy
Ages 5–16	Fingertip Tapping	Finger dexterity and motor speed; motor programming
Social Perception (if social concerns)		
(Ages 3–16)	(Affect Recognition)	Ability to recognize emotional affect
Visuospatial Processing		
Ages 3–16	Design Copying	Motor and visuoperceptual skills in copying 2-D designs
(Ages 5–16)	(Arrows)	Ability to judge line orientation

APPLICATION OF THE NEPSY-II IN DIAGNOSING LANGUAGE DISORDERS

Background

Language disorders are a group of disorders related to language processing abilities. The *DSM-IV-TR* recognizes five Communication Disorders: Expressive Language Disorder; Mixed Receptive-Expressive Language Disorder; Phonological Disorder, Stuttering; and Communication Disorder; Not Otherwise Specified. Phonological Disorder was previously known as Developmental Articulation Disorder. It does not refer to the phonological difficulties with sound symbol association that children with dyslexia experience, but rather refers to failure to use developmentally expected speech sounds that are appropriate for age and dialect (e.g., errors in sound production, use, representation, or organization such as, but not limited to, substitutions of one sound for another [use of /t/ for target /k/ sound] or omissions of sounds such as final consonants) (American Psychological Association, 2000, pp. 56–67).

Language disorders may be acquired or developmental. Acquired type refers to impairment that occurs after a period of normal development as a result of neurological or medical conditions (e.g., encephalitis, head trauma, irradiation). Developmental type indicates a significant delay or impairment in language development not associated with a neurological insult of known origin.

The NEPSY-II validity studies addressed Expressive and Mixed Receptive-Expressive Language disorders. The incidence of these two categories, also referred to collectively as specific language impairment (SLI), is approximately 10–15% in preschool children and 3–7% in school-age children. Expressive Language Disorder is associated with limited vocabulary, errors in tense, difficulty recalling words, difficulty producing sentences with developmentally appropriate length or complexity, and difficulty expressing ideas. Mixed Language Disorder is associated with all the deficits of Expressive Language Disorder plus receptive language deficits (e.g., difficulty understanding words, sentences, or specific types of words). In diagnosing Expressive or Mixed Receptive, Expressive Language Disorder, or Phonological Disorder, an Autism Spectrum Disorder must be ruled out, since language deficits are a part of that diagnosis. If Mental Retardation is diagnosed, or there is a motor-speech or sensory deficit, or environmental deprivation is present, the language difficulties must be in excess of those usually associated with these problems. Otherwise, the language problem is considered a part of the primary diagnosis (APA, 2000).

Most empirical research on language disorders has focused on specific language impairment (SLI). Children with SLI have nonverbal IQs within the normal range, but have below-average oral language ability (Leonard, 1998). Secondary problems include reading disorders (Flax et al., 2003; Schuele, 2004); spelling problems (Schuele, 2004); and increased rates of learning disorders and delays in academic achievement (Young et al., 2002).

Comorbidities of language disorder include autoimmune disorders (Choudhury & Benasich, 2003), with the most common psychiatric comorbidities being ADHD (19%), Oppositional Defiant Disorder and Conduct Disorder (7%), as well as anxiety disorders (10%) (Cantwell & Baker, 1991). (For additional evidence of ADHD in language disorder, see Cohen et al., 1998; Toppelberg & Shapiro, 2000; Westby & Watson, 2004). According to Beitchman and colleagues, language impairment at age 5 years predicts ADHD and anxiety (i.e., particularly social phobia) disorder at age 19 years. There may also be an increased risk of antisocial personality (Beitchman, Hood, Rochon, & Peterson, 1989; Beitchman, Wilson, Brownlie, Walter, & Lance, 1996; Beitchman et al., 2001). The latter might be connected to a common underlying genetic factor in some of the individuals with persistent language disorder.

Receptive deficits in language include errors when discriminating among phonemes, morphemes, and other speech sounds, particularly when a task is complex or involves high memory load (Bishop & McArthur, 2005; Burlingame, Sussman, Gillam, & Hay, 2005; Coady, Kluender, & Evans, 2005). Receptive deficits also include errors when discriminating among tones in a frequency discrimination task (McArthur & Bishop, 2004); when choosing agents in sentences that vary in syntactic complexity (Dick, Wulfeck, Krupa-Kwiatkowski, & Bates, 2004; Evans & MacWhinney, 1999); and when comprehending subject and object in long *Wh*-questions (Deevy & Leonard, 2004).

Expressive deficits include deficits when producing long, lexically complex sentences (Klee, Stokes, Wong, Fletcher, & Gavin, 2004); when producing long, syntactically complex sentences (Marinellie, 2004); when using verb tense/inflectional markers (*-end*), particularly when the marker occurs in a sentence internal rather than final position (Dalal & Loeb, 2005); and when saying nonwords in a nonword repetition task (Gray, 2003). Bishop and Snowling (2004) note that nonword repetition, in which the child must repeat meaningless but pronounceable strings of syllables (e.g., "blonterstaping"), is a primary marker in language disorders, as well as in dyslexia.

Research on attention deficits in language disorders is scarce. Available research indicates that children with language impairments show deficits in auditory sustained and selective attention (Noterdaeme, Amorosa, Mildenberger, Sitter, & Minow, 2001); and secondarily, attentional capacity limitations during simultaneous processing of verbal information (nonwords and sentences) (Marton & Schwartz, 2003). Because of their language deficits, these children may not be able to attend to language-based tasks, or they may be subject to comorbid attention problems. A similar capacity limitation, may, however, apply also to their executive functions. Studies have also shown that children with language disorders show executive dysfunction, including deficits in the ability to shift attention between two categories of geometric symbols (round and angular forms) (Noterdaeme et al., 2001); to remember digits or locations of X's on a computer screen under dual-task conditions (Hoffman & Gillam, 2004); and to process multiple nonwords simultaneously (Marton & Schwartz, 2003). Verbal working memory deficits (phonological and functional working memory) may be a clinical marker for language disorders and may be related to morphological and lexical language deficits (Montgomery, 2003). The ADHD children with specific language impairment show deficits in verbal working memory, whereas ADHD children without SLI show no such deficits (Jonsdottir, Bouma, Sergeant, & Scherder, 2005). Therefore, it would appear that the language disorders are additive to the ADHD profile.

Not surprisingly, language disorders are associated with verbal memory deficits, but they also appear to be associated with nonverbal memory deficits (Montgomery, 2003). Children with language impairments show verbal memory deficits on nonword repetition tests, in which they have difficulty repeating nonwords with many syllables (Montgomery, 2003); on complex working memory tests, in which they have trouble making semantic acceptability judgments about sentences while remembering words (Hansson, Forsberg, Lofqvist, Maki-Torkko, & Sahlen, 2004); and on verbal short-term memory tests, in which they have difficulty remembering words (Hick, Botting, & Conti-Ramsden, 2005). Further, children with language impairments show nonverbal memory deficits on visuospatial memory tests, in which they show poor spatial span, poor recall for spatial patterns, and difficulty associating spatial patterns with particular locations (Bavin, Wilson, Maruff, & Sleeman, 2005; see also Hoffman & Gillam, 2004). The memory deficits may be exacerbated when target information is presented at fast rather than slow rates (Fazio, 1998). The deficits may also impair performance on other language tasks. For example, poor phonological working memory in language disorders may result in poor sentence comprehension for long but not short sentences (Montgomery, 2003).

In social perceptual areas, some studies have examined whether children with language impairments show deficits in affect recognition in faces (see Creusere, Alt, & Plante, 2004). In one study (Trauner, Ballantyne, Chase, & Tallal, 1993), children with language impairment showed *no* deficits in identifying facial expressions on still photographs (perhaps because the task was not sufficiently demanding; see Creusere et al., 2004). They did show deficits in identifying affect on audiotape recordings. In another study (Dimitrovsky, Spector, Levy-Shiff, & Vakil, 1998), children with verbal learning impairments showed deficits in identifying facial affect expressions. In a third study, children with language impairments showed deficits in identifying facial affect expressions with unfiltered speech but not with filtered speech (Creusere et al., 2004). Two studies examined whether children with language impairments show theory of mind deficits. In one study (Miller, 2004), children with language impairments showed no deficits on a false belief task when linguistic complexity of the task was low. In another study (Miller, 2001), children with language impairments performed similar to *same-age* peers on a false belief task when linguistic complexity of the task was low but similar to *younger* peers when linguistic complexity was high.

Compared to controls, children with language impairments show significantly poorer social knowledge, often use inappropriate (nonverbal) negotiation and conflict resolution strategies, and demonstrate passive or withdrawn social behavior (Brinton, Fujiki, & McKee, 1998; Marton, Abramoff, & Rosenzweig, 2005). Children with language impairments are also more likely to rate themselves at risk of being bullied in school (Knox & Conti-Ramsden, 2003).

Visuospatial deficits in children with language disorders have been found on tests of executive function and memory, as noted before. Compared to controls, children with language impairments have shorter spatial span and are less accurate in recalling spatial patterns (Bavin et al., 2005); show slower development on a visuospatial short-term memory task (Hick et al., 2005); and show poorer recall of spatial locations (Hoffman & Gillam, 2004).

Motor deficits in children with developmental language impairments have been noted in several studies (e.g., Mandelbaum et al., 2006; Noterdaeme et al., 2001; Reinö-Habte Selassie, Jennische, Kyllerman, Viggedal, & Hartelius, 2005). The children displayed deficits in sensorimotor skills, oromotor skills, and praxis, compared to high-functioning autistic children, based on clinical impressions by a neurologist. It seems plausible that these motor programming problems may be part of the speech production and articulatory problems in expressive language disorders.

Children with language impairments also have deficits in processing speeds (namely, slow responding) on tasks involving particularly linguistic and but also some nonlinguistic stimuli. They have been slower on comprehending complex sentences (Dick et al., 2004); on reaction time tests, in which they respond more slowly to linguistic *and* nonlinguistic stimuli (Miller, Kail, Leonard, & Tomblin, 2001); lexical decision tests, in which they take longer to recognize words (Edwards & Lahey, 1996); and on speed of naming and vocalization tests, in which they take longer to name pictures and to respond to nonlinguistic stimuli (Lahey & Edwards, 1996).

To conclude, just as language is a very complex activity, children with language disorders exhibit a vast symptomatology, including underlying impairment of different components: auditory and phonological discrimination and processing, problems comprehending complex syntax, and motor programming. They also display many secondary or comorbid problems: in auditory attention, executive function, working memory as well as other verbal and nonverbal types of memory, processing speed, and social perception and knowledge.

NEPSY-II Validity Study for Language Disorders

This validity study was focused on Expressive and Mixed Receptive-Expressive Language disorders. A sample of 29 children diagnosed with one or the other of these conditions and meeting *DSM-IV-TR* criteria was assessed with the NEPSY-II to evaluate the influence of language impairment on other cognitive abilities. A control group matched for age, sex, race/ethnicity, and parent education level was derived from the NEPSY-II normative sample. Each child was required to have normal vision and hearing. Individuals with a history of psychiatric or neurological disorder were excluded from the sample.

As might be expected, in the Language domain children with language disorders performed significantly lower ($p < .01$) than matched controls on the

Comprehension of Instructions Total score with a large effect size (.89). Phonological Processing results were also lower ($p < .03$) than those matched controls, but effect size was moderate (.56). They also showed significantly poorer performance (see the following paragraphs) when compared to matched controls on predominately language-based subtest performance in other domains (i.e., Auditory Attention and Response Set, Inhibition, Narrative Memory, and Word List Interference). For instance, secondary verbal memory deficits were seen.

In the Memory and Learning domain, an effect size over 1.0 was seen on *Word List Interference Repetition* Total (effect size: 1.55). In other words, the children with language disorders were poorer ($p < .01$) at simply repeating short word series when compared to matched controls. The WI *Recall* score was also lower ($p < .01$) for word recall after interference and the difference showed a large effect size (.81). Secondary verbal memory deficits ($p < .01$) were further observed on *Narrative Memory* (NM) when story memory results from the children with language disorders were compared to matched controls. The NM Free Recall Total score and NM Free and Cued Recall Total score differences both displayed large effect sizes (.91 and .87, respectively). The NM Free and Cued vs. NM Recognition Contrast score revealed a moderate effect size (.56).

The language disorder sample also displayed a lower result ($p < .02$) on *Memory for Faces* than the matched controls with a moderate effect size (.71), but Memory for Faces Delayed performance was not significantly different. This suggests that the children need more time to consolidate the information over time. This hypothesis is supported by the results on the Memory for Designs vs. MD Delayed Contrast Score, where the clinical sample showed a significantly higher ($p < .01$) MD vs. MDD Contrast Score than did the matched controls with a moderate negative effect size (–.75).

In the Attention and Executive Functioning domain, the sample of children with language disorders displayed lower performances ($p < .01$) on many scores of two language-based measures of attention and executive functions. Effect sizes were moderate to high. *Response Set* (RS) Total Correct showed an effect size greater than 1.0 at 1.27, and the RS Combined Score effect size (.93) was not far below. The *Inhibition* subtest revealed combined scores (integrating time and errors) on two conditions with effect sizes greater than 1.0 and two time scores near that point: Inhibition (IN)-Naming Total Completion Time: .99; IN-Inhibition Total Completion Time Score: .92; IN Naming Combined Score: 1.04; IN Inhibition Combined Score: 1.31. In addition, IN Total Errors SS showed an effect size of 1.32. Rapid naming was an instrumental component on both RS and IN subtests. Only the IN Switching Total Completion Time score did not show a significant difference ($p < .36$) between the clinical and the control group. This reflects the fact that the typical children were slow on the complex Switching task, so there was not enough difference in time to completion to be significant. The IN-Switching Combined Score, integrating time and errors, was significantly lower ($p < .02$) than that of matched controls with a large effect size (1.03). This result suggests that the clinical group's errors in switching were where the difference in performance could be observed. Further, the IN Naming vs. IN Inhibition Contrast Scaled Score was lower ($p < .01$) for the clinical group than that of controls with a large effect size (.85). The IN Inhibition vs. IN Switching Contrast Scaled Score did not reach significance ($p < .23$), so it was the naming condition more than inhibition or switching that caused problems for the children with language disorders when compared to matched controls.

The language constraints of the *Auditory Attention* subtest are not as great as those on the more complex Response Set, but performance on the Auditory Attention Total Correct score was still lower ($p < .04$) for the clinical sample than matched controls, with a moderate effect size (.75). The AA Combined Score (integrating total correct and total commission errors) was also lower ($p < .05$) with a moderate effect size (.70). *Animal Sorting*, which can be mediated with language, showed the same profile on the AS Combined score, with lower performance ($p < .03$) for the clinical sample and a moderate effect size (.74).

In the Sensorimotor domain only the *Visuomotor Precision* Combined Score, integrating time and accuracy, was lower ($p < .02$) than the same score for matched controls. Effect size was moderate (.70). This demonstrated mild comorbid motor deficits. In the Social Perception domain, the *Affect Recognition* Total SS was lower ($p < .02$) than that of matched controls, but effect size was small (.54). This result may have been due to difficulty mediating the emotional recognition task with language.

The language disorder sample displayed a number of difficulties ($p < .01$) in the Visuospatial Processing Domain when performance was compared to matched controls. Large effect sizes were seen on nonmotor tasks, *Geometric Puzzles* (effect size: .83) and *Picture Puzzles* (.97), as well as on a visuospatial/visuomotor copying task, *Design Copying Process* (DCP) Total Score (effect size: 1.08), DCP Motor Score (.87), DCP Global Score (.98), and DCP Local Score (.92). *Arrows*, assessing judgment of line orientation, was significantly lower ($p < .05$), but effect size was only moderate (.61). Mediating these tasks with language would be difficult for the clinical sample, but, again, there does appear to be a comorbid motor deficit apparent on the DCP Motor Score.

Subtests unchanged from the 1998 NEPSY that showed significantly lower performance for a language disorder sample than for matched controls were: *Repetition of Nonsense Words* (p < .001), *Memory for Names* (p < .01), *Sentence Repetition* (p < .001), *Oromotor Sequences* (p < .01) and *Imitating Hand Positions* (p < .01). The first of these subtests is a phonological task; the MN and SR subtests call on naming ability and/or verbal memory; the Oromotor Sequences subtest requires oromotor coordination for articulation, and the last subtest is most easily performed if the child mediates with language, although motor programming is involved as well.

The lowest score across all subtests was Inhibition Total Errors at a mean score of 4.5. Scores lower than a 7 were obtained on Response Set, Inhibition, and Narrative Memory, all subtests requiring language skills.

Overall, the results of the clinical sample of children with language disorders show impairment in all cognitive domains assessed with the NEPSY-II. These findings highlight the global impact of language deficits in a child's functioning and also the tendency for rather widespread and diffuse symptomatology. One prevalent type of co-occurring problems is motor deficits, which occur in some children with language disorders.

The NEPSY-II Diagnostic Cluster for Language Disorders

The results from NEPSY-II suggest that children with Expressive Language Disorders and Mixed Receptive and Expressive Language Disorders show impairment across domains due to the global impact of Language Disorders.

- Primary deficits in:
  - Receptive language and phonological skills
  - Naming and name retrieval
  - Oromotor skills
- Secondary deficits in:
  - Verbal memory
  - Nonverbal short-term memory due to slow consolidation of visual information mediated with language
  - Attention/executive functions when tasks are language based
  - Visuospatial areas mediated with language
- Possible comorbid deficits in:
  - Visuomotor and motor skills

(See Rapid Reference 6.9 for the summary of the NEPSY-II diagnostic cluster for language disorder.)

≡ *Rapid Reference 6.9*

NEPSY-II Diagnostic Cluster for Language Disorder

Children with Expressive Language Disorders and Mixed Receptive and Expressive Language Disorders show impairment across domains on NEPSY-II due to the global impact of Language Disorders.

Primary deficits in:

- Receptive language and phonological skills
- Naming and name retrieval
- Oromotor skills

Secondary deficits in:

- Verbal memory
- Areas mediated with language or language-based
- Nonverbal short-term memory due to slow consolidation of visual information mediated with language
- Attention/executive functions when tasks are language-based
- Visuospatial areas mediated with language

Possible comorbid deficits in:

- Visuomotor and motor skills

Because children with language disorders can have such pervasive problems across domains, it is important to administer a nonverbal cognitive assessment that will make it possible to judge the child's cognitive ability more accurately than could be accomplished with a language-based cognitive measure. It is also essential to include a speech-language evaluation, preferably to be administered by a certified speech-language therapist. An adaptive behavior scale should be endorsed by parents, teachers, and the child, depending on age. Achievement tests should be included, and samples of classroom work can be important in helping understand what the child is experiencing in the classroom. On all assessments, test the limits whenever necessary to give a clearer picture of the child's problem-solving ability. Be sensitive to any signs of anxiety/depression in these children, who can become very discouraged. Checklists to assess these possibilities may be helpful. Add any additional NEPSY-II subtests to the Referral Battery that seem appropriate. Observational notes, results of a classroom observation (if possible), and the comprehensive history covering all educational, medical, developmental, and psychological factors should be combined with the NEPSY-II results, as well as all other assessments. Together these measures should yield enough information to ascertain if the child has a Language Disorder and to form the basis of a comprehensive intervention program.

Referral Battery for Language Disorders

(Note subtest age range. Subtests in parentheses are optional.)

Age	Subtest	Designed to Assess
Attention/Executive Functioning Domain		
Ages 3–6	Statue	Inhibition of motor response to interfering noise
Ages 5–16	Auditory Attention and Response Set	Selective auditory attention and vigilance (AA)
		Shift and maintenance of new auditory set; inhibit and switch
Ages 5–16	Inhibition	Shift and maintenance of new visual set; inhibit and switch
(Ages 7–16)	(Animal Sorting)	Concept formation; ability to transfer concepts to action; shift
(Ages 7–16)	(Clocks)	Planning and organization; visuospatial skills; concept of time
Language Domain		
Ages 3–4	Body Part Naming and Identification	Confrontation naming and name recognition, basic components of expressive and receptive language
Ages 3–12	Oromotor Sequences	Oromotor coordination for articulation
Ages 3–12	Repetition of Nonsense Words	Phonological encoding and decoding as the child repeats nonsense words presented aloud.
Ages 3–16	Comprehension of Instructions	Receiving, processing, and executing oral instructions
(Ages 3–16)	(Phonological Processing)	(phonological processing at the level of word segments [syllables] and letter sounds [phonemes])
Ages 3–16	Speeded Naming	Rapid semantic access and production of names

Age	Subtest	Designed to Assess
Memory and Learning Domain		
Ages 3–6	Sentence Repetition	Repetition and immediate recall of sentences
Ages 5–16	Memory for Names and MN Delayed	Name learning and short-term recall; long-term memory for names
Ages 7–16	Word List Interference	Verbal working memory; repetition and recall after interference
Sensorimotor Domain		
Ages 3–12	Imitating Hand Positions	Imitation of hand/finger positions; visuospatial analysis and motor programming
(Ages 3–12)	(Visuomotor Precision)	Graphomotor speed and accuracy
Social Perception (if social concerns)		
(Ages 3–16)	(Affect Recognition)	Ability to recognize emotional affect
Visuospatial Processing		
Ages 3–16	Geometric Puzzles	Mental rotation, visuospatial analysis, and attention to detail

APPLICATION OF THE NEPSY-II IN DIAGNOSING AUTISTIC SPECTRUM DISORDERS

Background

Autism Spectrum Disorder (ASD): The *DSM-IV-TR* includes a number of disorders under the heading of Pervasive Developmental Disorders: Autistic Disorder, Asperger's Disorder, Rett's Disorder, Childhood Disintegrative Disorder, and Pervasive Developmental Disorder, Not Otherwise Specified. For the purposes of the NEPSY-II validity studies only the first two most common of these autism spectrum disorders will be addressed in two separate studies. The National Institute of Mental Health (NIMH, 2004b) reported that prevalence estimates for all autism spectrum disorders (ASD) range from 2 to 6% per 1,000 children. Data released by the Center for Disease Control and Prevention's Autism and Developmental Disabilities Monitoring Network (ADDM) in 2009 showed that an average of 1 in 150 children has an autism spectrum disorder. If 4 million children are born in the United States every year, approximately 26,670 children will eventually be diagnosed with an ASD. Assuming the prevalence rate has been constant over the past two decades, we can estimate that about 560,000 individuals between the ages of 0 to 21 have an ASD. A meta-analysis of 40 studies indicated that the overall prevalence rate of Autism Spectrum Disorder was 20.0 per 10,000 ($p < .05$) (Williams, Goldstein, & Minshew, 2006). Prevalence estimates vary with diagnostic criteria (ICD-10 or DSM-IV), age of child screened, and study location (Japan or North America). Recent epidemiological research suggests that prevalence rates for ASD could be as high as 30 to 60 cases per 10,000, possibly due to better screening and to broadening of ASD definitions (Rutter, 2005).

Children on the autistic spectrum have autism-specific functional developmental problems (Greenspan, 2001). These include deficits in the ability to empathize and to see the world from another's perspective in both physical and emotional contexts (theory of mind) (Baron-Cohen, 1995; 2001) Beaumont and Newcombe (2006) investigated theory of mind and central coherence abilities in adults with high-functioning autism (HFA) or Asperger syndrome (AS) using naturalistic tasks. Twenty adults with HFA/AS correctly answered significantly fewer theory of mind questions than 20 controls on a forced-choice response task. On a narrative task, there were no differences in the proportion of mental state words between the two groups, although the participants with HFA/AS were less inclined to provide explanations for characters' mental states. No between-group differences existed on the central coherence questions of the forced-choice response task, and the participants with HFA/AS included an equivalent proportion of explanations for nonmental state phenomena in their narratives as did controls. Their results supported the ToM deficit account of autism spectrum disorders, and suggest that difficulties in mental state attribution cannot be exclusively attributed to weak central coherence and persist in some individuals into adulthood.

With early interventions, however, children on the autism spectrum can make significant progress in relating to and understanding others' mental states. Therefore, early and reliable diagnosis is essential to address the needs of these children.

Children with autism spectrum disorders often carry a previous diagnosis of ADHD (Holtman, Bölte, & Poustka, 2005). Gillberg (2003) states that many individuals with autism spectrum disorders show severe degrees of inattention and impulsivity and many meet the symptom criteria for ADHD of the *DSM-IV*. They display the DAMP profile (Deficits in Attention, Motor control, and Perception). Other pathological features may also lead to other diagnoses. Symptoms of anxiety are common in children with ASD (Tsai, 2006). Also, children with ASD, especially those with average cognitive ability, are reported to have an increased risk of developing a mood disorder when compared to typical peers. Symptoms often worsen with puberty (Ghaziuddin & Tsai, 1991; Gillberg, 1984). Kim and colleagues (2000) found that 16.9% of children and adolescents with ASD endorsing a checklist of depressive symptoms had elevated scores. Bipolar disorder has been reported in children and adolescents with ASD (Frazier, Doyle, Chiu, & Coyle, 2002), although bipolar occurred less often than unipolar depression.

Autistic Disorder is characterized by varying degrees of impairments in social interaction and communication and the presence of a restricted range of behaviors and interests. Intellectual functioning is often impaired and is strongly related to outcome (Spreen, Risser, & Edgell, 1995). The previously mentioned meta-analysis of 40 studies by Williams and colleagues (2006) found the prevalence of Autistic Disorder specifically to be 7.1 per 10,000 ($p < .05$). Gillberg (2001) noted that about 30% of children with autism have IQs over 70, which qualifies as "high-functioning autism." The prevalence of high-functioning autism would be 0.03 percent.

Children with Autistic Disorder display a number of possible comorbidities. The NIMH (2004b) reports that autistic individuals may have sensory problems such as being highly attuned or painfully sensitive to sounds, textures, tastes, and smells; may have mental retardation; and may experience seizures. Mesibov and colleagues (Mesibov, Klinger, & Adams, 1997) report that although people with autism share features with people with ADHD, the underlying reasons for the symptoms are different (p. 35). Gillott, Furniss, and Walter (2001) found that children with high-functioning autism demonstrated significantly more anxiety symptoms than did children with language impairment and typical children, with separation anxiety and obsessive-compulsive disorder occurring most frequently. Macrocephaly (head volume greater than the 97th percentile) was originally observed by Kanner (1943) and has been confirmed in approximately 20% of individuals with autism (Fombonne, 1999). Seizures occur in 3-30% of children with autism (Bertrand et al., 2001; Giovanardi-Rossi et al. 2000).

It is essential for clinicians engaged in diagnosis to know that autistic-like symptoms of varying degrees occur in children with Fragile-X syndrome (a chromosomal abnormality associated with mental retardation and physical abnormality); and with tuberous sclerosis (a rare genetic disorder that causes benign tumors to grow in the brain). All clinicians should be well-acquainted with symptoms of these disorders in order to avoid misdiagnosis. Nonetheless, only 5 to 10% of cases of autism are due to the result of other diseases (Cook, 1998; Rutter, 1994).

Autism can be reliably detected by the age of 3 years, and in some cases as early as 18 months. Children with autism may not babble, point, or make meaningful gestures by one year of age; may not speak one word by 16 months, or combine two words by 2 years; may not respond to their names; may not smile; may make no or poor eye contact with others; and may become attached to one particular toy or object (Gillberg, 2001). Children with autism, therefore, display problems in shared attention, including social referencing and problem-solving (Mundy, Sigman, & Kasari, 1990). In addition, deficits in the capacities for affective reciprocity (Baranek, 1999; Dawson & Galpert, 1990; Lewy & Dawson, 1992; Osterling & Dawson, 1994; Tanguay, 1999; Tanguay, Robertson, & Derrick, 1998); and functional (pragmatic) language (Wetherby & Prizant, 1998) also appear typical of autism. As adolescents, children with autism have problems with higher level abstract thinking, including making inferences (Minshew & Goldstein, 1998). Difficulty with the imagination, organizational skills, and problem solving required to cope easily in a new environment, see the big picture, predict likely outcomes, and understand other people's motivation are characteristics of AS students at the university level (Beaumont & Newcombe, 2006).

Specifically, an apparent core deficit in autism known as Theory of mind (ToM) refers to the ability to reflect on one's own mind and the minds of others. It is the ability to infer the full range of mental states (beliefs, desires, intentions, imagination, emotion, and so forth (Baron-Cohen, 2001). A meta-analysis indicated that individuals with autism show significantly pronounced ToM deficits compared to normal and mentally retarded individuals (Yirmiya, Erel, Shaked, & Solomonica-Levi, 1998). Children with Autistic Disorder performed less well than normally developing children on seven of eight ToM tests for false belief, level one; Smarties; deception; ignorance; picture story; false belief- level two; and other tasks, respectively, but not on ToM tests assessing desire.

Furthermore, autistic/normal differences were more pronounced as participants got older and as typical children's verbal abilities increased. The pattern of deficits in ToM is often not unique to autism, compared to other psychiatric disorders (e.g., mental retardation), but *is* usually more severe (Yirmiya et al., 1998; Shaked & Yirmiya, 2004). The ToM deficits in autism are linked to impairments such as deficits in understanding self-conscious emotions (e.g., shame and embarrassment; Heerey, Keltner, & Capps, 2003); deficits in empathetic ability (Dyck, Ferguson, & Shochet, 2001); and deficits in verbal ability (Yirmiya, Solomonica-Levi, & Shulman, 1996; Yirmiya & Shulman, 1996). Studies have shown that individuals with autism do show intact understanding of physiological (heart, lungs) and cognitive (brain, mind) systems using mentalistic explanations (peterson, 2005); intact understanding of thought bubbles representing thought (Kerr & Durkin, 2004); and intact understanding of others' intentions (Carpenter, Pennington, & Rogers, 2001).

Further, in addition to ToM deficits affecting social perception, processing affect can be problematical for individuals with autism, as well. They show deficits in recognizing human and canine emotions (Downs & Smith, 2004), and perform no better on facial affect recognition tasks when viewing full rather than partial faces (Gross, 2004). Performance is significantly poorer on facial affect recognition tests when compared to schizophrenic and normal individuals (Bölte & Poustka, 2003). Individuals with autism have problems making social judgments regarding the trustworthiness of faces (Adolphs, 2003). One study showed no deficit in the ability to recognize facial expression of emotion (Castelli, 2005), whereas another showed deficits in face affect recognition were eliminated with slow dynamic presentations of faces via strobe (Gepner, Deruelle, and Grynfeltt, 2001).

A core symptom in Autistic Disorder, in addition to those in social perception, is language delay or a total lack of development of language (American Psychiatric Association, 2000). Children who develop language deficits in pragmatics are most germane to autism. Specifically, autistic individuals show deficits in maintaining an ongoing topic of discourse (Hale & Tager-Flusberg, 2005); providing appropriate responses to requests for clarification during conversation (Volden, 2004); maintaining joint attention with a conversational partner (Charman, 2003); and maintaining central coherence in story comprehension (e.g., keeping overall story meaning in mind rather than focusing on details) (Norbury & Bishop, 2002).

Reading comprehension is a complex language activity in which individuals with autism show significantly poorer performance than age-matched controls (Minshew, Johnson, & Luna, 2001) despite intact phonological processing skills for single word decoding (Bishop et al., 2004). Along with intact reading decoding skills, good spelling and word association skills are also seen (Minshew et al., 2001). Because the individual reads words well, there is usually an expectation that he/she understands at the same level, which is often not the case. Deficits in verbal inference-making, comprehension of idioms and metaphors, and comprehension of complex language structure are deficits in individuals with autism that contribute to reading and story comprehension problems (Minshew et al., 2001) Further, the National Institute of Mental Health (2004b) reports that autism spectrum disorder is associated with abnormal speech production (e.g., inability to combine words into sentences, repeating the same word or phrase, and echolalia); conversational difficulties (e.g., inability to engage in conversational turn taking); and atypical gestures during conversations (e.g., mismatch between gestures and speech). (For a review of language deficits in autistic disorder, see Boucher, 2003.)

Language impairments in autism may mediate executive function deficits (e.g., failure to use verbal mediation strategies may produce deficits in maintaining goal-related information in working memory) (Joseph, McGrath,

& Tager-Flusberg, 2005). Autistic individuals show consistent deficits in many but not all aspects of executive functioning, specifically on planning tasks (e.g., Tower of Hanoi), in which they perseverated (Ozonoff, Pennington, & Rogers, 1991) and mental flexibility tests (e.g., Wisconsin Card Sorting Test) where they displayed both perseveration and category deficits (Ozonoff et al., 1991; Szatmari, Tuff, Finlayson, & Bartolucci, 1990). On category fluency tasks they generated fewer category exemplars, and they also displayed EF deficits on *some* inhibition tests on which they showed deficits in both prepotent inhibition and cognitive flexibility (Ozonoff, Strayer, McMahon, & Fillouz, 1994). By contrast, autistic individuals showed relatively intact inhibitory function with average reaction time and accuracy on the classic Stroop Color-Word test, suggesting relatively normal inhibition of prepotent responses (namely, reading color words); and visual working memory (Geurts, Verte, Oosterlaan, Roeyers, & Sergeant, 2004). (For reviews of EF deficits in Autistic Disorder, see Hill, 2004; and Sergeant, Geurts, & Oosterlaan, 2002.)

Deficits in both auditory and visual attention tasks, particularly on tests tapping social aspects of communication, are seen in individuals with autism. In visual attention tasks, autistic individuals show abnormalities on social monitoring tests, in which they show less attention to significant social stimuli (mouth, eye, body of an actor) and more attention to nonsignificant stimuli (inanimate objects in a social setting) (Klin, Jones, Schultz, Volkmar, & Cohen, 2002), and on gaze processing tests (pelphrey, Morris, & McCarthy, 2005). On auditory attention tasks, individuals with autism show deficits on auditory orienting tests with depressed physiological responses to an occasional oddball *vowel* in a sequence of standard vowels. This deficit was not obtained for non-vowel sounds and may be speech-sound specific (Ceponiene et al., 2003).

Specific, as opposed to general, memory deficits are seen in individuals with autism. They show deficits in spatial working memory (Williams et al., 2006; Williams, Goldstein, Carpenter, & Minshew, 2005); source memory for social aspects of context (O'Shea, Fein, Cillessen, Klin, & Schultz, 2005) source memory for words (internal, external, and reality sources) (Hale & Tager-Flusberg, 2005); and immediate and delayed recall of faces and of family scenes (Williams et al., 2005). In contrast, individuals with autism show intact associative learning ability, rote verbal working memory, and recognition memory (Williams et al., 2006); intact verbal working memory on an N-back letter test involving no complex cognitive demands (Williams, Goldstein, Carpenter, & Minshew, 2005); intact immediate and delayed memory for word pairs and stories on a verbal working memory task (Williams et al., 2006); intact short-term memory and paired associate learning (Minshew & Goldstein, 2001); and intact semantic priming (Ozonoff & Strayer, 2001).

Three areas in which recent research in autism is scarce include sensorimotor, visuospatial, and processing speed. The available research in sensorimotor deficits indicates the following deficits: impersistence and stereotypies (Mandelbaum et al., 2006); oculomotor deficits in pursuit eye movement (Takarae, Minshew, Luna, Krisky, & Sweeney, 2004); nonmeaningful combined hand-and-finger gestures in pragmatic language assessments (Freitag, Kleser, Schneider, & von Gontard, 2007); and slow performance on Grooved Pegboard and weak grip strength (Hardan, Kilpatrick, Keshavan, & Minshew, 2003). An early study revealed poor motor imitation abilities (Jones & Prior, 1985). A few studies have revealed visuospatial deficits related to weak central coherence (CC) (Pellicano, Mayberry, Durkin, & Maley, 2006). The concept of CC is defined as the ability to integrate elements into coherent wholes. A weakness in this area is marked by local processing (i.e., focus on details as a whole, rather than the global elements) on coherence tests such as the Children's Embedded Figures Test, Block Design, and the Rey Complex Figure Test (Pellicano, Gibson, Mayberry, Durkin, & Badcock, 2005). Weak CC is related to aspects of executive control but not to false-belief understanding (Pellicano, Mayberry, Durkin, & Maley, 2006) or to susceptibility to visual illusions (Ropar & Mitchell, 2001). Another study indicated autistic children showed deficits in exploration of containers (explored less time and explored fewer containers), which, the authors argued, is consistent with the DSM-IV criterion of "restricted interests" in autism (Pierce & Courchesne, 2001). The available research on processing speed in individuals with autism shows deficits in the speed with which they discriminate among faces and between objects (Behrmann et al., 2006). Other research indicates that autistic individuals show inspection times on laboratory tasks as fast as age-matched normally developing children (IQ +1 SD from the mean) and faster than mentally retarded children of the same age (Scheuffgen, Happe, Anderson, & Frith, 2000).

To conclude, children with autism exhibit a complex symptomatology. Their ability to empathize and to see the world from another's perspective is impaired, and perseverative tendencies or obsessive-compulsive traits characterize behavior. Language may be entirely absent but when functional, pragmatic aspects are poor, intellectual development and concept formation is impaired in a majority of the children. Sensorimotor development may be affected, and weak central coherence and/or poor social perception may lead to specific types of visual or visuospatial impairment. Further inattention and impulsivity, poor inhibition, and anxiety and mood disorders are frequently comorbid.

NEPSY-II Validity Studies for Autistic Disorder

The NEPSY-II validity group of 23 children with high-functioning autism (HFA) with IQ level ≤ 80 met the *DSM-IV-TR* criteria for Autistic Disorder. In addition to the aforementioned IQ level, group membership was determined by absence of neurological dysfunction not associated with autism, absence of concurrent psychiatric diagnoses, and absence of specific learning disabilities. Children could carry a codiagnosis of Oppositional Defiant Disorder and/or Attention Deficit Hyperactivity Disorder. Members of the clinical group were also required to have normal auditory acuity and normal or corrected visual acuity. Their performance on NEPSY-II was compared to that of the control sample randomly selected from the standardization population and matched for age, sex, race/ethnicity, and parent education level.

As a group, the children with HFA differed ($p < .01$) from matched controls on the *Animal Sorting* (AS) subtests of Attention/Executive domain with some very large effect sizes (AS Total Correct Sorts effect size: 2.18; AS Combined Scaled Score effect size: 2.47). This subtest assesses the executive functions needed to formulate concepts quickly and to transfer the concepts into action by sorting into categories, as well as being able to inhibit that category and shift to another. In relation to the control sample, the children with HFA performed poorly on *Auditory Attention and Response Set*. Greatest differences were seen on Response Set where they displayed a difference ($p < .02$) with effect size larger than 1.0 on the RS Combined Score (integrating correct responses and commission errors) (effect size: 1.02), and a difference ($p < .01$) on RS Total Correct Score with a large effect size of .97. The AA vs. RS Contrast Score (effect size: 85) also showed a difference ($p < .03$) with a large effect size (.85). Differences were also seen on Auditory Attention, however, but with moderate effect sizes: AA Total Correct ($p < .03$; effect size: .73) and AA Combined Score ($p < .02$; effect size: 79). The children with HFA seemed to perform better on visual attention and executive function tasks than on auditory tasks of the same type. For instance, on the Inhibition subtest only one score (IN Total Completion Time Score effect size: 1.55) showed a significant difference ($p < .01$) in performance when compared to match controls.

All of the Language domain subtest performances differed ($p < .01$) from matched controls with large effect sizes in the subtests *Comprehension of Instructions* (CI Total score effect size: 1.78); *Phonological Processing* (pH Total score effect size: 1.10); *Speeded Naming* (SN Total Completion Time effect size: 1.11; SN Combined Score effect size: 93). Therefore, the sample group of HFA children in comparison to matched controls was not able to understand and execute oral directions, had difficulty with phonological processing, and was slow and inaccurate in accessing semantics quickly and accurately. It should be noted that despite the fact that HFA children in this study were required to have an IQ of > 80, they still displayed language and communication problems, as expected in children with autism.

Again, as would be expected, the clinical sample of children with HFA showed secondary deficits in verbal memory, but nonverbal memory also appeared problematical on some subtests. Lower performances ($p < .01$) were found in *Narrative Memory* (NM) and *Word List Interference* (WI), with effect sizes greater than 1.0 (NM Free Recall Score effect size: 1.21; NM Free and Cued Recall: 1.28; WI Repetition: 1.68; WI Recall Total: 1.71). A difference ($p < .03$) was also observed in NM Free/Cued Recall vs. Recognition Contrast Score, with a large effect size: 1.06.

Lower scores in nonverbal memory performance for the clinical sample in comparison to matched controls were found in *Memory for Designs* (MD) and Memory for Designs Delayed (MDD). On the immediate memory task, the group with HFA showed a lower ($p < .03$) MD Content Score with moderate effect size (76), and the MD Total Score at the same confidence level also showed a moderate effect size (70). The lower ($p < .01$) MD Spatial Score had a larger effect size (88), however. As would be expected, the MD Content vs. Spatial Contrast Scaled Score was lower ($p < .02$) than matched controls with a moderate (.67) effect size. On the delayed design memory task, MDD, the clinical sample again displayed poorer performances ($p < .01$) than matched controls on the design memory tasks (MDD Content Score effect size: 1.00), but the MDD Spatial Score did not reach significance ($p < .09$). The MDD Total Score was lower ($p < .01$) with a large effect size (1.03). The contrast between immediate and delayed design memory was also lower ($p < .02$) than that of matched controls with a large effect size (1.01). Thus, children with HFA did display deficits in short-term and long-term design memory and immediate spatial memory, but long-term spatial memory was similar to matched controls.

The *Memory for Faces* performance of the children with HFA was lower ($p < .01$) than that of matched controls and the effect size of Memory for Faces Total was large (1.03). Given the social perception problems of children with autism, this result would not be surprising. Memory for Faces Delayed Total did not reach significance ($p < .06$); however, this appeared to have more to do with the matched controls performing at a slightly lower level on MFD than on MF, and the clinical sample performing slightly better than on the immediate. Nonetheless, the children with HFA still only achieved a MFD scaled score of 7.1 (mean = 10 ± 3), while the MF Total scaled score was 6.4. These scores were in comparison to the matched control group's scaled score of 10.0 on MF and 9.3 on MFD.

In the Social Perception domain, the HFA group performance was lower ($p < .01$) than that of the control sample on *Affect Recognition*, a test designed to assess recognition of facial emotions, and effect size was large (1.19). The *Theory of Mind* subtest revealed that 70% of the children with HFA achieved a score of 6 or less, which was considered weak, at less than the tenth percentile. Only 9% of the matched controls scored at that level. Therefore, children with HFA showed poorer ability to identify emotional facial affect and a majority of the sample displayed a deficit in understanding another's perspective and being able to match affect to social context. Along with their difficulty with immediate Memory for Faces, these results converge on the social perceptual difficulties that are a core symptom of Autistic Disorder.

Sensorimotor differences were seen between the clinical and matched control sample. Performance of simple finger tapping and more complex hand movement sequences taken together for the dominant hand was lower ($p < .04$) for the HFA group than for the control group, as seen on the *Fingertip Tapping Dominant Hand* Combined Score with a moderate effect size (.75), but not the corresponding measures of the nondominant hand. While simple finger tapping was similar for children with HFA and matched controls ($p < .33$), motor programming of the hands bilaterally (FT Sequences Combined SS) was significantly poorer ($p < .03$) for the HFA group compared to that of the matched controls, and effect size (.88) was large. Time to execute a pencil line through winding tracks on the Visuomotor Precision subtest (VP Total Completion Time) was similar ($p < .24$) for the two groups, but the VP Combined Score, integrating speed and accuracy, was lower ($p < .01$) for the group of children with HFA than for controls. Effect size was high (.86).

In the Visuospatial Processing domain, the two groups displayed differences ($p < .01$) in performance on a subtest requiring judgment of line orientation with a large effect size, as seen on the *Arrows* Total Score (effect size: 1.15). While this may be due to a visuospatial deficit, it is also true that attending to multiple stimuli (eight arrows) requires the executive functions of response inhibition and monitoring in order to consider each of the arrows carefully before making a choice. Further, there may have been difficulty understanding oral directions. A nonmotor visuospatial task, Geometric Puzzles, showed no differences ($p < .31$) in comparing the performance of the HFA group and matched controls, nor did the 3-D motoric construction task (Block Construction $p < .53$). The children with HFA showed poorer performance ($p < .02$) on *Picture Puzzles*, in which they had to deconstruct a picture mentally and recognize part to whole relationships in the ecological pictures. The pictures of everyday scenes and objects may have been the problem, as this was a nonmotor task and required similar understanding of part-whole relationships (as those seen in Geometric Puzzles) that they had been able to solve at the same level as matched controls. Relating to the geometric puzzles may have been easier for them than relating to pictures of real life scenes. Several differences ($p < .01$) in performance between the clinical group and matched controls were seen in visual-motor integration skills for two-dimensional geometric design copying. All effect sizes were large: *Design Copying* Process (DCP) Total (.89), DCP Motor (.82), DCP Global (.88), and DCP Local (.80). These results suggest that children with HFA have motor problems that interfere with paper-pencil tasks, as seen on Visuomotor Precision in the Sensorimotor domain. The children with HFA had problems with design configuration (DCP Global), as well as with copying details (DCP Local). This group of children with HFA did not seem to have significant central coherence (CC) deficits as seen in the study of Pellicano and colleagues (2006). CC refers to the ability to integrate elements into coherent wholes. Children with deficits in CC tend to focus on details as a whole, rather than the global elements. Pellicano and colleagues (2006) postulated that CC is related to aspects of executive control.

On the 1998 NEPSY (Korkman et al., 1998) subtests that were unchanged, significant differences were seen between an HFA clinical sample and matched controls. Differences in performance between the two groups occurred on *Design Fluency* ($p < .001$), an executive function task requiring planning and strategizing in order to create as many unique designs as possible. Performance may also have been affected by the graphomotor and time aspects of this task. Differences were also seen on Route Finding ($p < .001$), a schematic map-reading task that requires understanding of symbolic representations of space, as well as directionality and orientation. Children with autism have difficulty understanding symbolic representations (Fay & Schuler, 1980), which, along with visuospatial deficits, may have affected performance on Route Finding adversely.

The deficit in fine motor programming seen in the clinical group on the Fingertip Tapping subtest of NEPSY-II was also seen on the 1998 NEPSY Manual Motor Sequencing subtest ($p < .03$), when performance was compared to matched controls. Their motor programming deficit as well as visuospatial processing deficits may be related to the poor performance ($p < .01$) of the HFA group on the Imitating Hand Positions subtest. The IMH subtest involves integrating visual-spatial information, using motor programming, and using kinesthetic feedback from position to imitate the examiner's hand position. Additionally, the interpersonal aspects of Imitating Hand Positions and the difficulty children with autism have with imitation (Jones & Prior, 1985) may have related to poor performance on this subtest. Furthermore, the Imitating Hand Position subtest requires close inspection of the examiner's hand as it is held in position for the child to imitate. When the hand is in position, however, the examiner's face is in the child's field of vision, and this may have an adverse effect on performance because core symptoms for children with autism are avoidant eye contact and avoidance of close personal interaction. Additionally, the children with HFA performed poorly, as compared to matched controls, on List Learning, which requires verbal memory for learning a list of 15 items over five trials ($p < .03$). It also requires executive functions to inhibit extraneous intrusions and intrusions from one list to another and to employ strategies such as clustering the items efficiently.

In summary, in the NEPSY-II validity studies, children with HFA displayed a complex pattern of findings, in accordance with earlier studies. Executive dysfunction in formulating concepts fluently and sorting into categories was impaired. Executive dysfunctions in inhibition and cognitive flexibility were more problematical than auditory attention. Performance was better on visual attention tasks. The group also displayed difficulty in processing quickly. The children with HFA, despite IQs > 80, were not able to understand and execute oral directions, had difficulty with phonological processing, and were slow and inaccurate in accessing semantics quickly. They displayed deficits in verbal memory (NM and WI subtests) and nonverbal, visuospatial memory remembering designs and their locations in a grid (MD and MDD subtests), although spatial location consolidated over time.

Memory for Faces performance was poorer for children with HFA than for controls, although delayed memory did not show a significant difference in the two groups, due to small group sizes. The HFA group showed characteristic problems in recognizing emotional facial expressions on Affect Recognition. The majority (70%) of the sample displayed a deficit in understanding the perspectives of others, whereas only a small portion of the control subjects did. These results are consistent with the marked social perceptual problems of autism.

The children with HFA showed evidence that finger dexterity and motor programming were poor, particularly for the dominant hand. A clear deficit in bilateral motor programming of sequential motor movements was seen, however. Time and accuracy in executing a pencil line through a winding track was poor, as was copying of geometric figures. The copying was affected by motor problems as well as difficulty perceiving and reproducing the configuration and the details. Deconstructing an ecological picture mentally and recognizing part to whole relationships in pictures was problematical. The pictures of everyday scenes and objects may have been the problem.

The NEPSY-II Diagnostic Cluster for Autistic Disorder

The results from NEPSY-II suggest that children with high-functioning Autistic Disorder show characteristic social perception problems, executive dysfunction, and language disorders as well as other impairments across domains, many of which are due to the global impact of executive and language disorders.

- Primary deficits:
  - Executive Functions, including:
    - Formulation of concepts transferring concepts into action (sort into categories)
    - Inhibition of response
    - Shift of set, cognitive flexibility
  - Selective and sustained auditory attention
  - Language, receptive and expressive
    - Understanding of oral language
    - Naming deficit: slow semantic access inaccuracy of naming
    - Phonological processing deficit—the latter may possibly be secondary to auditory inattention on task
  - Social Perception:
    - Affect recognition and affect from social context
    - Theory of mind (74% of sample; understanding another's perspective, beliefs, intention; problems with literal interpretation)
  - Slow processing speed
  - Visuospatial processing
    - Visual perception of configuration and detail of geometric designs, part-whole relationships, spatial location
  - Motor programming of sequential hand movements bilaterally; mild problems with dominant hand tapping and sequencing
- Secondary deficits:
  - Ability to carry out oral instructions
  - Verbal memory, especially semantic and narrative memory
  - Visual memory: short-term memory for faces, designs, and spatial location; long-term memory for designs
  - Visuomotor copying and precision

(See Rapid Reference 6.10 for the summary of the NEPSY-II validity study diagnostic cluster for autistic disorder.)

≡ Rapid Reference 6.10

The NEPSY-II Diagnostic Cluster for Autistic Disorder

Children with high-functioning Autistic Disorder show characteristic social perception problems, executive dysfunction, and language disorders, as well as other impairments across domains on NEPSY-II. Many impairments are due to the global impact of executive and language disorders.

Primary deficits:
- Executive Functions, including:
  - Formulation of concepts transferring concepts into action (sort into categories)
  - Inhibition of response
  - Shift of set, cognitive flexibility
- Selective and sustained auditory attention
- Language, receptive, and expressive
  - Understanding of oral language
  - Naming deficit: slow semantic access and inaccuracy of naming
  - Phonological processing deficit—the latter may be secondary to auditory inattention to task
- Social Perception
  - Affect recognition and affect from social context
  - Theory of mind (74% of sample; understanding another's perspective, beliefs, intention; problems with literal interpretation)
- Slow processing speed
- Visuospatial processing
  - Visual perception of configuration and detail of geometric designs, part-whole relationships, spatial location
- Motor programming of sequential hand movements bilaterally; mild problems with dominant hand tapping and sequencing

Secondary deficits:
- Ability to carry out oral instructions
- Verbal memory, especially semantic and narrative memory
- Visual memory: short-term memory for faces, designs, and spatial location; long-term memory for designs
- Visuomotor copying and precision

The NEPSY-II Referral Battery for Social/Interpersonal Deficits

(Use for Autistic Spectrum Disorders [Autism and Asperger's Disorder]; Other Social/Interpersonal Concerns)

Age	Subtest	Designed to Assess
Attention/Executive Functioning Domain		
Ages 3–6	Statue	Inhibition of motor response to interfering noise
Ages 5–12	Design Fluency	Planning, strategizing, monitoring for rapid problem solution
Ages 5–16	Auditory Attention and Response Set	Selective auditory attention and vigilance (AA)
		Shift and maintenance of new auditory set; inhibition
Ages 5–16	Inhibition	Shift and maintenance of new visual set; inhibition
Ages 7–16	Animal Sorting	Concept formation; ability to transfer concepts to action; shift
Language Domain		
Ages 3–16	Comprehension of Instructions	Receiving, processing, and executing oral instructions
Ages 3–16	Speeded Naming	Rapid semantic access and production of names
Ages 3–16	Word Generation	Verbal productivity; generation of words in categories
(Ages 3–16)	(phonological Processing)	Phonological processing: word segments and phonemes
Memory and Learning Domain		
(Ages 3–16)	(Memory for Designs) (and MD Delayed)	Spatial memory for novel visual designs; immediate and long-term visuospatial memory
Ages 3–16	Narrative Memory	Encoding of story details with free and cued (questions) recall
Ages 5–16	Memory for Faces and MF Delayed	Encoding of facial features, as face discrimination and recognition; immediate and long-term memory for faces

(continued)

(*continued*)

Age	Subtest	Designed to Assess
Ages 7–16	Word List Interference	Verbal working memory; repetition and recall after interference

Sensorimotor Domain

Age	Subtest	Designed to Assess
Ages 3–12	Imitating Hand Positions	Imitation of hand/finger positions: visuospatial analysis and motor programming
Ages 3–12	Visuomotor Precision	Graphomotor speed and accuracy
(Ages 3–12)	(Manual Motor Sequences)	Imitation of rhythmic manual movement sequences (programming)
Ages 5–16	Fingertip Tapping	Finger dexterity and motor speed; motor programming

Social Perception (if social concerns)

Age	Subtest	Designed to Assess
Ages 3–16	(Affect Recognition)	Ability to recognize emotional affect
Ages 3–16	Theory of Mind	Ability to understand mental functions and another's point of view

Visuospatial Processing

Age	Subtest	Designed to Assess
Ages 3–6	Block Construction	Visuospatial and visuomotor ability to reproduce 3-D constructions from models or 2-D drawings
Ages 3–16	Geometric Puzzles	Mental rotation, visuospatial analysis, and attention to detail
Ages 3–16	Design Copying	Motor and visuoperceptual skills in copying 2-D designs
Ages 3–16	Geometric Puzzles	Visuospatial analysis, mental rotation, and attention to detail
(Ages 5–16)	(Arrows)	Ability to judge line orientation
Ages 7–16	(picture Puzzles)	Visual discrimination, spatial localization, visual scanning, and the ability to deconstruct a picture into constituent parts and recognize part-whole relationships

Although individual children in this clinical group may show much heterogeneity, as a group, children with HFA displayed a profile on NEPSY-II that included the characteristics shown in Rapid Reference 6.10. The NEPSY-II was not designed specifically to assign *DSM-IV-TR* (APA, 2000) diagnoses, but it can be used to determine the presence of deficits that are associated with this diagnosis. The assessment can also provide the opportunity to observe numerous other behaviors associated with autism. Even more important, the assessment provides an overview of the child's strengths and weaknesses as a basis for evaluating the child's education and intervention needs as well as resources on which to build. Of course, any such diagnosis must only be made within the context of the child's developmental, medical, social, and educational history, as well as the manner in which he or she functions in everyday life. With this diagnosis, in particular, but with many diagnoses of developmental disorders in general, it is wise to observe the child in a peer group setting in order to observe social interaction. Diagnoses of the more complex developmental disorders may require that even an abbreviated Referral Battery be administered over time, much less a Full NEPSY-II. The clinician can perform a few subtests in multiple 30-to-60 minute sessions, rather than attempting to assess the child in one long session with dubious results. If the clinician knows in advance that the referral question is to rule out Autistic Disorder, he or she should take the time for preparation, as noted in Chapter 3. This may make the difference between a successful and an unsuccessful evaluation.

Occasionally, a child is untestable in the first session. In these cases, the clinician should gather as much information as possible from parents, teachers, medical personnel, and caregivers, have adaptive behavior scales filled out, use the time to attempt interactive play with the child, and perform an in-depth observation of the child's behaviors. The clinician should discuss with the parents all aspects of the initial observation and interaction with the child and make recommendations for therapies. The clinician should schedule an appointment to see the child in about two to three months, after intensive therapies have been initiated, and attempt the evaluation again.

Asperger's Disorder is also an autistic spectrum disorder. Symptoms in the *DSM-IV-TR* (APA, 2000) are similar to those in Autistic Disorder. They include impaired social interaction and restricted, repetitive, and stereotyped patterns of behavior, interest, and activities. However, children with Asperger's Disorder or Asperger's syndrome (AS), as it is more commonly called, usually demonstrate fairly normal language acquisition and development. In some cases they may have an early delay in language that is overcome by approximately 3 to 4 years of age, by which time they are often communicating in a somewhat formal and precocious manner. Pragmatics may continue to be a problem, as is social perception. Children with AS are not usually intellectually impaired, as are many of the children with Autistic Disorder.

Asperger's syndrome is a relatively rare disorder. Prevalence has been estimated to be 0.003 to 0.03 % (APA, 2000; Sponheim & Skjeidal, 1998). More recently these prudent estimates have been questioned and it has been maintained that the disorder is more frequent (0.1%) than had been earlier thought (Chakrabarti & Fombonne, 2005).

In her early writings, Wing (1981; Bourgoine & Wing, 1983) described the main clinical features of AS as a lack of empathy, naïve inappropriate, one-sided interaction, little or no ability to form friendships, pedantic, repetitive speech, poor nonverbal communication, intense absorption in certain subjects, and clumsy with ill-coordinated movements and odd postures (Atwood, 1998, p. 13). Following these descriptions, Schopler and Mesibov (1983), Tantam (1988), and Gillberg (1984) published papers that, along with Wing's work, ignited interest in Asperger's syndrome. By the 1990s, the prevailing view was that AS is a variant of autism and a Pervasive Developmental Disorder or, the more recent term, an autism spectrum disorder. In the mid-1990s, Asperger's Disorder, as it was called, first entered the *DSM-IV* (APA, 1994). Research in AS has continued since that time in attempting to understand and categorize these children, as well as to differentiate them from autistic or other socially inept children. Differences in criteria for diagnosing Asperger's syndrome and high-functioning autism has made it difficult to review and compare studies on these disorders, and to interpret findings (Mayes & Calhoun, 2003a; 2003b).

Wing (1991) noted that most individuals with AS are in the average range of intelligence, although some fall into the mild range of mental retardation. Fine, Bartolucci, Szatmari, and Ginsberg (1994) found their sample of AS individuals had overall low average abilities with no difference between verbal and nonverbal abilities. In 1995, Klin, Volkmar, Sparrow, Ciccheti, and Rourke (1995) found that their subjects with AS demonstrated average overall intellectual abilities, and this level was similar to that of an HFA comparison group. The AS group had higher Verbal IQ than Performance IQ scores, a pattern not seen in the HFA group. This pattern was observed across all AS subjects. Ozonoff and colleagues, (1991) saw a similar level and pattern of intellectual abilities, and this pattern did separate the AS sample from the sample with HFA.

Neuropsychological impairments include executive functions, with respect to initiative and strategy formation, flexibility, and shared attention (Happé, Booth, Charlton, & Hughes, 2006; Hill & Bird, 2006; Kleinhans, Akshoomoff, & Delis, 2005; Ozonoff, 1995). Similar to autistic individuals, those with AS have been considered to have difficulties with central coherence. This is evident as overfocus on detail instead of general configuration (Háppe & Frith, 2006; Jolliffe & Baron-Cohen, 1999). Theory of Mind problems are also considered typical of these children although research findings have varied (Beaumont & Newcombe, 2006; Kaland et al., 2002). In addition, processing of facial affect is impaired. In some instances severe difficulties of processing faces may appear as prosopagnosia; that is, inability to recognize the identity of faces (Barton, Hefter, Cherkasova, & Manoach, 2007). Individuals with Asperger's have been noted to have changes in cerebral blood flow compared to controls with activation in cerebellum during ToM tasks presented by the auditory route. No support was found for right hemisphere dysfunction, however (Nieminen-von Wendt et al., 2003).

Language disorder is not connected with AS, but individuals with AS often have atypical prosody and intonation (Church, Alisanski, & Amanullah, 2000; Klin et al., 1995; Nieminen, Kulomäki, Ulander, & von Wendt, 2000). Their expressions may be overly detailed and comprehension of jokes and humor poor (Ghaziuddin & Gerstein, 1996). There is poorer performance in the AS group than the HFA group on fine motor skill tasks, visual-motor integration, visual-spatial perception, nonverbal concept formation, gross motor skills, and visual memory (Jansiewicz et al., 2006; Klin et al., 1995). On a daily basis individuals with Asperger's syndrome have difficulties managing their practical lives that contrasts with their good cognitive capacity (Gilotty, Kenworthy, Black, Wagner, & Sirian, 2002; Happé et al., 2006).

Psychiatric comorbidity is very frequent in Asperger's Syndrome. These include ADHD and learning disorders, Tourette's Syndrome and tic disorder, mood disorders, depression and anxiety, conduct and oppositional-defiant disorder, obsessive-compulsive disorder, mutism, and eating disorder (Duggal, 2007; Frazier et al., 2002; Ghaziuddin, Weidmer-Mikhail, & Ghaziuddin, 1998; Kadesjö & Gillberg, 2000; Ringman & Jancovic, 2000; Searcy, Burd, Kerbeshian, Stenhjem, & Franceshini, 2000; Wentz, Gillberg, Gillberg, & Råstam, 2001). According to Ghaziuddin (2002), every second child with Asperger's syndrome has ADHD as a comorbid disorder, but overall the frequency of comorbid disorders has not been systematically assessed in children and adolescents.

NEPSY-II Validity Study for Asperger's Disorder (Asperger's Syndrome)

A sample of 19 children with a *DSM-IV-TR* clinical diagnosis of Asperger's Disorder was assessed with the NEPSY-II. Additional inclusion criteria for this study were as follows: absence of a neurological dysfunction not typically associated with Asperger's Disorder, IQ greater than 85, no concurrent psychiatric diagnosis, and normal or corrected visual and auditory acuity. A control sample matched for age, sex, race/ethnicity, and parent education level was randomly selected from the normative sample for comparison of performance on the NEPSY-II.

Within the Attention and Executive Functioning domain measures of selective and sustained auditory attention: *Auditory Attention* (Combined Score effect size: 81), and complex auditory attention with executive maintenance and shift of set; *Response Set* (Combined Score effect size: 82) were impaired ($p < .01$) with large effect sizes. On the other hand, measures of nonverbal sorting (Animal Sorting, $p < .13$) and planning (Clocks, $p < .09$) were relatively intact. It is important to note that although differences were not significant for most Executive Functioning subtest scores, moderate to large effect sizes were observed for many of these scores. On the Inhibition (IN) Naming Total Completion Time (moderate effect size .78) and on the IN Inhibition Total Completion Time (large effect size .86), the children with Asperger's Disorder were slower ($p < .04$) than matched controls, suggesting slowed processing both in rapid semantic access and speed of inhibiting responses.

The Asperger's Disorder group also exhibited a deficit ($p < .01$) in visual memory: *Memory for Faces* Total Score with an effect size of 1.34, and a deficit ($p < .03$) on the *Memory for Designs Content* score with a large effect size (.82). Verbal memory abilities were similar to those seen in the matched controls. No impairment was observed on subtests in the Language domain, and affect recognition was not impaired. Of the Asperger's group, 26% showed low performance (low score = scaled score of ≤ 6; 10th percentile or below) on the *Theory of Mind* subtest. A higher percentage of children diagnosed with Asperger's Disorder obtained low scores (scaled score ≤ 6; 10th percentile or less) on the Theory of Mind subtest than in the matched control sample (10.5%). However, the sample of children with Autistic Disorder showed low performance by 70% of the group. Performance on all aspects of the *Fingertip Tapping* (FT) subtest and on the *Visuomotor Precision* (VP) subtest, both timed subtests in the Sensorimotor domain, was impaired ($p < .01$). All effect sizes on FT were greater than 1.0 (FT Dominant Hand Combined effect size: 1.12; FT Nondominant Hand Combined effect size: 1.30; FT Repetitions Combined: 1.08; FT Sequences Combined: 1:07). The VP Total Completion Time was slower than matched controls ($p < .02$) with a large effect size (.84). However, the children were accurate in making lines through winding tracks, even though they were slow in executing the lines. On the Visuospatial Processing domain, the children with Asperger's scored lower ($p < .03$) than controls on *Block Construction* (effect size: 80), and on the *Design Copying* subtests, results were impaired ($p < .01$): DCP Total effect size: 1.15; DCP Motor Score effect size: 1.06; DCP Local effect size:1.00. The DCP Global, which assesses the ability to perceive and copy the configuration (whole) of a design was also lower ($p < .05$), but effect size was moderate (.74). The Visuospatial Processing subtests not requiring a motor response (Geometric Puzzles and Picture Puzzles) were relatively intact. The lowest scores across all subtests were obtained on immediate Memory for Faces (ss: 6.6). Additional scores more than −1 SD from the mean were obtained on the Memory for Designs Delayed and Fingertip Tapping subtests.

Overall, the results suggest that children with Asperger's Disorder show impairment in visual memory, including facial memory; attention, fine motor abilities, speeded or timed tasks, and in visuoconstructive abilities. The findings highlight the relatively intact language and verbal memory abilities in Asperger's Disorder. These results point to better developed affect recognition and theory of mind in children with Asperger's Disorder when compared to those with Autistic Disorder (Korkman et al., 2007).

The NEPSY-II Diagnostic Cluster for Asperger's Disorder

The results from NEPSY-II suggest that children with Asperger's Disorder show impairment especially in fine motor skills and attention/executive functions.

- Primary deficits:
  - Selective and sustained auditory attention
  - Executive functions
    - Inhibition of response
    - Maintenance and shift of set for rapid auditory responses and on inhibition tasks
  - Slowed processing speed on naming, inhibition, and graphomotor execution
  - Social perception (26% of sample)
    - Theory of mind; understanding another's perspective, beliefs, intention; problems with literal interpretation
  - Visuospatial processing
    - Visual perception of faces and the configuration and details of geometric designs
    - 2-dimensional and 3-dimensional copying
  - Finger dexterity bilaterally, motor programming of hands bilaterally, graphomotor skills
- Secondary deficits in
  - Ability to focus on auditory tasks and shift from one to another quickly
  - Impulsivity, due to slow inhibition of response
  - Rapid processing/rapid access to language

- Visuoconstructive performance in the classroom, especially for writing and copying from board, but also including 3-D constructions
- Visual memory: short-term memory for faces and for designs; No problem for long-term memory; visual material consolidates over time due to slowed processing

(See Rapid Reference 6.11 for the summary of the NEPSY-II validity study diagnostic cluster for Asperger's Disorder.)

≣ *Rapid Reference 6.11*

The NEPSY-II Diagnostic Cluster for Asperger's Disorder

Children with Asperger's Disorder show impairment on NEPSY-II, especially in fine motor skills and attention/executive functions.

Primary deficits:

- Selective and sustained auditory attention
- Executive functions
  - Inhibition of response
  - Maintenance and shift of set for rapid auditory responses and on inhibition tasks
- Slowed processing speed on naming, inhibition, and graphomotor execution tasks
- Social perception (26% of sample)
  - Theory of mind; understanding another's perspective, beliefs, intention; problems with literal interpretation
- Visuospatial processing
  - Visual perception of faces and the configuration and details of geometric designs
  - 2-dimensional and 3-dimensional copying
- Finger dexterity bilaterally, motor programming of hands bilaterally, graphomotor skills

Secondary deficits:

- Ability to focus on auditory tasks and shift from one to another quickly
- Impulsivity, due to slow inhibition of response
- Rapid processing/rapid access to language

- Visuoconstructive performance in the classroom, especially for writing and copying from board, but also including 3-D constructions
- Visual memory: short-term memory for faces and for designs (no problem for long-term memory; visual material consolidates over time due to slowed processing)
- The Social/Interpersonal Referral Battery (pp. 313–314) is used for assessment of individuals with Autistic Disorder and with Asperger's syndrome.

Although individual children in this clinical group may show much heterogeneity, as a group, children with Asperger's syndrome (AS) displayed a profile on NEPSY-II that included the characteristics shown in Rapid Reference 6.10. NEPSY-II was not designed specifically to assign *DSM-IV-TR* (APA 2000) diagnoses. Still, it can be used to determine the presence of deficits that are associated with Asperger's Disorder. Of course, any such diagnosis must only be made within the context of the child's developmental, medical, social, and educational history, as well as the manner in which he or she functions in everyday life. With this diagnosis, as with Autistic Disorder, as with many diagnoses of developmental disorders in general, it is wise to observe the child in a peer group setting in order to observe social interaction, especially since children with Asperger's often relate better to adults than to peers. If the clinician knows in advance that the referral question is to rule out Asperger's Disorder, he or she should take the time for preparation as noted in Chapter 3, especially ascertaining stereotypical interests and if the child has frequent meltdowns when frustrated. If the latter is the case, the clinician may wish to schedule several shorter sessions. In general, children with Asperger's tend to cooperate well in assessment, and even to enjoy it, but, as with assessment of most developmental disorders, preparation is a key factor.

APPLICATION OF THE NEPSY-II IN ASSESSING TRAUMATIC BRAIN INJURY

The number of children who survive life-threatening illnesses, injuries, and congenital disorders has increased steadily with advances in medical technology (Farmer & Deidrick, 2006; Wallander & Thompson, 1995). Neurological impairments are common among survivors and can result in physical, cognitive, and behavioral disabilities (Farmer, Kanne, Grissom, & Kemp, 2009). Traumatic brain injury (TBI) in children represents a significant public health problem in the United States, causing, as of 2004, an estimated 435,000 emergency department visits and 37,000 hospitalizations annually among children aged 0 to 14 years (Langlois, Rutland-Brown, & Thomas, 2004). Mechanisms of injury vary based on age. Toddlers are significantly more likely to sustain TBI as a result of a fall, while older children and teenagers are more likely to experience TBI due to vehicular accidents and sports (Giza, 2006).

Advanced neuroimaging techniques are now used to expand our knowledge of traumatic brain injury, and increasingly, they are being applied to children. There are four methods of neuroimaging as they apply to children who present acutely after injury:

- Susceptibility weighted imaging is a three-dimensional high-resolution magnetic resonance imaging technique that is more sensitive than conventional imaging in detecting hemorrhagic lesions that are often associated with diffuse axonal injury.
- Magnetic resonance spectroscopy acquires metabolite information reflecting neuronal integrity and function from multiple brain regions and provides sensitive, noninvasive assessment of neurochemical alterations that offers early prognostic information regarding the outcome.
- Diffusion weighted imaging is based on differences in diffusion of water molecules within the brain and has been shown to be very sensitive in the early detection of ischemic injury. It is now being used to study the direct effects of traumatic injury as well as those due to secondary ischemia.
- Diffusion tensor imaging is a form of diffusion weighted imaging and allows better evaluation of white matter fiber tracts by taking advantage of the intrinsic directionality (anisotropy) of water diffusion in the human brain. It has been shown to be useful in identifying white matter abnormalities after diffuse axonal injury when conventional imaging appears normal.

An important aspect of these advanced methods is that they demonstrate that a "normal-appearing" brain in many instances is not normal; that is, there is evidence of significant undetected injury that may underlie a child's clinical status. Availability and integration of these advanced imaging methods will lead to better treatment and change the standard of care for use of neuroimaging to evaluate children with traumatic brain injury (Ashwal, Holshouser, & Tong, 2006). In assessing children with TBI the findings from the neuroimaging examinations are important, as they also provide a basis for understanding neuropsychological effects. In this respect, close teamwork, together with a pediatric neurologist, is essential. The assessment of these children also demands a neuropsychological understanding of brain-behavior relationships and special knowledge of neuropsychology.

Catroppa, Anderson, Morse, Haritou, and Rosenfeld (2007) examined functional outcomes following traumatic brain injury (TBI) during early childhood, to investigate impairments up to five years post-injury, and identify predictors of outcome. The study compared three groups of children (mild = 11, moderate = 22, severe = 15), aged 2.0 to 6.11 years at injury, to a healthy control group ($n = 17$). Using a prospective, longitudinal design, adaptive abilities, behavior, and family functioning were investigated acutely at 6 months, 30 months, and 5 years post-injury, with educational progress investigated at 30 months and 5 years post-injury. A strong association was suggested between injury severity and outcomes across all domains. Further, five-year *outcomes* in adaptive and behavioral domains were best predicted by preinjury levels of child function, and educational performance by injury severity. Children who sustain a severe TBI in early childhood are at greatest risk of long-term impairment in day-to-day skills in the long-term post-injury.

Clinically, children seem to recover from milder injuries with apparently little neurological or cognitive impairment. However, there is increasing evidence from sports injuries in adolescents and young adults that repeated concussion can be associated with long-term neuropsychological dysfunction (Collins et al., 2002; Field, Collins, Lovell, & Maroon, 2003; Matser, Kessels, Lezak, Jordan, & Troopst, 1999). A recent factor analysis study of children with post-concussive syndrome (pCS) demonstrated three replicable dimensions of PCS based on parent ratings: cognitive, somatic, and emotional symptoms both at baseline and three months post-injury. Behavioral symptoms appeared at baseline, but not at three months (Belanger, Kretzmer, Yoash-Gantz, Pickett, & Tupler, 2009). The lack of persistent behavioral symptoms may contribute to assumptions that mild TBI has little long-term effect.

Furthermore, TBI at a particular stage of maturation may result in specific deficits in cognitive domains undergoing development at that stage (Ewing-Cobbs, Prasad, Landry, Kramer, & DeLeon, 2004; Taylor & Alden, 2006). As many as 29,000 children experience new disability after TBI as a result of lasting changes in their physical, cognitive, social, and behavioral functioning. Children who sustain more severe injuries and who are injured at younger ages show greater evidence of long-term impairments and slower rates of acquisition for new skills (Ewing-Cobbs et al., 2005; Schutzman & Greenes, 2001). Despite its high incidence, TBI-related disability often goes unrecognized by caregivers, educators, and physicians. In particular, children's cognitive needs after TBI are commonly unmet or unrecognized. (Slomine et al., 2005). Traumatic Brain Injury was established as a special education disability category in the 1990 amendments to the Individuals with Disabilities Education Act, yet many children after TBI are either misclassified in the special education system or do not receive special education services at all (Glang, Tyler, Pearson, Todis, & Morvant, 2004; Ylvisaker et al., 2001).

Deficits in executive functioning are among the most frequently reported areas of cognitive impairment after TBI (Anderson & Catroppa, 2005; Brookshire, Levin, Song, & Zhang, 2004; Mangeot, Armstrong, Colvin, Yeates, & Taylor, 2002; Roncadin, Guger, Archibald, Barnes, & Dennis, 2004). Between 18% and 38% of the children with traumatic brain injury had significant executive dysfunction in the first year after injury, with greater dysfunction reported for children with more severe traumatic brain injury (Sesma, Slomine, Ding, & McCarthy, 2008). Typical development of these skills is protracted and depends on intact frontal-striatal circuits (Giedd et al., 1999; Luciana & Nelson, 1998). However, these circuits are frequently damaged from TBI because they are distributed networks that run through common lesion sites (i.e., frontal and prefrontal cortex) and are particularly vulnerable to the diffuse axonal injury that can occur from severe TBI (Levin et al., 1993). Children with preexisting difficulties with inattention and hyperactivity are at higher risk for developing ADHD after TBI ((Max et al., 2004; Schachar, Levin, Max, Purvis, & Chen, 2004).

Yeates and colleagues (2004) investigated short- and long-term social outcomes of pediatric TBI in a prospective, longitudinal study that included 53 children with severe TBI, 56 with moderate TBI, and 80 with orthopedic injuries, recruited between 6 and 12 years of age. Child and family functioning were assessed at baseline, at 6- and 12-month follow-ups, and at an extended follow-up a mean of 4 years post-injury. Growth curve analyses revealed that pediatric TBI yields negative social outcomes that are exacerbated by family environments characterized by lower socioeconomic status, fewer family resources, and poorer family functioning. After controlling for group membership, age, race, socioeconomic status, and IQ, path analyses indicated that long-term social outcomes were accounted for in part by specific neurocognitive skills, including executive functions and pragmatic language, and by social problem-solving. Deficits in these domains among children with TBI are likely to reflect damage to a network of brain regions that have been implicated in social cognition.

Over time, recovery rate slows down more for those with greater brain injury severity. The greatest slowing of recovery occurs in Performance IQ, adaptive problem solving, memory, and motor skills, as well as on a summary score of overall performance. Given this "plateauing" of recovery, achievement of parity with peers by the moderately and severely injured seems unlikely.

In conclusion, the neuropsychological impairments that frequently occur in this group of children are those of executive functions, attention, and social cognition. Also, children with mild injury may have impairments detected on closer assessment, but their recovery rate is faster than for children with severe injuries, unless they have repeated mild-moderate injuries that may lead to long-term effects.

NEPSY-II Validity Study for TBI

The NEPSY-II was administered to a very small sample of ten children with a single complicated mild-to-severe TBI. This study should therefore be considered very preliminary. For the purposes of the NEPSY-II validity study and based on previously developed classification criteria (Capruso & Levin, 1992), moderate TBI was defined as Glasgow Coma Scale, at admission, of 9–12, or 13–15 if there was a CT scan or MRI scan abnormality, a skull fracture, or a duration of impaired consciousness lasting between 1 and 24 hours. Severe TBI was defined as Glasgow Coma Scale, at admission, of less than or equal to 8, or a duration of impaired consciousness lasting more than 24 hours. Six children met the criteria for mild to moderate TBI and four children for severe TBI. Due to the small sample size, results are discussed in the text only (Korkman et al., 2007, p. 125).

The NEPSY-II assessment of children with TBI revealed performance that was lower than those scores obtained by the normative group, but significant differences were infrequent due to the small sample size. Scores that were significantly different between the two samples were on the *Inhibition, Fingertip Tapping*, and *Visuomotor Precision* subtests. In addition, several score differences produced moderate to high effect sizes, although they did not reach significance, probably due to clinical sample size: *Animal Sorting, Auditory Attention and Response Set, Speeded Naming, Memory for Designs, Memory for Faces*, and *Word List Interference*. The lowest scaled scores, more than one standard deviation below the mean, were found on *Auditory Attention and Response Set*.

APPLICATION OF THE NEPSY-II IN ASSESSING CHILDREN WITH HEARING IMPAIRMENT

There is not a Referral Battery for children with hearing impairment, but the NEPSY-II was administered to a small sample of 18 children who were deaf or hard of hearing. The group was fairly heterogeneous in terms of the etiology and severity of hearing impairment. Examiners modified subtests to accommodate the needs of the children, and eliminated subtests that were not possible for the children to complete (e.g., Auditory Attention and Response Set). All of the children assessed were required to have intellectual functioning in the low average range or higher and to be free of psychiatric disorders, specific learning disabilities, autism spectrum disorders, head injury, and seizures. Normal or corrected visual acuity was also necessary. As with all of the clinical groups, complete inclusion criteria are provided in Appendix F of the NEPSY-II *Clinical and Interpretive Manual*. Controls matched for age, sex, race/ethnicity, and parent education level were randomly selected from the normative sample for comparison (Korkman et al., 2007, p. 125).

NEPSY-II Validity Study of Children With Hearing Impairment

Given the modifications made during administration, only subtests administered to at least 10 children were reported in the validity study. For this reason, data were not reported for Response Set, Inhibition-Switching, or Word List Interference. Within the Attention and Executive Functioning domain, the modified administration of Auditory Attention yielded an *Auditory Attention* Combined score that was poorer ($p < .04$) than that of matched controls and showed a large effect size (.86). On subtests in the Language domain, the deaf/hard of hearing group displayed poorer performance ($p < .01$) than matched controls on the *Phonological Processing* Total score with a large effect size of 1.13. From the Memory and Learning domain, the *Memory for Designs* Content score and the *Memory for Designs* Total score for the clinical group are significantly poorer ($p < .03$ and $p < .04$, respectively) than that of controls. The *MD Content* score showed a moderate effect size of 75, while the *MD Total* score showed a large effect size (.89). None of the Sensorimotor, Social Perception, or Visuospatial Processing subtest performances for the clinical groups differed significantly from performances of matched patrols. Three scores approached significance, but did not reach it, yet had moderate effect sizes in the top of that range or a large effect size: *AA Total Correct* score ($p < .06$; effect size $-.83$); *Clocks Total* score ($p < .07$; effect size $-.73$); and *NM Free and Cued Recall vs. Recognition Contrast* score ($p < .07$; effect size $-.79$). It is likely that with a larger sample size, these three scores would also have shown a significant difference in performance when compared to matched controls.

Not surprisingly, the clinical group of children who were deaf and hard of hearing displayed impairments in auditory attention and phonological processing, but they also displayed a less expected impairment in immediate memory for designs. The children had significantly more difficulty remembering the designs, rather than their spatial location, which showed no difference with matched controls. It is also of interest that the Clocks subtest, which involves some visuospatial aspects as well as the need for naming skills and language understanding, and

Narrative Memory, which relies strongly on the child being able to encode receptive language and recall salient story details, approached significance and showed moderate to large effect sizes.

EVIDENCE OF RELIABILITY IN NEPSY-II

Test reliability is any indication of the degree with which a test provides a precise and stable measure of the underlying construct it is intended to measure. Classical test theory posits that a test score is an approximation of an individual's true score (i.e., the score he or she would receive if the test was perfectly reliable) and measurement error (i.e., the difference between an individual's true score and the individual's obtained score). A reliable test will have a relatively small measurement error and produce consistent results across administrations. The reliability of the test refers to the accuracy, consistency, and stability of test scores across situations (Anastasi & Urbina, 1997). The reliability of a test should be considered in the interpretation of obtained scores on one occasion and differences between scores obtained on multiple occasions.

The NEPSY-II *Clinical and Interpretive Manual* (Table 4.1, pp. 54–56) provides reliability coefficients for all primary and process scaled scores (Korkman et al., 2007). They were calculated for each age level separately and then averaged across four age bands (i.e., ages 3–4, 5–6, 7–12, 13–16). This was done because different patterns of tests make up the domains for the two different age groups.

CONVENTIONS FOR REPORTING RESULTS

Several conventions for reporting results were used for the NEPSY-II:

1. For those analyses that serve to evaluate the difference between two mean scores (e.g., test-retest reliability and counterbalanced validity studies and matched controls studies), mean scores in the tables are reported to one place. However, the standard difference, *t* values and probability (*p*) values, were calculated from grouped innings to two decimal places. Calculations of those values with reported means may vary slightly from those reported in the tables due to the rounding error.
2. All analyses use traditional values for significance level (alpha =.05).
3. Along with statistical significance and *p* values, effect sizes are reported as evidence of reliability and validity. The term *standard difference* refers to Cohen's *d*. The values described in the text follow Cohen's (1988) suggestions for effect size interpretation.

The use of descriptors should not replace review of the actual p values and effect sizes reported in the tables of the *Clinical and Interpretation Manual*. For example, although p equals .07 is not statistically significant, it would be evaluated differently if the effect size were .90 rather than .10. Similarly, a p value of .04 is a significant result, but when paired with an effect size of .03, the effect is probably too small to be meaningful. Moreover, depending on the situation the importance associated with a particular effect size might be very different from those suggested by Cohen's guidelines. In certain clinical situations, a small effect size might still represent an important finding. The reader is encouraged to evaluate the specifics of a given result when interpreting significance and effect size magnitudes.

(See Rapid Reference 6.12 for a summary of the conventions for reporting results.)

≡ *Rapid Reference 6.12*

Conventions for Reporting Results

Several conventions for reporting results were used for NEPSY-II.

1. For analyses that evaluate the difference between two mean scores (e.g., test-retest reliability, counterbalanced validity studies, and matched controls studies), mean scores in the tables were reported to one place. However, the standard difference, t values, and probability (p) values were calculated from grouped innings to two decimal places. Therefore, calculations of those values with reported means may vary slightly from those in the tables due to the rounding error.

2. All analyses use traditional values for significance level (alpha $= .05$).

3. Along with statistical significance and p values, effect sizes are reported as evidence of reliability and validity. The term *standard difference* refers to Cohen's d. The values described in the text follow Cohen's (1988) suggestions for effect size interpretation.

The use of descriptors should not replace review of the actual p values and effect sizes reported in the tables of the *Clinical and Interpretation Manual*.

- **Example**: Although p equals .07 is not statistically significant, it would be evaluated differently if the effect size were .90 rather than .10. Similarly, a p value of .04 is a significant result, but when paired with an effect size of .03, the effect is probably too small to be meaningful.

- Depending on the situation, the importance associated with a particular effect size might be very different from those suggested by Cohen's guidelines. In certain clinical situations a small effect size might still represent an important finding. The reader is encouraged to evaluate the specifics of a given result when interpreting significance and effect size magnitudes.

RELIABILITY PROCEDURES IN NEPSY-II

The NEPSY-II subtests vary widely across and within domains in terms of the stimulus presentation, administration procedures used, and the type of responses elicited. Some subtests have baseline conditions that provide a means of identifying the contribution of more basic cognitive skills from performance on the higher-level cognitive tasks (e.g., Inhibition). Other subtests have two or more conditions that measure different aspects of a domain (e.g., Phonological Processing). These factors vary across subtests and have a bearing on the nature and outcome of the reliability analyses performed. For example, internal consistency measures for Inhibition will be unaffected because the earlier conditions have lower cognitive demands than the later items. See Strauss, Sherman, and Spreen (2006) for a review of reliability and validity in neuropsychological instruments.

For many process measures and some primary measures of the NEPSY-II, reliability is influenced by a limited variability in normal samples (e.g., error scores and simple cognitive processes), particularly as a majority of individuals at a given age attain the skills needed to perform a task. In samples of typically-developing (nonclinical) children, some process scores yield a small range of raw scores (e.g., error scores), which hinders the psychometric properties of these variables in the normative sample due to limited ranges or skewed distributions. For example, in typically developing children, the ability to perceive another's point of view as measured by the theory of mind task is well developed by age 7. Therefore, the full range of scores is seen on the Theory of Mind subtest in children under age 7 where children are highly variable in the attainment of social perspective. After age 7, the distribution is highly skewed because a majority of the children successfully perform the task. The reliability of the score is much higher in younger age groups than in older age groups, where the skewed score distribution and range restriction is reflected in the change from the scaled score to a percentile.

Despite the limitations in obtaining reliability estimates for the scores in typically developing children, children with certain clinical diagnoses, such as Autistic Disorder or Reading Disorder, may exhibit test performances that are best captured by these process measures. Therefore, the clinical utility of the scores is high; the findings from the special group samples highlight the clinical utility of these measures and the importance of including them in an assessment. In addition, the psychometric properties of these variables may differ if the reliability is analyzed within clinical populations, due to the greater range and variability of scores obtained in clinical groups. The NEPSY-II process scores that often yield restricted distributions in normally functioning children and higher ranges and distributions in clinical populations include error rates, contrast scores, and scores in which perfect scores are expected in typically developing individuals (e.g., Theory of Mind after age 7) (Korkman et al., 2007, pp. 51–52).

The reliability procedures used in NEPSY-II vary among the subtests based on the properties of the subtest.

Reliability coefficients were obtained utilizing the split-half and alpha methods. The split-half of reliability coefficient of a subtest is the correlation between the total scores of the two half-tests, corrected for length of the test using the Spearman-Brown formula (Crocker & Algina, 1986; Li, Rosenthal, & Rubin, 1996). The internal consistency reliability coefficients were calculated with the formula recommended by Nunnally and Bernstein (1994). The average reliability coefficients were calculated using Fisher's z transformation (Silver & Dunlap, 1987; Strube, 1988).

Stability coefficients and decision-consistency procedures were used when the aforementioned methods were not appropriate.

Stability Coefficients

Test-retest stability is reported on those subtests for which parallel forms could not be created because the subtests' scores are based on item-level scores that are not strictly independent, due either to an allowed latency time within which the child can respond and receive credit for an item (e.g., Auditory Attention and Response Set) or to the use of speed of performance as a scoring criterion (e.g., Fingertip Tapping, Speeded Naming). The stability coefficients used as reliability estimates are the correlation of scores on the first and second testing, corrected for variability of the normative sample (Allen & Yen, 1979; Magnusson, 1967).

Decision-Consistency

Several subtests have highly skewed score distributions and are not scaled, but rather are presented as percentile rank scores. In addition, the combined and contrast scores demonstrate the same restriction of score range. For these scores, a test-retest correlation coefficient would be artificially depressed due to restricted score ranges; therefore, a decision-consistency methodology was used to demonstrate reliability. A cutoff score is used to create two categories and the consistency of the classification (i.e., percent agreement) from test to retest is assessed. The decision-consistency reliability indicates the concordance of the decisions in terms of percent of classification. The following cutoff scores were used.

- For percentile ranks: 10th percentile
- For scaled scores: scaled score of 6
  - Percentiles classified into *less than* 10th percentile, *equal to* 10th percentile, and *greater than* 10th percentile
  - Scaled scores classified into *less than* 6, *equal to* 6, and *greater than* 6

Along with statistical significance and p values, effect sizes are reported as evidence of reliability and validity. Most NEPSY-II subtests have adequate to high internal consistency or stability.

Effect Size Ranges
- Small effect sizes: .20–.49
- Moderate effect sizes: .50–.79
- Large effect sizes: .80 and greater are reported as large effect sizes

Reliability coefficients are provided in the NEPSY-II Clinical and Interpretative Manual (Korkman et al., 2007, pp. 54–59) for all subtest primary and process scores. Consistent with other neuropsychological instruments, verbal tests have higher reliabilities, and executive functions tend to have modest reliability (Strauss et al., 2006).

The highest reliability coefficients are seen in Rapid Reference 6.13 across four age bands.

≡ Rapid Reference 6.13
....

Reliability Procedures Used in NEPSY-II

The reliability procedures used in NEPSY-II vary among the subtests, based on the properties of the subtest.

Reliability coefficients were obtained utilizing the split-half and alpha methods
- The split-half reliability coefficient of a subtest is the correlation between the total scores of the two half-tests, corrected for length of the test using the Spearman-Brown formula.
- The internal consistency reliability coefficients were calculated with the formula recommended by Nunnally and Bernstein.
- The average reliability coefficients were calculated using Fisher's z transformation.

Stability Coefficients and decision-consistency procedures were used if the above methods were not appropriate
- Test-retest stability is reported on those subtests for which parallel forms could not be created because the subtests' scores are based on item-level scores that are not strictly independent:
  - Due either to an allowed latency time within which the child can respond and get credit for an item or to the use of speed of performance as a scoring criterion.

(continued)

(continued)
- The stability coefficients used as reliability estimates are the correlation of scores on the first and second testing, corrected for variability of the normative sample.

Decision-Consistency
- Several subtests have highly skewed score distributions and are not scaled, but rather are presented as percentile rank scores.
- The combined and contrast scores demonstrate the same restriction of score range.

For these scores, a test-retest correlation coefficient would be artificially depressed due to restricted score ranges; therefore, a decision-consistency methodology was used to demonstrate reliability.

- A cutoff score is used to create two categories and the consistency of the classification (i.e., percent agreement) from test to retest is assessed.
- The decision consistency reliability indicates the concordance of the decisions in terms of percent of classification. The following cutoff scores were used:
  - For percentile ranks: 10th percentile
  - For scaled scores: scaled score of 6
  - Percentiles classified into *less than* 10th percentile, *equal to* 10th percentile, and *greater than* 10th percentile
  - Scaled scores classified into *less than* 6, *equal to* 6, and *greater than* 6

Effect Size Ranges: Along with statistical significance and *p* values, effect sizes are reported as evidence of reliability and validity. Most NEPSY-II subtests have adequate to high internal consistency or stability.
- Small effect sizes: .20–.49
- Moderate effect sizes: .50–.79
- Large effect sizes: .80 and greater are reported as large effect sizes

Overall, the lowest reliabilities for NEPSY-II subtests coefficients are those calculated with test-retest reliability: Response Set Total Correct, Inhibition Total Errors, Memory for Designs Spatial and Total Scores, Memory for Designs Delayed Total Scores. Lower reliability on the error scores was likely a result of practice effects and range-restriction on the test-retest reliability, as errors tend to decline with experience on a task and small changes in performance result in a large change in classification. The reliability coefficients for scores in the Memory and Learning domain are consistent with findings that memory subtests tend to produce lower reliability on test-retest due to the heavy influence of practice effects on memory tasks. (See Rapid Reference 6.14 for the highest reliability coefficients.)

≡ Rapid Reference 6.14

The Highest Reliability Coefficients of NEPSY-II Scaled Scores for Normative Sample by Age

Subtests	(Average r^2)			
	Ages 3-4	Ages 5-6	Ages 7-12	Ages 13-16
Comp. of Instructions Total	.86	.82	.75	.62
Design Copying Process Total	.88	.85	.78	.82
FT Dominant Hand Combined	—	.87	.90	.75
FT Nondominant Hand Combined	—	.84	.94	.83
FT Repetitions Combined	—	.94	.92	.83
FT Sequences Combined	—	.84	.98	.92
Imitating Hand Positions Total	.89	.82[a]	.82[a]	—
List Memory and LM Total Correct	—	—	.91	—
Memory for Names and MND Total	—	.89	.89	.79
Phonological Processing Total	.88	.92	.86	.66
Picture Puzzles Total	.85	.81	—	—
Sentence Repetition Total	.89	.87	—	—

Note: Internal consistency (alpha or split-half reliability coefficients) are reported unless otherwise noted.

a) Average reliability coefficients were calculated for ages 5–12.

Reliabilities in the Special Groups

The reliability information for the special groups supports the generalizability of the instrument. The evidence of internal consistency for the special groups was obtained by the same methods as those used with the normative sample. Detailed demographic information can be found in Chapter 5 of the NEPSY-II

Clinical and Interpretive Manual, and descriptions of inclusion criteria can be found in Appendix F of that same volume. Rapid Reference 6.15 shows the highest reliability coefficients of selected primary and process scores for the special groups averaged across two age bands (5–6 and 7–12). As predicted, reliability coefficients calculated with the clinical sample were higher than those in the normative group. These results suggest that NEPSY-II is a reliable tool for the use of assessment of children with clinical diagnoses (Korkman et al., p. 56).

≣ Rapid Reference 6.15

Reliability Coefficients of Selected NEPSY-II Primary and Process Scaled Scores for Special Groups

	Average r by Age Bands	
Subtest Scores by Domain	5-6 yrs.	7-12 yrs.
Attention and Executive Functioning		
Clocks (CL) Total Score	–	.88
Inhibition (IN) Naming Total Completion Time	.94	.84
IN Inhibition Total Completion Time	.80	.80
IN Switching Total Completion Time	–	.86
Language		
Comprehension of Instructions (CI) Total	.83	.80
Phonological Processing (pH) Total Score	.92	.90
Memory and Learning		
Memory for Designs (MD) Content Score	.77	.86
Memory for Designs (MD) Spatial Score	.96	.88
MD Total Score	.95	.93
Sentence Repetition Total Score	.96	–
Word Interference (WI) Repetition Score	–	.80
WI Recall Total Score	–	.67
Subtest Scores by Domain	5-6 yrs.	7-12 yrs.

Subtest Scores by Domain	Average r by Age Bands	
	5-6 yrs.	7-12 yrs.
Social Perception		
Affect Recognition Total Score	.90	.88
Theory of Mind Total Score	.85	–
Visuospatial Processing		
Arrows (AW) Total Score	.92	.92
Block Construction (BC) Total Score	.94	.85
Design Copying (DCP) Motor Score	.89	.74
DCP Global Score	.78	.73
DCP Local	.77	.74
DCP Total	.91	.88
Geometric Puzzle (GP) Total Score	–	.82
Picture Puzzle (pP) Total Score	–	.89

Evidence of Inter-Rater Agreement

All NEPSY-II protocols were double-scored by two independent scorers, and evidence of interscorer agreement was obtained using all cases entered for scoring, including clinical and normative cases. For subtests where the criteria were simple and objective, inter-rater agreement was very high (.98–.99). Clocks and Design Copying require detailed and interpretive scoring based on established criteria. Memory for Names and Theory of Mind require a small degree of interpretation in scoring unusual responses. Word Generation requires the application of a series of rules to determine whether words are credible, and Visuomotor Precision requires judgment about the number of segments containing errors. To determine the degree to which trained raters were consistent in scoring these subtests during standardization, interrater reliability was calculated as percent agreement rates between trained scorers. Agreement rates ranged from 93–99% (Clocks 97%, Design Copying 94–95% across scores, Memory for Names 99%, Theory of Mind 99%, Word Generation 93%, and Visuomotor Precision 95%). The results show that although these subtests require some judgment in scoring, they can be scored with a very high degree of reliability between raters. (Rapid Reference 6.16 summarizes inter-rater reliability for NEPSY-II.)

≡ *Rapid Reference 6.16*

Inter-Rater Reliability for NEPSY-II

To determine the degree to which trained raters were consistent in scoring these subtests during standardization, inter-rater reliability was calculated as percent agreement rates between trained scorers. Agreement rates ranged from 93 to 99%:

Clocks 97%

Design Copying 94–95% across scores

Memory for Names 99%

Theory of Mind 99%

Word Generation 93%

Visuomotor Precision 95%

The results show that although these subtests require some judgment in scoring, they can be scored with a very high degree of reliability between raters.

CONCLUDING REMARKS

In this chapter, we have reviewed the types of developmental and acquired disorders for which a *NEPSY-II* assessment (Korkman et al., 2007) is appropriate. We have also discussed patterns observed in representative disorders in the NEPSY-II validity studies that are reflected in the Referral Batteries and can guide the clinician in selecting subtests to aid diagnosis, as well as having reviewed reliability of the NEPSY-II. Now in Chapter 7, we move to the final step in the assessment process, the reporting of test results, by looking at illustrative case reports.

 TEST YOURSELF

1. **Across the years, many studies have shown that a core deficit of dyslexia is in phonological processing.**

   True or False?

2. **The Speeded Naming and Word Generation subtests were most sensitive to impairments in RD.**

   True or False?

3. **Math disabilities often coexist with language, spatial, attentional, and psychomotor disabilities.**

   True or False?

4. In the math sample, the lowest scores on **NEPSY-II** were obtained on **Memory for Designs.**

   True or False?

5. The clinical group with mathematics disorder showed a primary deficit in executive functions.

   True or False?

6. For the **ADHD** group, only Clocks performance did not reach significance in A/E domain.

   True or False?

7. Affect Recognition results from the Social Perception domain were lower ($p < .01$) in the clinical **ADHD** group than in matched controls, and the effect size was large (1.17).

   True or False?

8. On **NEPSY-II** the math group showed fairly typical language, social perception, and sensorimotor function.

   True or False?

9. The sample of children with autism in the **NEPSY-II** validity studies were high-functioning (IQ > 100).

   True or False?

10. The social and imitative aspects of Imitating Hand Positions may affect performance in autism.

    True or False?

    Match the letter of the correct answer with the corresponding number.

11. _____These factors are associated with later math deficits.   (a) 75%

12. _____of the Asperger's group show a Theory of Mind deficit.   (b) standard

13. _____A very common cognitive impairment after TBI.   (c) 93–99%

14. _____Effect size reflects this difference.   (d) SGA/VLBW

15. _____Inter-rater agreement on **NEPSY-II.**   (e) executive dysfunction

Fill in the blanks:

16. Referral Batteries serve to _____ the clinician to subtests that address the referral question. They should not replace _____ and judgment.

17. Along with statistical significance and p values, _____ sizes are reported as evidence of _____ and validity.

18. An effect size of .03 when paired with $p < .04$ is probably _____ to be meaningful.

19. None of the _____, Social Perception, or _____, subtest performances for the group with hearing impairment differed significantly from performances of matched controls.

20. There is increasing evidence from _____, injuries in adolescents and young adults, that repeated _____, can be associated with long-term neuropsychological dysfunction.

Answers:

1. True; 2. False; 3. True; 4. True; 5. True; 6. False; 7. False; 8. True; 9. False; 10. True; 11. d; 12. a; 13. e; 14. b; 15. c; 16. guide, clinical experience; 17. effect, reliability; 18. too small; 19. Sensorimotor, Visuospatial Processing; 20. sports, concussion

Seven

ILLUSTRATIVE CASE REPORTS

This chapter synthesizes the principles and concepts presented in the first six chapters of the book and guides you through the process of presenting the wealth of data available from a NEPSY-II evaluation in a clear, understandable manner. Hypotheses should be validated through results on NEPSY-II, other assessments, the comprehensive history, and school and medical records. This chapter contains three case studies of children referred for neuropsychological evaluation. The case studies are organized around the use of the NEPSY-II Referral Batteries in order to guide you in their use. With increasing economic and time constraints, a clinician may find that it is not always possible to administer a full NEPSY-II, though that is the most comprehensive and thorough path for assessment. When constraints are present, the NEPSY-II Referral Batteries will be useful tools for addressing a more general referral question (GRB) or to focus your assessment on a common referral question using a specific Diagnostic Referral Battery (DRB).

It is important to understand that there is no standardized report format; therefore, these reports are presented in several different formats. You may follow a prescribed format recommended by your agency, clinic, hospital, or the like. On the other hand, if you are in a position to develop your own format, it is essential to keep in mind the parties to whom you will be communicating the test results (e.g. parents, medical professionals, school personnel, and so forth). The referral statement focuses the reader on the referral question immediately. It provides comprehensive background information so the readers understand how the child's developmental, medical, psychosocial, and educational background may provide clues to or may have contributed to the problem. It presents test results divided into sections, usually by domain or function that make the wealth of information manageable to read. It describes the task that the child was performing that yielded the test results. It is essential to supply comparative information for scores by providing means, percentiles, and descriptors. Charts and graphs can be very helpful to understanding results, whether they appear in the body of the report or on a data page attached to the back of the report. Interpretations should be straightforward and readable without too much technical lingo. The authors find that designating the primary, secondary, and co-occurring deficits is a helpful device to help parents and professionals understand the influence of deficit areas on the subcomponents of complex functions and how that impacts the child's performance in specific areas. Discuss the influence of deficits across domains so your reader can understand how a primary deficit in one domain can influence performance in several other domains. Verify your interpretation by relating findings to the referral question, and to developmental, educational, or medical factors that are impacting the child's functioning in everyday life. Your interpretation should speak directly to the interventions that you recommend. There is no point in interpreting findings and then attaching interventions that have little or no connection to interpreted findings. It is hoped that the following illustrative case reports will help you understand the use of NEPSY-II Referral Batteries and different approaches to compiling and interpreting test results that will lead to meaningful interventions.

The first case study is a brief report of an evaluation with a General Assessment Battery due to a vague referral question. It reveals how important diagnostic information can be gleaned from such an assessment, and the results can be used to build a further assessment, if necessary, and to design a treatment plan. It is also a demonstration of how subtests can be used clinically when scoring them would be misleading.

The second case is the report of a child with math difficulties who is not responding to interventions, and his parents question whether or not he is receiving appropriate remediation. He was assessed with the focused Learning Difference-Mathematics Referral Battery.

The third case is the report of a child with high-functioning autism who was re-evaluated with the Social/Interpersonal Referral Battery in order to help with the decision whether or not to place him in a regular classroom. It also demonstrates how subtests not needed can be eliminated from the Referral Battery and more pertinent subtests can be substituted.

CASE STUDY #1: GENERAL REFERRAL BATTERY

Neuropsychological Report

Text in italics and enclosed by brackets ([ ]) is intended to be interpretive for the reader of this volume and is not a part of the assessment report.

NAME: Julianne D.   **DOB:** 04-20-02
DOE: 09-22-08   **CA:** 6.5 years
EXAMINER: ABC, Ph.D.

Referral Statement

Julianne D. is a 6.5-year-old girl who resides with both parents. She has no siblings. Julianne is presently in kindergarten at Sunshine Elementary School. Julianne was brought for evaluation by her parents because they and Julianne's teacher are confused by her learning profile. She is very verbal and expressive, but has marked difficulty with any type of spatial activities (puzzles, copying, etc.). Julianne's teacher, Ms. N., referred Julianne for assessment through the school, and the school psychometrist administered a brief cognitive screening (see following) that revealed an intellectual deficit. The psychometrist felt that developmental immaturity might have negatively affected Julianne's results, because her vocabulary level was average. The psychometrist noted, however, that Julianne should have a full evaluation, but reported that it would be several months before she would be able to undertake any further testing for Julianne. The D. family feared that Julianne would fall further behind in school in that amount of time; therefore, they sought an outside evaluation through this clinic. (See Rapid Reference 7.1 concerning information to include in referral section.)

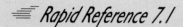

Rapid Reference 7.1

Information for Referral Section

- Identify the child by full name, age, and gender (nickname can be put in quotation marks)
- Brief description of child's family and with whom the child lives
- Referral source(s)
- Brief description of presenting problem (this focuses the report immediately on the referral question(s) to be answered)

Relevant History

History was obtained from a review of the history form filled out by Julianne's parents and the parent interview prior to Julianne's assessment, as well as a review of school records, and a telephone conference with the school psychometrist and Julianne's teacher.

Julianne is an only child born to apparently caring parents in an intact family. Mr. D. is a draftsman for an engineering firm and Mrs. D. works as a baker in a local grocery store. Both parents report that they were average students and are high school graduates. Father had an additional year of technical training. Mother's family history is unremarkable for any neurodevelopmental disorders, but Julianne's father was adopted and he has no biological family medical history.

Mr. and Mrs. D. report that Julianne's general health is good. She was the product of a full-term, uneventful pregnancy, and an uncomplicated natural birth. She weighed 6 lbs 1 oz. Parents are of average size, but Julianne has always been petite. Mr. and Mrs. D. have assumed that one of Mr. D's biological parents had a short stature. Parents reported that developmental landmarks were attained within normal limits for the most part, but these landmarks were not documented medically. Little health history is available for Julianne, as she has not been seen by a doctor since her birth, with the exception of three visits in as many years to the emergency room of the local hospital for fever and earache. Julianne's parents explained that they do not have health insurance. This clinic has sliding scale fees, so Mr. and Mrs. D. were able to make payment arrangements for her evaluation.

Julianne's parents characterized her as an "easy, very social" infant. She has always been sensitive to noises in the environment, however. Sometimes, these seem to be noises that other children do not mind (e.g. a small bell ringing). Julianne will also comment on an airplane coming before the sound is audible to others in the family. Mother reported that Julianne was a little slow in talking at first, but became very talkative and expressive by the time she was 18 months. She loves to tell stories, and her parents feel that these are quite advanced for Julianne's age. The one developmental area that has caused Mr. and Mrs. D. concern is Julianne's inability to assemble puzzles, to build constructions from a picture, and to copy a picture, or do craft activities at a level that they would expect for her age. For this reason, and because Julianne's maternal grandmother was able to continue taking care of her on the three days that Mrs. D. worked, her parents delayed Julianne's entry into kindergarten for an extra year. They felt that this extra time might allow her to "catch up." Julianne's vision was tested just before school began, because Mr. and Mrs. D. thought that Julianne's vision might be causing her problems in working with shapes, puzzles, and constructional tasks. Her vision was within normal limits, however.

A month after school began, the kindergarten teacher requested a meeting with Julianne's parents because their daughter was already experiencing marked learning problems. The teacher reports that despite her well-developed expressive language, Julianne is having trouble learning basic concepts, such as *above/below, inside/outside, over/under,* and she becomes confused when trying to follow oral directions that include spatial concepts. Although she can say the names of the four basic shapes, Julianne cannot identify them if she is given the oral label, nor can she attach the correct names to the correct shapes. Likewise, Julianne can sing the "Alphabet Song" but she has trouble identifying the symbols A, B, and C, because she confuses the shapes. The same is true for numbers. Julianne can count to eight correctly, but mixes up the visual symbols. Mr. & Mrs. D state that Julianne is a year older than her classmates, so her parents feel she should be mastering these concepts easily. Instead, she is falling further and further behind them in learning. Parents have wondered if Julianne might be dyslexic.

Julianne has always been well-liked by children in the neighborhood, according to Mr. and Mrs. D. They have noticed, however, that she prefers to play with children who are younger than she is. They feel that that may be partly because she is petite and feels more confident with them. The teacher reports that she socializes well at school and loves to play in the puppet center where she can make up puppet plays. She is very imaginative in doing this, and the other children enjoy doing the plays with her. The teacher and Julianne's parents feel, however, that a significant gap is opening up between Julianne's spatial abilities and those of her peers, yet she converses easily with them and with adults.

Previous Testing

On 09-01-08, the *Wechsler Abbreviated Scale of Intelligence* (WASI), a brief cognitive measure, was administered to Julianne by M. S., MA, the psychometrist at Julianne's school. The two subtests (Vocabulary and Matrix Reasoning) version was chosen. It yielded an estimated FSIQ of 68 (2nd percentile), with a significant difference between verbal and nonverbal reasoning. The psychometrist noted that this cognitive ability level seemed to be at variance with Julianne's good language development, since vocabulary is usually a good general estimate of cognitive ability.

Behavioral Observations

Julianne is a right-handed young girl with blonde hair, blue eyes, and elfin features. She was well-groomed, and appeared well-nourished, though small-for-age. Julianne was very friendly and talkative as she entered the testing session. She separated easily from her mother and settled quickly at the testing table, chatting with the examiner happily. Eye contact was good. When chatting with this clinician, Julianne was verbally and affectively expressive, using very nicely crafted phrases spontaneously. Despite her good language skills, however, Julianne appeared immature for chronological age. For instance, in the waiting area and in this examiner's office during the break, she chose to play with the toddler toys, rather than toys usually chosen by 6 year-olds.

It was notable during the testing that when a task required visuospatial skills or even when the stimuli on a task from a different domain were spatial, Julianne's performance would slow and she would become confused. This was first evident on the Inhibition subtest that has circles, squares, and directional arrows as stimuli. With just a little reassurance, however, Julianne was ready to try the task. Julianne used a fragmented piecemeal approach to Design Copying. She rarely was able to produce the correct overall configuration. She tended to focus on producing the inner details, but even then they were not integrated. She attempted to talk her way through visuospatial tasks, but was rarely successful, even with verbal mediation. Julianne attended well for the most part, but would become confused with visuospatial stimuli. She was extremely cooperative, and gave very good effort to the assessment. Even when she knew a task would be difficult, she did not become upset, and was willing to try her best. Therefore, this assessment is felt to be a reliable reflection of Julianne's abilities, given the caveats on certain subtest results presented in this report.

Test Battery Administered

NEPSY-II, General Assessment Battery.

[*Because the referral question was vague and time was of the essence, the clinician selected the NEPSY-II General Assessment Battery, knowing that she could get a quick overview of skills in that way, but that, if needed, she could then add any subtests that she felt were necessary in order to delineate Julianne's primary and secondary deficits more fully.*]

Test Results

Attention and Executive Functioning Domain

Julianne's performance on the **Auditory Attention subtest** showed an AA Total Correct Scaled Score of 9 in relation to the NEPSY-II subtest mean of 10 ± 3. This performance was *At Expected Level* for age. Julianne was required to listen for the word *red* among many other distracter words. When she heard the word *red*, she was to touch the correct color on an array with a yellow, a blue, a black, and a red circle.

The AA Combined Score integrated her AA Total Correct Scaled Score and the AA Total Commission Errors Percentile Rank (26th–50th percentile), both *At Expected Level*. A commission error occurs when the child touches the wrong color or touches the correct one more than 2 seconds after hearing the word. Julianne made 3 commission errors, which is average for age. Therefore, her AA Combined Scaled Score (9) was also *At Expected Level*.

Julianne displayed two instances of inattention on the Behavioral Observations for AA Inattentive Off-Task Behavior Total, which fell *At Expected Level*

(Cumulative Percentage of 26–75) when compared to the normative sample for age. Response Set is the second task in this subtest and a part of the General Assessment Battery, but it is intended for ages 7–16, so it was not administered to Julianne.

On the **Inhibition subtest,** the Naming condition assesses the ability to name shapes and directions from visual stimuli (*circles* and *squares* and arrows pointing *up* and *down*) quickly, while the Inhibition condition assesses the ability to inhibit a well-learned response in order to say the opposite. Upon seeing the first stimulus picture of circles and squares, Julianne commented that she sometimes gets "mixed up on shapes." This examiner wanted to proceed with the task in order to observe how Julianne performed with spatial stimuli on a task that was not in the Visuospatial domain. In other words, would she have difficulty with spatial material only on a visuospatial task, or would she also have problems with spatial stimuli in other domains? This clinician reassured her by explaining that the task might be a little difficult, but she should just do her best so that the examiner could see how to help her. She was willing to try and did not appear tearful or anxious, so testing proceeded. Despite her good humor and effort, Julianne displayed marked difficulty, especially on the second section of the test where she had to name the opposite shape for the one shown and the opposite direction for an arrow pointing up or down. Even on the first part, the Inhibition Naming trial, however, Julianne had a difficult time because she was not always sure if she was looking at a *circle* or a *square*. Based on a subtest mean (average) scaled score of 10 ± 3 and a mean (average) percentile rank of 50, Julianne's Primary Scores, including Combined Scores, were all deficient:

> IN Naming Total Completion SS: 1 (<2nd percentile)
> INN Total Errors Percentile Rank: <2nd percentile
> INN Combined SS: 1 (<2nd percentile)
> IN Inhibition Total Completion Time SS: 3 (2nd percentile)
> INI Total Errors Percentile Rank: <2nd percentile
> INI Combined SS: 1 (2nd percentile)
> IN Total Error (both shapes and arrows) SS: 2 (2nd percentile)
> INN vs. INI Contrast Scaled Score: 3 (2nd percentile)

Process scores for Julianne on the Inhibition subtest were also *Well Below Expected Level* for Uncorrected Errors, Self-Corrected Errors, and Total Errors. The clinician felt that because of Julianne's significant visuospatial problems with the stimuli, this test could not be used as an assessment of either naming or inhibition. Therefore, this was noted on the Record Form, but results were interpreted clinically to demonstrate that even on a task in another domain, visuospatial stimuli caused significant problems for Julianne. She showed marked difficulty with the visuospatial concepts of shape and direction, especially under time constraints, and most especially when she had to alternate concepts of which she was unsure in the first place.

Because the **Statue subtest** had no visuospatial stimuli, it was used to assess inhibition, instead of the Inhibition subtest. Statue is designed to assess the ability to inhibit motor response to intruding auditory stimuli. Julianne performed *At Expected Level* (Statue SS: 9). On the Statue Process Score Percentile Ranks for Body Movement (51st–75th percentile) and Eye Opening (26th–50th percentile); therefore, Julianne performed *At Expected Level* in inhibiting body movement, and not opening her eyes when there was an interfering noise. She did startle and open her eyes when this examiner knocked on the table and later coughed as distracters, but her 2 errors on Eye Opening were within normal limits at her age. Predictably, because of her talkative nature, she had difficulty inhibiting vocalizations (3 errors, 11th–25th percentile), but even this area was *Borderline*. It would not meet the stringent cutoff at the 10th percentile for significant abnormalities. Julianne's ability to inhibit response appeared to be within normal limits for age, except for mildly distracting herself with talking.

Language Domain

On assessment of language skills, Julianne's performance revealed **Comprehension of Instructions** *At Expected Level* (scaled score of 9 at the 37th percentile in relation to the NEPSY-II Test Mean of 10 ± 3). These results indicated that Julianne's receptive language understanding was within normal limits for age, despite the fact that it was necessary to start her on Item 1, the level for age 5, because she failed one of the prerequisite items when she had to point to a cross. Julianne made no errors on the "bunny" items (e.g. "Show me a yellow bunny;" "Show me a big blue bunny."). The second section with circles and crosses as stimuli has such items as "Point to the white one and a circle," and "Point to the blue cross and the yellow cross." By the time Julianne reached the items that had circles and crosses for stimuli again, she had made the connection between the cross that she saw at church and the stimulus cross, so she passed enough items to score in the average range.

On the **Speeded Naming (SN) subtest**, Julianne showed an interesting pattern. Again, because she had to confront circles and squares, she had difficulty. Her SN Total Completion Time Scaled Score (7) was *Borderline* (11th–25th percentile), but the clinician noted that her performance would have been faster if she had not experienced marked difficulty handling Item 4, which involved size/color/shape naming. Julianne's performance slowed very significantly as she began Item 4. Interestingly, she made no errors on the colors on either Item 3 (color/shape) or Item 4, but she did not seem to be able to label the spatial words well. Even on Item 3, Julianne named only six *shapes* correctly and self-corrected only two errors. In other words, she was still confusing circles and squares. On Item 4, although all of the colors were correct, she named only six *shapes* correctly and eight *sizes*. She self-corrected an additional three *size* words and one *shape* word. Thus, of a possible 84 points on the two items, Julianne scored only 58 points, and 32 of those were for correct colors. This performance did not appear to be a problem in naming, because Julianne had no trouble accessing color names. Rather, it appeared to be a visuospatial deficit that prevented her from developing automaticity in naming shapes and sizes.

Julianne's SN Total Correct Percentile Rank was at less than the 2nd percentile for age. She made only six self-corrections, suggesting that she did not always realize that she had identified a shape or size incorrectly. Her SN Self-Corrected Errors Percentile Rank was also at the < 2nd for age. These results were *Well Below Expected Level* for Julianne's age.

Memory and Learning Domain

On **Narrative Memory (NM),** in relation to the NEPSY-II subtest mean of 10 ± 3, Julianne performed *At Expected Level* (26th–75th percentile) on the NM Free Recall Scaled Score (8) and the NM Free and Cued Recall (9) In relation to the subtest mean percentile of 50, Julianne's NM Recognition performance was also *At Expected Level* (51st–75th percentile). Therefore, the NM Free and Cued Recall vs. Recognition Contrast Scaled Score (8) was *At Expected Level,* as well. In other words, Julianne showed average story memory for age in freely recalling the story details, responding to questions about the story, and recognizing story details when she heard them.

Julianne's performance on Memory for Faces was exceptional in relation to the NEPSY-II mean of 10 ± 3 and to Julianne's own mean (10.7) on the memory subtests scores overall, with Julianne selecting 13 out of 16 faces correctly. This placed her performance *Above Expected Level* at an MF scaled score of 15 at the 95th percentile for immediate memory, and Memory for Faces Delayed was also *Above Expected Level* with Julianne selecting 15 out of 16 faces correctly (SS: 17; 99th percentile). Interestingly, Julianne's facial recognition skills appeared to be dissociated from her significant visuospatial deficits.

The Word List Interference subtest is also a part of the General Assessment Battery, but it is given to children ages 7–16, so it was not appropriate for Julianne.

Sensorimotor Domain

On the **Visuomotor Precision (VP)** subtest, Julianne showed a VP Time to Completion Scaled Score of 8, *At Expected Level* (26th–75th percentile), again pointing to motor speed within normal limits, though at the bottom of that classification. On the other hand, she displayed a VP Total Error Percentile Rank of 2nd–5th percentile (average is 50th percentile). The clinician noted that Julianne did not seem to perceive or anticipate the curves in the track as she was drawing pencil lines between the winding tracks, so her pencil tracing frequently strayed outside the tracks, causing errors. The integration of the VP Time to Completion and VP Total Error scores produced a VP Combination Scaled Score of 3, *Well Below Expected Level*. Again, the problem appeared to be visuospatial rather than motoric.

Social Perception Domain
[The General Referral Battery of the NEPSY-II does not include either of the subtests on the Social Perception Domain unless the child is displaying social/interpersonal deficits, which was not the case for Julianne.]

Visuospatial Processing Domain
As expected, Julianne performed poorly on the Visuospatial Processing domain subtests. In relation to the NEPSY-II subtest mean of 10 ± 3, she displayed a Design Copying Process Total Scaled Score of 4 at the 2nd percentile with a classification *Well Below Expected Level* in relation to other children of her age.

DC Motor Scaled Score (SS): 8, *At Expected Level* (26th–75th percentile)
DC Global Scaled Score: 2, *Well Below Expected Level* (<2nd percentile)
DC Local Scaled Score: 6, *Below Expected Level* (3rd–10th percentile)

Julianne's fine motor skills for copying were acceptable, but she performed poorly in reproducing the global configuration of the designs. While her DC Local SS was significantly better than the Global SS, it still indicated that Julianne had significant difficulty in reproducing the design details. Her copy designs showed better reproduction of details than of the outside configuration of the design, but even then the details were poorly integrated and randomly placed.

Julianne's Global vs. Local Contrast Scaled Score was at a scaled score of 11, *At Expected Level* (26th–75th percentile). This does not mean that her performance on both tasks was average. Rather, it means that given her very poor performance in reproducing the configuration of the design (Global), the poor level of her ability to reproduce small features within the design is approximately what one would expect. In other words, Julianne has marked difficulties reproducing both global and local elements of a design, though her motor control was within normal limits for age. Thus, it appeared that the deficits lay in Julianne's visuospatial perception rather than in her fine motor control.

The above interpretation of a visuospatial deficit rather than a motor deficit was supported by Julianne's poor performance on the nonmotor **Geometric Puzzles** subtest, a purely visuospatial task that assesses mental rotation, visuospatial analysis, and attention to detail. Julianne was presented with a grid containing geometric shapes. For each item, she was required to match two shapes outside of the grid to two shapes within the grid. A point is awarded for each correct shape matched. Julianne earned only 5 out of 24 possible points, a performance that placed her at less than the 2nd percentile for age, *Well Below Expected Level.*

CLINICAL IMPRESSIONS AND SUMMARY

Julianne D's history, clinical observations, and the results of her testing revealed a complex and somewhat confusing profile. Attention/executive functions (response inhibition to noise distracters), language, and verbal memory skills were average for age and significantly better than Julianne's pervasively poor visuospatial abilities. The former were weak even on tasks that were not directly assessing visuospatial functioning, but that had visuospatial stimuli. Therefore, several subtests were only interpreted clinically to demonstrate the negative impact that Julianne's poor visuospatial abilities can have on activities in other areas in everyday life. Specifically, this effect was seen on NEPSY-II subtests assessing other areas, such as inhibition, naming, and visuomotor precision. Despite her significantly poor visuospatial perception, Julianne displayed facial recognition skills that were excellent. Results will be summarized for each domain in more detail in the following discussion.

On the Attention/Executive Functioning domain subtests administered to her, Julianne displayed average auditory selective attention for age. Her ability to inhibit motor response to interfering auditory stimuli was also average. Julianne had significant difficulty, however, on the Inhibition subtest in both the naming and inhibition conditions because of the visuospatial stimuli on this subtest. Her performance was very weak, not because she could not name or inhibit, but because of her visuospatial deficits. The clinician, therefore, did not interpret this test for executive functioning. However, clinically, the results were valuable for demonstrating the marked difficulty Julianne has with the visuospatial concepts in all domains, not just on specific visuospatial tasks.

Despite apparently good receptive language on Comprehension of Instruction and in expressive language skills observed informally during testing, rapid naming performance was borderline for completion time and very poor for correct naming. These scores were not valid, and it would be wrong to assume from these results that Julianne had a naming deficit. Clinical observation during testing revealed that Julianne did not have a problem with naming per se, because she accessed color names with no errors. Rather, the problem appeared to be Julianne's confusion in recognizing shapes, so she often did not realize that she had identified them incorrectly. Her completion time was borderline due to her marked confusion on the second part of the test where she had to deal with two visuospatial concepts (shape/size) in addition to color that she was able to name with no difficulty. Since her problems with the Speeded Naming subtest were due to visuospatial confusion, not naming problems, this subtest, too, was only interpreted clinically. It did, however, contribute to the picture of Julianne's difficulty in handling visuospatial stimuli in areas other than on tasks of visuospatial processing.

In the Memory and Learning domain, in addition to Julianne's average performance for free recall, free/cued recall, and recognition of story details on a subtest of story memory, Narrative Memory, Julianne was also administered the Memory for Faces and Memory for Faces Delayed subtests. Her performance on both the immediate and the delayed MF tasks was excellent, a finding that appears to be uniquely dissociated from her visuospatial deficits.

In the Sensorimotor domain, Julianne's performance on Visuomotor Precision revealed average time to completion, suggesting no difficulties with motor speed, but poor accuracy in straying outside the tracks. Again, the problem appeared to be visuospatial rather than motoric. The clinician noted that Julianne did not seem to perceive and/or anticipate the curves as she was drawing the pencil lines between the winding tracks. Therefore, her pencil line frequently strayed outside the tracks on a curve, causing numerous errors. Therefore, this subtest was interpreted clinically for total errors, since they seemed to be the result of her visuospatial deficits, rather than poor motor coordination.

On specific visuospatial assessment in the Visuospatial Processing domain, Julianne displayed poor ability to solve nonmotor geometric puzzles and poor design copying overall. Her process scores on Design Copying showed average motor performance, which correlates with Julianne's Visuomotor Processing Time to Completion performance, mentioned before. However, she displayed very poor ability to perceive and reproduce the outside configuration (global processing) of a figure and poor ability to reproduce and integrate small features within the design (local processing). Although Julianne's local processing of details was poor, this area was significantly better than global processing for the outside configuration of the design. Visuospatial processing is purported to be subserved by right posterior functioning, particularly right parietal.

On subtests that could be scored reliably, rather than interpreted clinically, Julianne's profile of strengths, weaknesses, and average abilities in relation to children of her age are summarized (see the following pages).

Classification of Test Results—Julianne D.

Classification	Scaled Score Range (mean = 10 + 3)	Percentile Rank Range
Above Expected Level	13–19	> 75
Immediate and delayed facial recognition skills		
At Expected Level	8–12	26–75
Selective auditory attention		
Off-task behavior on an auditory attention task		
Inhibition of motor response to sound distracters (ability to stand still with eyes closed)		
Comprehension of oral language instructions of increasing complexity		
Story memory for free recall of details, for free and cued recall, and for recognition		
Fine motor coordination for untimed paper-pencil design copying task		
Borderline	6–7	11–25
Inhibition of motor response to sound distracters—vocalizations:		
when a noise distractor was heard, talked, but not a significant weakness		
Below Expected Level	4–5	3–10
Visuospatial perception, analysis, and reproduction of details of a 2-D design		
Well Below Expected Level	1–3	< 2
Motor and visuospatial skills integrated for copying 2-dimensional figures		
Visuospatial skills were the confounding factor; fine motor coordination for copying was average (see above)		
Visuospatial perception, analysis, and reproduction of configuration of a 2-D design		
Mental rotation, visuospatial analysis, and attention to detail on a nonmotor geometric matching task		

Summary Graphs of NEPSY-II Scores–Julianne D.
(Graphed in relation to the subtest mean for age of 10 ± 3)
Average range: 8–12

Attention/Executive Functioning Scaled Scores

Subtest Score Name	1	2	3	4	5	6	7	8	9	10	11	12	13	14	15	16	17	18	19
Auditory Attention Total Correct Scaled Score									X										
Auditory Attention Combined Scaled Score									X										
Inhibition–interpreted clinically only	–	–	–		–	–	–	–	–	–	–	–	–	–	–	–	–	–	–
Statue Total Scaled Score									X										

Language Scaled Scores

Subtest Score Name	1	2	3	4	5	6	7	8	9	10	11	12	13	14	15	16	17	18	19
Comp. of Instructions SS									X										
Speeded Naming – interpreted clinically only	–	–	–	–	–	–	–	–	–	–	–	–	–	–	–	–	–	–	–

Memory and Learning Scaled Scores

Subtest Score Name	1	2	3	4	5	6	7	8	9	10	11	12	13	14	15	16	17	18	19
Memory for Faces Total SS															X				
MF Delayed Total SS																	X		
Narrative Memory–Free Recall SS									X										
NM Free/Cued SS										X									

Sensorimotor Scaled Scores

Subtest Score Name	1	2	3	4	5	6	7	8	9	10	11	12	13	14	15	16	17	18	19
Visuomotor Precision Total Completion Time								X											
Visuomotor Precision Combined SS (time/error) – interpreted clinically only	–	–	–	–	–	–	–	–	–	–	–	–	–	–	–	–	–	–	–

Social Perception

No subtests included in the General Assessment Battery unless it is a problem area.

Visuospatial Processing

Subtest Score Name	1	2	3	4	5	6	7	8	9	10	11	12	13	14	15	16	17	18	19
Design Copying Process Total Score				X															
Design Copying Process Motor Score								X											
Design Copying Process Global Score			X																
Design Copying Process Local Score						X													
Geometric Puzzles Total Score	2nd percentile																		

Along with Julianne's area of strength in facial recognition skills in terms of the typical child of her age (mean = 10 ± 3), she displayed relative strengths in language and verbal memory, both at the 37th percentile in relation to her cognitive ability at the 2nd percentile. This is an unusual profile. In addition, Julianne's NEPSY-II results revealed the following primary and secondary deficits, as well as a diagnostic cluster pointing to a preliminary diagnosis.

> **Primary deficit:** Visuospatial processing (with dissociation of face recognition, which is a strength).
>
> **Secondary deficits** that stem from this primary deficit include the following:
>
> - **Understanding visuospatial words** such as *inside/outside*, and confusion in naming shapes and directions despite average language overall on this assessment. Further assessment of the subtleties of language should be undertaken, however. (A secondary deficits, because Julianne had marked weaknesses in visuospatial perception and processing.)
> - **Slow naming performance on tasks with visuospatial components.** (Due to visuospatial confusion, not a naming or processing speed deficit. A naming deficit could be ruled out as Julianne had no difficulty naming colors quickly.)
> - **Poor copying skills and visuomotor precision on tasks with visuospatial components.** (Due to primary deficits in perceiving visuospatial forms and stimuli, not due to motor deficits. A primary motor problem could be ruled out, as she performed WNL on the Motor Scaled Score of Design Copying (untimed) and VP Completion Time (timed).)
> - **Difficulty recognizing the shapes of letters and numbers** negatively impacting acquisition of **basic reading and math skills.** Later, the math learning problems may become accentuated.

The pattern of Julianne's strengths and primary and secondary deficits along with the physical and behavioral characteristics of short stature, elfin face, friendly nature, possible mild–moderate intellectual disability, very well-developed language and poor visuospatial skills with good facial recognition abilities converge on a diagnostic behavioral cluster consistent with William's syndrome. This is a genetic syndrome that includes neurological maldevelopment characterized by good language abilities, but also by very significant visuospatial deficits. These children have excellent facial recognition skills that appear to be dissociated from other visuospatial deficits. Their cognitive deficits are initially masked by their talkative, happy nature, and very expressive language, so it is not unusual for these children to go undiagnosed until approximately six years of age. Children with William's syndrome are also subject to cardiac problems and other possible medical complications. Therefore, it is essential that Julianne be seen by a multidisciplinary pediatric team to confirm or rule out Williams Syndrome.

PRELIMINARY DIAGNOSIS

Rule out/in William's syndrome. (This is a prospective diagnosis. A confirmatory medical diagnosis should be completed as soon as possible.)
Rule out/in Intellectual Disability. (To be confirmed or ruled out in subsequent cognitive assessment.)

RECOMMENDATIONS

1. Julianne's preliminary diagnosis should be confirmed by a pediatric neurologist and/or developmental pediatrician who are part of a multidisciplinary pediatric team, including a pediatric cardiologist. This psychologist would be glad to help with this referral, if desired. The Speech/Language therapist and occupational therapist should be a part of the assessment team. A treatment plan can then be formulated by the pediatric team.

2. A full cognitive assessment is recommended for Julianne and further neuropsychological assessment, as well, with the balance of the subtests from the NEPSY-II. Adaptive behavior checklists, and achievement testing should be completed to provide the full picture of Julianne's potential. This psychologist would be happy to continue following Julianne as part of the multidisciplinary team, if Julianne's parents wish it.

3. With parents' permission, on completion of the full assessment, these results will be shared with them and with the pediatric team in order to facilitate treatment planning, if that is the course Mr. and Mrs. D choose.

4. This psychologist will supply Julianne's parents with information concerning William's syndrome and will discuss it with them in detail during the parent feedback session to help prepare them for their meeting with the medical team.

5. If Mr. and Mrs. D. desire it, this psychologist will seek a meeting at Julianne's school to include them, her teacher, and the Special Services Team. Consideration will need to be given to Julianne's educational placement.

6. Interventions for school and home need to be formulated immediately, so Julianne can begin to receive remediation and adaptive techniques for her significant visuospatial deficit and the effect that it has on early learning. At the school meeting, plans for Response to Intervention (RTI) can be discussed, so the school can formulate the plan as soon as possible. After the full assessment is completed, interventions can be modified, if needed.

7. The following are recommendations for Julianne's parents and the Special Services Team at school to consider:

   (a) At this point the most advantageous arrangement appears to be a split placement, with Julianne continuing in the mainstream classroom for all areas where she is finding success (e.g., language, social relationships, etc.) and to have special education placement for intensive interventions for specific visuospatial learning and for those areas influenced by it.

   (b) The school occupational therapist should work with Julianne, preferably 30 min. x 2/week, on 3-D constructional skills, working up to 2-D copying skills and any other areas the pediatric team and the school occupational therapist feel would be beneficial.

   (c) If subtle problems with language are noted in her speech-language evaluation, Julianne may need 30 minutes of speech-language therapy/week with the speech-language therapist at school.

   (d) Adaptive technology should be implemented where appropriate.

   (e) Julianne will need to work through her good language skills in order to help her in visuospatial areas. She needs a quiet spot in which to work so she can "talk" herself through visuospatial tasks. Kinesthetic tracing and language descriptions will be helpful: Julianne traces a sandpaper or carpet shape with her finger and describes the shape at the same time. The rough surface of the shape gives Julianne kinesthetic feedback to help her link the visuospatial concept to its name: "Square. A square has four sides that are the same (tracing the sides). Square." This is repeated five times; then Julianne performs the same task with a circle and repeats. She then looks at a shape on a card and repeats the process. She is then shown the cards and asked to identify the two shapes (when instructed to "Show me a circle," she points). When she is able to identify those two shapes, she is presented with the cards and asked to name the two shapes. This process is used with all of the basic shapes, two at a time, reviewing those already learned, until Julianne has mastered identifying them and naming them on the cards. The same process can be used with letters and with numbers, but they should not be mixed in presentation until she is approaching mastery.

(f) Real objects in the shapes Julianne is learning should be handled and talked about. ("This plate is a circle; that box is square.") Two objects in each shape should be presented and the number increased progressively until Julianne has mastered identifying them and naming them. She can have a treasure hunt, looking in the classroom and at home for the target shapes.

(g) Preschool/kindergarten software that presents shapes with their names slowly and repetitively should be included in her interventions. Letters and numbers can be practiced in this way as well.

(h) When Julianne has mastered enough letters to begin spelling simple words, she can proceed to that step. She has well-developed phonological skills, so she can learn sound-symbol association. Whole word learning would rely too much on the visuospatial configuration of the word for Julianne.

(i) When Julianne has mastered the first five numbers, she can begin some very simple number activities (e.g., counting up objects to equal a number, etc.). She should continue with mastery of the next five numbers as described before, however. Arithmetic will likely be very difficult for Julianne due to underlying visuospatial concepts.

(j) Julianne can begin work with very large, simple floor puzzles with no pictures on them and with a template for their placement outlined in tape on the floor. As she masters this activity, the template can be removed, and she will work toward completing the puzzles without the template. By having plain puzzle pieces, Julianne has to attend to the shape of the puzzle piece for solution, rather than matching the pictures.

(k) Work on visuospatial words can be included in Julianne's interventions with her acting out the concept (e.g., *in/out*) as she repeats the word. This can also be done with dolls and a dollhouse as well. The school speech-language therapist might be involved in this learning for 30 min. x 1/wk. Again, having Julianne use her body in learning will give her proprioceptive feedback to help link the concepts to the words and meaning.

    (l) Julianne's parents should be given a program for working with her at home for no more than 20 min./day in order to reinforce the interventions that she is receiving through her school program.

8. Julianne has relative strengths in language that should help build her confidence. Since verbal memory is also a relative strength, she might enjoy a basic class for children in improvisation and drama games. Julianne would also enjoy story times at the library and dictating her own stories to her parents or teacher. Simple read-along story books would also be enjoyable.

9. Parents can help Julianne continue to build social relationships by arranging a play date for her every week or so.

10. As much as possible, Julianne should be treated as a typical child in school and at home. Give Julianne praise when she is obeying family rules and working well in school. Praise effort, not grades. Family rules need to be simple and clear cut. Use Time Out (1 minute per year) in a nonjudgmental, nonthreatening manner when Julianne makes a poor behavioral choice. When Time Out is over, resume interactions in a positive manner. Always be mindful, however, that one must be patient with Julianne if she becomes confused by any task or activity with visuospatial components.

11. Mr. and Mrs. D. will be provided with the name of a social worker who can help them access services available through the state for children with disabilities. They will also be given the contact number for a support group for parents of children with disabilities that meets locally once a month, and also plans family activities.

12. This psychologist is available for guidance at any stage in the above process. Please feel free to contact her with questions or concerns.

Follow-up to the Report of Case #1

Given the diagnostic cluster of skills with which Julianne was reported to have had difficulty at home and school, this psychologist, drawing on her background in developmental neuropsychology, had formed a preliminary hypothesis of William's syndrome fairly early in the assessment process. Administering the General Assessment Battery gave the clinician a preliminary scanning of Julianne's strengths and weaknesses in a limited amount of time. Indeed, considering Julianne's pattern of strengths and weaknesses, the NEPSY-II results converged on a diagnostic cluster consistent with William's syndrome. Further, the clinician could verify her findings with concerns reported from school, home, other testing, and the neuropsychological literature.

William's syndrome is a rare genetic disorder, first identified in 1961 by the cardiologist Williams and colleagues (Williams, Barratt-Boyes, & Lowe, 1961). They described four children with supravalvar aortic stenosis in association with mental retardation and a characteristic elfin facial appearance (Jones & Smith, 1975). It is now recognized that the syndrome also commonly includes other abnormalities of the cardiovascular system, as well as of the renal, musculoskeletal, endocrine, and other organ systems. The overall incidence of WMS has been estimated at a rare 1 in 50,000 live births (Bellugi, Wang, & Jernigan, 1994).

In William's syndrome, there is neurological maldevelopment characterized by a mild to moderate intellectual deficit with good language abilities, but significant visuospatial deficits (Bellugi, Bihrle, Jernigan, Trauner, & Doherty, 1990). Belugi and colleagues (Bellugi, Bihrle, Neville, Jernigan, & Doherty, 1992) have also demonstrated that in William's syndrome there appears to be a dramatic preservation of facial discrimination ability despite other significant deficits and biases in spatial processing, and despite the usual pattern of right-hemisphere specialization for these tasks. More recently, Mobbs and colleagues (2004) have observed in MRI studies, significant increases in activation in the right fusiform gyrus (FuG, the face processing center) and in several frontal and temporal regions for a William's syndrome clinical group. By comparison, controls showed activation in the bilateral FuG, occipital, and temporal lobes. The clinician's neuropsychological background in genetic syndromes was very helpful as she was able to connect Julianne's elfin appearance (short palpebral fissures, epicanthal folds, and long philtrum) (Jones & Smith, 1975; Newton, 1995), marked visuospatial deficits, "friendly and loquacious" personality, and "unusual command of language" (Von Arnim & Engel, 1964) to the possibility of this genetic metabolic syndrome that can include cardiac problems (supravalvular stenosis) and often mild-moderate mental retardation (Loring, 1999).

The above case is an example of the importance in diagnostic work of having a broad background in pediatric neuropsychology with current knowledge of the literature. The clinician felt that further testing was needed in order to gain a fuller picture of Julianne's cognitive functioning. However, because it was important for Julianne to be evaluated medically for William's syndrome, the clinician was able to share her preliminary diagnosis with Julianne's parents on the basis of her findings from the General Assessment Battery, and to make a referral to a developmental pediatrician and pediatric cardiologist who agreed to see Julianne pro bono at a nearby university medical center with which she was affiliated. The physicians would work with a medical team to pursue the final medical diagnosis and to be sure that Julianne was screened for cardiac problems as well as any other affected organ systems. The team, of which the clinician was a part, would be sure that Julianne received any other evaluations needed. Further, the clinician referred the parents to a social worker who could help them apply for a special state insurance plan for children with disabilities.

Parents gave permission for the preliminary findings from the NEPSY-II General Assessment Battery to be shared with the medical team and the teacher so that special services and interventions could be initiated as soon as possible. The school psychologist administered academic testing and adaptive behavior scales, while the neuropsychologist continued with a full NEPSY-II. In this way, assessment was expedited and plans for educational interventions could be formulated. The clinican worked with the teacher and school psychologist on preliminary RTI (response to intervention) plans. Julianne's good language and motor skills provided good channels for remediation, while her primary and secondary deficits could be addressed through specific interventions.

When all assessments were completed and all data were gathered by the pediatric and school teams, all personnel, including the psychologist and Julianne's parents, would meet to further refine the treatment and RTI plans.

CASE STUDY 2: REFERRAL BATTERY: LEARNING DIFFERENCES–MATHEMATICS

Neuropsychological Report

NAME: Peter L.   **DOB:** 06-09-1995
DOE: 12-19-2006   **CA:** 11.6 years
EXAMINER: XYZ, PhD

Referral Statement

Peter L. is a young boy of 11.6 years who was brought for evaluation by his mother and father with whom he makes his home. According to his parents, Peter has experienced significant problems in learning mathematics since first grade. For the past two years, Peter has received individualized help in math through Resource Room services (40 minutes, 5 days/week). He is making little progress, however, so his parents sought this evaluation in order to ascertain if there is an underlying problem and some manner in which Peter might be helped.

Relevant History

History was obtained from a review of the history form filled out by Peter's parents and the parent interview prior to his assessment, as well as a review of school records provided by them. Mr. and Mrs. L. did not wish for the school to be contacted prior to testing as they were concerned that such a contact might jeopardize Peter's present Resource Room services.

Peter is the middle son of an apparently caring, intact family. He has an older brother, 13, and a younger sister, 9 years of age, neither of whom has any learning disabilities. Peter's mother is a college graduate who works in the home as the primary caregiver, and Peter's father is an attorney.

Peter was born at 31-weeks gestational age in an emergency Cesarean-section delivery after an uneventful pregnancy. He was 5 lbs, 1 oz at birth. He was in the Neonatal Intensive Care Unit of Central Hospital for a month, receiving assisted ventilation and came home on an apnea monitor. After a few weeks the monitor was removed, and he progressed well. Peter and his parents bonded well, despite the initial complications. Peter's development has been followed by a pediatrician since birth, and all developmental landmarks were attained within normal limits correcting for prematurity in the first year. Development has been on a normal trajectory since that time, as documented by his pediatrician. He has mild seasonal allergies, but otherwise his general health is excellent.

Peter attended a private preschool for two years before entering kindergarten at 5 years of age. Peter loved school, and he was successful in all areas of learning in preschool and first grade. In second grade, however, he began to experience problems in mathematics, and these difficulties appear to have grown worse each year, according to his parents. They are very concerned that he does not seem to be "catching up" even with the 40 minutes of Resource Room help that he receives each day. They are not sure whether he is actually getting individualized help or just extra time to finish his work. There are five children in the Resource Room at the time Peter attends it, and the teacher must work with each of them in the 40-minute period. Peter's grades are generally in the C/B range in all areas except math, in which he is presently receiving a D. His math teacher reports that Peter applies himself, but just does not seem to be able to understand math concepts and operations. Mr. and Mrs. L. are concerned that Peter is getting discouraged and may "give up" the struggle before long.

An active, social child, Peter is well-liked by his peers and is generally even-tempered. He has a best friend his age at school, and the boys spend a lot of time playing together. In his neighborhood, there are three other boys with whom he plays regularly. Peter plays on a Little League baseball team and is a good athlete, according to Dad. He interacts well with all members of the team, according to Mr. L., who is his assistant coach. Peter enjoys tennis and is learning to play golf from his Dad. Peter grumbles about chores, but generally does them, but his parents report that homework can be a battle, especially math. Peter works at the kitchen table but is "up and down constantly" when he is supposed to be working, according to his mother. (See Rapid Reference 7.2 concerning information in the Background History section.)

≡ Rapid Reference 7.2

Relevant History Section: What to Include

- **Sources of history information:** who provided it and in what form. Interview, school records, history form, etc.
- **Additional family information:** parents' occupations; any family tensions, sibling rivalries, relationship with parents, family history of physical/psychological/neurological disorders, etc.
- **Pregnancy, delivery, and perinatal history:** any complications, interventions, perinatal care in hospital, bonding.
- **Developmental and medical history:** developmental landmarks WNL or delayed? sleeping/eating patterns, significant illnesses or surgeries, head injury or repeated mild concussions; activity level, repetitive behaviors, etc.
- **Schooling:** – preschool, school experience since that time, successes, learning problems; child's attitude toward school, teachers, homework, etc; participation in school activities, athletics.
- **Psychosocial history – social interactions:** school and neighborhood friends, child's temperament, emotional status, behavioral problems, any counseling and with whom.

Previous Testing

School evaluation: 02–10–2006:

Wechsler Intelligence Scale for Children –III (WISC-III)

Verbal IQ: 92 (Mean = 100 ± 15), 30th percentile, average
Performance IQ: 87, 19th percentile, low average
Full Scale IQ: 88, 21st percentile, low average

Wechsler Individual Achievement Test – II (WIAT-II)

Math Composite–69, 2nd percentile, weak
Math Operations–70, 2nd percentile, weak
Math Reasoning–73, 4th percentile, weak

(–19 pt. discrepancy between cognitive ability measure and Math Composite score on standardized measures of achievement)

Test battery Administered

NEPSY-II—Referral Battery for Learning Differences-Mathematics

Test Observations

Peter appeared relaxed on being introduced to this psychologist. He smiled and made good eye contact. He is a boy of average height and build for his 11.6 years, with brown hair and hazel eyes. Peter was animated in conversing with the examiner about school, and he seemed to enjoy school except for math. Peter commented, "I just don't get it," in referring to math. He doesn't feel that his Resource Room sessions are helping because, "mostly we just do worksheets, and they are boring." He reported that there are four other students in the Resource Room at the same time he is, and everyone is working on different worksheets. Peter likes athletics, especially baseball, but he is also excited about learning how to play golf with his dad. If he could have three wishes, Peter would "play ball in the World Series, meet Tiger Woods, and be better at math."

When testing began, Peter applied himself well for about 20–30 minutes, but then he would begin to look around and his work pace would slow. If he had a 5–10 min. break then, he would resume work with no difficulty, and again apply himself well. Visuospatial tasks were obviously difficult for him, especially Memory for Designs. Peter displayed a mature pencil grip, but the movement of his hand when copying designs was not fluid. (See Rapid Reference 7.3)

≡ *Rapid Reference 7.3*

Test Observations: What to Include

During the assessment, make notes of:

- Physical description of the child.
- Interaction with examiner: forms rapport easily, shy, defensive, anxious, etc.
- Client interview: converses easily, smiles, eye contact, able to discuss any problems, discouragement, etc.
- Record HOW the child performs during testing: problem-solving skills, organized strategies, distracted, fatigued, topics that were easy or difficult, awkward pencil grip, slow/fast, etc.

Include:

- Factors that may compromise the validity or reliability of test results (e.g. attention, obsessiveness in being sure test pieces are perfectly placed slowing performance, administered in second language, etc.)
- Factors that may be symptomatic of brain disease or important differential information concerning psychiatric or developmental disorders (e.g. emotional lability, unusual thought processes, elfin face or other unusual physical features, stereotypies, etc.) (Armengol, Kaplan, & Moes, 2001).

- Your observations are *a part of your assessment* and very important to the interpretation of results and formulation of interventions.

Test Results

Attention and Executive Functioning Domain

Auditory Attention and Response Set Subtest: Peter's performance on the Auditory Attention subtest reflected average selective auditory attention when he was required to listen for the word *red* among many distracters and touch a red circle in response. In relation to the NEPSY-II subtest mean of 10 ± 3, Peter displayed:

AA Total Correct SS: 12 (75th percentile), *At Expected Level*
AA omission errors: 51st–75th percentile, *At Expected Level*
AA commission errors: 11th–25th percentile, *Borderline*
AA Inhibitory errors: 26th–50th percentile, *At Expected Level*.
Behavioral Observation: AA Off Task Behavior–Inattentive/Distracted (11th–25th percentile), *Borderline*

On the more complex auditory Response Set (RS) task, when Peter had to inhibit the impulse to touch "red" when he heard *red* and touch "yellow" instead, he made numerous commission and inhibitory errors. In other words, he had significant difficulty in inhibiting an automatic response to touch "red" and switch to the alternate response, *yellow*. On the same task, he was also required to use selective attention to touch "blue" when he heard the word *blue*. The multiple requirements of the Response Set (RS) subtest appear to have caused a breakdown in Peter's executive functioning, making it difficult for him to inhibit response and switch set, as well as to focus his attention on a matching response.

RS Total Correct SS: 8 (26th–75th percentile), *At Expected Level*
RS Combined SS: 5 (5th percentile), *Below Expected Level*

(Commission and inhibitory errors were integrated with his RS Total Correct.)

Peter made an appropriate number of correct responses, but he could not monitor his performance well enough to inhibit incorrect responses in order to avoid making commission errors (touching an incorrect color or touching a color more than 2 seconds after hearing the target word).

AA vs. RS Contrast Score: 4 (3rd–10th percentile), *Well Below Expected Level*

(Derived by contrasting the AA and RS Combined Scores.)

The AA Combined Score was *At Expected Level,* but the RS Combined Score was *Below Expected Level.* This contrast between the two tasks caused Peter's AA vs. Response Set Contrast Score to be *Well Below Expected Level* for his age. This means that given Peter's average performance on A, one would expect a much better RS performance than was seen on the RS task. Instead, his performance deteriorated to *Well Below Expected Level* because of the executive functions required on the Response Set.

Inhibition Subtest: When the Inhibition (IN) subtest (designed to assess executive functions) was administered, Peter showed a similar pattern. He displayed an average completion time in naming shapes or directions rapidly on the Naming condition in relation to the subtest mean of 10 ± 3):

IN Naming Completion Time SS: 11(26th–75th percentile), *At Expected Level*
IN Naming Combined SS: 14 (>75th percentile [91st percentile]), *Above Expected Level* (integrating time and errors)
IN Naming Total Errors: >75th percentile for age, *Above Expected Level*

Thus, the integrated speed and accuracy of Peter's performance was at the 91st percentile for his actual IN Combined Score and was better than that of 91 out of 100 children of his age. The percentile rank range for his age was >75th percentile range. Peter made no errors, so the accuracy of his performance was excellent. Therefore, slowed speed of access to semantics (words) could be ruled out as having an adverse effect on the subsequent trials of the Inhibition subtest. For that matter, rapid performance was *At Expected Level* on all three conditions of this subtest.

On the Inhibition condition of the Inhibition subtest, Peter was required to inhibit the previously learned response in order to give an opposite response. That is, when he looked at a circle, he had to call it a *square,* and vice versa. Likewise, when he looked at an arrow pointing *up* or *down,* Peter had to respond with the opposite direction. In relation to the NEPSY-II mean (average) of 10 ± 3, Peter displayed the following scores:

IN Inhibition Total Correct SS: 12 (75th percentile), *At Expected Level*
IN Inhibition Total Error: 11th–25th percentile rank, *Borderline*
IN Inhibition Combined SS: 8 (26th–75th percentile), *At Expected Level*

(IN Inhibition Total Correct integrated with IN Total Errors)
(IN Inhibition Total Correct integrated with Total Error Percentile)

Peter made five errors on the Inhibition condition. He did manage to self-correct three of them, however. This beginning slide in the executive functions of inhibition and cognitive flexibility when shifting set was apparent with increasing demands for monitoring performance.

In the third condition of the Inhibition subtest, Switching condition, Peter's executive functioning deteriorated further. On this task, when he saw a white shape, he had to say the name of the shape, but when he saw a black shape, he had to say the opposite shape. In the same way, when he saw a white arrow, he had to say the direction the arrow was pointing, but if the arrow was black, he had to say the opposite direction. The more executive functions were required to facilitate cognitive flexibility and the monitoring of a task, the more difficulty Peter experienced.

IN Switching Completion Time Total SS of 11 (63rd percentile) was *At Expected Level.*
IN Switching Total Errors Percentile Rank of 11th–25th percentile was *Below Expected Level.*
IN Switching Combined SS was 6 (9th percentile) and *Below Expected Level* (time and errors integrated).

At an average speed on the Inhibition–Switching task, Peter's accuracy was poor. He made 14 errors and of these only 6 were self-corrected, indicating that his ability to monitor his accuracy and correct himself (Self-corrected Errors) was *Borderline*. His monitoring and accuracy in terms of uncorrected errors (Uncorrected Errors) was *Below Expected Level*.

Looking at the three conditions of the Inhibition subtest, one sees that accuracy was good on the Naming condition, but he made 5 errors on the Inhibition condition and 14 on the Switching condition, so across all three conditions accuracy was poor:

IN Total Errors SS: 6 (9th percentile), *Below Expected Level*

The errors all occurred on the last two conditions (Inhibition and Switching), however, which assess executive functions. When one compares his IN-Naming (INN) condition performance to IN-Inhibition (INI) condition performance:

INN vs. INI Contrast SS: 6 (9th percentile), *Below Expected Level*

This contrast score meant that given Peter's ability to access names quickly and accurately being *Above Expected Level* for age, one would expect his IN-Inhibition time and error performance to be approximately equal to or better than his IN-Naming Combined score. Rather, Peter's IN-Inhibition Combined SS was at the bottom of the average range, indicating deteriorating performance when more executive functioning was required by the task.

INI vs. INS Contrast SS of 6 (9th percentile), *Below Expected Level*

Comparing the Inhibition condition to the Switching condition one can see greater deterioration in executive functioning between the IN-Inhibition condition *At Expected Level* and the IN-Switching condition than one would expect, with the latter being *Below Expected Level*. Peter displayed progressively more executive dysfunction the more the task demanded monitoring of performance and cognitive flexibility.

Language Domain

Comprehension of Instructions: Peter's performance revealed receptive language skills *At Expected Level* for understanding oral instructions of increasing complexity (Comprehension of Instructions Total SS: 8; 25th percentile), although performance was at the bottom of the average range.

Speeded Naming: On a task designed to assess rapid access to semantics (names of colors, shapes; colors and shapes; size color and shape; and letters and numbers), in relation to the NEPSY-II subtest mean of 10 ± 3, Peter displayed a:

SN Total Completion Time SS: 11 (63rd percentile), *At Expected Level*
SN Total Correct Percentile Rank: 51st–75th percentile, *At Expected Level*

Both time to completion and accuracy in naming were average for age, so the integrated score for time and total correct was also average (below):

Speeded Naming Combined SS: 11(63rd percentile), *At Expected Level*

Peter made no errors on the task, which was average for age. Therefore, his math difficulties do not appear to have a significant language contribution, nor does speed of access to basic language (naming) appear to be confounding math performance.

Memory and Learning Domain

Memory for Faces: In the visual memory area on Memory for Faces, Peter performed well:

Memory for Faces Total SS: 16 (99th percentile), *Above Expected Level*

Peter remembered all 16 faces immediately after a 5 second exposure to each. He appears able to encode facial characteristics very well.

MF Delayed Total SS: 9 (75th percentile), *At Expected Level*

There was, however, a significant 7 point discrepancy between Peter's immediate MF performance and his delayed recall of the faces. This drop suggests that there may be some mild memory decay present, but Peter is still recalling the faces at an average level 15–25 minutes after seeing them. The discrepancy between immediate and delayed recall of faces is reflected in the

MF vs. MFD Contrast SS: 4 (3rd–10th percentile), *Well Below Expected Level*

In other words, given Peter's excellent performance on MF, one would expect him to perform on the MF Delay at a higher level, rather than his performance dropping from the 99th percentile to the 75th percentile. This drop may be due to an inability to inhibit interference of other information between the immediate and delayed trials, since Peter displayed significant difficulties with executive functions, especially inhibition.

Memory for Designs: Peter's visuospatial memory for abstract geometric designs in the short and long term reflected a significant area of concern.

Memory for Designs Total SS: 1 (<2nd percentile), *Well Below Expected Level*

Immediate design memory overall was very poor for age. Essentially, this score means that fewer than 2 children out of 100 of Peter's age are worse at immediate recall of designs than he is. Peter's immediate recall of the designs themselves was poor:

MD Content Total SS: 4 (3rd percentile), Below Expected Level

Recall of the locations of the designs in a grid was also very poor:

MD Spatial Total SS: 3 (2nd percentile), Well Below Expected Level

Therefore, Peter shows weaknesses in recalling the configuration and details of the design itself as well as the spatial location of the design within the grid.

MD Content vs. MD Spatial Contrast SS: 5 (5th percentile), *Below Expected Level*

Given the level of Peter's immediate memory for content (the designs), one would expect at least an equal performance on immediate memory for spatial location, instead of a decline from *Below Expected Level* to *Well Below Expected Level* for age. Therefore, the contrast is *Below Expected Level*.

Memory for Designs Delayed: Looking at long-term visuospatial memory, one sees:

MD Delayed Total SS: 5 (5th percentile), *Below Expected Level*

This score provides evidence that Peter appears to consolidate visuospatial memory a little over time, but his performance is still poor. Immediate memory for designs overall was *Well Below Expected Level* with a scaled score of 1, so there was a + 1 $\frac{1}{4}$ standard deviation gain from immediate to delayed performance. It is still deficient, however.

MDD Content Total SS: 6 (9th percentile), *Below Expected Level*

Reflects how poorly Peter remembered the design itself over time , in relation to the subtest mean of 10 ± 3.

MDD Spatial Total SS: 1 (< 2nd percentile), *Well Below Expected Level*

The same pattern of weaker memory for spatial locations than for the configuration and details of the designs existed in both short- and long-term visuospatial memory for Peter.

MDD Content vs. MDD Spatial Contrast SS: 1 (< 2nd percentile), *Well Below Expected Level*

Given the MDD Content Total falling at the 9th percentile, one would expect that the MMD Spatial Total would at least meet that level, rather than falling at

<2nd percentile. Both are, however, poor. Nonetheless, long-term memory for spatial location was significantly weaker than long-term memory for designs per se.

MD vs. MDD Contrast Total SS: 11 (63rd percentile), *At Expected Level*

Given the level of performance on immediate Memory for Designs, performance on Memory for Designs Delayed is about what one would expect.

Because specific memory deficits in children are usually secondary to a broader primary deficit, one has to consider the fact that Peter's problems on this subtest may be due to primary visuoperceptual, visuospatial deficits. Indeed, test results in that domain revealed just such deficits, which will be discussed further under the Visuospatial Processing domain results to follow.

Word List Interference: This subtest is designed to assess verbal working memory, repetition, and word recall following interference. Since Peter's language was *At Expected Level* (Comprehension of Instructions Total SS: 8), it may have been recall after interference that negatively affected Peter's results on this subtest, as inhibiting interference is an executive function. We saw that Peter displayed executive dysfunction previously on the Inhibition Subtest and the Response Set of the Auditory Attention subtest.

On Word List Interference (WI), Peter was presented with two series of words and was asked to repeat each sequence following its presentation. Each series became an interference trial for the next one on the repetition trial and again when he was required to recall each series in order.

Word List Interference–Repetition Total SS: 7 (16th percentile) was *Borderline*.

When Peter was just repeating the series, one after the other, his performance was marginal, but when required to recall the series in the order of presentation from memory, Peter's performance was poor.

Word List Interference–Recall Total SS: 6 (9th percentile), *Below Expected Level*

Given Peter's *Borderline* performance on the repetition trial, one would not have expected the drop in his recall trial to *Below Expected Level*.

WI Repetition vs. Recall Contrast SS: 7 (16th percentile) was *Borderline*.

These results suggest that Peter's executive dysfunction is interfering with verbal working memory and will impact mathematics as well, since working memory is an integral part of math problem solution.

Sensorimotor Domain

Visuomotor Precision: On the Visuomotor Precision (VP) subtest, Peter was required to make pencil lines through winding tracks as quickly as possible without straying outside the borders of the tracks. He executed the lines at an average speed for age, as seen below:

> VP Total Completion Time SS: 11 (63rd percentile), *At Expected Level*

However, Peter's accuracy was not good, as seen in his next score:

> VP Total Errors Percentile Rank: 11th–25th percentile, *Borderline*

So, when time and errors were integrated, Peter showed a marginal performance for age:

> VP Combined SS: 7 (16th percentile), *Borderline*

He performed well, however, in only lifting his pencil from the paper once as he executed his lines (VP Pencil Lift Total Percentile Rank: > 75, *Above Expected Level*). In other words, he did not need to lift the pencil point in order to execute a curve.

It appears that Peter's graphomotor speed was within normal limits, but his graphomotor control for speed and accuracy combined is better than that of only 16 out of 100 children of his age. Inefficient graphomotor control may impede Peter's written math performance, especially if he has to copy numerous problems from the board or the textbook to his paper. When accuracy in copying is not good due to poor graphomotor control, Peter is apt to copy problems incorrectly or write numerals in the wrong columns. Without interventions and modifications in this area Peter could well become resistant to written work of any kind because it is so effortful for him.

Visuospatial Processing Domain

Design Copying: In the Visuospatial Processing domain, Peter displayed scores below:

> Design Copying Process (DCP) Total SS: 6 (9th percentile), *Below Expected Level*

This score reflected his overall performance for paper/pencil copying of progressively more detailed geometric figures.

The Process Scores on Design Copying take apart the various components comprising the task, so their individual contributions to the total performance can be studied more fully:

DCP Global SS: 11(63rd percentile), *At Expected Level*

The above score shows that Peter is able to perceive the outside configuration of designs and is able to produce the same on an untimed copying task. His ability to perceive and reproduce the details, however, was poor:

DCP Local SS: 5 (5th percentile), *Below Expected Level*

Keeping in mind that mathematics is a very detail-oriented discipline, this problem could have a significant impact on math performance. Peter also displayed a poor fine motor copying performance for age.

DCP Motor SS: 3 (2nd percentile), *Below Expected Level*

Therefore, his ability to reproduce geometric designs with pencil and paper is affected by both motoric and visuospatial deficits. The finding of a motoric deficit reinforces the results seen earlier in poor graphomotor control on Visuomotor Precision subtest.

Geometric Puzzles and Picture Puzzles are nonmotor tasks, but nonetheless, performance was marginal for age on Picture Puzzles and poor on Geometric Puzzles.

Picture Puzzles Total SS: 7 (16th percentile), *Borderline*

Geometric Puzzles Total SS: 6 (9th percentile), *Below Expected Level*

While the Design Copying subtest might have been affected by motor control, the Geometric Puzzles and Picture Puzzles subtests did not have any motor constraints, so they revealed pure visuospatial difficulties. The Geometric Puzzles subtest is designed to assess mental rotation and visuospatial analysis, while Picture Puzzles looks at visual discrimination, spatial location, and visual part-to-whole relationships in pictures from everyday life. Peter seemed to have a bit more difficulty with performance on the task involving abstract geometric designs than on Picture Puzzles that used ecological pictures. His poor performance on Geometric Puzzles reflects a primary deficit in visuospatial processing, which is contributing to secondary effects in copying details on Design Copying and in encoding and recalling designs and spatial locations on Memory for Designs and Memory for Designs Delayed. (See Rapid Reference 7.4 concerning reporting test results.)

≡ *Rapid Reference 7.4*

Reporting Test Results

- Present results by domain or functional area.
- Break down each section into subheadings by test.
- For each test, describe the task, so parents understand what the child was being asked to do.
- Report the scores with means and percentiles for comparisons.
- Explain unusual or atypical results or if a test has been interpreted clinically rather than psychometrically.
- Report any modifications of test administration.
- Explain child's problem-solving strategies as they relate specifically to each test.

CLINICAL IMPRESSIONS AND SUMMARY:

Peter L. is a young boy of 11.6 years who is experiencing marked difficulty in math. He receives 40 minutes of Resource Room help in mathematics, five times a week, but does not appear to be responding well to interventions, according to his parents. He has received special services for three years with little progress, which concerns his parents significantly. Assessment by the school psychologist on 2-10-2006 revealed a WISC-III Verbal IQ: 92 (Mean $= 100 \pm 15$) at the 30th percentile in the average range. His Performance IQ of 87 (19th percentile) was low average, as was the Full Scale IQ of 88 (21st percentile).

In relation to the Standard Score mean (average) of 100 ± 15, the WIAT-II Math Composite was weak at 69 (2nd percentile). The composite score comprised weak to borderline Math Operations at 70 (2nd percentile) and borderline Math Reasoning at 73 (4th percentile) There was a –19 pt. discrepancy between Peter's cognitive ability measure (WISC-III FSIQ: 88) and his score on a standardized measure of achievement (WIAT-II Math Composite score: 69).

Area of Strength

In the present assessment with the NEPSY-II Referral Battery for Learning Differences–Mathematics, Peter displayed a strength in immediate memory for facial recognition at the 99th percentile. He was able to remember all 16 faces immediately after a 5 second exposure to each. Although it was still at expected level for age,

Peter's delayed facial recognition skills dropped a significant 2 $\frac{1}{3}$ standard deviation from his immediate memory scaled score of 16 to his delayed score of 9. This is more than would be expected, according to the contrast score between Memory for Faces and Memory for Faces Delayed, and may suggest some mild memory decay over time, or it may be due to executive dysfunction in inhibiting interference from intervening tasks. These excellent facial recognition skills help Peter in the social arena, where he is well accepted and well liked. Interestingly, it appears that Peter's well-developed facial recognition skills appear to be dissociated from his visuospatial deficits.

Average Abilities

Peter displayed average performance in receptive language in comparison to age-mates, and it was within the range of his cognitive ability. He was able to understand oral instructions of increasing complexity. On a rapid naming task he also displayed average speed of lexical access and accuracy. On another naming task that was an introductory part of the Inhibition subtest, Peter's integrated speed and accuracy performance was better than that of 91 out of 100 children of his age. Therefore, his math difficulties do not appear to have a significant language contribution, nor does speed of access to words appear to be contributing to poor math performance. Peter showed average ability to perceive and reproduce the basic outside configuration of a geometric design on a paper/pencil copying task.

Primary, Secondary, and Co-occuring Deficits

There are several deficit areas that may well impact math performance negatively.

Primary Deficits

- **Executive Functions**: Executive dysfunction was seen in Peter's problems inhibiting response and adopting, maintaining, and shifting set. He displayed difficulty in monitoring his performance for accuracy in order to self-correct errors. Peter was unable to inhibit interfering stimuli efficiently. These executive functions are essential for good mathematics performance.
- **Visuospatial Processing**: Poor performance was seen on a nonmotor visuospatial task requiring mental rotation and visuospatial analysis. Borderline performance occurred on another nonmotor task of visual discrimination, spatial localization, and part-whole relationships. Total performance on a paper/pencil geometric design copying task was

poor, influenced both by deficits in local processing and reproduction of design details. Mathematics relies on well-developed visuospatial perception, processing, and analysis.

Secondary Deficits

- *Visuospatial Memory:* Because specific memory deficits in children are usually secondary to a broader primary deficit, Peter's problems with visual design memory and spatial memory, both immediate and delayed, appear to be secondary to his primary deficit in visuospatial processing. Retaining the visuospatial material that is an integral part of mathematics will be very difficult for Peter.
- *Verbal Working Memory:* Secondary to executive dysfunction; observed on Word List Interference. This weakness may be secondary to the more general inhibition problem. Working memory is an integral part of mathematics performance.
- *Mathematics Disorder:* Secondary to visuospatial deficits, executive dysfunction, and visuospatial and verbal working memory. Mathematics is going to be a significantly difficult area for Peter.

Co-occuring Deficits

- *Graphomotor Control and Visuomotor Precision Deficits:* On the Design Copying Motor score, Peter's fine motor copying performance fell at the 2nd percentile, below expected level for age.
- A **secondary visuomotor precision deficit** was produced by Peter's co-occurring fine motor control deficit in combination with his primary visuospatial deficits. On the Visuomotor Precision subtest, Peter's accuracy was not good in just drawing a line through a winding track. This was due to an apparent inability to perceive or anticipate the curves. The combination of poor visual perception and weak fine motor control is producing visuomotor precision problems.

Area for Consideration

ADHD, Predominately Inattentive Type, is not always as obvious to those around the individual as it would be if he or she were hyperactive. It is notable that Peter sustained attention for about 20–30 minutes during testing and then needed a break before he was able to sustain attention again. He displayed borderline inattentive/distractible behavior in relation to the base rate for age in the normative sample on the Auditory Attention subtest. Mother has noted that Peter is "up and down" frequently during homework time. Attention Deficit Hyperactivity

Disorder can have an enormous additive, negative effect on math performance and other school learning, especially working memory. Because, as we discussed, Peter could not have sustained his attention for further testing during his initial session, we have scheduled another testing session to consider math operations in greater depth and to review adaptive behaviors; therefore, the ADHD testing could be included at that time. (See Rapid Reference 7.5 concerning clinical impressions and summary in assessment report.)

Summary of Test Results

In summary, Peter is a young man of low average to average cognitive ability who is social and well-liked. He has a history of prematurity, but, otherwise, is in good health. He displayed significant weaknesses in mathematics on school testing. He has received interventions in school for the past three years through the Resource Room for 40 minutes a day with little improvement. Peter's assessment with the NEPSY-II Referral Battery for Learning Differences–Mathematics showed a strength in facial recognition skills that is helpful to him in the social arena where he is well accepted and well liked. Although in the average range, his delayed Memory for Faces performance dropped significantly from his strong immediate memory, which appears to be due to the executive dysfunction that Peter displayed in inhibiting interfering stimuli.

Receptive-expressive language was within normal limits (WNL) for age., and speed and accuracy of lexical access was a strength on one assessment and average on another. Since no language deficits were revealed in assessment, this would not appear to be a confounding factor in his weak math performance. As a matter of fact verbal mediation should help Peter in math problem solution. Peter showed average ability to perceive and reproduce the basic outside configuration of a geometric design on a paper/pencil copying task. This was one of the few visuospatial/visuomotor tasks that Peter was able to complete WNL.

Peter displayed primary deficits in executive functions and visuospatial processing that underlie his weak mathematics skills. Executive dysfunction was seen in Peter's problems with inhibiting interference and/or response; adopting, maintaining, and shifting set, and monitoring performance are all essential to good math performance. For good math achievement, one needs cognitive flexibility and the ability to inhibit interfering stimuli in order to organize, plan, and strategize for problem solution. It is essential to monitor performance for pertinent details and self-correction.

Peter's primary deficit in the visuospatial area reveals problems with local processing, that is, focusing on details. While he was able to copy the outside configuration of a shape at the average level, he showed poor ability to perceive and reproduce the details of the design. In math, it is essential to notice details such as operational signs (e.g.,+, − , =), place value, decimal points, and so forth. Underlying math performance are visuospatial skills (visuospatial analysis, spatial location, part-whole relationships, mental rotation, etc.), all of which are problematical for Peter. His NEPSY-II test profile of particular weaknesses in visuospatial and visuomotor functions and executive functions is compatible with that typical of prematurely born children although the degree of prematurity of Peter was not alarming per se (Korkman, Kirk, & Kemp, 2008; Mikkola et al., 2005).

Because of his primary deficit in visuospatial perception and analysis, Peter displayed secondary deficits in the immediate and long-term ability to recall visual designs and spatial locations. Well-developed visuospatial memory is a key need for good math skills. His deficit in verbal working memory was secondary to Peter's executive dysfunction because he displayed a weakness in inhibiting interfering stimuli. Interference to working memory, which is a core need in mathematics, is a significant problem for Peter.

Peter's primary deficits in visuospatial skills and in executive function led to secondary deficits in visuospatial memory and in verbal working memory, both of which are contributing significantly to Peter's weakness in mathematics. These primary and secondary deficits converge on the diagnostic cluster of symptoms for Mathematics Disorder, which is, in itself, a secondary deficit. A Mathematics Disorder is manifested as a deficit in the visuospatial concepts and procedural competencies that define the mathematical domain, and these, in theory, would be due to underlying deficits in the central executive or in the information representation or manipulation (i.e., working memory) systems of the language or visuospatial domains (Zorzi et al., 2002). Mathematics is going to be a significantly difficult area for Peter, and he may well need to conclude math studies when he has fulfilled basic requirements in high school. In the meantime, however, in order to make progress in this area, he must have intensive individually targeted interventions.

Along with Peter's primary and secondary deficits discussed above, Peter displayed a comorbid (co-occurring) deficit in graphomotor control and a secondary visuomotor precision deficit. The fine motor control of Peter's paper/pencil copying performance was weak, and his accuracy was not good in just drawing a line through a winding track. This latter problem was secondary to an apparent inability to perceive or anticipate the curves. Put together with Peter's problems in fine motor control, a visuomotor precision deficit was produced. Inefficient graphomotor control may impede Peter's written math performance, especially if he has to copy numerous problems from the board or from his textbook. It will also make graphing and similar operations difficult. This is especially true because spatial localization is also a problem. Children who have graphomotor problems are generally dysgraphic in all areas demanding writing or copying and often cannot finish written tests.

Finally, this psychologist noted a number of symptoms that may point to ADHD in Peter, which would certainly be detrimental to math performance that, by its nature, demands good attention and concentration. Although, it may turn out that executive dysfunction alone is responsible for Peter's difficulty with focus, it is recommended that ADHD be ruled out for Peter, so that we are sure that we have tapped all areas that may be influencing his weak math skills.

All of the above results relate to the problems that Peter is experiencing every day in mathematics. Interventions need to address underlying deficits specifically to help Peter achieve more in mathematics. Peter has made little progress with mathematics in the Resource Room, because his intervention has not addressed the deficits underlying his Mathematics Disorder. Peter's NEPSY-II test profile of particular weaknesses in visuospatial and visuomotor functions and executive functions is compatible with the profile typical of premature infants although Peter's progress following his premature birth was good. With his pervasive visuospatial deficits, Peter may not wish to pursue mathematics beyond the required level for graduation. Even then, tutoring may be advisable. If ADHD is confirmed and treated, however, that may well address some of his distractibility and working memory problems, and, thus, improve his mathematics performance somewhat, despite the visuospatial deficits. Executive dysfunction should be addressed regardless whether or not ADHD is present. Developing Peter's executive functioning should also help him improve math performance by learning to plan, strategize and monitor his performance, as well as to inhibit response and switch set as needed for cognitive flexibility (see Rapid Reference 7.5).

⟱ *Rapid Reference 7.5*

Formulating Clinical Impressions and Summary

- Restate the child's name, the presenting problem, and the referral question in the first sentence or two.
- Summarize previous testing briefly.
- Interpretation should be broken down into manageable sections across domains.

Possible divisions:

  - Areas of strength
  - Average abilities

- Primary deficit(s)
- Secondary deficits
- Co-occuring deficits
- Diagnostic cluster pointing to the diagnosis
- Areas for consideration—possible need for further assessment of symptoms noted during evaluation
- Summarize and verify all findings by relating them to the child's history and problems at home and school in everyday life.

DIAGNOSIS

Axis I: 294.9 Cognitive Disorder–NOS (visuospatial processing deficit, executive dysfunction [the latter may be secondary to ADHD])

315.1 Mathematics Disorder (secondary to visuospatial and executive function deficits)

315.40 Developmental Coordination Disorder – Dysgraphia

Rule out 314.00 Attention Deficit Hyperactivity Disorder, predominately inattentive type

Axis II: V71.09 No diagnosis or condition

Axis III: No current medical issues; history of prematurity.

Axis IV: Educational difficulties

Axis V: GAF = 60 (moderate)

(See Rapid Reference 7.6 for possible formats for reporting diagnoses.)

Rapid Reference 7.6

Formats for Diagnosis Section of Report:

- Include rule out diagnoses in any coded diagnosis section
- For insurance reimbursement:
  - Use required format for the clinician's agency/institution
  - If free to choose format:
    - Full DSM-IV-TR Five-Axis Format with Codes
    - Use of at least one DSM-IV-TR or ICD 10 Code
- For parent/school/agency if not insurance reimbursable
  - Can use narrative form or codes (include rule out diagnoses)

Recommendations

1. Rule out ADHD, Inattentive Type, with addition of about six more NEPSY-II subtests needed to complete ADHD Referral Battery, adaptive behavior rating scales filled out by parents and teachers, and a continuous performance test. Adaptive behavior scales will be given to parents during this feedback session if they choose to take this course, so they can be returned before the next testing session.

2. With parents' permission, this psychologist recommends a meeting be set up at Peter's school in order to work out a Response to Intervention (RTI) plan for Peter as soon as possible.

3. Recommendations for Math Learning:

   (a) Peter needs individualized math learning with manipulatives, hands-on techniques, and sequenced computer programs. The coverage of fewer math topics in more depth, and with coherence, is very important for students who struggle with mathematics. Only when whole numbers are understood fully, for instance, should the child move to rational numbers. The focus on rational numbers should include understanding the meaning of fractions, decimals, ratios, and percents, using visual representations (including placing fractions and decimals on number lines, and solving problems with fractions, decimals, ratios, and percents). Accurate and fluent arithmetic with whole numbers is necessary before understanding fractions is possible.

   (b) The National Mathematics Advisory Panel recommends explicit instruction for students struggling with math. It defines *explicit instruction* as follows (2008, p. 23):

   - "Teachers provide clear models for solving a problem type using an array of examples.
   - Students receive extensive practice in use of newly learned strategies and skills.
   - Students are provided with opportunities to think aloud (i.e., talk through the decisions they make and the steps they take.)
   - Students are provided with extensive feedback."

   When the teacher feels the child truly understands the process, then shift the emphasis to Peter talking himself through the process.

(c) Provide about 5–10 minutes in each intervention session for practice to help students become automatic in retrieving basic arithmetic facts. The goal is quick retrieval of facts using the digits 0 to 9 without any access to pencil and paper or manipulatives.

(d) "Math Blaster" or a similar computer program at Peter's performance level is helpful for drill and practice at school and at home.

(e) Any math worksheet should contain some earlier math processes for review, as well as the new process being presented. In this way Peter continues to review processes that he has learned earlier. Worksheets should only be used for beginning 5-minute drills and for homework, so Peter does not have to copy out the problems. Peter should only compete with himself. Most of Peter's math learning should be hands-on.

4. Interventions for Executive Dysfunction underlying Math Disorder:

(a) Peter needs to work with his Resource Room teacher on "stop, think, check" techniques for completing his work carefully and accurately. This will help him develop the ability to inhibit and think through a process before responding impulsively. Then he checks to be sure he has provided his best answer, monitoring his performance and correcting if needed. This will help him internalize controls. Use "stop, think" techniques at home, as well.

(b) Write out new or difficult math processes in numbered steps on cards for Peter and laminate them, so he can refer to the cards when working on a particular process.

(c) Interventions that teach students the structure of word problem types and how to discriminate superficial from substantive information to know when to apply the solution methods they have learned can positively and significantly affect proficiency in solving word problems.

(d) A quiet spot in the classroom where Peter can give himself oral feedback will be helpful. A cardboard study carrel on a table at the back of the room can work well. A checklist taped to his desk can remind him of checking steps.

(e) Playing chess or checkers with Dad, Mom, or his older brother will be helpful for developing the ability to inhibit impulsive responding, and to plan and strategize before proceeding.

(f) To help Peter with planning, use a large white, wipe-off calendar to plan long-term projects such as reports. Mount it where it is readily visible. Entries are made for each day of the week to highlight the work to be completed that day. Put all other activities/appointments for Peter on the calendar, as well, so Peter can see how much time he actually has to complete the task. As he completes each step, he marks it off. Entries can be color-coded for subject/activity.

(g) Set a study time and help Peter set up a tray with all materials easily available. Peter plans the order in which he will do his work and what materials he needs. No phone or texting during that time. Television needs to be off. Every 30 minutes he can take a break for 10 min., but he should not be allowed to pop up and down at will. The kitchen table is a good place for studying and often works better than Peter studying in his room alone, but be sure that there is not too much activity there while Peter is studying. Mom or Dad can be on hand as a resource, but do not sit right beside him and work him through his lessons. If he asks a question, answer it, and demonstrate it, if needed, but then let him proceed on his own, so he learns that he is capable of accomplishing his work by himself.

(h) It will be helpful if parents work out a point system with Peter for every lesson accomplished completely during homework time. Let Peter keep track of these points so he can see that he is making progress toward a goal he has set with his parents. He can monitor his progress in this way. Keep rewards reasonable; do not be too extravagant. Try to avoid monetary rewards. Remember to reward the effort to complete his work well, rather than rewarding the ultimate grade that he receives. Do not make the goal points so high that Peter feels that he can never reach the goal; but high enough that he is not reaching a goal too easily. Set the goals together. When he has earned one goal, plan another to work for.

Good rewards: Time with Dad playing golf; a sleep-over for his neighborhood and/or school friends; a special meal with his family at his favorite restaurant. If he is working toward a special toy or game, keep it reasonable.

5. Interventions for Visuospatial Deficits underlying Math Disorder:

(a) Because of his visuospatial deficit, Peter needs to be able to use hands-on, kinesthetic materials to understand visual perceptual and spatial components of mathematics. For instance, rather than drawing a number line, he will learn better with a wooden balance bar where he can see how adding or subtracting a number changes the balance. When he understands the concept, then he can begin drawing and labeling a number line.

(b) Give concrete examples whenever possible. For instance, when Peter is learning the different types of triangles, have plastic models of each, so he can feel how they differ and learn the names for each. Find examples in real life. Then use flash cards if needed to make the final step to the 2-D picture that he names.

(c) If Peter is learning fractions, have him measure different fractional amounts of sand to and see what they equal when added together. Then subtract fractional amounts. Double or triple the amounts. Divide them. When he is handling fractions well, let him follow an actual recipe.

(d) When Peter must commit something to memory, such as multiplication tables or a math formula, it may help him to walk about to a rhythm as he says the information or looks at it. Writing or drawing in sand or on a rug as he says the information can be helpful.

(e) As much as possible, all math learning should use manipulatives, such as Cuisiennaire rods for learning place value, because he cannot visualize how a number could have one value if it is in the first decimal place, but a different value if it is one more space to the right or left of the decimal point. When he understands the concept, then he can move to written math.

6. The following are recommendations for Peter's dysgraphia:

(a) If Peter does not receive printed math worksheets for homework, parents may be able to copy math book pages so he can perform his calculations right on the page, rather than copying them out.

(b) When he is copying only a few problems, teach him to fold a sheet of paper in half lengthwise and then in thirds horizontally. Unfold and he will have six "boxes" into which a math problem can be placed. This separates each problem into its own "space" and prevents errors from math problems being crowded onto one another.

(c) Peter will control his pencil more easily if he has a fat-barreled automatic pencil. Grippers on wooden pencils can be uncomfortable, but are helpful for some children.

(d) Because of his difficulty with fine motor control, Peter should learn keyboarding as soon as possible. A sturdy computer notebook or Alpha-smart will be very helpful for school if there are not computers available in the classroom. He should compose creative or expository writing directly into the computer, and then go back and edit. This will allow his ideas to be unimpeded by motor output. This summer he might take a keyboarding class. The fine motor coordination needed for typing is less refined than that needed for graphomotor control.

(e) Copying from the board or from his book to paper should be kept to a minimum for Peter.

Behavioral Recommendations:

8. Continue to help Peter build his confidence through his athletics by supporting him in the endeavors where he succeeds as well as in the effort he is making in school.

9. Family rules need to be simple and clear cut. When Peter breaks a family rule the consequences should be employed immediately, but in a nonjudgmental, nonthreatening manner. He needs much positive reinforcement for positive actions.

Intervention for Math—Resource Room x 5/week; 40 min. each

Subtests from Referral Battery for Math only

Attention and Executive Functioning Domain					
Subtest Score Name	Raw Scores	Scaled Scores	Percentile Ranks	Cumulative Percentages	Classification
Auditory Attention Total Correct	30	12	75		At Expected Level
Auditory Attention Combined Scaled Score	–	11	63		At Expected Level
Auditory Attention Total Omission Errors	0	–	51–75	–	At Expected Level
Auditory Attention Total Commission Errors	1	–	11–25	–	Borderline
Auditory Attention Total Inhibitory Errors	0	–	26–50		At Expected Level
Response Set Total Correct	32	8	25	–	At Expected Level
Response Set Combined Scaled Score	–	5	5	–	Below Expected Level
Response Set Total Omission Errors	2	–	51–75	–	At Expected Level
Response Set Total Commission Errors	10	–	2–5	–	Below Expected Level
Response Set Total Inhibitory Errors	8	–	2–5	–	Below Expected Level
AA vs. RS Contrast Scaled Score	–	4	2	–	Well Below Expected Level
Inhibition–Naming Completion Time Total	42	11	63	–	At Expected Level
IN–Naming Combined Scaled Score	–	14	91	–	Above Expected Level
IN–Naming Total Errors	0	–	>75	–	Above Expected Level

(continued)

	Attention and Executive Functioning Domain				
Subtest Score Name	Raw Scores	Scaled Scores	Percentile Ranks	Cumulative Percentages	Classification
IN–Naming Total Self-Corrected Errors	0	–	51–75	–	At Expected Level
IN–Naming Total Uncorrected Errors	0	–	51–75	–	At Expected Level
IN–Inhibition Completion Time Total	53	12	75	–	At Expected Level
IN–Inhibition Combined Scaled Score	–	8	25	–	At Expected Level
IN–Inhibition Total Errors	5	–	11–25	–	Borderline
IN–Inhibition Total Self-Corrected Errors	3	–	11–25	–	Borderline
IN–Inhibition Total Uncorrected Errors	2	–	26–50	–	At Expected Level
IN–Switching Completion Time Total	99	11	63	–	At Expected Level
IN–Switching Combined Scaled Score	–	6	9	–	Below Expected Level
IN–Switching Total Errors	14	–	2–5	–	Below Expected Level
IN–Switching Total Self-Corrected Errors	6	–	11–25	–	Borderline
IN–Switching Total Uncorrected Errors	8	–	6–10	–	Below Expected Level
IN–Naming vs. Inhibition Contrast Scaled Score	–	6	9	–	Below Expected Level
IN–Inhibition vs. Switching Contrast Scaled Score	–	6	9	–	Below Expected Level
IN Total Errors Scaled Score (overall)	19	6	9	–	Below Expected Level

Attention/Executive Functioning Scaled Scores –Referral Battery: Math

Subtest Score Name	1	2	3	4	5	6	7	8	9	10	11	12	13	14	15	16	17	18	19
Auditory Attention Total Correct												X							
Auditory Attention Combined Scaled Score											X								
Response Set Total Correct								X											
Response Set Combined Scaled Score					X														
Inhibition–Naming Completion Time Total											X								
Inhibition–Naming Combined Scaled Score														X					
Inhibition–Inhibition Completion Time Total												X							
Inhibition–Inhibition Combined Scaled Score								X											
Inhibition–Switching Completion Time Total											X								
Inhibition–Switching Combined Scaled Score						X													
Inhibition Total Errors						X													

Attention/Executive Functioning Process Scores Percentile Ranks

Subtest Score Name	<2	2–10	11–25	26–75	>75
Auditory Attention Total Omission Errors					X
Auditory Attention Total Commission Errors			X		
Auditory Attention Total Inhibitory Errors				X	
Response Set Total Omission Errors					X
Response Set Total Commission Errors		X			
Response Set Total Inhibitory Errors		X			
Inhibition–Naming Total Errors					X
Inhibition–Naming Total Self-Corrected Errors				X	
Inhibition–Naming Total Uncorrected Errors				X	
Inhibition–Inhibition Total Errors			X		
Inhibition–Inhibition Total Self-Corrected Errors			X		
Inhibition–Inhibition Total Uncorrected Errors				X	
Inhibition–Switching Total Errors		X			
Inhibition–Switching Total Self-Corrected Errors			X		
Inhibition–Switching Total Uncorrected Errors		X			

Subtests from Referral Battery for Math Only

Subtest Score Name	Language Domain			
	Raw Scores	Scaled Scores	Percentile Ranks	Classification
Comprehension of Instructions Total Score	24	8	25	At Expected Level
Speeded Naming Total Completion Time	38	11	63	At Expected Level
Speeded Naming Total Correct	75	–	51–75	At Expected Level
Speeded Naming Combined Scaled Score	–	11	63	At Expected Level
Speeded Naming Total Self-Corrected Errors	0	–	51–75	At Expected Level

Language Scaled Scores

Subtest Score Name	1	2	3	4	5	6	7	8	9	10	11	12	13	14	15	16	17	18	19
Comprehension of Instructions Total Score								X											
Speeded Naming Total Completion Time											X								
Speeded Naming Combined Scaled Score											X								

Language Percentile Ranks

Subtest Score Name	<2	2–10	11–25	26–75	>75
Speeded Naming Total Correct				X	
Speeded Naming Total Self-Corrected Errors				X	

(continued)

(continued)

Subtests from Referral Battery for Math Only

Subtest Score Name	Memory and Learning Domain				
	Raw Scores	Scaled Scores	Percentile Ranks	Cumulative Percentages	Classification
Memory for Faces Total Score	16	16	99	–	Above Expected Level
MFD Total Score	12	9	75	–	At Expected Level
MF vs. MFD Contrast Scaled Score	–	4	2	–	Below Expected Level
Memory for Designs Total Score	63	1	<2	–	Well Below Expected Level
Memory for Designs Content Score Total	35	4	2		Below Expected Level
Memory for Designs Spatial Score	22	3	<2	–	Well Below Expected Level
Memory for Designs Delayed Total Score	25	5	5	–	Below Expected Level
MDD Content Score	15	6	9	–	Below Expected Level
MDD Spatial	6	1	<2	–	Well Below Expected Level
Memory for Designs Content vs. MD Spatial Contrast Scaled Score	–	5	5	–	Below Expected Level
Memory for Designs Delayed Content vs. MDD Spatial Contrast Scaled Score	–	1	<2	–	Well Below Expected Level
Memory for Designs vs. Memory for Designs Delayed Total Score	–	11	63	–	At Expected Level
Word List Interference–Repetition Total Score	14	7	16	–	Borderline
Word List Interference–Recall Total Score	13	6	9	–	Below Expected Level
WI Repetition vs. Recall Contrast Scaled Score	–	7	16	–	Borderline

Subtests from Referral Battery for Math Only
Memory and Learning Scaled Scores

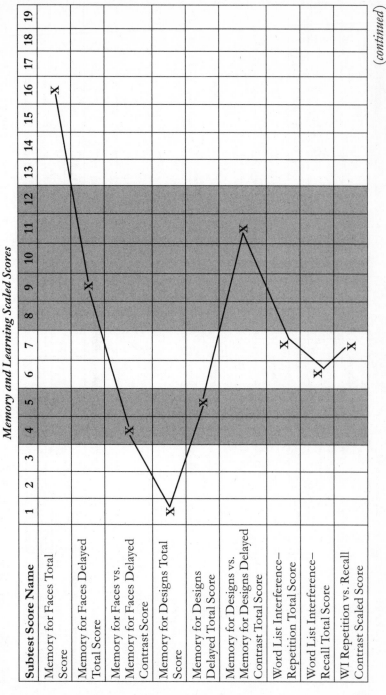

Subtest Score Name	1	2	3	4	5	6	7	8	9	10	11	12	13	14	15	16	17	18	19
Memory for Faces Total Score																X			
Memory for Faces Delayed Total Score									X										
Memory for Faces vs. Memory for Faces Delayed Contrast Score				X															
Memory for Designs Total Score	X																		
Memory for Designs Delayed Total Score					X														
Memory for Designs vs. Memory for Designs Delayed Contrast Total Score											X								
Word List Interference–Repetition Total Score							X												
Word List Interference–Recall Total Score						X													
WI Repetition vs. Recall Contrast Scaled Score							X												

(*continued*)

391

Sensorimotor Domain

Subtest Score Name	Raw Scores	Scaled Scores	Percentile Ranks	Cumulative Percentages	Classification
Visuomotor Precision Total Completion Time	82	11	63	–	At Expected Level
Visuomotor Precision Total Errors	8	–	11–25	–	Borderline
Visuomotor Precision Combined Scaled Score	–	7	16	–	Borderline
Visuomotor Precision Pencil Lift Total	1	–	>75	–	Above Expected Level

Sensorimotor Scaled Scores

Subtest Score Name	1	2	3	4	5	6	7	8	9	10	11	12	13	14	15	16	17	18	19
Visuomotor Precision Total Completion Time											X								
Visuomotor Precision Combined Scaled Score							X												

Sensorimotor Percentile Ranks

Subtest Score Name	<2	2–10	11–25	26–75	>75
Visuomotor Precision Total Errors			X		
Visuomotor Precision Pencil Lift Total					X

Social Perception

Referral Battery for Mathematics does not contain subtests from this domain unless social problems are evident, which was not the case for Peter.

Subtests from Referral Battery for Math Only

Visuospatial Processing

Subtest Score Name	Raw Scores	Scaled Scores	Percentile Ranks	Classification
Design Copying Process Total Score	74	6	9	Below Expected Level
Design Copying Process Motor Score	27	3	2	Below Expected Level
Design Copying Process Global Score	32	11	63	At Expected Level
Design Copying Process Local Score	15	5	5	Below Expected Level
DCP Global vs. Local Contrast Scaled Score	–	3	2	Below Expected Level
Geometric Puzzles Total Score (7–16 yr. only)	6	1	9	Below Expected Level
Picture Puzzles Total Score	11	7	16	Borderline

(Block Construction is a subtest in this Referral Battery for 3- to 6-year-olds only.)

Visuospatial Scaled Scores

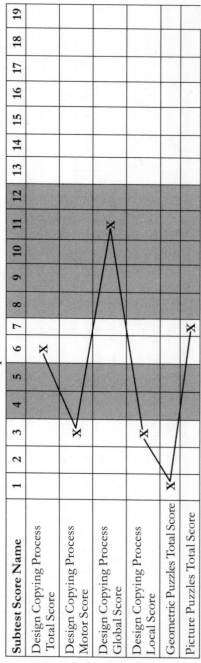

393

Behavioral Observations across Domains

Attention and Executive Functioning Domain

Subtest Score Name	Raw Score	Cumulative Percentages	Percent of Normative Sample
Auditory Attention and Response Set			
Inattentive/Distracted—Off Task Behaviors Total	2		11–25
Out of Seat/Physical Movement in Seat—Off Task Behaviors Total	0		–
Inhibition			
INN Points to Stimuli Total	0	26–75	–
INI Points to Stimuli Total	0	>75	–
INS Points to Stimuli Total	1	26–75	–

Language Domain

Subtest Score Name	Raw Score	Cumulative Percentages	Percent of Normative Sample
Comprehension of Instructions			
Asks for Repetition Total	0		–

Memory and Learning Domain

Subtest Score Name	Raw Score	Cumulative Percentages	Percent of Normative Sample
Memory for Designs and Memory for Designs Delayed			
Rule Violation Total	0		—
Word List Interference			
Asks for Repetition Total	0		—

Sensorimotor Domain

Subtest Score Name	Raw Score	Cumulative Percentages	Percent of Normative Sample
Visuomotor Precision			
Pencil Grip–Mature	Y	—	87

Social Perception: No subtests included in this Referral Battery from this domain.

Visuospatial Scaled Scores: No quantified Behavior Observations in this domain.

CASE STUDY # 3

A SOCIAL/INTERPERSONAL REFERRAL BATTERY USED IN FOLLOW-UP EVALUATION OF A PREVIOUSLY DIAGNOSED CLIENT

NAME: Allen B.   **DOB:** 4-16-1998
DOE: 4-2-2006   **CA:** 7.11 years
EXAMINER: C.D., PhD

Referral Statement

Allen is a young boy of 7.11 years diagnosed with Autistic Disorder, high functioning (HFA). His school is recommending him for inclusion in the regular classroom in the fall. Response to Intervention monitoring shows him at first grade level in all areas. Parents requested this evaluation in order to help them make a good decision about Allen's educational placement.

Relevant History

Allen was diagnosed with HFA at 3 years of age by this psychologist, and has been followed by her since that time. He was referred to a nonprofit developmental center near his home where a full range of therapies was available. Within a month of his diagnosis, he had begun speech and language therapy, including Applied Behavioral Analysis (ABA) for 30 minutes x 2/week, physical therapy for 30 minutes x 1/week., and occupational therapy for 30 minutes x 1/week. Mrs. B. was very diligent in making sure that she followed through with his home program. He has made very good, steady progress since that time. This therapy regimen was followed until he entered public school, and has been continued in the summer vacation since he has been in school full-time. During the school year, Allen has been in a special classroom for autistic children through which he receives multiple therapies, including social skills training. He has continued additional speech/language therapy x 1/week during the school year at the developmental center, as well.

Family history is positive for Allen's father being uncomfortable in social situations, having a fascination with numbers, and being able to quote quantities of a certain types of statistics from memory. His father also showed a language delay in childhood and communicates little in adulthood, except with his wife, family, and a few close friends. He avoids crowds. Mother is a social, very gentle, caring individual who handles all the organizational and financial matters for the family. Allen's little brother, Donald, age 4.6 years, also has HFA. There is no history in the maternal family of neurodevelopmental disorders, and neither the maternal nor the paternal side shows any psychological or neurological disorders or chronic illnesses, according to Mrs. B.

In addition to his therapies, Allen attended the Headstart program in his small town until he was 4 years of age. At 5 years, with the help of an individual aide, he entered kindergarten at the local elementary school. At mid-year, Allen was placed in a new program for children with autism. He has been in this program since, but Allen's special education teacher feels that he is now ready for inclusion in the regular classroom in the fall. He would enter second grade at that time, but the special education teacher would continue to work with him one period a day and would consult weekly with his regular classroom teacher. The developmental center would continue with his speech language therapy for 30 minutes, x 1/week, according to his mother.

Parents report that Allen has made excellent progress socially since he was last seen by this psychologist. Mother feels that eye contact has also improved greatly. He has begun Cub Scouts and loves it. The leader's own child has a developmental disability, so he has been particularly empathetic toward Allen. With the leader's guidance, the other boys in the troop are usually very kind in helping him. Allen also participates in Sunday School and enjoys playing soccer on a recreation department team that is especially for children with disabilities. He talks about friends now, though he often doesn't know their names, but he does seem to be interacting more with peers, both in school and in extracurricular activities. One very nurturing little girl tends to "take care" of Allen much of the time at school. Mother notes that he is still quite literal and continues to be fixated on animals. He learns every fact he can about each of them and loves watching nature programs. Parents limit television, however, as Allen will become transfixed by it otherwise and begins scripting commercials verbatim. Only occasionally does Allen "hand-flap" now, according to Mother.

Previous Testing

08-20-2001: Allen was first evaluated by this psychologist at 3.4 years of age with the **Leiter International Performance Scale–Revised,** which yielded a non-verbal Brief IQ of 85 (25th percentile) in the low average range.

The Bayley Scales of Infant Development

Mental Development Index of <–50, largely due to poor language development. The latter was reflected in the **Preschool Language Scale–3rd Edition,** on which he displayed:

Auditory Comprehension at 69 (mean = 100 ± 15) was weak.
Expressive Communication was borderline at 77.
Total Language was at the bottom of the borderline range: 70 at the 2nd percentile for age.

On the **Vineland Adaptive Behavior Scale–Interview Edition** *(VADS)*, Allen displayed weak adaptive behavior skills overall for age (Adaptive Behavior Composite of 60; mean = 100 ± 15). On the subscales, Allen showed weak communication skills (Communication: 54), daily living skills (Daily Living Skills: 60), and socialization (Socialization: 54), with borderline motor skills (Motor Skills: 72).

The **Childhood Autism Rating Scales (CARS)** were endorsed by Mother (36), Father (36), and Allen's Headstart preschool teacher (35), separately with all ratings being positive for mild-moderate autism (30–38).

The **Gilliam Autism Rating Scales (GARS)** endorsed by Allen's mother, revealed an Autism Quotient of 105 (mean = 100 ± 15). Problems with Stereotypical Behaviors (12) and Social Interactions (13) were high average (mean = 10 ± 3). Development was rated as average (10) and Communication (8) was in the low average range.

Modified Checklist for Autism in Toddlers (M-CHAT) filled out retroactively by Allen's parents revealed symptoms of autism spectrum disorder before 3 years: *no response to being called by his name, poor eye contact, poor joint attention, wandering aimlessly, and repetitive behaviors.*

Informal Play Evaluation: An individual play evaluation with this psychologist revealed no imaginative play, though a few instances of imitative play (feeding the baby doll, "drinking" from a cup). Eye contact was poor, and Allen was fairly unresponsive to his name. He did show affection to his mother. Allen liked to line up blocks, and even separated them by color. He played repetitively at watching blocks fall off the edge of the slide, after studying the edges of them. Hand-flapping was observed frequently, along with verbatim dialogue from the cartoon *Blue's Clues,* about which his mother noted that he was obsessive.

School Observation: revealed that Allen interacted little with other children, although he did talk a little with the teacher. He did not engage in imaginative play; rather, he preferred to spin the wheels on a truck, drop blocks into a wide-mouthed jar repetitively, and wander aimlessly on the playground. When an aide tried to engage him in play with a farm set, he remained for a few minutes manipulating a horse in an aimless way and then wandered off again. He enjoyed coloring (age-appropriate scribbling) and remained with this activity for about 10 minutes. Allen would put his head against the edge of the teacher's desk and study the edge of it.

07-12-2003: The **Differential Ability Scales (DAS)–Upper Preschool** (mean = 100 ± 15) were administered to Allen with the following results:

GCA of 83 ± 7, 13th percentile, Low average
Verbal Cluster of 69 ± 10, 2nd percentile, Weak
Nonverbal Cluster of 104 ± 10, 61st percentile, Average

There was a significant –35 point discrepancy between Allen's weak verbal abilities and average nonverbal abilities. Individual subtest performance on the DAS revealed the following results in relation to the subtest mean of 50 ± 10):

Copying: 54
Pattern Construction: 53
Picture Similarities: 50
Early Number Concepts: 36
Naming Vocabulary: 32
Verbal Comprehension: 32

08-04-2004: The **Differential Ability Scales (DAS)–Upper Preschool** were administered to Allen again in 2004, a year after the first administration. Allen achieved the following scores:

GCA: 90 ± 7, 25th percentile
Verbal Cluster: 73 ± 10, 4th percentile
Nonverbal Cluster 102 ± 10, 55th percentile)

Subtest scores in relation to the subtest mean of 50 ± 10 were as follows:

Copying: 43
Pattern Construction: 63
Picture Similarities: 49
Early Number Concepts: 49
Naming Vocabulary: 33
Verbal Comprehension: 35

Sensory Profile – Dunn Mother's ratings of Allen's sensory hypo- and hyper-sensitivities were compared to those of normally developing children of his age:

Definite Differences: Auditory Filtering, Taste/smell Sensitivity, and Total Sensory Score.

Probable Differences: Tactile Sensitivity, Underresponsive/Seeks Sensation.
Typical Performance: Movement Sensitivity, Low energy/Weak Visual/
   Auditory sensitivity.

Allen's mother rated him as having definite differences with others his age in being able to filter out auditory stimuli, in hypersensitivities to taste/smell, and in sensory sensitivities in general. He frequently avoided certain tastes or food smells, would only eat certain tastes, and limited himself to particular food texture/temperatures. Allen ate mainly chicken nuggets, fish sticks, applesauce, and baby food green beans. He frequently limited himself to crunchy foods, such as chips. He showed borderline differences in being sensitive to touch and in being either underresponsive to sensory stimuli or in seeking out sensory stimulus. Movement, visual, and auditory stimuli were within normal limits, according to Mother. She did not rate Allen as having low energy or being weak.

Test Battery Administered

NEPSY-II Social/Interpersonal Referral Battery

Test Observations

Allen is a well-groomed, left-handed young boy with brown hair and blue eyes. He made good eye contact and smiled shyly when this psychologist greeted him. Eye contact was fleeting to good across the testing session, however. Allen separated from his mother with no difficulty. In order to reestablish rapport with Allen, a short play session was initiated with him. He chose to play with the animal figures. He told the examiner many facts about the various animals. When this psychologist began an imaginary game, however, Allen did join in on a fairly basic level. He made use of another object (the bottom of a box) as an imaginary barn and he was the zookeeper going around to check on the animals. He felt best directing the play, telling this psychologist what role she should play (the helper) and what she should say. When it was time to work, Allen cleaned up cooperatively, noting that he has to clean up at school.

Allen settled into the assessment easily and did not appear anxious. Only two instances of very brief hand-flapping were noted. He enjoyed the Design Copying task the most, and experienced the most difficulty with the Auditory Response Set and the Inhibition subtests. On the Fingertip Tapping subtest, Allen's pointer finger and thumb frequently slid into a pincer movement, rather than making an

"O" configuration, although this is not unusual in a child of seven. Overflow movement was evident around the mouth when Allen was performing sequential finger movements, but again, nearly a quarter of 7-year-olds still show this involuntary movement. Allen impulsively made rule violations on Memory for Designs. He was quite wiggly and squirmy during the assessment, but he did not leave his chair. He did become distracted, however, especially during the Auditory Attention subtest. Ten-minute breaks were taken approximately every 20 minutes, including a snack time. During breaks, Allen immediately headed for the animal figures and started talking about them factually, rather than playing an imaginary game. Allen always returned to work cooperatively. Several times when this examiner and Allen were talking, he launched into his factual discourse on animals, his current stereotypical interest. Allen did display a short attention span, but worked hard, nonetheless.

Test Results

Attention and Executive Functions Domain

Animal Sorting (AS): This subtest requires executive functioning for concept formation and transferring the concept into action by sorting cards into categories. At first, Allen wanted to tell this examiner factual information about the animals on the cards. When he was reminded of the task at hand, he handled it well and resumed work, but then had one brief return to his stereotypical interest of animal facts before continuing to the end of the task. He made one very obvious sort (blue cards/yellow cards) and then when asked to try another one, he moved the cards around, but didn't seem to grasp what he was to do with the pictures, so he sorted into the blue and yellow background colors again. He appeared to have significant difficulty with the abstract task of formulating concepts in order to sort the cards, despite the fact that he had appeared to understand the Teaching Example. Because he had used up quite a bit of the time allowed, he ran out of time before he sorted any more categories. He performed *Below Expected Level* for age (Animal Sorting Total Correct scaled score [SS]: 5, (5th percentile) when compared to the NEPSY-II subtest mean of 10 ± 3. He made one Repeated Error and no Novel Errors, so his error rate was *At Expected Level* (51st–75th percentile). These errors were integrated with the correct responses to derive the AS Combined SS of 6 at the 9th percentile. Allen's performance was still only *Borderline* for age. Allen appears to have difficulty with the executive functions of inhibiting his stereotypical interest and of formulating concepts by which to sort pictures into categories.

Auditory Attention and Response Set (AA/RS): On Auditory Attention (AA), Allen was required to listen for the word *red* among many distracter words and touch a red circle in response. His AA Total Correct SS of 8 was *At Expected Level* for age. He made an average number of omission errors (26th–51st percentile), but numerous commission and inhibitory errors (both < 2nd percentile) placed Allen *Well Below Expected Level*. This suggested that he was not able to inhibit response well, so he responded when he should not have done so. When AA Total Correct SS (8) was integrated with the percentile rank for commission errors (< 2), the AA Combined SS of 5 (5th percentile) was *Below Expected Level*, reflecting the negative impact of Allen's commission error rate on his correct performance. This suggested executive dysfunction for Allen, because he displayed poor ability to inhibit response.

On the second part of this subtest, Response Set, Allen was required to employ executive functions more extensively and inhibit the impulse to act according to concrete stimuli. This task was very difficult for him, and his RS Total Correct SS: 1 (0.1 percentile), *Well Below Expected Level* for age, reflected that fact. While Allen made few correct responses, however, he also made few commission or inhibitory errors, scoring *At Expected Level* on those dimensions. Nonetheless his omission errors were high. His commission and inhibitory errors were lower than they were on AA, because he often did not respond to targets at all (omission errors), as he seemed to be trying to sort out what his response should be. Therefore, Allen's RS Omission Errors percentile rank fell at the 2nd–5th percentile for age. Allen's RS Combined SS of 7 (16th percentile) was higher than RS Total Correct SS of 1, because when the Commission Errors percentile rank at the 26th–51st percentile (*At Expected Level*) was integrated with it, Allen's AA Combined SS was improved. This was because he only made an average number of commission errors, and these are the types of errors integrated into the combined score. Nonetheless, his RS Combined SS of 7 (16th percentile) was still only *Borderline* (11th–25th percentile). Therefore, on the AA vs. RS Contrast Score the result was *At Expected Level*, because given Allen's *Below Average* AA Combined score, his RS Combined score was approximately at the level one would expect. Executive functions appear to be a pervasive problem area for Allen.

Inhibition (IN): This subtest has three conditions—Naming, Inhibition, and Switching. In the first condition, IN-Naming, Allen looked at an array of black and white circles and squares and named the shape of each quickly. He then saw an array of arrows, pointing up or down, and he had to name the direction each was pointing. This trial was to establish his naming speed and accuracy. His IN-Naming Completion Time SS: 11 (63rd percentile) was *At Expected Level* for age. He made no naming errors, so IN Naming Total Errors was *Above Expected Level* for age. When the latter score was integrated into the former score to reflect the effect of time and accuracy on his performance, Allen's IN-Naming Combined Scaled Score (SS) of 14 (91st percentile) was *Above Expected Level* for Allen's age. Therefore, there was no reason to fear that Allen's naming ability would negatively impact the second and third conditions of the Inhibition subtest. His ability to perform a rapid naming task at this high level reflects much improvement in lexical access for Allen, as long as he has to name only two shapes.

In the second condition (IN-Inhibition), Allen had to name the opposite shape or direction for each shape or arrow seen. This task required executive functioning for inhibition of the automatic response in order to make an alternate response. Allen's performance on the Inhibition condition showed a marked difference with the Naming condition. The IN-Inhibition Completion Time Total SS of 5 was *Below Expected Level* (3rd–10th percentile) for age. Introducing the executive functioning requirements slowed Allen's performance significantly in comparison to his speed on the naming condition. He made 10 errors overall, but did manage to self-correct them all. Allen did not inhibit efficiently and responded impulsively, but then was able to self-correct the errors. Because he had to self-correct the errors rather than inhibiting response first his performance on IN-Inhibition Total Self-Corrected Errors was *Below Expected Level*. On the other hand, because he had no uncorrected errors, that dimension was *Above Expected Level* (IN-Inhibition Total Uncorrected Errors: >75th percentile rank). Overall on this condition, Allen's IN-Inhibition Total Error percentile rank was 11th–25th percentile in the *Borderline* range. When his *Below Expected Level* completion time was integrated with Allen's *Borderline* total errors score, his IN-Inhibition Combined SS was 6 (9th percentile) in the *Borderline* (11th–25th percentile) range for age. The introduction of executive functions in the IN-Inhibition condition caused performance to fall to a *Below Average* level for age (9th percentile) in relation to the good performance he attained on the Naming condition combined score (91st percentile).

The third condition, Inhibition–Switching, required even more executive functioning. When the shape was black, Allen had to name that shape, but if it was white, he was required to name the opposite shape. The same was true for the arrow stimuli where he had to name the direction of the arrow or the opposite. Allen's IN-Switching Completion Time Total SS of 7 (16th percentile) in relation to the subtest mean of 10 ± 3, revealed *Borderline* speed for age on this task. Allen made four errors that he was able to self correct for a performance *At Expected Level* (51st–75th percentile) for age. He also had four uncorrected errors that scored at the same level, so his IN-Switching Total Errors percentile rank was 51st–75th *At Expected Level*. When the *Borderline* IN-Switching Completion Time score was integrated with the IN-Switching Total Errors (*At Expected Level*),

IN-Switching Combined SS was 9 (37th percentile) *At Expected Level*. So, while, Allen was faster on the Switching condition than on the Inhibition condition, he seemed to be inhibiting a little better and making fewer errors. The practice during the Inhibition task may have helped him inhibit response more efficiently. Also, typical children tend to have more problems on this condition, so there is less difference in the performance of the child with a developmental disorder and that of the typical child. It does appear, however, that Allen is developing executive functions that are aiding his ability to inhibit and switch, which may result in more cognitive flexibility. His performance on the IN Inhibition and IN Switching conditions is also evidence of learning in Allen.

Looking at summary scores for the Inhibition subtest, one sees that across the test the IN Total Errors SS of 4 (3rd percentile) was *Below Expected Level* (3rd–10th percentile) for age. The IN-Naming vs. IN-Inhibition Contrast SS: 10 (26th–75th percentile), is average, but given Allen's good performance on IN-Naming (91st percentile), one would expect a much better performance on the IN-Inhibition Combined score, which was *Below Expected Level*. This marked contrast between IN-Naming and IN-Inhibition suggests that Allen's poor executive functions in the IN-Inhibition Condition were the confounding factor in the comparison of the two conditions. On the IN-Inhibition vs. IN-Switching Contrast SS: 10 (26th–75th percentile), *At Expected Level*, one can see that the performances on these two conditions were both relatively equal (*At Expected Level*, 26–75th percentile), so the contrast between them is what one would expect.

[*On this Referral Battery, Statue is a subtest for 3- to 6-year-olds; therefore, it was not administered to Allen. Design Fluency is also a part of the battery, but this psychologist chose to eliminate this test for Allen because there was already much information available on executive functions for Allen. She wished to include the optional Phonological Processing subtest in the Language Domain, instead, since it is key to reading acquisition. This change is a demonstration of the flexibility of choice on the NEPSY-II.*]

Language Domain

Comprehension of Instructions (CI): This subtest is designed to assess receptive language understanding of progressively more complex oral instructions. For each item, Allen pointed to the correct stimuli in response to the oral instructions. His performance (CI Total SS: 10) was *At Expected Level* (26–75th percentile) in relation to the NEPSY-II subtest mean of 10 ± 3. Allen has obviously made excellent progress with his language therapy and other interventions that have strengthened language skills.

Phonological Processing Skills (PP): This optional test for this Referral Battery was administered to Allen. His phonological skills for sound-symbol association in reading are at the top of the average range (Phonological Processing Total SS: 12, *At Expected Level* [26th–75th percentile]). These results are supported by the teacher's report that Allen is now reading at first-grade level.

Speeded Naming (SN): On this subtest that assesses rapid naming, a basic expressive language function, Allen was required to name size/color/shape of each shape in an array as quickly as possible. He then had to name upper- and lowercase letters and numbers as quickly as possible. His SN Total Completion Time SS: 7 was *Borderline* (11th–25th percentile) in relation to the subtest mean of 10 ± 3. The SN Total Correct Percentile Rank of 2nd–5th percentile was *Below Expected Level* for age. Allen had 124 correct responses out of a possible 135, but no self-corrected errors. Therefore, he had more uncorrected errors than expected. When time and accuracy were integrated on the SN Combined SS: 5 (5th percentile), results were *Below Expected Level* (3rd–10th percentile) for age. These results suggest that Allen still has difficulty with rapid lexical access when more than two types of stimuli must be named on the same task. On the IN-Naming subtest, Allen merely had to say the individual names of two shapes, circle and square—his combined score for speed and accuracy was at the 91st percentile, while the combined score for Speeded Naming (completion time integrated with accuracy) was at the 5th percentile when he had to name three concepts. These results show that Allen continues to have subtle deficits in language. He has overcome many of his original language deficits, but this basic problem persists and may affect reading speed, if not accuracy. Inhibition may also play a role when there are multiple stimuli and Allen has to inhibit and switch constantly.

Word Generation (WG): This subtest is designed to assess verbal productivity through the ability to generate words within specific semantic and initial letter categories. Allen was given semantic categories (animals and eat/drink) and then he was asked to produce as many words as possible in 60 seconds for each category. He was then required to repeat the task with two initial letter categories (words beginning with *F* and with *S*). Allen produced no words in 60 seconds for either type of category, despite seeming to understand the example. The task under time pressure appeared to place him under too much pressure to perform. Results were *Well Below Expected Level* (≤2nd percentile). (WG-Semantic Total SS: 1; WG Initial Letter Total SS: 3). The WG Semantics vs. Initial Letter Contrast SS was 5 (5th percentile) and *Below Expected Level* (3rd–10th percentile) for age. Therefore, basic language functions, such as rapid naming of more than two labels and rapid verbal production of words, were deficient for Allen, despite the fact that he could understand oral directions and had average phonological skills for age. The time pressure may be the confounding factor that is impeding the executive function of initiation.

Memory and Learning Domain

Memory for Faces (MF): This subtest is designed to assess the ability to encode facial details and recall them immediately and to recognize the faces on a delay task. Immediately after a 5-second exposure to each of 16 black and white photos of children's faces, Allen was shown arrays of three faces and asked to identify the one in each array of three that he had seen before. His performance on the immediate face recognition task was *Below Expected Level* (3rd–10th percentile) for age (MF Total SS: 5; 5th percentile). On the MF Delayed task, however, administered 25 minutes later, Allen performed *At Expected Level* (26th–75th percentile). It appears that over the intervening period, between Memory for Faces and MF Delayed, Allen consolidated the facial cues and then was able to perform within the average range for age. His facial recognition performance increased from the 5th percentile to the 63rd percentile. It appears that slow processing of faces is causing the lag, but there is consolidation over time. Obviously, however, there are adverse social implications for a child who is unable to encode and recognize facial cues immediately. Given Allen's poor performance on MF immediate recall, his recall 25 minutes later is significantly better than expected (*Above Expected Level* [>75th percentile] on the MF vs. MFD Contrast SS: 15; 94th percentile). These results suggest that Allen may develop more facial recognition skills over time, which would be very beneficial for his social perception.

Narrative Memory (NM): This is a subtest of story memory under free recall, cued recall, and recognition conditions. Allen listened to a story and was then asked to repeat the story (free recall). He was then asked questions to elicit missing details from his recall of the story (cued recall). On the recognition task, he was asked which of two details the story contained. On NM Free Recall, Allen remembered 2 details out of a possible 20 (NM Free Recall Total SS: 4; 3rd percentile) for a performance *Below Expected Level* (3rd–10th percentile) or age. When cued with questions on missing details, Allen was able to access 7 more details from memory, so he had encoded them when the story was read, but was unable to access them in free recall. Nonetheless, his NM Free and Cued Recall Total SS: 3; 1st percentile, was *Well Below Expected Level* (≤2nd percentile). On the NM Recognition Trial, Allen had no correct answers, so his performance was *Well Below Expected Level* (<2nd percentile). Given Allen's performance on NM Free and Cued Recall, which was *Well Below Expected Level*, his poor performance on the NM Recognition task is about what one would expect. Therefore, the NM Free and Cued Recall vs. NM Recognition Contrast SS was *At Expected Level*. Because children's memory deficits are usually due to a primary deficit in language, Allen's problems with verbal memory and executive functions are a further indication of his underlying subtle language problems, despite average comprehension of oral instructions.

Word List Interference (WI): Verbal working memory, repetition, and word recall following interference were assessed on this subtest. Allen was presented with two series of two to three words each and was asked to repeat each sequence following its presentation. Then he was asked to recall each sequence in the order of presentation. Allen was unable to repeat any of the sequences accurately, suggesting that underlying subtle language deficits were affecting performance. He was also unable to recall the word series after interference, suggesting that the interplay of subtle language deficits and the ability to inhibit interfering stimuli influenced Allen's performance. Therefore, his WI performance overall was *Well Below Expected Level* ($\leq$ 2nd percentile) at the 1st percentile for age.

[*Memory for Designs and MD Delayed are optional on the Social/Interpersonal Referral Battery and were not administered to Allen in the interest of time, since visuospatial abilities have been good in previous assessments.*]

Sensorimotor Domain

Fingertip Tapping (FT): There are two parts to this subtest, fingertip tapping and sequential finger movement. The first part is designed to assess the child's finger dexterity and motor speed; the second part assesses fine motor programming. The score for fingertip tapping is based on time for 20 taps of the pointer finger tip on the pad of the thumb. Allen's FT Dominant Hand (left) Repetitions Completion Time was *Above Expected Level* at >75th percentile. The score for the sequential finger movement is based on time for five correct sequences. Allen's FT Dominant Hand–Sequences Completion Time (51st–75th percentile) was *At Expected Level* (26th–75th percentile). Performance for both tapping and sequencing with the Dominant Hand showed an FT Dominant Hand Combined SS:12; 75th percentile, *At Expected Level*. Allen's FT Nondominant (right) Hand Repetitions and Hand Sequences Completion Times were both *Above Expected Level* at >75th percentile. Therefore, FT Nondominant Hand Combined SS of 14 (91st percentile) was *Above Expected Level*. The FT Dominant Hand vs. FT Nondominant Hand Contrast SS of 14 (91st percentile) was *Above Expected Level* (>75th percentile). This score indicates that given the dominant hand performance *At Expected Level*, one would expect the same or lower classification for the nondominant hand. Instead, the nondominant hand performed *Above Expected Level*. It is of interest that Allen's nondominant right hand performed more efficiently than his dominant left hand, which is the opposite of the usual configuration for the dominant hand. The scaled score difference between the two combined scores was only 2 points; however, which is not a significant difference.

Looking at Repetitions across both hands, one sees an FT-Repetitions Combined SS: 14; 91st percentile, *Above Expected Level*. Combining sequences across hands produced an FT-Sequences Combined SS of 12; 75th percentile, *At Expected Level*. The FT Repetitions vs. Sequences Contrast SS: 11; 63rd percentile, suggests that given Allen's ability to perform repetitions with both hands (*Above Expected Level*), his ability to perform sequences *At Expected Level* would be appropriate, because sequences require more time to produce for the same number of finger movements. Overall, one notes that fine motor movement is *At or Above Expected Level,* and Allen's nondominant right hand appears to be a little more efficient than his dominant left, but not significantly so.

Visuomotor Precision (VP): This subtest is designed to assess graphomotor speed and accuracy. Allen was required to make pencil lines through winding tracks quickly without making marks outside the lines (errors). Allen's graphomotor speed was *Borderline* (11th-25th percentile). VP Total Completion SS: 6. He only made 1 error, however, which placed him *Above Expected Level* for accuracy on Visuomotor Precision Total Errors. Time and errors integrated produced a Visuomotor Precision Combined SS: 12 (75th percentile), *At Expected Level.* He did not lift his pencil in drawing his line, so motor control was good, but motor speed was slow.

Imitating Hand Positions (IH): The ability to imitate static finger/hand positions bilaterally is assessed by this subtest. The task integrates fine motor programming, visuospatial analysis, and kinesthetic feedback. The examiner formed a hand position out of Allen's sight, and then the hand position was brought into view and held for 20 seconds while Allen imitated it. All of the hand positions are formed first with the dominant hand and then all are formed with the nondominant hand. Allen's performance overall (IH Total SS: 9; 37th percentile) was *At Expected Level* (26th–75th percentile). (Both the Dominant Left Hand and Nondominant Hand scores were in the 26th–75th percentile [9 points for Dominant Hand and 10 points for Nondominant], so there was no difference.)

[*Manual Motor Processing is an optional subtest in the Sensorimotor Domain and was not administered to Allen, as all other sensorimotor subtests produced average or above average results.*]

Social Perception Domain

Affect Recognition (AR): The first subtest in the Social Perception domain is designed to assess the ability to recognize affect (emotion) from colored photos of children's faces. Allen's Affect Recognition Total SS: 11 (63rd percentile) reflected performance *At Expected Level* in relation to the subtest mean of 10 ± 3. Therefore, Allen appears to be recognizing emotions on faces as well as the typical child of his age. This has been an emphasis of his therapy in the last two years. This is an optimistic sign for development of Allen's social skills in the future.

Theory of Mind (ToM): This subtest is designed to assess the ability to understand mental functions, such as belief, intention, deception, pretending, and so forth, as well as the ability to understand that another's point of view might be different from one's own. Further, it addresses the understanding of figurative language and the ability to understand how emotion relates to social context. In the Verbal task, the examiner read various scenarios to Allen or displayed pictures. He was then asked questions that tapped into the afore-mentioned ToM concepts. On the Contextual task, Allen was shown a picture depicting a social context and was then asked to select one of four photos that showed the appropriate affect for one of the people in the picture. Allen's ToM–Verbal Percentile Rank was at the 26th–90th percentile, *At Expected Level* to *Above,* demonstrating that all of the work that Allen has done in this area through his speech/language therapy and the autistic program has been benefi-cial. However, he is clearly still having difficulty matching the appropriate emo-tion to social context, for he only had 2 correct responses on the Contextual Task, causing his ToM Total Percentile Rank to drop into the *Borderline* range (11th–25th percentile). After intensive social skills therapy, Allen can now iden-tify facial affect in isolation and is gaining an average understanding of other people's points of view, but he continues to show difficulty in making the link between social context and the emotional reaction to it. This will be an impor-tant addition to his therapy work.

Visuospatial Processing Domain

Design Copying–Process Scoring (DCP): This untimed subtest assesses mo-tor and visual-perceptual skills associated with the ability to copy two-dimensional geometric figures. Allen was required to copy geometric figures displayed in the Response Booklet. The Processing Scoring was used rather than General Scoring, because the latter provides separate diagnostic scores for different components of the task.. In Allen's case, he displayed performance *Above Expected Level* on all aspects: DCP Total SS: 17 (99th percentile); DCP Motor SS: 17 (99th percentile); DCP Global SS: 16 (98th percentile); DCP Local SS: 16 (98th percentile); and DCP Global vs. DCP Local Contrast SS: 13 (84th percentile). Essentially, what these scores indicate is that Allen's visuospatial and graphomotor skills for copy-ing on an untimed task are excellent. He is able to reproduce both the outside con-figuration (Global score) and the details (Local score) of the design equally well, at an above-average level, so that overall (Total score), Allen's untimed paper/pencil design copying skills are at the 99th percentile for age. This is an area of significant strength for Allen. He did, however, show slow motor speed on the timed Visuomotor Precision subtest in the Sensorimotor domain.

Geometric Puzzles (GP): This is a nonmotor subtest designed to assess mental rotation, visuospatial analysis, and attention to detail. Allen was presented with a picture of a large grid containing geometric shapes. Outside of the grid were four smaller pictures taken from sections of the larger picture. For each item, he was required to match two shapes outside the grid to two shapes within the grid. Allen performed *At Expected Level:* GP Total SS: 11(63rd percentile).

Picture Puzzles (PP): This is also a nonmotor subtest designed to assess visual discrimination, spatial location, and visual scanning, as well as the ability to deconstruct a picture into its constituent parts and to recognize part-whole relationships in ecological (real-life) pictures, rather than geometric designs. Allen was presented with a large photo divided by a grid and four smaller photos taken from sections of the large picture. He was required to identify the location on the grid of the larger picture from which each of the smaller pictures was taken. Allen performed *At Expected Level:* PP Total SS: 11 (63rd percentile). While Allen's performance on these two non-motor visuospatial assessments was average, he appears to perform significantly better on a visuospatial task with motor output. Using a pencil for design reproduction may focus Allen better than the purely visual tasks.

[*Arrows and Picture Puzzles were optional subtests on the Social/Interpersonal Referral Battery. The former was not administered, but the latter was, since it contains ecological pictures. This examiner wanted to see if he would perform better on the nonmotor visuospatial task with real-life pictures than he would on the nonmotor geometric task. Performance was the same, however. On this Referral Battery, the Block Construction subtest is recommended for ages 3–6, so it was not administered.*]

Clinical Impressions and Summary:

Allen B. is a young boy of 7.11 years who was diagnosed with Autistic Disorder, high-functioning (HFA), at 3.4 years of age by this examiner. He is left-hand dominant. Allen's younger brother is also diagnosed with HFA.

Allen has had intensive therapies since his diagnosis (speech/language therapy, Applied Behavioral Analysis, physical therapy, and, initially, occupational therapy). He attended Headstart for two years and is presently in a special public school program for children with autism. His teacher feels that Allen is ready for inclusion in the regular classroom. The RTI monitoring shows him now achieving at first-grade level in all areas. Allen's parents requested this evaluation to integrate the information with the school data in order to help them make the best placement decision for Allen.

The Social/Interpersonal Referral Battery of the NEPSY-II was administered to Allen in order to ascertain areas of strengths and weakness in which he has or has not progressed and that will serve to help shape new goals for intervention in his therapies and educational program. The information will also help to inform Mr. and Mrs. B's decision for Allen's educational placement.

Areas of Strength

Visuospatial/Fine Motor and Visuomotor Skills: Allen displayed a significant strength in this area in relation to typical children of his age in the visuospatial/ visuomotor skills associated with untimed paper/pencil copying of progressively more complex geometric designs. Allen's DCP Total scaled score of 17 (99th percentile) was $+ 2\frac{1}{3}$ standard deviations above the NEPSY-II mean of 10 ± 3. His DCP Total Score reflected superior visuomotor performance and superior ability to perceive and reproduce both the outside configuration and the inner details of geometric designs. Allen's Repetitive fingertip tapping bilaterally was also *Above Expected Level* for age at the 91st percentile. Good fine motor coordination underlies his well-developed graphomotor skills. Allen's Nondominant (right hand) showed strong ability to make repetitive and sequential finger movements with a scaled score of 14 at the 91st percentile. It is notable, however, that, while the dominant left hand was *At Expected Level* with a scaled score of 12 (75th percentile), the performances were not significantly different. On a visuomotor precision task, Allen displayed fine motor control for accuracy above the level expected for age.

Simple Naming Speed: When Allen had to access labels for each of two objects, his IN-Naming performance was at the 91st percentile. This strength in lexical access deteriorated rapidly, however, when he had to name three attributes for each of two objects (size/color/circle or square) rapidly or alternate between upper and lowercase number and letters (see Secondary Deficits).

Average Areas

Inhibition-Switching–Learning: The IN-Switching Combined Score was average. Allen was faster on the IN-Switching condition than on the IN-Inhibition condition. He was inhibiting a little better and making fewer errors. The practice during the IN-Inhibition task may have helped him inhibit response more efficiently. This may be a hopeful sign for Allen being able to develop more executive functioning.

Receptive Language/Phonological Processing: Allen displayed average receptive language understanding of oral directions and average phonological processing skills. The latter results support the teacher's findings that

Allen has developed the phonological skills to allow him to achieve grade level reading.

Memory for Faces Delayed: On the Memory for Faces Delayed subtest (63rd percentile), Allen performed *At Expected Level.* It appears that although his immediate facial recognition skills were poor, Allen consolidated the facial cues over the 25-minute period and was then able to perform within the average range for age.

Affect Recognition and Theory of Mind (Verbal Task): The Social Perception domain is an important one in Allen's assessment because he is subject to HFA. On the Affect Recognition subtest, Allen was able to recognize emotions on faces as well as the typical child of his age. This has been an emphasis of his therapy in the last two years, and it appears to have been beneficial. On the Theory of Mind Verbal task, Allen displayed average understanding of another's point of view and understood mental functions and figurative language.

Non-motor Visuospatial Tasks: In the Visuospatial domain, Allen performed at the level expected for age on two nonmotor visuospatial tasks, Geometric Puzzles and Picture Puzzles. Evidently motor performance was helpful to Allen on the Design Copying subtest, as on that apparently more difficult subtest he showed a very strong performance, as previously noted in Areas of Strength.

Visuomotor Precision and Imitating Hand Positions: When time and errors were integrated for the Visuomotor Precision subtest, Allen's performance was average. He also displayed average ability to imitate static hand positions bilaterally, employing visuospatial analysis, motor programming, and kinesthetic feedback.

Borderline Area

Slowed Processing: Allen displayed *Borderline* Speeded Naming Time to Completion, despite good naming ability, and *Borderline* motor speed on the Visuomotor Precision subtest in spite of good accuracy. He also displayed *Borderline* time to completion on IN-Inhibition and IN-Switching, but in both cases that appeared to be due to:

Primary and Secondary Deficits

There are several deficit areas for Allen, explained in the following list.

Primary Deficits
- *Executive Functions:* Among a number of executive functions are included concept formation and the ability to transfer concepts into action, the ability to plan and strategize, as well as the ability to inhibit response in order to adopt, maintain, and/or shift set. Allen displayed

ability to learn how to inhibit response and shift to an alternative response over time, but he did display other executive dysfunction typical of autism:

- Significant difficulty inhibiting his stereotypical interest in animals and demonstrating cognitive flexibility.
- On a task of simple, selective auditory attention, Allen displayed a lack of response inhibition.
- On tasks with complex auditory and visual stimuli, Allen showed varying ability to inhibit response and shift to an alternate response.

- *Residual Language Disorder; Possible Secondary Effects from Executive Dysfunction:*
    - Although Allen displays average comprehension of oral instructions and phonological processing skills, residual language deficits remain as part of his HFA. This is one of the reasons that it is so important for children with HFA to continue in speech/language therapy even after they are talking well.
    - Allen performed well on the Naming condition of the Inhibition subtest because he was just quickly accessing one name for each shape. Allen's overall performance on the more complex rapid naming task (Speeded Naming) with alternating stimuli was below the level expected for his age. It is possible that his poor performance on SN may be a secondary effect of executive dysfunction on Allen's average naming skills.
    - On Word List Interference, Allen was unable to repeat any of the word sequences accurately. Being unable to repeat 2–3 words suggests a residual language disorder.
    - Allen also experienced problems with verbal productivity while generating words within specific semantic and initial letter categories. Results on Word Generation were well below the level expected for age. Again, these results may also be influenced by executive dysfunction, because Allen was required to categorize on one task and to search across category "files" on the second task to locate quickly words that began with a certain letter.
- *Social Perception*
    - *Understanding of Emotions from Social Context:* Allen demonstrated poor understanding of emotions of others related to social context pictures on the Contextual task of the Theory of Mind subtest. So, while Allen was observed to have increasing social skills and

he demonstrated understanding of another person's point of view on the ToM language items, he is still unable to connect the appropriate affect to social context.

- ***Immediate Memory for Faces:*** Although Allen recognizes individual facial affect at an average level on an untimed test, he displayed a poor performance for encoding facial features rapidly and recalling the faces immediately. Facial processing skills are subserved at least in part by the Fusiform Gyrus of the brain. Allen's problem with immediate processing of faces appears to be a primary processing deficit. Nonetheless, he does consolidate facial features over time, suggesting that this specific processing may improve over time.
- There are adverse social implications for a child who is unable to encode and recognize facial cues immediately.

Secondary Deficits:

- ***Verbal memory due to effects of Residual Language Deficit and Executive Dysfunction:*** Allen's Narrative Memory free recall performance was poor. When cued with questions concerning details he had not recalled, he was able to access more story details, suggesting that they were encoded in memory but he could not access them efficiently. Narrative memory for free and cued recall taken together were well below the level expected for age, and recognition memory for story details was well below the level expected for age. Verbal memory deficits are a known secondary effect of primary language problems. On the second part of the Word List Interference subtest, Allen experienced significant problems inhibiting interference so that he could recall words.
- Because of the interplay of secondary verbal memory deficits and executive dysfunction, Allen is apt to experience the following problems:
  - Difficulty learning and remembering procedures, language, and story information.
  - Difficulty with working memory in all learning tasks, particularly as complexity increases.
  - Problems inhibiting interfering stimuli on learning tasks.
- ***Variable Speed Issues–Secondary Effect of Task Demands:*** Allen's speed varies from very fast, as on Repetitive Fingertip Tapping, to average on a simple naming task (on Inhibition), to borderline on Visuomotor Precision, Speeded Naming, and Inhibition-Switching, to below expected level for age on the Inhibition condition of the Inhibition subtest and in consolidation of facial cues over time. While these

are all types of tasks, it would appear that the variance in the speed is driven more by the task constraints than the speed, affecting results. If the task is simple, Allen performs quickly. When the task is complex or requires more executive functions, Allen's speed is apt to be slow. The one exception to this would seem to be his slow consolidation of facial cues, which is a primary brain function.

- **Social skills problems** due to inability to connect appropriate affect to social context and to recognize facial cues immediately.

Essentially, the results of this testing show definite progress for Allen, but there remain some significant concerns. He has made such fine gains since he was first diagnosed that we want to see that trajectory continue. In observing Allen clinically throughout this assessment, this psychologist can see benefits to inclusion in the regular classroom to challenge him and benefits to leaving him in the autistic program for one more year, as he is thriving there. The fear is that with his residual language problems and significant executive dysfunction, not to mention the social percepual issues, Allen would be overwhelmed in the regular classroom and regress or possibly shut down. He is due to have academic achievement testing and adaptive behavior rating scales for parents and teachers endorsed this week through his school program. Then Allen's parents, the teacher, and this psychologist will meet to discuss the issue.

At this point, it is this psychologist's clinical judgment that inclusion should be a gradual process for Allen, although ultimately it is needed and will be beneficial. Possibly, he could begin with an hour a day in the regular classroom for two weeks, then expand inclusion to 2 hours for two more weeks. At that point, assuming all is going well and he is adjusting and able to achieve in the new setting, he would remain for 3 hours in the regular classroom for the remainder of the fall semester. At the end of the semester, we would meet again to evaluate his progress and make a decision about full inclusion or continuing partial inclusion for the remainder of the year. Allen's therapy time in the autistic program is so valuable that we don't want to curtail that in any way. Yet it will be difficult for him to get the amount of social skills, speech and language, and behavior modification that he is getting now if he is in full inclusion. For this reason, I would lean toward the 3-hour inclusion arrangement for a year, so Allen can continue to receive the one-on-one and small group services that he is getting now.

In addition to academics, there is much work to be done in developing executive functions. Residual language and verbal memory problems, as well as social perception, must continue to be addressed, so a cooperative inclusion arrangement would be advantageous for Allen in this psychologist's clinical judgment. None-theless, it is wise to go forward with the meeting set up for parents, teachers, and this psychologist, so we can look objectively at all sides of the question.

Diagnosis

299.00 Autistic Disorder, high-functioning

Recommendations

Inclusion Considerations

1. Parents, teachers, and this psychologist will meet next week to discuss pros and cons of inclusion for Allen in the next school year. Recommendations for inclusion, if this is the course to be followed:

    (a) That Allen continue in all of his school-based therapies for at least a year before we consider cutting back on the same. It is especially important that he continues with his language therapy and social skills work.

    (b) It is strongly recommended that inclusion be faded in over a month or more, if needed, as children with autism do not always handle change well. For any period of time in the day that Allen has inclusion, it is strongly recommended that he have an individual certified paraprofessional working with him who can anticipate his needs and help him cope with the regular classroom work demands, social interactions, sensory stimulus, and so forth. The object is not to have someone doing things for Allen, but rather guiding him in doing as much as he can for himself.

    (c) If Allen goes into a regular classroom, he will need a nurturing teacher with training in teaching children with autism, who also has clearly defined boundaries, is calm, nonjudgmental, and is not easily manipulated. He needs a structured classroom with a predictable environment and expectations. A cluttered, unpredictable, ever-changing environment will only confuse the child with an autism spectrum and make him anxious.

    (d) If he is in a regular classroom, Allen will need a structured picture schedule taped to his desk and to his notebook, so he knows where he should be at all times. Children with autism respond to structure and rules.

Interventions for Executive Functions

1. With all learning Allen will need help to:
    - Identify the main idea in new information
    - Draw associations between new knowledge and already acquired knowledge
    - See and understand the "whole picture" before focusing on details

2. Allen needs an organized sequential approach to acquiring executive functioning skills. The teacher helps Allen to learn to:
    - Describe the problem.
    - Set a goal.
    - Establish a procedure for reaching the goal.
    - The teacher supervises the child carrying out the established procedure.
    - The teacher and Allen evaluate whether or not the established procedure was followed and if the goal was met. If not, the teacher and Allen discuss changes that would help Allen reach his goal.

The object is to teach Allen how to monitor and self-regulate eventually. He learns to self-initiate a task, sustain his focus on it, shift set when needed by inhibiting automatic responses and interfering stimuli, and stopping when appropriate. Help him keep an Executive Notebook for his plans.

When he is able to complete simple procedures, begin to try more complex procedures with multiple steps. After establishing a procedure for reaching the goal, add two more steps:

- Break the procedure into achievable steps.
- Develop a logical order for the steps.

Then the teacher supervises the child completing the first step and helps with the next few.

- Then, procedure is evaluated.

When Allen can complete the first step independently, then he tries the first two steps and the teacher helps with the next few, and so on over time until he can complete the multi-step procedure independently.

Remember to evaluate how it went each time the procedure is completed until Allen is handling it easily.

3. Executive functioning skills can be taught at home, as well. Help Allen learn task step by step from laminated cards. He does first step, then parent helps with following steps. Then moves to first two steps and parent helps until all can be handled with supervision. Then fade the supervision.

- Complete chores
- Get up, get ready, and out the door
- Self care/hygiene
- Keep track of possessions
- Follow time limits
- Tolerate uncertainty and changes

Be sure to identify chores and responsibilities that Allen can handle and provide appropriate structure (i.e., index cards, etc., to clearly lay out the plan and steps involved in completing a task).

Interventions for Residual Language Disorder

1. Allen must continue with his school-based speech and language therapy twice a week for 30 minutes in order to be sure that he continues to progress and develops pragmatic language skills and verbal memory. He should also continue speech language once a week for 30 minutes at the developmental center.
2. If Allen enters the regular classroom, it is essential for the teacher and aide to realize that although Allen now speaks fairly well, he still has a residual language disorder. They should meet with the speech/language therapist before Allen enters the classroom to learn the techniques that will be most helpful for Allen.
3. Allen will be a visual learner who needs to talk his way through tasks as well. Use simple, colorful charts, models, and manipulatives. Picture clues will help him retain information. Use concrete examples with simple, direct speech.
4. Avoid using figurative or abstract language with Allen when teaching or correcting behavior (e.g., "Don't count your chickens before they're hatched"), but teach such sayings at a separate time.

Interventions for Learning at Home and School

1. When Allen is learning something that requires sequential steps, use the chaining method with a sequence of pictures arranged horizontally to cue him.
2. If Allen is making comments that are tangential to the school subject, establish a nonverbal cue to stop him when he deviates from the topic. Stop him, refocus, and restate the question. Have a designated time each day when he can talk for 5 minutes about his subject of interest. The rest of the time he is redirected to another activity rather than

being allowed to have a unilateral discourse on one subject for an extended period of time.

3. Reinforcers for Allen must be activities or objects that are reinforcing for him. If a child does not care about the reinforcer, it will not be a reward to him, so you will not see an increase in the desired behavior. A possible reinforcer for Allen would be 10 minutes on a video game.

4. Arrange activities in reverse order of preference. In this way the preferred activity following the nonpreferred activity will act as a natural reinforcer.

5. For all learning, continue to give concrete examples. Use picture materials and teach through Allen's strength.

6. No more than 30 minutes/day for video games, preferably in short sessions as rewards. The more video games Allen plays, the more remote and repetitive he becomes. Keep him engaged with people as much as possible.

7. Do not rush Allen, as he is apt to become anxious. Be aware that processing time can be variable

Interventions for Social Perception and Social Skills at Home and School:

1. Continue to work on eye contact. When he talks to you make sure that he also establishes eye contact with you. He has made good progress but we are not there yet. Prompt with "Look at me," if necessary.

2. Continue to work on nonverbal cues (facial and body language). When Allen has a disagreement or makes a mistake because he did not pick up a social cue, ask him to think back about what the other individual's face looked like just before he or she got upset with him. (What did the voice sound like? Did it sound deeper? How did the individual use his or her body? Were the hands on the hips? Was the foot tapping? etc.)

3. Take pictures of different facial expressions or purchase the same. Use magazine pictures to depict a social situation, and ask Allen to match the facial expression card to the event. Scenes should be appropriate for happy, sad, disgusted, fearful, angry, and so forth.

4. For poor social interaction/not reading nonverbal cues, develop a pre-established and practiced nonverbal cue to alert Allen that his behavior is inappropriate. Take time to explain what was wrong with behavior and what would have been appropriate.

5. Role-play new situations several times, so he is comfortable with the situation.

6. Continue to write Social Stories with Allen to help him prepare for events, activities, and so forth.

7. Establish a cue with Allen that will help him curtail repetitive, long discourses on his stereotypical interests. The more repetitive he is, the less he will interact. This applies to any type of activity.

8. Keep Allen involved in his Cub group and invite one friend at a time over to play.

9. Mother feels that Allen has made progress in his maturity level due to her pulling back and not overfunctioning for him. Therefore, focus needs to be continued on Allen not to manipulate his parents. Curtailing manipulation needs to be undertaken in a calm, nonjudgmental manner so that it does not become a battle. It is essential to keep going on this track or he will have no reason to handle things on his own. If he can handle a task on his own, have him do it, even if an adult would do the job better. Praise effort, just as you do with school work.

A special note:

Allen's parents, school team, and therapists have done an excellent job of helping Allen emerge from his shell. Congratulations! Let's continue to think and plan together for Allen's bright future. The list of recommendations for Allen is long, because this psychologist wanted Mr. and Mrs. B to have a comprehensive picture of Allen's needs. Since there are many suggestions, select the ones you wish to implement first, but be sure to continue forward when Allen begins to conquer a task. On follow-up, other recommendations may then be reviewed and added.

DATA SHEET: ALLEN B., AGE 7.11 YEARS
Summary of Diagnostic Referral Battery–Social Interpersonal

Attention and Executive Functioning Domain					
Score Name	Raw Scores	Scaled Scores	Percentile Ranks	Cumulative Percentages	Classification
Animal Sorting Total Correct Subtest	1	5	5	–	Below Expected Level
Animal Sorting Total Errors	0	–	>75	–	Above Expected Level
Animal Sorting Combined Scaled Score	–	6	9	–	Borderline
Animal Sorting Total Repeated Sort Errors	0	–	>75	–	Above Expected Level
Animal Sorting Total Novel Sort Errors	0	–	51–75	–	At Expected Level
Auditory Attention Total Correct	26	8	25	–	At Expected Level
Auditory Attention Combined Scaled Score	–	5	5	–	Below Expected Level
Auditory Attention Total Omission Errors	4	–	26–50	–	At Expected Level
Auditory Attention Tot. Commission Errors	26	–	< 2	–	Well Below Expected Level
Auditory Attention Total Inhibitory Errors	25	–	< 2	–	Well Below Expected Level
Response Set Total Correct	0	1	0.1	–	Well Below Expected Level
Response Set Combined Scaled Score	–	9	37	–	At Expected Level
Response Set Total Omission Errors	36	–	< 2	–	Well Below Expected Level
Response Set Total Commission Errors	0	–	>75	–	Above Expected Level
Response Set Total Inhibitory Errors	0	–	>75	–	Above Expected Level
AA vs. RS Contrast Scaled Score	–	11	63	–	At Expected Level

(continued)

421

(continued)

Attention and Executive Functioning Domain

Score Name	Raw Scores	Scaled Scores	Percentile Ranks	Cumulative Percentages	Classification
IN–Naming Completion Time Total	57	11	63	–	At Expected Level
IN–Naming Combined Scaled Score	–	14	91	–	Above Expected Level
IN–Naming Total Errors	0	–	>75	–	Above Expected Level
IN–Naming Total Self-Corrected Errors	0	–	>75	–	Above Expected Level
IN–Naming Total Uncorrected Errors	0	–	51–75	–	At Expected Level
IN–Inhibition Completion Time Total	154	5	5	–	Below Expected Level
IN–Inhibition Combined Scaled Score	–	6	9	–	Borderline
IN–Inhibition Total Errors	10	–	11–25	–	Borderline
IN–Inhibition Total Self-Corrected Errors	10	–	2–5	–	Below Expected Level
IN–Inhibition Total Uncorrected Errors	0	–	>75	–	Above Expected Level
IN–Switching Completion Time Total	171	7	16	–	Borderline
IN–Switching Combined Scaled Score	–	9	37	–	At Expected Level
IN–Switching Total Errors	8	–	51–75	–	At Expected Level
IN–Switching Total Self-Corrected Errors	4	–	51–75	–	At Expected Level
IN–Switching Total Uncorrected Errors	4	–	51–75	–	At Expected Level
IN–Naming vs. Inhibition Contrast SS	–	4	2	–	Below Expected Level
IN–Inhib. vs. Switching Contrast SS Score	–	10	50	–	At Expected Level
IN Total Errors (across test)	18	10	50	–	At Expected Level

Attention and Executive Functioning Scaled Scores

Subtest Score Name	1	2	3	4	5	6	7	8	9	10	11	12	13	14	15	16	17	18	19
Animal Sorting Total Correct Sorts					X														
Animal Sorting Combined Scaled Score						X													
Auditory Attention Total Correct								X											
Auditory Attention Combined Scaled Score					X														
Response Set Total Correct	X																		
Response Set Combined Scaled Score									X										
Inhibition–Naming Completion Time Total											X								
Inhibition–Naming Combined Scaled Score														X					
Inhibition–Inhibition Completion Time Total					X														
Inhibition–Inhibition Combined Scaled Score						X													
Inhibition–Switching Completion Time Total							X												
Inhibition–Switching Combined Scaled Score									X										
Inhibition Total Errors										X									

423

Language Domain

Subtest Score Name	Raw Scores	Scaled Scores	Percentile Ranks	Classification
Comprehension of Instructions SS	23	10	50	At Expected Level
Phonological Processing Total SS	35	12	75	At Expected Level
Speeded Naming Total Completion Time SS	218	7	16	Borderline
Speeded Naming Total Correct	124	–	2–5	Below Expected Level
Speeded Naming Combined SS	–	5	5	Below Expected Level
Speeded Naming Total Self-Corrected Errors	0	–	>75	Above Expected Level
Word Generation–Semantic Total SS	0	1	0.1	Well Below Expected Level
Word Generation–Initial Letter Total SS	0	3	1	Well Below Expected Level
WG Semantic vs. Initial Letter Contrast SS	–	5	5	Below Expected Level

Language Scaled Scores

Subtest Score Name	1	2	3	4	5	6	7	8	9	10	11	12	13	14	15	16	17	18	19
Comprehension of Instructions Total Score										X									
Phonological Processing Total Score												X							
Speeded Naming Total Completion Time							X												
Speeded Naming Combined Scaled Score					X														
Word Generation–Semantic Total Score	X																		
Word Generation–Initial Letter Total Score			X																

Memory and Learning

Subtest Score Name	Raw Scores	Scaled Scores	Percentile Ranks	Cumulative Percentages	Classification
Memory for Faces Total Score	7	5	5	–	Below Expected Level
Memory for Faces Delayed Total Score	11	11	63	–	At Expected Level
MF vs. MFD Contrast Scaled Score	–	15	95	–	Above Expected Level
Narrative Memory Free and Cued Recall Total Score	9	3	1	–	Well Below Expected Level
NM Free Recall Total Score	2	4	2	–	Below Expected Level
NM Recognition Total Score	0	–	< 2	–	Well Below Expected Level
NM Free and Cued Recall vs. Recognition Contrast Scaled Score	–	8	25	–	At Expected Level
Word List Interference—Repetition Total	0	1	0.1	–	Well Below Expected Level
Word List Interference—Recall Total SS	0	1	0.1	–	Well Below Expected Level
WI Repetition vs. Recall Contrast SS	–	3	1	–	Well Below Expected Level

Memory and Learning Scaled Scores

Subtest Score Name	1	2	3	4	5	6	7	8	9	10	11	12	13	14	15	16	17	18	19
Memory for Faces Total Score					X														
Memory for Faces Delayed Total Score											X								
Memory for Names Total Score	X																		
Memory for Names Delayed Total Score		X																	
Memory for Names and Memory for Names Delayed Total Score	X																		
Narrative Memory Free and Cued Recall Total Score			X																
Narrative Memory Free Recall Total Score				X															
Word List Interference-Repetition Total Score	X																		
Word List Interference-Recall Total Score	X																		

Sensorimotor Domain					
Subtest Score Name	Raw Scores	Scaled Scores	Percentile Ranks	Cumulative Percentages	Classification
Fingertip Tapping—Dominant Hand Repetitions Completion Time	6	–	>75	–	Above Expected Level
Fingertip Tapping—Dominant Hand Sequences Completion Time	11	–	51–75	–	At Expected Level
Fingertip Tapping—Nondominant Hand Repetitions Completion Time	5	–	>75	–	Above Expected Level
Fingertip Tapping—Nondominant Hand Sequences Completion Time	11	–	>75	–	Above Expected Level
Fingertip Tapping—Dominant Hand Combined Scaled Score	–	12	75	–	At Expected Level
Fingertip Tapping—Nondominant Hand Combined Scaled Score	–	14	91	–	Above Expected Level
Fingertip Tapping—Repetitions Combined Scaled Score	–	14	91	–	Above Expected Level
Fingertip Tapping—Sequences Combined Scaled Score	–	12	75	–	At Expected Level
FT Dominant Hand vs. Nondominant Hand Contrast Scaled Score	–	14	91	–	Above Expected Level
FT Repetitions vs. Sequences Contrast Scaled Score	–	11	63	–	At Expected Level
Imitating Hand Positions	19	9	37	–	At Expected Level
Visuomotor Precision Total Completion Time	183	6	9	–	Borderline
Visuomotor Precision Total Errors	1	–	>75	–	Above Expected Level
Visuomotor Precision Combined Scaled Score	–	12	75	–	At Expected Level
Visuomotor Precision Pencil Lift Total	0	–	>75	–	Above Expected Level

Sensorimotor Scaled Scores

Subtest Score Name	1	2	3	4	5	6	7	8	9	10	11	12	13	14	15	16	17	18	19
Fingertip Tapping–Dominant Hand Combined Scaled Score												X							
Fingertip Tapping–Nondominant Hand Combined Scaled Score														X					
Fingertip Tapping–Repetitions Combined Scaled Score														X					
Fingertip Tapping–Sequences Combined Scaled Score												X							
Visuomotor Precision Total Completion Time						X													
Visuomotor Precision Combined Scaled Score												X							

Social Perception Domain

Subtest Score Name	Raw Scores	Scaled Scores	Percentile Ranks	Classification
Affect Recognition Total Score	26	11	63	At Expected Level
Theory of Mind Total Score	16	–	11–25	Borderline
Theory of Mind–Verbal Score	14	–	26–50	At Expected Level

Social Perception Scaled Scores

Subtest Score Name	1	2	3	4	5	6	7	8	9	10	11	12	13	14	15	16	17	18	19
Affect Recognition Total Score											X								

Visuospatial Processing

Subtest Score Name	Raw Scores	Scaled Scores	Percentile Ranks	Classification
Arrows Total Score	26	11	63	At Expected Level
Design Copying Process Total Score	95	17	99	Above Expected Level
Design Copying Process Motor Score	39	17	99	Above Expected Level
Design Copying Process Global Score	32	16	98	Above Expected Level
Design Copying Process Local Score	24	16	98	Above Expected Level
DCP Global vs. Local Contrast Scaled Score	–	13	84	Above Expected Level
Design Copying General Total Score	13	–	>75	Above Expected Level
Geometric Puzzles Total Score	26	11	63	At Expected Level
Picture Puzzles Total Score	7	11	63	At Expected Level

Visuospatial Processing Scaled Scores

Subtest Score Name	1	2	3	4	5	6	7	8	9	10	11	12	13	14	15	16	17	18	19
Arrows Total Score											X								
Block Construction Total Score										X									
Design Copying Process Total Score																	X		
Design Copying Process Motor Score																	X		
Design Copying Process Global Score																X			
Design Copying Process Local Score																X			
Geometric Puzzles Total Score											X								
Picture Puzzles Total Score											X								

Behavioral Observations across Domains

Attention and Executive Functioning Domain

Subtest Score Name	Raw Score	Cumulative Percentages	Percent of Normative Sample
Auditory Attention and Response Set			
Inattentive/Distracted–Off Task Behaviors Total	2	26–75	–
Out of Seat/Physical Movement in Seat–Off Task Behaviors Total	26	< 2	–
Inhibition			
INN Points to Stimuli Total	1	26–75	–
INI Points to Stimuli Total	2	26–75	–
INS Points to Stimuli Total	2	26–75	–

Language Domain

Subtest Score Name	Raw Score	Cumulative Percentages	Percent of Normative Sample
Comprehension of Instructions			
Asks for Repetition Total	1	26–75	–
Phonological Processing			
Asks for Repetition Total	0	26–75	–

(continued)

Behavioral Observations across Domains

Memory and Learning Domain

Subtest Score Name	Raw Score	Cumulative Percentages	Percent of Normative Sample
Memory for Designs and Memory for Designs Delayed			
Rule Violation Total	2	3–10	–
Word List Interference			
Asks for Repetition Total	0	26–75	–

Sensorimotor Domain

Subtest Score Name	Raw Score	Cumulative Percentages	Percent of Normative Sample
Fingertip Tapping			
Visual Guidance	Y	–	72
Incorrect Position	Y	–	40
Posturing	N	–	68
Mirroring	N	–	84
Overflow	Y	–	23
Visuomotor Precision			
Pencil Grip–Mature	Y	–	63

Social Perception Domain

Subtest Score Name	Raw Score	Cumulative Percentages	Percent of Normative Sample
Affect Recognition			–
Spontaneous Comments Total	1	26–75	

Appendix: NEPSY-II Data Worksheet

NEPSY-II DATA WORKSHEET						
NAME _____ DATE OF BIRTH _____ AGE _____						
Attention and Executive Functioning Domain						
Score Name	**Raw Scores**	**Scaled Scores**	**#S.D. from Mean**	**%ile Rank**	**Cum. %ages**	**Classification**
Auditory Attention (AA) Total Correct Scaled Score and Percentile Rank					–	
Auditory Attention Combined Scaled Score					–	
Auditory Attention Total Omission Errors Percentile Rank					–	
Auditory Attention Total Commission Errors Percentile Rank					–	
Auditory Attention Total Inhibitory Errors Percentile Rank					–	
Response Set (RS) Total Correct Scaled Score and Percentile Rank					–	
Response Set Combined Scaled Score					–	
Response Set Total Omission Errors Percentile Rank					–	
Response Set Total Commission Errors Percentile Rank					–	
Response Set Total Inhibitory Errors Percentile Rank					–	
Auditory Attention. vs. Response Set Contrast Scaled Score					–	
Clocks (CL) Total Scaled Score					–	
Design Fluency (DF) Total Scaled Score					–	
Design Fluency Structured Array Cumulative Percentage				–		
Design Fluency Random Array Cumulative Percentage				–		

(continued)

(*continued*)

Score Name	Raw Scores	Scaled Scores	#S.D. from Mean	%ile Rank	Cum. %ages	Classification
Inhibition–Naming (INN) Completion Time Total Scaled Score					–	
Inhibition–Naming Combined Scaled Score					–	
Inhibition–Naming Total Errors Percentile Rank					–	
Inhibition–Naming Total Self-Corrected Errors Percentile Rank					–	
Inhibition–Naming Total Uncorrected Errors Percentile Rank					–	
Inhibition–Inhibition (INI) Completion Time Total Scaled Score					–	
Inhibition–Inhibition Combined Scaled Score					–	
Inhibition–Inhibition Total Errors Percentile Rank					–	
Inhibition–Inhibition Total Self-Corrected Errors Percentile Rank					–	
Inhibition–Inhibition Total Uncorrected Errors Percentile Ranks					–	
Inhibition–Switching (INS) Completion Time Total Scaled Score					–	
Inhibition–Switching Combined Scaled Score					–	
Inhibition–Switching Total Errors Percentile Rank					–	
Inhibition–Switching Total Self-Corrected Errors Percentile Rank					–	
Inhibition–Switching Total Uncorrected Errors Percentile Rank					–	
IN–Naming vs. IN-Inhibition Contrast Scaled Score					–	
IN–Inhibition vs. IN-Switching Contrast Scaled Score					–	
Inhibition Total Errors Scaled Score					–	
Statue (ST) Total Scaled Score					–	
Statue Body Movement				–		
Statue Eye Opening				–		
Statue Vocalization				–		

	Language Domain					
Score Name	Raw Scores	Scaled Scores	#S.D. from Mean	%ile Rank	Cum. %ages	Classification
Comprehension of Instructions (CI) SS					–	
Phonological Processing (PH) SS					–	
Repetition of Nonsense Words (RN) SS					–	
Speeded Naming (SN) Total Completion Time Scaled Score					–	
Speeded Naming Total Correct Percentile Rank					–	
Speeded Naming Combined Scaled Score					–	
Speeded Naming Total Self-Corrected Errors Percentile Rank					–	
Word Generation (WG) Semantic Scaled Score					–	
Word Generation Initial Letter Scaled Score					–	
WG Semantic vs. Initial Letter Contrast SS					–	
	Memory and Learning Domain					
List Memory (LM) Scaled Score						
LM Repetitions Cumulative Percentage				–		
LM Novel (Non-List) Cumulative Percentage				–		
LM Interference (Wrong List) Cumulative Percentage				–		
LM Learning Effect Cumulative Percentage				–		
LM Interference Effect Cumulative Percentage				–		
LM Delayed (LMD) Scaled Score						
LM Delay Effect Cumulative Percentage				–		
Memory for Designs (MD) Total Scaled Score					–	
MD Content Scaled Score					–	
MD Spatial Scaled Score					–	
MD Content vs. MD Spatial Contrast Scaled Score						

(*continued*)

(continued)

Score Name	Raw Scores	Scaled Scores	#S.D. from Mean	%ile Rank	Cum. %ages	Classification
Memory – Designs Delayed (MDD) SS					–	
MDD Content Scaled Score					–	
MDD Spatial Scaled Score					–	
MDD Content vs Spatial Contrast Scaled Score					–	
MD vs. MDD Contrast Scaled Score					–	
Memory for Faces (MF) Total Scaled Score					–	
Memory for Faces Delayed (MFD) Total Scaled Score					–	
MF vs. MFD Contrast Scaled Score					–	
Memory for Names (MN) Scaled Score					–	
MN Delayed Scaled Score					–	
MN and MN Delayed Scaled Score					–	
Narrative Memory (NM) Free Recall Scaled Score					–	
NM Free and Cued Recall Scaled Score					–	
NM Recognition Percentile Rank						
NM Free and Cued Recall vs. Recognition Contrast Scaled Score					–	
Sentence Repetition Scaled Score					–	
Word List Interference (WI) Repetition Total Scaled Score					–	
WI-Recall Total Scaled Score					–	
WI Repetition vs. Recall Contrast Scaled Score					· –	

Score Name	Raw Scores	Scaled Scores	#S.D. from Mean	%ile Rank	Cum. %ages	Classification
Sensorimotor Domain						
Fingertip Tapping (FT) Repetitions Combined Scaled Score (Both Hands)					−	
Fingertip Tapping (FT) Sequences Combined Scaled Score (Both Hands)				−		
FT Dominant Hand Combined Scaled Score (Both Movements)					−	
FT Nondominant Hand Combined Scaled Score (Both Movements)					−	
FT Dominant vs. Nondominant Contrast Scaled Score					−	
FT Repetitions vs. Sequences Contrast Scaled Score					−	
FT Dominant Hand Repetitions Completion Time					−	
FT Dominant Hand Repetitions Percentile Rank					−	
FT Nondominant Hand Repetitions Completion Time						
FT Nondominant Hand Repetitions Percentile Rank						
FT Dominant Hand Sequences Completion Time						
FT Dominant Hand Sequences Percentile Rank						
FT Nondominant Hand Sequences Completion Time					−	
FT Nondominant Hand Sequences Percentile Rank					−	
Imitating Hand Positions (IH) Scaled Score					−	
IH Dominant Hand Cumulative Percentage						
IH Nondominant Hand Cumulative Percentage						
Manual Motor (MM) Sequences Total Scaled Score					−	
MM Percentile Rank					−	

(continued)

(continued)

Score Name	Raw Scores	Scaled Scores	#S.D. from Mean	%ile Rank	Cum. %ages	Classification
Visuomotor Precision Total Completion Time					–	
Visuomotor Precision Total Errors					–	
Visuomotor Precision Combined Scaled Score					–	
Visuomotor Precision Pencil Lift Total					–	
Social Perception						
Affect Recognition Total Scaled Score						
AR Happy Errors Percentile Rank						
AR Sad Errors Percentile Rank						
AR Neutral Errors Percentile Rank						
AR Fear Errors Percentile Rank						
AR Angry Errors Percentile Rank						
AR Disgust Errors Percentile Rank						
Theory of Mind Scaled Score/ Percentile Rank						
Visuospatial Processing						
Arrow Scaled Score						
Block Construction Scaled Score						
Design Copy General Percentile Rank *or*						
Design Copying Process Total Score						
Design Copying Process Motor Score						
Design Copying Process Global Score						
Design Copying Process Local Score						
DCP Global vs. Local Contrast Scaled Score						
Geometric Puzzles Total Scaled Score						
Picture Puzzles Total Scaled Score						

Behavioral Observations – Attention and Executive Functioning			
Subtests and Behavioral Observations	Raw Score	Cum. %ages	% of Norm. Sample
Auditory Attention and Response Set			
Inattentive/Distracted–Off Task Behaviors Total			–
Out of Seat/Physical Movement in Seat–Off Task Behaviors Total			–
Inhibition			
INN Points to Stimuli Total			–
INI Points to Stimuli Total			–
INS Points to Stimuli Total			–
Language			
Subtests and Behavioral Observations	Raw Score	Cum. %ages	% of Norm. Sample
Comprehension of Instructions			
Asks for Repetition Total			–
Oromotor Sequences			
Rate Change			–
Oromotor Hypotonia	Y N	–	
Stable Misarticulation	Y N	–	
Phonological Processing			
Asks for Repetition Total			–
Repetition of Nonsense Words			
Stable Misarticulation	Y N	–	
Memory and Learning			
Memory for Designs and Memory for Designs Delayed			
Rule Violation Total			–
Memory for Faces and Memory for Faces Delayed			
Spontaneous Comments Total			–
Sentence Repetition			
Asks for Repetition Total			–
Word List Interference			
Asks for Repetition Total			–

(*continued*)

(*continued*)

Sensorimotor			
Subtests and Behavioral Observations	Raw Score	Cum. %ages	% of Norm. Sample
Fingertip Tapping			
Rate Change			–
Visual Guidance	Y N	–	
Incorrect Position	Y N	–	
Posturing	Y N	–	
Mirroring	Y N	–	
Overflow	Y N	–	
Imitating Hand Positions			
Mirroring	Y N	–	
Other Hand Helps	Y N	–	
Manual Motor Sequences			
Rate Change			–
Overflow	Y N	–	
Perseveration	Y N	–	
Loss of Asymmetrical Movement	Y N	–	
Body Movement	Y N	–	
Forceful Tapping	Y N	–	
Visuomotor Precision			
Pencil Grip Mature Intermediate Immature Variable		–	
Social Perception			
Affect Recognition			
Spontaneous Comments Total			–

References

Adolphs, R. (2003). Cognitive neuroscience of human social behaviour. *National review of neuroscience, 4*, 165–178.

Achenbach, T. M., & Edelbrock, C. (1991). *Manual for the child behavior checklist –Revised.* Burlington: University of Vermont.

Allen, L. I., & Yen, W. M. (1979). *Introduction to measurement theory.* Monterey, CA: Brooks/Cole.

American Educational Research Association, American Psychological Association, & National Council on Measurement in Education. (1999). *Standards for educational and psychological testing.* Washington, DC: Author.

American Psychiatric Association. (1994). *Diagnostic and statistical manual of mental disorders* (4th ed.). Washington, DC: Author.

American Psychiatric Association. (2000). *Diagnostic and statistical manual of mental disorders* (4th ed., text revision). Washington, DC: Author.

Anastasi, A., & Urbina, S. (1997). *Psychological testing* (7th ed.). Upper Saddle River, NJ: Prentice Hall.

Anderson, V., & Catroppa, C. (2005). Recovery of executive skills following paediatric traumatic brain injury (TBI): A 2 year follow-up. *Brain injury, 19*, 459–470.

Angold, A., Costello, E. J., Erkanli, A., & Worthman, C. M. (1999). Pubertal changes in hormone levels and depression in girls. *Psychological Medicine, 29*, 1043–1053.

Armengol, C., Kaplan, E., & Moes, E. (Eds.), (2001). *The consumer-oriented neuropsychological report.* Lutz, FL: Psychological Assessment Resources, Inc.

Ashwal, S., Holshouser, B., & Tong, K. (2006). Use of advanced neuroimaging techniques in the evaluation of pediatric traumatic brain injury. *Developmental Neuroscience, 28*, 309–326.

Atwood, T. (1998). *Asperger's syndrome.* London: Jessica Kingsley.

Baranek, G. T. (1999). Autism during infancy: A retrospective video analysis of sensory-motor and social behaviors at 9–12 months of age. *Journal of Autism and Developmental Disorders, 29*, 213–224.

Barkley, R. A. (1990, 1998, 2006). *Attention-deficit hyperactivity disorder: A handbook for diagnosis and treatment* (3rd ed.). New York: Guilford Press.

Barkley, R. A. (1996). Critical issues in research on attention. In G. R. Lyon & N. A. Krasnegor (Eds.), *Attention, memory, and executive function* (pp. 45–56). Baltimore: Brookes.

Barkley, R. A. (1997). Behavioral inhibition, sustained attention, and executive functions: Constructing a unifying theory of ADHD. *Psychological Bulletin, 12*, 65–94.

Barkley, R. A. (2004). Adolescents with ADHD: An overview of empirically based treatments. *Journal of Psychiatric Practice, 10*, 39–56.

Barkley, R. A., Fischer, M., Edelbrock, C., & Smallish, L. (1990). The adolescent outcome of hyperactive children diagnosed by research criteria: I. An 8-year prospective follow-up study. *Journal of the American Academy of Child & Adolescent Psychiatry, 29*, 546–557.

Baron, I. S. (2004). *Neuropsychological evaluation of the child.* New York: Oxford University Press.

Baron-Cohen, S. (1995). Mindblindness: An essay on autism and theories of mind. Cambridge, MA: MIT Press.

Baron-Cohen, S. (2001). Theory of mind and autism: A review. *International Review of Research in Mental Retardation, 23*, 169–184.

Baron-Cohen, S., Ring, H., Moriarty, J., Schmitz, B., Costa, D., & Eli, P. (1994). Recognition of mental state terms: Clinical findings in children with autism and a functional neuroimaging study of normal adults. *British Journal of Psychiatry, 165,* 640–649.

Barton, J., Hefter, R., Cherkasova, M., & Manoach, D. (2007). Investigations of face expertise in the social developmental disorders. *Neurology, 69,* 860–870.

Bavin, E. L., Wilson, P. H., Maruff, P., & Sleeman, F. (2005). Spatio-visual memory of children with specific impairment: Evidence for generalized processing problems. *International Journal of Language and Communication Disorders, 40,* 319–332.

Beaumont, R., and Newcombe, P. (2006) Theory of mind and central coherence in adults with high-functioning autism or Asperger syndrome, *Autism, 10,* 365–382.

Beery, K. E. (1982). *Developmental test of visual motor integration.* Cleveland, OH: Modern Curriculum Press.

Behrmann, M., Avidan, G., Leonard, G. L., Kimchi, R., Luna, B., Humphreys, K., et al. (2006). Configural processing in autism and its relationship to face processing. *Neuropsychologia, 44,* 110–129.

Beitchman, J. H., Hood, J., Rochon, J., & Peterson, M. (1989). Empirical classification of speech/language impairment in children. II. Behavioral characteristics. *Journal of the American Academy of Child and Adolescent Psychiatry, 28,* 118–123.

Beitchman, J. H., Wilson, B., Brownlie, E. B., Walters, H., & Lance, W. (1996). Long-term consistency in speech/language profiles. I: Developmental and academic outcomes. *Journal of the American Academy of Child and Adolescent Psychiatry, 35,* 804–814.

Beitchman, J. H., Wilson, B., Johnson, C., Atkinson, L., Young, A., Adlaf, E., et al. (2001). Fourteen-year follow-up of speech/language-impaired and control children: Psychiatric outcome. *Journal of the American Academy of Child & Adolescent Psychiatry, 40,* 75–82.

Belanger, H., Kretzmer, T., Yoash-Grantz, R., Pickett, T., & Tupler, L. (2009). Cognitive sequelae of blast-related versus other mechanisms of brain trauma. *Journal of the International Neuropsychological Society, 15,* 1-8.

Bellugi, U., Bihrle, A., Jernigan, T., Trauner, D., & Doherty, S. (1990). Neuropsychological, neurological, and neuroanatomical profile of Williams syndrome. *American Journal of Medical Genetics Supplement, 6,* 115–125.

Bellugi, U., Bihrle, A., Neville, H., Jernigan, T., & Doherty, S. (1992). Language, cognitive, & brain organization in a neurodevelopmental disorder. In M. R. Gunnar & C. A. Nelson, (Eds.), *Developmental neuroscience* (pp. 201–232). Hillsdale, NJ: Erlbaum.

Bellugi, U., Wang, P., & Jernigan, T. (1994). Williams syndrome: An unusual neuropsychological profile. In S. Broman & J. Grafman (Eds.), *Atypical Cognitive Deficits in Developmental Disorders: Implications for Brain Function.* Hillsdale, NJ: Erlbaum.

Benner, G., Nelson, J. R., Allor, J., Mooney, P., & Dai, T. (2008). Academic processing speed mediates the influence of both externalizing behavior and language skills on the academic skills of students with emotional disturbance. *Journal of Behavioral Education, 17,* 63–78.

Benton, A. L., Hamsher, K., Varney, N. R., & Spreen, O. (1983). *Contributions to neuropsychological assessment: A clinical manual.* New York: Oxford University Press.

Bernstein, J., & Waber, D. (1990). Developmental neuropsychological assessment: The systemic approach. In A. A. Boulton, G. B. Baker, & M. Hiscock (Eds.), *Neuromethods: Vol. 17. Neuropsychology* (pp. 311–371). Clifton, NJ: Humana Press.

Bertrand, J., Mars, A., Boyle, C., Bove, F., Yeargin-Allsopp, M., & Decoufle, P. (2001). Prevalence of autism in a United States population: The Brick Township, New Jersey, investigation. *Pediatrics, 108,* 1155–1161.

Biederman, J., Faraone, S. V., Keenan, K. (1992). Further evidence for family-genetic risk factors in attention deficit hyperactivity disorder. *Archives of General Psychiatry, 49,* 728–738.

Biederman, J., Newcorn, J., & Sprich, S. (1991). Comorbidity of attention deficit hyperactivity disorder with conduct, depressive, anxiety, and other disorders. *American Journal of Psychiatry, 148*, 564–577.

Bishop, D. V. M. (2006). Children's communication checklist (2nd. ed., U.S. edition). San Antonio, TX: Harcourt Assessment.

Bishop, D. V. M., Mayberry, M., Wong, D., Maley, A., Hill, W., & Hallmayer, J. (2004). Are phonological processing deficits part of the broad autism phenotype? *American Journal of Medical Genetics Part B (Neuropsychiatric Genetics), 128*, 54–60.

Bishop, D. V. M., & McArthur, G. M. (2005). Individual differences in auditory processing in specific language impairment: A follow-up study using event-related potentials and behavioural thresholds. *Cortex, 41*, 327–341.

Bishop, D. V. M., & Snowling, M. J. (2004). Developmental dyslexia and specific language impairment: Same or different? *Psychological Bulletin, 130*, 858–886.

Boehm, A. (1986). Boehm test of basic concepts - Revised. San Antonio, TX: The Psychological Corporation

Bölte, S., & Poustka, F. (2003). The recognition of facial affect in autistic and schizophrenic subjects and their first-degree relatives. *Psychological Medicine, 33*, 907–915

Bölte, S., & Poustka, F. (2006). The broader cognitive phenotype of autism in parents: How specific is the tendency for local processing and executive dysfunction? *Journal of Child Psychology and Psychiatry, 47*, 639–645.

Borger, N., & van der Meere, J. (2000). Visual behaviour of ADHD children during an attention test: An almost forgotten variable. *Journal of Child Psychology and Psychiatry, 41*, 525–532.

Boucher, J. (2003). Language development in autism. *International Congress Series, 1254*, 247–253.

Bourgoine E., & Wing, L. (1983). Identical triplets with Asperger's syndrome. *British Journal of Psychiatry, 126*, 261–265.

Bracken, B. A. (1992). The interpretation of tests. In M. Zeidner & R. Most (Eds.), *Psychological testing: An inside view* (pp.119–156). Palo Alto, CA: Consulting Psychologists Press.

Bracken, B. A. (2006a). Bracken basic concept scale-Third edition: Receptive. San Antonio, TX: Harcourt Assessment.

Bracken, B. A. (2006b). Bracken basic concept scale-Third edition: Expressive. San Antonio, TX: Harcourt Assessment.

Bradley, L. (1989). Predicting learning disabilities. In J. Dumont & H. Nakken (Eds.), *Neuropsychological foundations of learning disabilities: Vol. 2. Cognitive, social, and remedial aspects* (pp. 1–17). Amsterdam: Swets & Zeitlinger.

Brinton, B., Fujiki, M., & McKee, L. (1998). Negotiation skills of children with specific language impairment. *Journal of Speech, Language, and Hearing Research, 41*, 927–940.

Brookshire, B., Levin, H. S., Song, J., & Zhang, L. (2004). Components of executive function in typically developing and head-injured children. *Developmental Neuropsychology, 25*, 61–83.

Brown, T. E. (2001). *Brown attention-deficit disorder scales for children and adolescents.* San Antonio, TX: The Psychological Corporation.

Burlingame, E., Sussman, H. M., Gillam, R. B., & Hay, J. E. (2005). An investigation of speech perception in children with specific language impairment on a continuum of formant transition duration. *Journal of Speech, Language, and Hearing Research, 48*, 805–816.

Byrne, B., Fielding-Barnsley, R., & Ashley, L. (2000). Effects of phoneme identity training after six years: Outcome level distinguished from rate of response. *Journal of Educational Psychology, 92*, 659–667.

Cantwell, D. P., & Baker, L. (1991). *Psychiatric and Developmental Disorders in Children with Communication Disorders.* Washington, DC: American Psychiatric Press.

Capruso, D. X., & Levin, H. S. (1992). Cognitive impairment following closed head injury. *Neurologic Clinics, 10*, 879–893.

Carpenter, M., Pennington, B. F., & Rogers, S. J. (2001). Understanding of others' intentions in children with autism. *Journal of Autism and Developmental Disorders, 31,* 589–599.

Casey, R. J. (1996). Emotional competence in children with externalizing and internalizing disorders. In M. Lewis & M. W. Sullivan (Eds.), *Emotional development in atypical children* (pp. 161–183). Mahwah, NJ: Erlbaum.

Castelli, F. (2005). Understanding emotions from standardized facial expressions in autism and normal development. *Autism, 9,* 428–449.

Catroppa, C., Anderson, V., Morse, S., Haritou, F., & Rosenfeld, J. (2007). Children's attentional skills 5 years post-TBI. *Journal of Pediatric Psychology, 32*, 354–369.

Center for Disease Control and Prevention: Autism and Developmental Disabilities Monitoring Network (ADDM). (2009). *Autism spectrum disorders.* Washington, DC: Author.

Ceponiene, R., Lepisto, T., Shestakova, R., Vanhala, P. A., Naatanen, R., & Yaguchi, K. (2003). Speech-sound-selective auditory impairment in children with autism: They can perceive but do not attend. *Proceedings of the National Academy of Science USA, 100*, 5567–5572.

Chakrabarti, S., & Fombonne, E. (2005). Pervasive developmental disorders in preschool children: Confirmation of high prevalence. *American Journal of Psychiatry, 162,* 1133–1141.

Charman, T. (2003). Why is joint attention a pivotal skill in autism? *Philosophical Transactions of the Royal Society, London: Biological Sciences, 358*, 315–324.

Choudhury, N., & Benasich, A. A. (2003). A family aggregation study: The influence of family history and other risk factors on language development. *Journal of Speech, Language, and Hearing Research, 46,* 261–272.

Christensen, A. L. (1975). *Luria's neuropsychological investigation.* Copenhagen, Denmark: Munksgaard.

Christensen, A. L. (1984). The Luria method of examination of the brain-impaired patient. In P. E. Logue & J. M. Schear (Eds.), *Clinical neuropsychology: A multidisciplinary approach* (pp. 5–28). Springfield, IL: Thomas.

Church, C., Alisanski, S., & Amanullah, S. (2000). The social behavioral and academic experiences of children with Asperger Syndrome. *Focus on Autism and Other Developmental Disabilities, 15*, 12–20.

Coady, J. A., Kluender, K. R., & Evans, J. L. (2005). Categorical perception of speech by children with specific language impairments. *Journal of Speech, Language, and Hearing Research, 48,* 944–959.

Cohen, J. (1988). *Statistical power analysis for the behavioral sciences* (2nd ed.). Hillsdale, NJ: Lawrence Erlbaum Associates.

Cohen, M. J. (1997). Children's memory scale. San Antonio, TX: The Psychological Corporation.

Cohen, M. J., Ricci, C. A., Kibby, M. Y., & Edmonds, J. E. (2000). Developmental progression of clock face drawing in children. *Child Neuropsychology, 6,* 64–76.

Cohen, N. J., Menna, R., Vallance, D. D., Barwick, M. A., Im, N., & Horodezky, N. B. (1998). Language, social cognitive processing, and behavioral characteristics of psychiatrically disturbed children with previously identified and unsuspected language impairments. *Journal of Child Psychology and Psychiatry, 39,* 853–864.

Colarrusso, P., and Hamill, D. (1972). *Motor Free Visual Perception Test.* Novato, CA: Academic Therapy Publications.

Collins, M. W., Lovell, M. R., Iverson, G., Cantu, R., Maroon, J., & Field, M. (2002). Cumulative effects of concussion in high school athletes. *Neurosurgery, 51*, 1175–1181.

Conners, C. K. (2000). *Conners' Rating Scales–Revised Technical Manual.* North Tonawanda, New York: Multi Health Systems.

Cook, E. H., Jr. (1998). Genetics of autism. *Mental Retardation & Developmental Disabilities Research Reviews, 4,* 113–120.

Cope, N., Harold, D., Hill, G., Moskvina, V., Stevenson, J., Holmans, P., et al. (2005). Strong evidence that KIAA0319 on chromosome 6p is a susceptibility gene for developmental dyslexia. *American Journal of Human Genetics, 76,* 581–591.

Corbett, B., & Glidden, H. (2000). Processing affective stimuli in children with attention-deficit hyperactivity disorder. *Child Neuropsychology, 6,* 144–155.

Creusere, M., Alt, M., & Plante, E. (2004). Recognition of vocal and facial cues to affect in language-impaired and normally-developing preschoolers. *Journal of Communication Disorders, 37,* 5–20.

Crocker, L., & Algina, J. (1986). *Introduction to classical and modern test theory.* Fort Worth, TX: Harcourt Brace Jovanovich.

Dalal, R. H., & Loeb, D. F. (2005). Imitative production of regular past tense -ed by English-speaking children with specific language impairment. *International Journal of Language and Communication Disorders, 40,* 67–82.

Dawson, G., & Galpert, L. (1990). Mother's use of imitative play for facilitating social responsiveness and toy play in young autistic children. *Development and Psychology, 2,* 151–162.

Dawson, G., Webb, S. J., & McPartland, J. (2005). Understanding the nature of face processing impairment in autism: Insights from behavioral and electrophysiological studies. *Developmental Neuropsychology, 27,* 403–424.

Deevy, P., & Leonard, L. B. (2004). The comprehension of Wh questions in children with specific language impairment. *Journal of Speech, Language, and Hearing Research, 4,* 7802–7815.

Delis, D. C., Kaplan, E., & Kramer, J. H. (2001). Delis-Kaplan executive function system. San Antonio, TX: The Psychological Corporation.

Denckla, M. B. (1973). Development of speed in repetitive and successive finger-movements in normal children. *Developmental Medicine and Child Neurology, 15,* 635–645.

Denckla, M. B. (1985). Motor coordination in dyslexic children: Theoretical and clinical implications. In E H. Duffy & N. Geschwind (Eds.), *Dyslexia: A neuroscientific approach to clinical evaluation* (pp. 187–195). Boston: Little, Brown.

Denckla, M. B., & Rudel, R. (1976). Rapid "automatized" naming (R.A.N.): Dyslexia differentiated from other learning disabilities. *Neuropsychologia, 14,* 471–479.

Dennis, M., Fletcher, J. M., Rogers, I., Hetherinzu, F. D. J. (2002). Object-based and action-based in visual perception children with spina bifida and hydrocephalus. *International Neuropsychological Society, 8,* 95–106.

De Renzi, E., & Faglioni, P. (1978). Normative data and screening power of a shortened version of the Token Test. *Cortex, 14,* 41–49.

Dick, F., Wulfeck B., Krupa-Kwiatkowski, M., & Bates, E. (2004). The development of complex sentence interpretation in typically developing children compared with children with specific language impairments or early focal unilateral focal lesions. *Developmental Science, 7,* 360–377.

Dimitrovsky, L., Spector, H., Levy-Shiff, R., & Vakil, E. (1998). Interpretation of facial expressions of affect in children with learning disabilities with verbal or nonverbal deficits. *Journal of Learning Disabilities, 31,* 286–292.

Doehring, D. G. (1985). Reading disability subtypes: Interaction of reading and nonreading deficits. In B. P. Rourke (Ed.), *Neuropsychology of learning disabilities* (pp. 372–406). New York: Guilford Press.

Downs, A., & Smith, T. (2004). Emotional understanding, cooperation, and social behavior in high-functioning children with autism. *Journal of Autism and Developmental Disorders, 34,* 625–635.

Drake, W. (1968). Clinical and pathological findings in a child with a developmental learning disability. *Journal of Learning Disabilities, 1,* 468–475.

Duggal, H. S. (2007). Ziprasidone for maladaptive behavior and attention-deficit/hyperactivity disorder symptoms in autistic disorder. *Journal of Child and Adolescent Psychopharmacology, 2,* 261–263.

Dyck, M. J., Ferguson, K., & Shochet, I. M. (2001). Do autism spectrum disorders differ from each other and from non-spectrum disorders on emotion recognition tests? *European Child & Adolescent Psychiatry, 10,* 105–116.

Edwards, J., & Lahey, M. (1996). Auditory lexical decisions of children with specific language impairment. *Journal of Speech and Hearing Research, 39,* 1263–1273.

Elliott, C. D. (2007). *Differential ability scales–Second edition.* San Antonio, TX: Harcourt Assessment.

Evans, J. L., & MacWhinney, B. (1999). Sentence processing strategies in children with expressive and expressive-receptive specific language impairments. *International Journal of Language and Communication Disorders, 34,* 117–134.

Ewing-Cobbs, L., Barnes, M., Fletcher, J., Levin, H., Swank, P., & Song J. (2005). Modeling of longitudinal academic achievement scores after pediatric traumatic brain injury. *Developmental Neuropsychology, 25,* 107–133.

Ewing-Cobbs, L., Prasad, M., Landry, S., Kramer, L., & DeLeon, R. (2004). Executive functions following traumatic brain injury in young children: A preliminary analysis. *Developmental Neuropsychology, 26,* 487–512.

Farmer, J. E., & Deidrick, K. M. (2006). Introduction to childhood disability. In J. E. Farmer, J. Donders, & S. Warschausky (Eds.), *Treating neurodevelopmental disabilities: Clinical research and practice* (pp. 3–20). New York: Guilford Press.

Farmer, J. E., Kanne, S. M., Grissom, M. O., & Kemp, S. (2009). Pediatric neuropsychology in medical rehabilitation settings. In R. Frank & T. R. Elliott (Eds.), *Handbook of rehabilitation psychology* (2nd ed.), (pp. 315–328). Washington, DC: American Psychological Association.

Fay, W. & Schuler, A. (1980). *Emerging language in autistic children.* Baltimore, MD: University Park Press.

Fazio, B. B. (1998). The effect of presentation rate on serial memory in young children with specific language impairment. *Journal of Speech, Language, and Hearing Research, 41,* 1375–1383.

Field, M., Collins, M., Lovell, M., & Maroon, J. (2003). A comparison of high school and collegiate athletes. *Journal of Pediatrics, 142,* 546–553.

Fine, J., Bartolucci, G., Szatmari, P., & Ginsberg, G. (1994). Cohesive discourse in pervasive developmental disorders. *Journal of Autism and Developmental Disorders, 24,* 315– 329.

Flax, J. F., Realpe-Bonilla, T., Hirsch, L. S., Brzustowicz, L. M., Bartlett, C. W., & Tallal, P. (2003). Specific language impairment in families: Evidence for co-occurrence with reading impairments. *Journal of Speech, Language, and Hearing Research, 46,* 530–543.

Fletcher, J. (2009). Dyslexia: The evolution of a scientific concept. *Journal of the International Neuropsychological Society, 15,* 501–508.

Flynn, J. R. (1984). The mean IQ of Americans: Massive gains 1932 to 1978. *Psychological Bulletin, 95,* 29–51.

Flynn, J. R. (1987). Massive IQ gains in 14 nations: What IQ tests really measure. *Psychological Bulletin, 101,* 171–191.

Fombonne, E. (1999). The epidemiology of autism: A review. *Psychological Medicine, 29,* 769–786.

Fraser, J., & Conti-Ramsden, G. (2008). Contribution of phonological and broader language skills to literacy. *International Journal of Language and Communication Disorder, 43,* 552–569.

Frazier, J. A., Doyle, R., Chiu, S., Coyle, J. T. (2002) Treating a child with Asperger's disorder and comorbid bipolar disorder. *American Journal of Psychiatry, 159,* 13–21.

Freedman, M., Leach, L., Kaplan, F., Winocur, G., Shulman, K., & Delis, D. C. (1994). Clock drawing: A neuro-psychological analysis. New York: Oxford University Press.

Freitag, C. M., Kleser, C., Schneider, M., & von Gontard, A. (2007). Quantitative assessment of neuromotor function in adolescents with high functioning autism and Asperger syndrome. *Journal of Autism and Developmental Disorders, 37,* 948–959.

Gadow, K., Sprafkin, J., & Nolan, E. (2001). DSM–IV symptoms in community and clinic preschools. *Journal of American Academy of Child and Adolescent Psychiatry, 40,* 1383–1392.

Galaburda, A., & Eidelberg, D. (1982). Symmetry and asymmetry in the human posterior thalamus: II. Thalamic lesions in a case of developmental dyslexia: A case study. *Annals of Neurology, 39,* 333–336.

Galaburda, A., & Kemper, T. (1979). Cytoarchitectonic abnormalities in developmental dyslexia: A case study. *Annals of Neurology, 6,* 94–100.

Galaburda, A., Sherman, G., Rosen, G., Aboitiz, E., & Geschwind, N. (1985). Developmental dyslexia: Four consecutive cases with cortical anomalies. *Annals of Neurology, 18,* 222–233.

Geary, D. (1993). Mathematical disabilities: Cognitive, neuropsychological, and genetic components. *Psychological Bulletin, 114,* 345–362.

Geary, D. (2000). Math disorders: An overview for educators. *Perspectives, 26,* 6–9.

Geary, D. (2003). Learning disabilities in arithmetic: Problem-solving differences and cognitive deficits. In H. L. Swanson, K. Harris, & S. Graham (Eds.), *Handbook of learning disabilities.* New York: Guilford Press.

Geary, D., Brown, S., & Samaranayake, V. (1991). Cognitive addition: A short longitudinal study of strategy choice and speed-of-processing differences in normal and mathematically disabled children. *Developmental Psychology, 27,* 787–797.

Geary, D. C., Hamson, C. O., & Hoard, M. K. (2000). Numerical and arithmetical cognition: A longitudinal study of process and concept deficits in children with learning disability. *Journal of Experimental Child Psychology, 77,* 236–263.

Geary, D., & Hoard, M. K. (2001). Numerical and arithmetical deficits in learning-disabled-children: Relation to dyscalculia and dyslexia. *Aphasiology, 15,* 635–647.

Gepner, B., Deruelle, C., & Grynfeltt, S. (2001). Motion and emotion: A novel approach to the study of face processing by young autistic children. *Journal of Autism and Developmental Disorders, 31,* 37–45.

Georgiou, G., Parrila, R., & Kirby, J. (2006). Rapid naming speed components and early reading acquisition. *Scientific Studies of Reading, 10,* 199–220.

Geurts H. M., Verte, S., Oosterlaan, J., Roeyers, H., & Sergeant, J. A. (2004). How specific are executive functioning deficits in attention deficit hyperactivity disorder and autism? *Journal of Child Psychology and Psychiatry, 45,* 836–854.

Ghaziuddin, M. (2002). Asperger Syndrome: Associated Psychiatric and Medical Conditions. *Focus on Autism and Other Developmental Disabilities, 17,* 3, 138-144.

Ghaziuddin, M., & Gerstein, L. (1996). Pedantic speaking style differentiates Asperger's syndrome from high-functioning autism. *Journal of Autism and Developmental Disorders, 26,* 585–595.

Ghaziuddin, M., & Tsai, L. (1991). Depression in autistic disorder. *The British Journal of Psychiatry, 159,* 721–723.

Ghaziuddin, M., Weidmer-Mikhail, E., & Ghaziuddin, N. (1998). Comorbidity of Asperger syndrome: A preliminary report. *Journal of Intellectual Disability Research, 42,* 279–283.

Giedd, J., Blumenthal, J., Jeffries, N., Castellanos, F., Liu, H., Zijdenbos, A., et al. (1999). Brain development during childhood and adolescence: A longitudinal MRI study. *Nature Neuroscience, 2,* 861–863.

Gilger, J. W., Pennington, B. F., & DeFries, J. C. (1992). A twin study of the etiology of co-morbidity: Attention-deficit hyperactivity disorder and dyslexia. *Journal of the American Academy of Child and Adolescent Psychiatry, 31,* 343–348.

Gillberg, C. (1984). Infantile autism and other childhood psychoses in a Swedish urban region: Epidemiological aspects. *Journal of Child Psychology & Psychiatry, 25,* 35–43.

Gillberg, C. (2001). Asperger syndrome and high-functioning autism. *The British Journal of Psychiatry, 179,* 375–375.

Gillberg, C. (2003). Deficits in attention, motor control, and perception: A brief review. *Archives of Disease in Children, 88,* 904–910.

Gillott, A., Furniss, F., & Walter, A. (2001). Anxiety in high-functioning children with autism. *Autism, 5,* 277–286.

Gilotty, L., Kenworthy, L., Black, D., Wagner, A., & Sirian, L. (2002). Adaptive skills and executive functioning in Asperger's syndrome and autism. *Child Neuropsychology, 8,* 90–101.

Giovanardi-Rossi, P., Posar, A., & Parmeggiani, A. (2000). Epilepsy in adolescents and young adults with autistic disorder. *Brain & Development, 22,* 102–106.

Ginsburg, H., (1997). Mathematics learning disabilities: A view from developmental psychology. *Journal of Learning Disabilities, 30,* 20–33.

Giza, C. C. (2006). Is being plastic fantastic? Mechanisms of altered plasticity after developmental traumatic brain injury. *Developmental Neuroscience, 28,* 364–379.

Glang, A., Tyler, J., Pearson, S., Todis, B., & Morvant, M. (2004). Improving educational services for students with TBI through statewide resource teams. *NeuroRehabilitation, 19,* 219–231.

Gray, S. (2003). Diagnostic accuracy and test–retest reliability of nonword repetition and digit span tasks administered to preschool children with specific language impairment. *Journal of Communication Disorders, 36,* 129–151.

Greenspan, S. I. (2001). *The developmental basis of the psychotherapeutic process.* New York: Marcel Dekker, Inc.

Grigorenko, E., & Naples, A. (Eds.). (2007). *Single-word reading: Behavioral and biological perspectives.* New York: CRC Press.

Gross, T. F. (2004). The perception of four basic emotions in human and nonhuman faces by children with autism and other developmental disorders. *Journal of Abnormal Child Psychology, 32,* 469–480.

Gross-Tsur, V., Manor, O., & Shalev, R. S. (1996). Developmental dyscalculia: Prevalence and demographic features. *Developmental Medicine and Child Neurology, 38,* 25–33.

Hale, C., & Tager-Flusberg, H. (2005). Social communication in children with autism: The relationship between theory of mind and discourse development. *Autism, 9,* 157–178.

Hanich, L. B., Jordan, N. C., Kaplan, D., & Dick, J. (2001). Performance across different areas of mathematical cognition in children with learning difficulties. *Journal of Educational Psychology, 93,* 615–626.

Hansson, K., Forsberg, J., Lofqvist, A., Maki-Torkko, E., & Sahlen, B. (2004). Working memory and novel word learning in children with hearing impairment and children with specific language impairment. *International Journal of Language and Communication Disorders, 39,* 401–422.

Happé, F., Booth, R., Charlton, R., & Hughes, C. (2006). Executive function deficits in autism spectrum disorders and attention-deficit/hyperactivity disorder: Examining profiles across domains and ages. *Brain and Cognition, 61,* 25–39.

Happé, F., & Frith, U. (2006). The weak coherence account: Detail-focused cognitive style in autism spectrum disorders. *Journal of Autism Developmental Disorders, 36,* 5–25.

Harcourt Assessment. (2005). *Wechsler Individual Achievement Test–Second edition.* San Antonio, TX: Author.

Hardan, A., Kilpatrick, M., Keshavan, M., & Minshew, N. (2003). Motor performance and anatomic magnetic resonance imaging (MRI) of the basal ganglia in autism. *Journal of Child Neurology, 18*, 317–324.

Harrison, P. L., & Oakland, T. (2003). Adaptive behavior assessment system. Second edition. San Antonio, TX: The Psychological Corporation.

Hartlage, L. C., & Long, C. J. (1998). Development of neuropsychology as a professional psychological specialty. In C. R. Reynolds and E. Fletcher-Janzen (Eds.), *Handbook of Clinical Child Psychology* (2nd edition), (pp 3–16). New York: Plenum Press.

Heerey, E., Keltner, D., & Capps, L. (2003). Making sense of self-conscious emotion: Linking theory of mind and emotion in children with autism. *Emotion, 3*, 394–400.

Hern, K., & Hynd, G. W. (1992). Clinical differentiation of the attention deficit disorder subtypes: Do sensorimotor deficits characterize children with ADD/WO? *Archives of Clinical Neuropsychology, 7*, 77-83.

Hick, R., Botting, N., & Conti-Ramsden, G. (2005). Cognitive abilities in children with specific language impairment: Consideration of visuo-spatial skills. *International Journal of Language and Communication Disorders, 40*, 137–149.

Hill, E. L. (2004). Executive dysfunction in autism. *Trends in Cognitive Science, 8*, 26–32.

Hill, E. L., & Bird, C. (2006). Executive processes in Asperger syndrome: Patterns of performance in a multiple case series. *Neuropsychologia, 44*, 2822–2835.

Hoffman, L. M., & R. B. Gillam. (2004). Verbal and spatial information processing constraints in children with specific language impairment. *Journal of Speech, Language, and Hearing Research, 47*, 114–125.

Holtmann, M., Bölte, S., & Poustka, F. (2005). ADHD, Asperger syndrome, and high-functioning Autism. *Journal of the American Academy of Child & Adolescent Psychiatry, 44*, 11, 1101.

Howell, R., Sidorenko, E., & Jurica, J. (1987). The effects of computer use on the acquisition of multiplication facts by a student with learning disabilities. *Journal of Learning Disabilities, 20*, 336–341.

Huang-Pollock, C., & Nigg, J. (2003). Searching for the attention deficit in attention deficit hyperactivity disorder: The case of visuospatial orienting. *Clinical Psychology Review, 23*, 6, 801–830.

Hynd, G., & Hynd, C. (1984). Dyslexia: Neuroanatomical/neurolinguistic perspectives. *Reading Research Quarterly, 4*, 482–498.

Individuals with Disabilities Education Act Amendments of 1997, 20 U.S.C. 1431 *et seq.* (Fed. Reg. 34, 1997).

Individuals with Disabilities Education Improvement Act of 2004, Pub. L. No. 108–446, *U.S. Statutes at Large 118* (2004): 2647.

International Dyslexia Association (2008). *Fact sheet: Definition of dyslexia*. Baltimore, MD.

Iuculano, T., Tang, J., Hall, C. W. B., & Butterworth, B. (2008). Core information processing deficits in developmental dyscalculia and low numeracy. *Developmental Science, 11*(6), 895-895.

Ivnik, R. J., Smith, G. E., Cerhan, J. H., Boeve, B. F., Tangalos, E. G., & Petersen, R. C. (2001). Understanding the diagnostic capabilities of cognitive tests. *The Clinical Neuropsychologist, 15*, 114–124.

Iwanaga, R., Ozawa, H., Kawasaki, C., & Tsuchida, R. (2006). Characteristics of the sensory-motor, verbal, and cognitive abilities of preschool boys with attention deficit/hyperactivity disorder combined type. *Psychiatry Clinical Neuroscience, 60*, 37–45.

Jansiewicz, E. M., Goldberg, M. C., Newschaffer, C. J., Denckla, M. B., Landa, R., & Mostofsky, S. H. (2006). Motor signs distinguish children with high functioning autism and Asperger's syndrome from controls. *Journal of Autism and Developmental Disorders, 36*, 613–621.

Jolliffe, T., & Baron-Cohen, S. (1999). The strange stories test: A replication with high-functioning adults with autism or Asperger's syndrome. *Journal of Autism and Developmental Disorders, 29,* 395–406.

Jones, K., & Smith, D. (1975). The Williams elfin facies syndrome: A new perspective. *Journal of Pediatrics, 86,* 718–723.

Jones, M., Branigan, H., & Kelly, M. L. (2009). Dyslexic and nondyslexic reading fluency: Rapid automatized naming and the importance of continuous lists. *Psychonomic Bulletin & Review, 16,* 567–572.

Jones, V., & Prior, M. (1985). Motor imitation abilities and neurological signs in autistic children. *Journal of Autism and Developmental Disorders, 15,* 37–46.

Jonsdottir, S., Bouma, A., Sergeant, J. A., & Scherder, E. J. (2005). The impact of specific language impairment on working memory in children with ADHD combined subtype. *Archives of Clinical Neuropsychology, 20,* 443–456.

Jordan, N. C., & Montani, T. O. (1997). Cognitive arithmetic and problem solving: A comparison of children with specific and general mathematics difficulties. *Journal of Learning Disabilities, 30,* 624–634.

Joseph, R. M., McGrath, L. M., & Tager-Flusberg, H. (2005). Executive dysfunction and its relation to language ability in verbal school-age children with autism. *Developmental Neuropsychology, 27,* 361–378.

Kadesjö, B., & Gillberg, C. (2000). Tourette's disorder: Epidemiology and comorbidity in primary school children. *Journal of the American Academy of Child and Adolescent Psychiatry, 39,* 548–555.

Kaland, N., Moeller-Nielsen, A., Callesen, K., Mortenson, E., Gottlieb, D., & Smith, L. (2002). A new, advanced test of theory of mind: Evidence from children with autism. *Journal of Child Psychology & Psychiatry, 43,* 517–528.

Kanner, L. (1943). Autistic disturbance of affective contact. *Nervous Child, 2,* 217–250.

Kaplan, E. (1988). A process approach to neuropsychological assessment. In T. Boll & B. K. Bryant (Eds.), *Clinical neuropsychology and brain function: Research, measurement, and practice* (pp. 129–167). Washington, DC: American Psychological Association.

Kätsyri J., Saalasti, S., Tiippana, K., von Wendt, L., & Sama, M. (2008) Impaired recognition of facial emotions from low-spatial frequencies in Asperger syndrome. *Neuropsychologia, 46*(7):1888–1897.

Kaufman, A., & Lichtenberger, E. (1999). *The Essentials of WAIS-III assessment.* New York: Wiley.

Kemp, S., Kirk, U., & Korkman, M. (2001). *Essentials of NEPSY.* Hoboken, NJ: Wiley.

Kerr, S., & Durkin, K. (2004). Understanding of thought bubbles as mental representations in children with autism: Implications for theory of mind. *Journal of Autism & Developmental Disorders, 34,* 637–648.

Kim, J., Szatmari, P., Bryson, S., Streiner, D., & Wilson, F. (2000). The prevalence of anxiety and mood problems among children with autism and asperger syndrome. *Autism, 4*(2), 117–132.

Klee, T., Stokes, S. F, Wong, A. M. Y., Fletcher, P., & Gavin, W. I. (2004). Utterance length and lexical diversity in Cantonese–speaking children with and without specific language impairment. *Journal of Speech, Language, and Hearing Research, 47,* 1396–1410.

Kleffner, F., & Landau, W. (2009). The Landau-Kleffner syndrome. *Epilepsia, 50*(suppl 7:3). Witchita, KS.

Kleinhans, N., Akshoomoff, N., & Delis, D. C. (2005). Executive functions in autism and Asperger's Disorder: Flexibility, fluency, and inhibition. *Special issue: Autistic Spectrum Disorders. Developmental Neuropsychology, 27,* 379–402.

Klenberg, L., Korkman, M., & Lahti-Nuuttila, P. (2001). Differential development of attention and executive functions in 3- to 12-year-old Finnish children. *Developmental Neuropsychology, 20,* 407–428.

Klin, A., Jones, W., Schultz, R., Volkmar, F., & Cohen, D. (2002). Defining and quantifying social phenotype in autism. *Archives of General Psychiatry, 59,* 809–816.

Klin, A., Volkmar, F. R., Sparrow, S. S., Cicchetti, D. V., & Rourke, B. P. (1995). Validity and neuropsychological characterization of Asperger syndrome: Convergence with nonverbal learning disabilities syndrome. *Journal of Child Psychology & Psychiatry, 36,* 1127–1140.

Knox, E., & Conti-Ramsden, G. (2003). Bullying risks of 11-year-old children with specific language impairment (SLI): Does school placement matter? *International Journal of Language and Communication Disorders, 38,* 1–12.

Korkman, M. (1980). *NEPS. Lasten neuropsykologinen tutkimus* [NEPS. Neuropsychological assessment of children]. Helsinki, Finland: Psykologien Kustannus Oy.

Korkman, M. (1988a). *NEPS. Lasten neuropsykologinen turkimus Uudistettu versio.* [NEPSY. Neuropsychological assessment of children. Rev. ed.]. Helsinki, Finland: Psykologien Kustannus Oy.

Korkman, M. (1988b). NEPSY. A proposed neuropsychological test battery for young developmentally disabled children: Theory and evaluation (Academic dissertation, University of Helsinki, 1988).

Korkman, M. (1988c). NEPSY—An adaptation of Luria 's investigation for young children. *The Clinical Neuropsychologist, 2,* 375–392.

Korkman, M. (1990). *NEPSY Neuropsykologisk undersokning: 4–7 år.* Svensk version [NEPSY. Neuropsychological assessment: 4–7 years. Swedish version]. Stockholm: Psykologi förlaget.

Korkman, M. (1993). *NEPSY Neuropsykologisk undersogelse: 4–7 ar.* Dansk vejleding [NEPSY. Neuropsychological assessment: 4–7 years. Danish manual]. (K. Holm, K. Fransden, J. Jordal, & A. Trillingsgaard, Trans.). Denmark: Dansk Psykologisk Forlag.

Korkman, M. (1999). Applying Luria's diagnostic principles in the neuropsychological asessment of children. *Neuropsychology Review, 9,* 89–105.

Korkman, M., Mikkola, K., Ritari, N., Tommiska, V., Salokorpi, T., & Fellman, V., for the Finnish ELBW cohort study group (2008). Neurocognitive test profiles of extremely low birth weight five-year-old children differ according to neurological abnormalities. *Developmental Neuropsycholology, 33*(5), 637-655.

Korkman, M (2000). NEPSY. Neuropsykologisk bedömning 3:0—12:11 år. Handbok (NEPSY Manual in Swedish). Stockholm, Sweden: Psykologiförlaget.

Korkman, M., Kemp, S. L., & Kirk, U. (2001a). Effects of age on neurocognitive measures of children ages 5 to 12: A cross-sectional study on 800 children from the U.S.A. *Developmental Neuropsychology, 20,* 331–354.

Korkman, M., Kemp, S. L., & Kirk, U. (2001b). Developmental assessment of neuropsychological function with the aid of the NEPSY. In A. S. Kaufman & N. L. Kaufman (Eds.), *Specific learning disabilities and difficulties in children and adolescents: Psychological assessment and evaluation.* New York: Cambridge University Press.

Korkman, M., Kirk, U., & Kemp, S. L. (1997). *NEPSY. Lasten neuropsykologinen tutkimus* [NEPSY: A developmental neuropsychological assessment]. Helsinki, Finland: Psykologien kustannus.

Korkman, M., Kirk, U., & Kemp, S. L. (1998). *NEPSY. A developmental neuropsychological assessment.* San Antonio, TX: The Psychological Corp.

Korkman, M., Kirk, U., & Kemp, S. L. (2000). *NEPSY. Neuropsykologisk bedömning 3:0—12:11 år.* Administreringsanvisningar [NEPSY-II validity studies and interpretation rules in Swedish]. Stockholm, Sweden: Psykologiförlaget, 65.

Korkman, M., Kirk, U., & Kemp, S. L. (2007). *NEPSY-II.* San Antonio, TX: The Psychological Corporation.

Korkman, M., Kirk, U., & Kemp, S. L. (2008). *NEPSY II—Lasten neuropsykologinen tutkimus.* Helsinki, Finland: Psykologien kustannus.

Korkman, M., & Pesonen, A. E. (1994). A comparison of neuropsychological test profiles of children with attention deficit-hyperactivity disorder and/or learning disorder. *Journal of Learning Disabilities, 27,* 383–392.

Knox, E., & Conti-Ramsden, G. (2003). Bullying risks of 11-year-old children with specific language impairment (SLI): Does school placement matter? *International Journal of Language and Communication Disorders, 38,* 1–12.

Lahey, M., & Edwards, J. (1996). Why do children with specific language impairment name pictures more slowly than their peers? *Journal of Speech and Hearing Research, 39,* 1081–1091.

Lahey, B. B., McBurnett, K., & Loeber, R. (2000). Are attention deficit/hyperactivity disorder and oppositional defiant disorder developmental precursors to conduct disorder? In A. J. Sameroff, M. Lewis, & S. M. Miller (Eds.), *Handbook of Developmental Psychopathology,* 2nd ed. (pp. 431–446). New York: Plenum.

Lahey, B., Schwab-Stone, M., Goodman, S., Waldman, I., Canino, G., Rathouz, P., et al. (2000). Age and gender differences in oppositional behavior and conduct problems: A cross-sectional household study of middle childhood and adolescence. *Journal of Abnormal Psychology, 109,* 488–503.

Landau, W. M., & Kleffner, F. R. (1957). Syndromes of acquired aphasia with convulsive disorder in children. *Neurology, 7,* 523–530.

Langlois J. A., Rutland-Brown, W., & Thomas K. E. (2004). *Traumatic brain injury in the United States: Emergency department visits, hospitalizations, and deaths.* Atlanta, GA: Dept. of Health and Human Services (U.S.), Centers for Disease Control and Prevention, National Center for Injury Prevention and Control.

Leonard, L. B. (1998). *Children with specific language impairment.* Cambridge, MA: MIT Press.

Levin, H. S., Culhane, K. A., Mendelsohn, D., Lilly, M. A., Bruce, D., Fletcher, J., et al. (1993). Cognition in relation to magnetic resonance imaging in head-injured children and adolescents. *Archives of Neurology, 50,* 897–905.

Lewy, A. L., & Dawson, G. (1992). Social stimulation and joint attention in young autistic children. *Journal of Abnormal Child Psychology, 20,* 555–566.

Li, H., Rosenthal, R., & Rubin, D. B. (1996). Reliability of measurement in psychology: From Spearman-Brown to maximal reliability. *Psychological Methods, 1,* 98–107.

Light, J. G., & DeFries, J. C. (1995). Comorbidity of reading and mathematics disabilities: Genetic and environmental etiologies. *Journal of Learning Disabilities, 28,* 96–106.

Lovegrove, W. (1994). Visual deficits in dyslexia: Evidence and implications. In A. Fawcett & R. Nicolson (Eds.), *Dyslexia in children: Multidisciplinary perspectives* (pp. 113–135). New York: Harvester Wheatsheaf.

Livingstone, M., Rosen, G., Drislane, F., & Galaburda, A. (1991). Physiological and anatomical evidence for a magnocellular defect in developmental dyslexia. *Proceedings of the National Academy of Science USA, 88,* 7943–7947.

Loring, D. (Ed.) (1999). *INS Dictionary of Neuropsychology.* New York: Oxford University Press.

Luciana, M., & Nelson, C. A. (1998). The functional emergence of prefrontally-guided working memory systems in four- to eight-year-old children. *Neuropsychologia, 36,* 273–293.

Lundberg, I., & Hoien, T. (2001). Dyslexia and phonology. In A. Fawcett (Ed.), *Theory and good practice* (pp. 109–123). London: Whurr Publishers.

Luria, A. R. (1966). *The working brain.* New York: Penguin Press.

Luria, A. R. (1973). *The working brain: An introduction to neuropsychology* (B. Haigh, Trans.). London: Penguin.

Luria, A. R. (1980). *Higher cortical functions in man* (2nd ed.) (B. Haigh, Trans.). New York: Basic Books. (Original work published 1962.)

Lyon, G. R., Shaywitz, S. E., & Shaywitz, B. A. (2003). Defining dyslexia, comorbidity, teachers' knowledge of language and reading: A definition of dyslexia. *Annals of Dyslexia, 53,* 1–14.

Magnusson, D. (1967). *Test theory.* Reading, MA: Addison-Wesley.

Mandelbaum, D. E., Stevens, M., Rosenberg, E., Wiznitzer, M., Steinschneider, M., Filipek, P., et al. (2006). Sensorimotor performance in school-age children with autism, developmental language disorder, or low IQ. *Developmental Medicine and Child Neurology, 48,* 33–39.

Mangeot, S., Armstrong, K., Colvin, A. N., Yeates, K. O., & Taylor, H. G. (2002). Long-term executive function deficits in children with traumatic brain injuries: Assessment using the Behavior Rating Inventory of Executive Function (BRIEF). *Child Neuropsychology, 14,* 271–284.

Marinellie, S. A. (2004). Complex syntax used by school-age children with specific language impairment (SLI) in child–adult conversation. *Journal of Communication Disorders, 37,* 517–533.

Martinussen, R., Hayden, J., Hogg-Johnson, S., & Tannock, R. (2005). A meta-analysis of WM with attention-deficit/hyperactivity disorder. *Journal of the American Academy of Child and Adolescent Psychiatry, 44,* 377–384.

Marton, K., Abramoff, B., & Rosenzweig, S. (2005). Social cognition and language in children with specific language disorders. *Journal of Communication Disorders, 48,* 143–162.

Marton, K., & Schwartz, R. G. (2003). Working memory capacity and language processes in children with specific language impairment. *Journal of Speech, Language, and Hearing, 46,* 1138–1153.

Mason, D., Humphreys, G., & Kent, L. (2003). Exploring selective attention in ADHD: Visual search through space and time. *Journal of Child Psychology & Psychiatry, 44,* 1–20.

Matser, J. T., Kessels, A. G., Lezak, M. D., Jordan, B. D., & Troopst, J. (1999). Neuropsychological impairment in amateur soccer players. *Journal of the American Medical Association, 282,* 971–973.

Max Jeffrey, E., Lansing, A., Koele, S., Castillo, C., Bokura, H., Schachar, R., et al. (2004). Attention deficit hyperactivity disorder in children and adolescents following traumatic brain injury. *Developmental Neuropsychology, 25,* 159–77.

Mayes, S., & Calhoun, S. (2003a). Ability profiles in children with autism: Influence in age and I.Q. *Autism, 7,* 65–80.

Mayes, S., & Calhoun, S. (2003b). Analysis of WISC-III, Stanford-Binet-IV, and academic achievement test scores in children with autism. *Journal of Autism and Development Disorder, 33,* 329–341.

Mazzocco, M. (2001). Math learning disability and Math LD subtypes. *Journal of Learning Disabilities, 34,* 520–533.

Mazzocco, M., & Myers, G. (2003). Complexities in identifying and defining mathematics learning disability in the primary school-age years. *Annals of Dyslexia, 53,* 218–253.

McArthur, G. M., & Bishop, D. V. (2004). Frequency discrimination deficits in people with specific language impairment: Reliability, validity, and linguistic correlates. *Journal of Speech, Language, and Hearing Research, 47,* 527–541.

McCarthy, R., & Warrington, E. (1990). *Cognitive neuropsychology: Clinical Introduction.* San Diego: Academic Press.

McGrew, K., & Murphy, S. (1995). Uniqueness and general factor characteristics of the Woodcock-Johnson Tests of Cognitive Ability-Revised. *Journal of School Psychology, 33,* 235-245.

Meng, H., Smith, S. D., Hager, K., Held, M., Liu, J., Olson, R. K., et al. (2005). DCDC2 is associated with reading disability and modulates neuronal development in the brain. *Proceedings of the National Academy of Sciences of the United States of America, 102,* 17053–17058.

Mesibov, G., Klinger, L., & Adams, L. (1997). *Autism: Understanding the disorder.* New York: Kluwer Academic/Plenum.

Mikkola, K., Ritari, N., Tommiska, V., Salokorpi, T., Lehtonen, L., Tammela, O., et al. (2005). Neurodevelopmental outcome at 5 years of age of a national cohort of extremely low birth weight infants who were born in 1996–1997. *Pediatrics, 116,* 1391–1400.

Miller, C. A. (2001). False belief understanding in children with specific language impairment. *Journal of Communication Disorders, 34,* 73–86.

Miller, C. A. (2004). False belief and sentence complement performance in children with specific language impairment. *International Journal of Language and Communication Disorders, 39,* 191–213.

Miller, C., Kail, R., Leonard, L. B., & Tomblin, J. (2001). Speed of processing in children with specific language impairment. *Journal of Speech, Language, and Hearing Research, 44,* 416–433.

Milsom, A., & Glanville, J. (2009). Factors mediating the relationship between social skills and academic grades in a sample of students diagnosed with learning disabilities or emotional disturbance. *Remedial and Special Education.,* 0: 0741932508327460v1.

Minshew, N. J., & Goldstein, G. (1998). Autism as a complex disorder of information-processing. *Mental Retardation and Developmental Disabilities Research Reviews, 4,* 129–136.

Minshew N. J., Goldstein G. (2001). The pattern of intact and impaired memory functions in autism. *Journal of Child Psychology and Psychiatry and Allied Disciplines, 42,* 1095–1101.

Minshew, N. J., Johnson, C., & Luna, B. (2001). The cognitive and neural basis of autism: A disorder of complex information-processing and dysfunction of neocortical systems. *International Review of Research in Mental Retardation, 23,* 111–138.

Mirsky, A. F. (1996). Disorders of attention: A neuropsychological perspective. In G. R. Lyon & N. A. Krasnegor (Eds.), *Attention, memory, and executive function* (pp. 71–95). Baltimore: Brookes.

Mobbs, D., Garrett, A., Menon, V., Rose, F., Bellugi, U., & Reiss, A (2004). Anomalous brain activation during face and gaze processing in Williams syndrome. *Neurology, 62,* 2070–2076.

Montgomery, J. (2003). Working memory and comprehension in children with specific language impairment: What we know so far. *Journal of Communication Disorders, 36,* 221–231.

Mortimore, T. (2003). *Dyslexia and learning style.* London: Whurr Publishers.

Mosconi, M., Nelson, L., & Hooper, S. R. (2008). Confirmatory factor analysis of the NEPSY for younger and older school-age children. *Psychological Reports, 102,* 861–866.

Mundy, P., Sigman, M., & Kasari, C. (1990). A longitudinal study of joint attention and language development in autistic children. *Journal of Autism and Developmental Disorders, 20,* 115–128.

Murphy, M., Mazzocco, M., Hanich, L., & Early, M. (2007). Cognitive characteristics of children with mathematics learning disability (MLD) vary as a function of the cutoff criterion used to define MLD. *Journal of Learning Disabilities, 40,* 458–478.

Naglieri, J. A., LeBuffe, P. A., & Pfeiffer, S. I. (1994). *Devereux scales of mental disorders.* San Antonio, TX: The Psychological Corporation.

Narrow, W. E., Regier, D. A., Goodman, S. H., Rae, D. S., Roper M. T., Bourdon, K. H., et al. (1998). A comparison of federal definitions of severe mental illness among children and adolescents in four communities. *Psychiatric Services, 49,* 1601–1608.

National Dissemination Center for Children with Disabilities. (2001). *NICHY fact sheet number 5 (FS5): Emotional disturbance.* Washington, DC: Author

National Institute of Mental Health: MTA Cooperative Group. (2004a). Multimodal treatment study of ADHD follow-up: 24-month outcomes of treatment strategies for attention-deficit/hyperactivity disorder. *Pediatrics, 113,* 754–761.

National Institute of Mental Health. (2004b). *What are the autism spectrum disorders?* Washington, DC: Author.

the National Mathematics Advisory Panel. (2008). *Foundations for Success: The Final Report of the National Mathematics Advisory Panel*, U.S. Department of Education: Washington, DC.

Newton, R., (Ed.). (1995). *A Color Atlas of Pediatric Neurology.* London: Mosby-Wolfe Publishing.

Niemi, J., Gundersen, H., Leppasaari, T., & Hugdahl, K. (2003). Speech lateralization and attention/executive functions in a Finnish family with specific language impairment. *Journal of Clinical and Experimental Neuropsychology, 25,* 457–464.

Nieminen, T., Kulomäki, T., Ulander, R., & von Wendt, L. (2000). Aspergerin oireyhtymä. *Lääkärilehti, 55,* 967–972.

Nieminen-von Wendt, T., Metsähonkala, L., Kulomäki, T., Aalto, S., Autti, T. H., & Vanhala, R., (2003). Changes in cerebral blood flow in Asperger syndrome during theory of mind tasks presented by the auditory route. *European Child and Adolescent Psychiatry, 12,* 178–189.

Norbury, C. F., & Bishop, D. V. M. (2002). Inferential processing and story recall in children with communication problems: A comparison of specific language impairment, pragmatic language impairment, and high functioning autism. *International Journal of Language and Communication Disorders, 37,* 227–251.

Noterdaeme, M., Amorosa, H., Mildenberger, K., Sitter, S., & Minow, F. (2001). Evaluation of attention problems in children with autism and children with a specific language disorder. *European Child and Adolescent Psychiatry, 10,* 58–66.

Nunnally, J., & Bernstein, I. H. (1994). *Psychometric theory (3rd ed.).* New York: McGraw-Hill.

Olson, R. K. (2006). Genes, Environment, and Dyslexia: The 2005 Norman Geschwind Memorial Lecture. *Annals of Dyslexia, 56,* 205–238.

Olson, R. K., & Wise, B. (2006). Computer-based remediation for reading and related phonological disabilities. In M. McKenna, L. Labbo, R. Kieffer, & D. Reinking (Eds.), *Handbook of literacy and technology*, Vol. 2 (pp. 57–74). Mahwah, NJ: Erlbaum.

O'Shea, A. G., Fein, D., Cillessen, A. H. N., Klin, A., & Schultz, R. T. (2005). Source memory in children with autism spectrum disorders. *Developmental Neuropsychology, 27,* 337–360.

Ostad, S. A. (2000). Cognitive subtraction in a developmental perspective: Accuracy, speed-of-processing and strategy-use differences in normal and mathematically disabled children. *Focus on Learning Problems in Mathematics, 22,* 18–31.

Osterling, J., & Dawson, G. (1994). Early recognition of children with autism: A study of first birthday home videotapes. *Journal of Autism and Developmental Disorders, 24,* 247–257.

Ozonoff, S. (1995). Reliability and validity of the Wisconsin card sorting test in studies of autism. *Neuropsychology, 9,* 491–500.

Ozonoff, S., Pennington, B. F., & Rogers, S. J. (1991). Executive function deficits in high-functioning autistic individuals: Relationship to theory of mind. *Journal of Child Psychology & Psychiatry, 32,* 1081–1105.

Ozonoff, S., & Strayer, D. L. (2001). Further evidence of intact working memory in autism. *Journal of Autism and Developmental Disorders, 31,* 257–263.

Ozonoff, S., Strayer, D. L., McMahon, W. M., & Fillouz, F. (1994). Executive function abilities in autism and Tourette syndrome: An information-processing approach. *Journal of Child Psychology & Psychiatry, 35,* 1015–1032.

Paracchini, S., Scerri, T., Monaco, A. P. (2006). The genetic lexicon of dyslexia. *Annual Review of Genomics and Human Genetics, 8,* 57.

Pellicano, E., Gibson, L., Mayberry, M., Durkin, K., & Badcock, D. R. (2005). Abnormal global processing along the visual pathway in autism: A possible mechanism for weak visuospatial coherence. *Neuropsychologia, 43,* 1044–1053.

Pellicano, E., Mayberry, M., Durkin, K., & Maley, A. (2006). Multiple cognitive capabilities/deficits in children with an autism spectrum disorder: "Weak" central coherence and its relationship to theory of mind and executive control. *Developmental Psychopathology, 18,* 77–98.

Pelphrey, K. A., Morris, J. P., & McCarthy, G. (2005). Neural basis of eye gaze processing deficits in autism. *Brain, 128,* 1038–1048.

Pennington, B. F. (2006). From single to multiple deficit models of developmental disorders. *Cognition, 101,* 385–413.

Pennington, B. F., McGrath, L. M., Barnard, H., Rosenberg, J., Smith, S. D., Willcutt, E. G., et al. (2009). Gene x environment interactions across the phenotypic distribution: Evidence from reading disability and attention-deficit/hyperactivity disorder. *Developmental Psychology, 45,* 77–89.

Peterson, C. C. (2005). Mind and body: Concepts of human cognition, physiology and false belief in children with autism or typical development. *Journal of Autism and Developmental Disorders, 35,* 487–497.

Pierce, K., & Courchesne, E. (2001). Evidence for a cerebellar role in reduced exploration and stereotyped behavior in autism. *Biological Psychiatry, 49,* 655–664.

Raskind, W., Hsu, L., Berninger, V., Thomson J., & Wijsman, E. (2008). Familial aggregation of dyslexia phenotypes. *Behavior Genetics, 30,* 385–396.

Reddy, L., Newman, E., DeThomas, C., & Chun, V. (2008). Effectiveness of school-based prevention and intervention programs for children and adolescents with emotional disturbance: A meta-analysis. *Journal of School Psychology, 47,* 77–99.

Reinö-Habte Selassie, G., Jennische, M., Kyllerman, M., Viggedal, G., & Hartelius, L. (2005). Comorbidity in severe developmental language disorders: Neuropediatric and psychological considerations. *Acta Paediatrica, 94,* 471-478.

Reitan, R. M. (1979). *Manual for administration of neuropsychological test batteries for adults and children.* Tucson, AZ: Reitan Neuropsychological Laboratories.

Rice, C. (2007). Prevalence of Autism Spectrum Disorders–Autism and Developmental Disabilities monitoring network, 14 sites, United States, 2002. *Morbidity and Mortality Weekly Report, 56,* SS1; 12. (Abstract obtained from Autism and Developmental Disabilities Monitoring Network Surveillance Year 2002 Principal Investigators.)

Ringman, J. M., & Jankovic, J. (2000). Occurrence of tics in Asperger's Syndrome and Autistic Disorder. *Journal of Child Neurology, 15,* 394–400.

Roncadin, C., Guger, S., Archibald, J., Barnes, M., & Dennis, M. (2004). Working memory after mild, moderate, or severe childhood closed head injury. *Developmental Neuropsychology, 25,* 21–36.

Ropar, D., & Mitchell, P. (2001). Susceptibility to illusions and performance on visuospatial tasks in individuals with autism. *Journal of Child Psychology and Psychiatry, and Allied Disciplines, 42,* 539–549.

Rourke, B., Fisk, J., & Strang, J. (1986). *Neuropsychological assessment of children: A treatment oriented approach.* New York: Guilford Press.

Rutter, M. (1994). Beyond longitudinal data: Causes, consequences, changes, and continuity. *Journal of Consulting Clinical Psychology, 62,* 928–940.

Rutter, M. (2005). Incidence of autism spectrum disorders: Changes over time and their meaning. *Acta Paediatrica, 94,* 2–15.

Schachar, R., Levin, H., Max, J., Purvis, K., & Chen, S. (2004). Attention deficit hyperactivity disorder symptoms and response inhibition after closed head injury in children: Do preinjury behavior and injury severity predict outcome? *Developmental Neuropsychology, 25,* 179–198.

Scheuffgen, K., Happe, F., Anderson, M., & Frith, U. (2000). High intelligence, low IQ? Speed of processing and measured IQ in children with autism. *Development and Psychopathology, 12,* 83–90.

Schopler, E., & Mesibov, G. (1983). *Autism in Adolescents and Adults.* New York: Plenum Press.

Schuele, C. M. (2004). The impact of developmental speech and language impairments on the acquisition of literacy skills. *Mental Retardation and Developmental Disabilities Research Reviews, 10,* 176–183.

Schumacher, J., Anthoni, H., Dahdouh, F., Konig, I. R., Hillmer, A. M., Kluck, N., et al. (2006). Strong genetic evidence of *DCDC2* as a susceptibility gene for dyslexia. *American Journal of Human Genetics, 78,* 52–62.

Schutzman, S. A., & Greenes, D. S. (2001). Pediatric minor head trauma. *Annals of Emergency Medicine, 37,* 65–74.

Semrud-Clikeman, M., Kathryn, G., Griffin, J., & Hynd, G. (2000). Rapid naming deficits in children and adolescents with reading disabilities and attention deficit hyperactivity disorder. *Brain & Language, 74*(1), 70-83.

Searcy, E., Burd, L., Kerbeshian, J., Stenehjem, A., & Franceschini, L. A. (2000). Asperger's syndrome, x-linked mental retardation (MRX23), and chronic vocal tic disorder. *Journal of Child Neurology, 15,* 699–702.

Sergeant, J. A., Geurts, H., & Oosterlaan, J. (2002). How specific is a deficit of executive functioning for attention deficit/hyperactivity disorder? *Behavioral Brain Research, 130,* 3–28.

Sesma, H. W., Slomine, B. S., Ding, R., & McCarthy, M. L. (2008). Executive functioning in the first year after pediatric traumatic brain injury. *Pediatrics 2008, 121,* 1686–1695.

Shaked, M., & Yirmiya, N. (2004). Matching procedures in autism research: Evidence from meta-analytic studies. *Journal of Autism and Developmental Disorders, 34,* 35–40.

Shalev, R. S., & Gross-Tsur, V. (2001). Developmental dyscalculia. *Pediatric Neurology, 24,* 337–342.

Shalev, R. S., Manor, O., Kerem, B., Ayali, M., Badichi, N., Friedlander, Y., et al. (2001). Developmental dyscalculia is a familial learning disability. *Journal of Learning Disabilities, 34,* 59–65.

Shaywitz, S. E., & Shaywitz, B. A. (2003). The science of reading and dyslexia. *American Association for Pediatric Ophthalmology and Strabismus, 7,* 158–166.

Silver, N. C., & Dunlap, W. P. (1987). Averaging correlation coefficients: Should Fisher's z transformation be used? *Journal of Applied Psychology, 72,* 146–148.

Simos, P. G., Breier, J. I., Fletcher, J. M., Foorman, B. R., Bergman, E, Fishbeck, K., et al. (2000). Brain activation profiles in dyslexic children during non-word reading: A magnetic source imaging approach. *Neuroscience Letters, 90,* 61–65.

Slomine, B. S., McCarthy, M., Ding, R., MacKenzie, E., Durbin, D., Christensen, J., et al. (2005). Service utilization and needs following pediatric traumatic brain injury. *Rehabilitation Psychology* (April), Midyear Meeting. Baltimore, MD.

Snowling, M. J., Bishop, D. V. M., Stothard, S. E., Chipcase, B., & Kaplan, C. (2006). Psychosocial outcomes at 15 years of children with a preschool history of speech-language impairment. *Journal of Child Psychology & Psychiatry, 47,* 759–765.

Snowling, M. J., & Hayiou-Thomas, M. E. (2006). The dyslexia spectrum: Continuities between reading, speech, and language impairments. *Topics in Language Disorders, 26,* 108–124.

Sponheim, E., & Skjeidal, O. (1998). Autism and related disorders: Epidemiological findings in a Norwegian study using ICD-10 criteria. *Journal of Autism and Developmental Disorders, 31,* 363–364.

Spreen, O., Risser, A. H., & Edgell, D. (1995). *Developmental neuropsychology.* New York: Oxford University Press.

Stanovich, K. (2000). *Progress in understanding reading: Scientific foundations and new frontiers.* New York: Guilford Press.

Stein, J. (1994). A visual defect in dyslexics. In A. Fawcett & R. Nicolson (Eds.), *Dyslexia in children: Multidisciplinary perspectives* (pp.137–156). New York: Harvester Wheatsheaf.

Stinnett, T. A, Oehler-Stinnett, J. O., Fuqua, D. R., & Palmer, L. S. (2002). Examination of the underlying structure of the NEPSY: A developmental neuropsychological assessment. *Journal of Psychoeducational Assessment, 20,* 66–82.

Strauss, E., Sherman, E., & Spreen, O. (2006). *A compendium of neuropsychological tests: Administration, norms, and commentary* (3rd ed.). New York: Oxford University Press.

Stroop, J. R. (1935). Studies of interference in serial verbal reactions. *Journal of Experimental Psychology, 18,* 643–662.

Strube, M. J. (1988). Some comments on the use of magnitude-of-effect estimates. *Journal of Counseling Psychology, 35,* 345–345.

Swaab-Barneveld, H., de Sonneville, L., Cohen-Kettenis, P., Gielen, A., Buitelaar, J., & van Engeland, H. (2000). Visual sustained attention in a child psychiatric population. *Journal of the American Academy of Child and Adolescent Psychiatry, 39,* 651–659.

Szatmari, P., Tuff, L., Finlayson, M. A., & Bartolucci, G. (1990). Asperger's syndrome and autism: Neurocognitive aspects. *Journal of the American Academy of Child Adolescent and Psychiatry, 30,* 152–153.

Takarae, Y., Minshew, N. J., Luna, B., Krisky, C. M., & Sweeney, J. A. (2004). Pursuit eye movement deficits in autism. *Brain, 127,* 2584–2595.

Tanguay, P. E. (1999). The diagnostic assessment of autism using social communication domains. Paper presented at the Interdisciplinary Council on Developmental and Learning Disorders' Third Annual International Conference, Autism and Disorders of Relating and Communicating. McLean, VA, November 12–14.

Tanguay, P. E., Robertson, J., & Derrick, A. (1998). A dimensional classification of autism spectrum disorder by social communication domains. *Journal of the American Academy of Child and Adolescent Psychiatry, 37,* 271.

Tannock, R. (2000). Attention-deficit/ hyperactivity disorder with anxiety disorders. In T. E Brown (Ed.), *Attention-deficit disorders and comorbidities in children, adolescents, and adults* (pp.125–170). Washington, DC: American Psychiatric Press.

Tantam, D. (1988). Lifelong eccentricity and social isolation. I. Psychiatric, social, and forensic aspects. *British Journal of Psychiatry, 153,* 777–782.

Taylor, C. T. & Alden, L. E. (2006). Parental overprotection and interpersonal behavior in generalized social phobia. *Behavior Therapy, 47,* 11–22.

Taylor, H. G., Espy, K., & Anderson, P. (2009). Mathematics deficiencies in children with very low birth weight or very preterm birth. *Developmental Disabilities Research Review, 15,* 52–59.

Taylor, H. G., & Fletcher, J. (1990). Neuropsychological assessments of children. In G. Goldenstein & M. Hersen (Eds.), *Handbook of Psychological Assessment* (pp. 228–255). New York: Pergamon Press.

Toppelberg, C. O., & Shapiro, T. (2000). Language disorders: A 10-year research update review. *Journal of the American Academy of Child and Adolescent Psychiatry, 39,* 143–152.

Trauner, D. A., Ballantyne, A., Chase, C., & Tallal, P. (1993). Comprehension and expression of affect in language-impaired children. *Journal of Psycholinguistic Research, 22,* 445–452.

Tsai, L. Y. (2006). Diagnosis and treatment of anxiety disorders in individuals with autism spectrum disorder. In M. G. Baron, J. Groden, G. Groden, & L. P. Lipsitt (Eds.) *Stress and coping in autism* (pp. 388–440). New York: Oxford University Press.

U.S. Bureau of the Census. (2004). *Current population survey, October 2003. School enrollment and computer use supplement* (Machine-readable data file). Washington, DC: Author.

U.S. Department of Education. (2001). *Twenty-fourth annual report to Congress on the implementation of the Individuals with Disabilities Education Act.* Washington, DC: Author.

Venger, L. A., & Holmomskaya, V. V. (Eds.). (1978). *Diagnostika umst vernogo nazvitja doskolnekov.* [Diagnosing the cognitive development of preschool children]. Moscow: Pedagogika.

Volden, J. (2004). Nonverbal learning disability: A tutorial for speech-language pathologists. *American Journal of Speech and Language Pathology, 13,* 128–141.

Von Arnim, G., & Engel, P. (1964). Mental retardation related to hypercalcemia. *Developmental Medicine and Child Neurology, 6,* 366–377.

Wagner, M., & Davis, M. (2006). How are we preparing students with emotional disturbances for the transition to young adulthood? *Journal of Emotional and Behavioral Disorders, 14*(2), 86–98.

Wallander, J. L., & Thompson, R. J. (1995). Psychosocial adjustment of children with chronic physical conditions. In M.C. Roberts (Ed.), *Handbook of pediatric psychology* (2nd ed.) (pp. 124–141). New York: Guilford.

Wang, P. P., Doherty, S., Rourke, S. B., & Bellugi, U. (1995). Unique profile of visuo-perceptual skills in a genetic syndrome. *Brain and Cognition, 29,* 54–65.

Wechsler, D. (2003). *The Wechsler Intelligence Scale for Children–Fourth edition.* San Antonio, TX: The Psychological Corporation.

Wechsler, D., & Naglieri, J. A. (2006). *The Wechsler Nonverbal Scale of Ability.* San Antonio, TX: Harcourt Assessment.

Wentz, E., Gillberg, C., Gillberg, C., & Råstam, M. (2001). Ten-year follow-up of adolescent-onset Anorexia Nervosa: Psychiatric disorders and overall functioning scales. *Journal of Child Psychology & Psychiatry, 42*(5), 613–622.

Westby, C., & Watson, S. (2004). Perspectives on attention deficit hyperactivity disorder: Executive functions, working memory, and language disabilities. *Seminars in Speech and Language, 25,* 241–254.

Wetherby, A. M., Prizant, B. M., & Hutchinson, T. (1998). Communicative, social-affective, and symbolic profiles of young children with autism and pervasive developmental disorder., *American Journal of Speech-Language Pathology, 7,* 79–91.

Willcutt, E. G., DeFries, J. C., Pennington, B. F., Smith, S. D., Cardon, L. R., & Oison, R. K. (2003). Genetic etiology of comorbid reading difficulties. In R. Piomin, J. C. DeFries, I. W. Craig, & P. McGuffin (Eds.), *Behavioral genetics in the postgenomic era* (pp. 227–246). Washington, DC: American Psychological Association.

Willcutt, E. G., Doyle, A. E., Nigg, J. T., Faraone, S. V., & Pennington, B. F. (2005). Validity of the executive function theory of Attention-Deficit/Hyperactivity Disorder: A meta-analytic review. *Biological Psychiatry, 57,* 1336–1346.

Willcutt, E. G., Pennington, B. F., Olson, R. K., & DeFries, J. C. (2007). Understanding co-morbidity: A twin study of reading disability and attention-deficit/hyperactivity disorder. *American Journal of Medical Genetics Part B: Neuropsychiatric Genetics, 144B,* 709–714.

Williams, J. C., Barratt-Boyes, B. G., & Lowe, J. B. (1961). Supravalvular aortic stenosis. *Circulation, 24,* 1311–1318.

Williams, D. L., Goldstein, G., Carpenter, P. A., & Minshew, N. (2005). Verbal and spatial working memory in autism. *Journal of Autism and Developmental Disorders, 35,* 747–756.

Williams, D. L., Goldstein, G., & Minshew, N. J. (2005). Impaired memory for faces and social scenes in autism: Clinical implications of memory dysfunction. *Archives of Clinical Neuropsychology, 20,* 1–15.

Williams, D. L., Goldstein, G., & Minshew, N. J. (2006). The profile of memory function in children with autism. *Neuropsychology, 20,* 21–29.

Williams, J. G., Higgins, J. P. T., & Brayne, C. E. G. (2006). Systematic review of prevalence studies of autism spectrum disorders. *Archives of Disease in Childhood, 91,* 8–15.

Wing, L. (1981). Asperger's syndrome: A clinical account. *Psychological Medicine, 11,* 115–129.

Wing, L. (1991). The relationship between Asperger's Syndrome and Kanner's Autism. In U. Frith, (Ed.), *Autism and Asperger Syndrome.* Cambridge: Cambridge University Press.

Wolf, M., Bowers, P., & Biddle, K. (2000). Naming-speed processes, timing, and reading: A conceptual review. *Journal of Learning Disabilities, 33*(4), 387–407.

Wolf, M., & Bowers, P. G. (1999). The double-deficit hypothesis for the developmental dyslexias. *Journal of Educational Psychology, 91,* 415–438.

Wood, C., Maruff, P., Levy, F., Farrow, M., & Hay, D. (1999). Covert orienting of visual spatial attention in Attention Deficit Hyperactivity Disorder: Does comorbidity make a difference? *Archives of Clinical Neuropsychology, 14,* 179–189.

Yeates, K. O., Swift, E., Taylor, H. G., Wade, S. L., Drotar, D., Stancin, T., et al. (2004) Short- and long-term social outcomes following pediatric traumatic brain injury. *Journal of the International Neuropsychological Society, 10,* 412–426.

Yeates, K., & Taylor, H. G. (1997). Predicting premorbid neuropsychological functioning following pediatric traumatic brain injury. *Journal of Clinical and Experimental Neuropsychology, 19,* 825–837.

Yirmiya, N., Erel, O., Shaked, M., & Solomonica-Levi, D. (1998). Meta-analyses comparing theory of mind abilities of individuals with autism, individuals with mental retardation, and normally developing individuals. *Psychological Bulletin, 124,* 283–307.

Yirmiya, N., & Shulman, C. (1996). Seriation, conservation, and theory of mind abilities in individuals with autism. *Child Development, 67,* 2045–2059.

Yirmiya, N., Solomonica-Levi, D., & Shulman, C. (1996). The ability to manipulate behavior and to understand manipulation of beliefs: A comparison of individuals with autism, mental retardation, and normal development. *Developmental Psychology, 32,* 62–69.

Ylvisaker, M., Todis, B., Glang, A., Urbanczyk, B., Franklin, C., DePompei, R., et al. (2001). Educating students with TBI: Themes and recommendations. *Journal of Head Trauma Rehabilitation, 16,* 76–93.

Young, A. R., Beitchman, J. H., Johnson, C., Douglas, L., Atkinson, L., Escobar, M., et al. (2002). Young adult academic outcomes in a longitudinal sample of early identified language impaired and control children. *Journal of Child Psychology & Psychiatry, 43,* 635–645.

Zabel, R. H. (1988). Preparation of teachers for behaviorally disordered students: A review of literature. *Handbook of Special Education Research and Practice, 2.* Oxford, England: Pergamon Press.

Zorzi, M., Priftis, K., & Umiltá, C. (2002). Neglect disrupts the mental number line. *Nature, 417,* 138.

Annotated Bibliography

Baron, I. S. (2004). *Neuropsychological evaluation of the child*. New York: Oxford University Press. Well written and organized, this book presents neuropsychological tests according to domain. Also general guidelines for assessment and for communicating results are provided. An excellent desk reference.

Barkley, R. A. (2006). *ADHD: Handbook for diagnosis and treatment* (3rd ed.). New York: Guilford Press. This volume covers all aspects of ADHD based on Barkley's self-regulation theory, including diagnosis, associated and comorbid conditions, and a thorough discussion of treatments: medical, psychological, and combined.

Bowler, D. (2007). *Autism spectrum disorder. Psychological theory and research*. Chichester, West Sussex, UK: Wiley. This book presents a neuropsychological view of autism spectrum disorders, explaining characteristic neurocognitive impairments such as social perception and executive dysfunction as well as what is known and thought about underlying brain dysfunction.

Ellison, P. A. T., & Semrud-Clikeman, M. (2009). *Child Neuropsychology: Assessment and interventions for neurodevelopmental disorders* (2nd ed.). New York: Springer. A basic but comprehensive treatment of neuropsychology for students. This volume covers basic anatomy, physiology, functional neuroanatomy, electrophysiology, and imaging on through neuropsychological assessment, instruments, interpretation, and a broad range of developmental, psychological, and acquired disorders, as well as neuropsychological interventions and pediatric psychopharmacology.

Fletcher, J. M., Lyon, G. R., Fuchs, L. S., & Barnes, M. A. (2007). *Learning disabilities: from identification to intervention*. New York: Guilford Press. This book presents an excellent in-depth analysis of each aspect of reading disabilities individually: word recognition, fluency, and comprehension. Also thoroughly addresses math disabilities and written expression disabilities, including handwriting fluency and compositional fluency. It presents a balanced view of evidenced-based research and a full discussion of Response to Intervention, which all neuropsychologists need to understand, whether or not they are in agreement with its approach. (See Fletcher-Janzen & Reynolds, 2008, below.)

Fletcher-Janzen, E., & Reynolds, C. (Eds.). (2000). *Handbook of cross-cultural neuropsychology*. New York: Kulwer Academic/Plenum Publishers. A diverse group of experienced researchers and educators were asked to answer four of six questions concerning how to translate the advances in neuroscience into educational actions that will advance the art of diagnosing and providing effective interventions to students with learning disabilities. Further, they were asked how to reconcile and maximize the contributions of neuroscience, neuropsychology, and RTI to the development of the most accurate, efficient, and effective identification and intervention model (Shaywitz, 2008, foreword, pp. xi-xii). An important discussion emerging from the diverse responses concerns the role of RTI as a strategy for the identification of children as learning disabled.

Fletcher-Janzen, E., & Reynolds, C. (Eds.) (2008). *Neuropsychological perspectives on learning disabilities in the era of RTI: Recommendations for diagnosis and intervention*. Hoboken, NJ: Wiley.

461

This is an important resource for investigating the many issues involved in cross-cultural assessment of specific groups (i.e. Asian American, Native American, African-American, Hispanics, gay and lesbian, women, elders, and children), as well as special populations (i.e. brain injury, epilepsy, medical disorders, and HIV). Among other issues, it also addresses specific problems with assessment instruments and psychometric considerations, as well as ethnobiological variations in responsiveness to medication.

Frank, R., Rosenthal, M., & Caplan, B. (Eds.). (2009). *Handbook of rehabilitation Psychology* (2nd. ed.). Washington, D.C.: American Psychological Association.

Although there is only one section of this book that addresses the pediatric population specifically, it is an important resource for looking at the rehabilitation process as a whole, especially the role of the family as caregivers, which is not often addressed in neuropsychological literature.

Genese, F., Paradis, J., & Crago, M. (2004): *Dual language development and disorders: A handbook on bilingualism & second language learning.* Baltimore, MD: Brookes Publishing.

This book provides some understanding of the specific problems of children who are bilingual and have primary problems in language development.

Glidden, L. M. (Ed.) (2001). *International review of research in mental retardation: Autism.* San Diego, CA: Academic Press.

A thorough and very readable review of etiology, diagnosis, characteristics, and functioning, and the implications of both for later development and for family members. It should be supplemented by Bowler's volume (see above), which supplies more recent research. Nonetheless, the present volume provides an excellent, readable, and succinct overview of autism.

Johnson, M. H. (2005). *Developmental cognitive neuroscience* (2nd ed.). Malden, MA: Blackwell Publishing.

For those who wish to increase their background knowledge of the development and organization of brain functions. It is easy to read even for novices in the field.

Shaywitz, S. (2003). *Overcoming dyslexia: A new and complete science-based program for reading problems at any level.* New York: Alfred A. Knopf.

An excellent book that covers all aspects of current research in dyslexia and evidence-based interventions. Written for parents and dyslexics themselves, it is important reading for the clinician, not only because of the discussions of assessment, diagnosis, and intervention, but also in developing empathy for the struggles met daily by those suffering from dyslexia and many other developmental and acquired neurological disorders. Shaywitz writes with a clarity and compassion that all neuropsychologists should strive to develop.

Snowling, M., & Stackhouse, J., (Eds.). (2006). *Dyslexia, speech, and language: A practitioner's handbook* (2nd ed.). Hoboken, NJ: Wiley.

This is a very practically oriented book on dyslexia. The authors provide links from theory to their applications in the treatment and special education of dyslexia. The book does not cover all aspects of dyslexia, however. The reader should supplement with more theory and research oriented reading as well as texts treating naming problems that may also underlie dyslexia.

Yeates, K., Ris, M. D., & Taylor, H. G. (Eds.) (2000). *Pediatric neuropsychology: Research, theory, and practice.* New York: Guilford Press.

With contributions from highly respected researchers in child neurology/neuropsychology (i.e. Denckla, Rovet, Welsh & Pennington, etc.), this is a clear, well-written resource for investigating primary disorders of the CNS, as well as CNS dysfunction in other medical disorders not so frequently addressed. It also contains excellent discussions of developmental neuropsychological assessment and child neuropsychological evaluations by veterans Jane Bernstein and Ida Sue Baron.

About the Authors

Sally Kemp is a developmental psychologist with a subspecialty in neuropsychology. In semi-retirement for the past three years, Dr. Kemp now holds an appointment as an Adjunct Professor of Health Psychology in the Health Psychology Program at the University of Missouri, Columbia. She frequently presents at conferences and training workshops in the US and abroad and is involved in research with NEPSY-II. Research interests center on autism, Asperger's syndrome, dyslexia, and ADHD. For nearly 20 years, Dr. Kemp practiced with Tulsa Developmental Pediatrics and Center for Family Psychology, a multidisciplinary practice in Tulsa, Oklahoma, and was a partner in her last 10 years there. During those years, she also served as an adjunct Associate Professor of Pediatrics at the University of Oklahoma Medical College—Tulsa and as a practicum supervisor in the Clinical Psychology program at the University of Tulsa. Dr. Kemp began her training in nursing, and later trained as a teacher. For 20 years she taught middle school, worked with LD children and was a school psychometrist in several settings, both public and private, across the country. Always, she had concerns about the children who were not learning for reasons that appeared to be beyond their ability to change. Her medical background caused her to question the neurological bases of such difficulties. Her pursuit to find some answers for these youngsters finally took her to Teachers College, Columbia University, for doctoral study with Ursula Kirk, a pioneer in addressing the neurological underpinnings of learning and developmental disorders. She was privileged to collaborate with Dr. Kirk, and, in 1987, Drs. Kirk and Kemp began their collaboration on NEPSY with Marit Korkman, who, at that time, first brought her Finnish NEPSY to Columbia for Dr. Kirk's review. Dr. Kemp is the third author of NEPSY and NEPSY-II with Drs. Korkman and Kirk (Korkman, Kirk, & Kemp, 1998; Korkman, Kirk, & Kemp, 2007).

Marit Korkman is a pioneer in the field of child neuropsychology, having developed the first neuropsychological assessment designed specifically for children and based on Lurian principles. She holds her doctorate from the Helsinki University, Helsinki, Finland. The original NEPSY was her doctoral dissertation, but she continued to hone and develop it, publishing it in her native Finland, as well as Denmark and Sweden, before beginning her collaboration with Drs. Kirk and Kemp on the American NEPSY. Dr. Korkman is now a professor at the University of Helsinki. Her main responsibility is to chair the national Finnish postgraduate specialization program in clinical neuropsychology. The senior author of the NEPSY and NEPSY-II, Dr. Korkman was for many years a senior pediatric neuropsychologist at the Children's Castle Hospital in Helsinki and at Helsinki University Central Hospital, Hospital for Children and Adolescents, Helsinki, Finland. She is a highly respected researcher and internationally productive investigator in a wide-ranging array of acquired and developmental disorders. Further, Dr. Korkman has taught pediatric neuropsychology at the University of Helsinki, at the University of Maastricht (Netherlands), and at Åbo Academy University in Finland. Particular research interests include language disorders, epilepsy, the effects of extremely low birth weight, and Fetal Alcohol Syndrome. She is a frequent presenter at conferences and workshops all over the world.

REVIEWER BIOGRAPHY

Dr. Stephen R. Hooper is a Professor of Psychiatry at the University of North Carolina School of Medicine where he also is the Associate Director of the Center for Development and Learning at the Carolina Institute for Developmental Disabilities. He holds clinical appointments in the Department of Pediatrics, the Department of Psychology, and the School of Education. Clinically, he is the Director of the Child and Adolescent Neuropsychology Service at the Center. Dr. Hooper received his doctoral degree from the University of Georgia and completed a Postdoctoral Fellowship in Child Neuropsychology at Brown University Medical School. Current research interests include examining the neurobiological bases and neuropsychological outcomes of a variety of childhood disorders including pediatric kidney disease, early onset childhood schizophrenia, pediatric traumatic brain injury, written language disorders, and childhood maltreatment and neglect. Dr. Hooper maintains grant funding from the National Institutes of Health, the Department of Education, and the Maternal Child Health Bureau. Dr. Hooper has written or edited 13 books, and nearly 200 peer-reviewed articles and book chapters. He is an editor on several professional journals and regularly provides scientific reviews for numerous journals in the field of child psychology and child neuropsychology.

Index

A

A.R. Luria (*See* Lurian Theory)

About the Authors, 463–464

Accessing language, 196, 202.
(*See also* Subtests: SN; IN; BPN; MN)
learning disabilities (*see* Referral Batteries)

Administration of NEPSY-II
(*See also* Subtests):
breaks to avoid spoiling delayed trials, 38
examiner practice for certain subtests, 54
item repetition, 58
modified (*see* Modified Administration)
order, 39
physical environment, 34–35
prompting, querying, 58
recording responses, 55
self-correction, 58
start/discontinue, rules for, 55
subtest administration (*see* Subtests)
subtest-by-subtest, rules for, 59
(*see* Subtests)
teaching tasks, 58
timing, 58

Affect Recognition (*See* Subtests-Social Perception Domain)

Age:
calculating chronological age, 131

ranges for subtests, 16–21

Animal Sorting (*See* Subtests – Attention and Executive Functioning Domain)

Annotated bibliography, 461–462

Appendices for scoring, 131

Appendix (NEPSY-II Data Worksheet), 433–440

Arrows (*See* Subtests- Visuospatial Domain)

Asperger's Disorder, 14, 21–22, 241, 299, 317–321. (*See* Clinical Applications)

Assessment: 46–53
conditions for special needs assessments:
attention problems (ADHD), 43–44
Autistic Spectrum Disorder (ASD), 45–46
blind child, 43, 52–53
deaf and hearing-impaired, 48–50
emotional disturbance, 47
language disorder, 46–47
learning differences, 48
reading, 48
mathematics, 48
mild intellectual deficit, 50–51
motor deficits, 51–52
dissociation of subcomponents, 353
flexibility of, 15

465

W